SELECTED □ FILM CRITICISM 1912-1920 □

edited by
Anthony Slide

THE SCARECROW PRESS, INC.
METUCHEN, N.J., & LONDON
1982

Frontispiece: Julian Johnson

In Preparation:

Selected Film Criticism: 1921-1930
Selected Film Criticism: 1931-1940
Selected Film Criticism: 1941-1950

Library of Congress Cataloging in Publication Data
Main entry under title:

Selected film criticism.

Contents: 1. 1912-1920.
1. Moving-pictures--Reviews.   I. Slide, Anthony.
PN1995.S426   791.43'75   81-23344
ISBN 0-8108-1525-7 (v. 1)   AACR2

This volume is dedicated to the memory of the screen's first serious critic, Julian Johnson

☐ CONTENTS

vii

□ PREFACE

Selected Film Criticism: 1912-1920 is the first of four volumes
providing extensive coverage of contemporary American film criticism
from the early teens through the late forties. This present volume
offers contemporary reviews of almost two hundred films, American
and foreign, features and shorts, released during the cinema's form-
ative years. The selection of films represented here has been based
on the production's importance in terms of its director or its performers, its historical value and its contemporary relevance. Several
films have been included not so much because they were major films
of the teens, but rather because they happen to be among the small
percentage of films from that era which have survived and, as such,
are frequently screened today. With more than 6,000 features being
released in this nine-year period, readers will appreciate that the
selection process was not an easy one.

Reviews have been selected from thirteen periodicals: Exceptional Photoplays, The Green Book Magazine, Life, Motion Picture
Classic, Motion Picture Magazine, Motion Picture News, Motography,
The Moving Picture World, The New York Dramatic Mirror, Photoplay, Photo-Play World, Picture-Play, and Variety. It would be
wrong to claim that many of these reviews are particularly well written or that they can be considered high-quality commentaries from
today's viewpoint, but rather they do provide a broad spectrum of the
types of film reviews being published in the teens, from the strictly
trade paper (is it box-office?) approach of the semi-illiterate Variety
and The Moving Picture World to the highly literate and at times
over-blown comments by Julian Johnson and Burns Mantle in Photoplay. And, of course, most importantly they indicate contemporary
feelings towards the cinema, demonstrating that even then reviewers

were complaining that films were overlong or that sometimes even a D. W. Griffith production was not perfect (as with the reviews of True Heart Susie, which today we can recognize as a far greater film than did contemporary critics).

A volume such as this can provide pleasant surprises. One is the superior quality of the frank reviews published in the early teens by The New York Dramatic Mirror, under the guidance of Frank Woods. Another is the excellent work of Frederick James Smith in Motion Picture Classic. Smith joined the Classic in January of 1918, after a sojourn with The New York Dramatic Mirror, and his comments are probably the closest to those by exponents of current popular film criticism. He died in 1941 while still a relatively young man.

Julian Johnson's reviews I have praised in previous books. He had been editor of Photoplay prior to James R. Quirk's reign, and it was he who introduced criticism to fan magazines with his "Department of Comment and Criticism of Current Photoplays" in the November 1915 issue of the magazine. In the twenties, Johnson contributed the titles for many major silent films, including Man-handled (1924), The Canadian (1926), Moana (1926), The Sorrows of Satan (1927), The Way of All Flesh (1927), Beggars of Life (1928), The Docks of New York (1928), and Wings (1929). In 1932, he became story editor at Fox and remained with the company until his retirement, as head of the story department, in 1957. Johnson died November 12, 1965, at the age of seventy-nine.

It is interesting to note that in some publications, such as The New York Dramatic Mirror, the quality of the reviews deteriorated as the decade progressed. In others, such as The Moving Picture World and Variety, the standards became higher; Variety in particular has grown in strength through the years. The quality of film reviewing in fan magazines reached its zenith about 1919, when one had Smith in Motion Picture Classic and Julian Johnson and Burns Mantle in Photoplay, while Adele Whitely Fletcher and Hazel Simpson Naylor were not doing too bad a job in Motion Picture Magazine, and Peter Milne had left Motion Picture News to take the critical helm at Picture-Play. Standards in fan magazine reviewing went slowly downhill in the twenties and have steadily declined. As far as the non-film periodicals are concerned, it has been an uphill trend. It could not be much else simply because few general periodicals bothered to recognize the cinema's existence in the teens, let alone to take its product seriously. Life, with its occasional film reviews by the drama critic in the late teens, had particularly high standards, which it carried through into the twenties, when Robert E. Sherwood and Robert Benchley were its reviewers. There is no comparison between the reviews in, say, Life and those mediocre early efforts in The New York Times (not included here because they are readily available in reprint form elsewhere).

As an added bonus, I have included a couple of samples of the yearly critical overviews popular in fan magazines of the late teens: one by Julian Johnson from Photoplay and one by Frederick James Smith from Motion Picture Classic. These overviews appear as appendixes following the individual reviews.

My thanks to the Margaret Herrick Library of the Academy of Motion Picture Arts and Sciences, the Los Angeles Public Library, the Theatre Arts Library of the University of California at Los Angeles, and the Library of Congress. Thanks also to Stanley Appelbaum of Dover Publications, George Pratt, Herb Sterne, and especially Elias Savada for his help in checking copyright registrations. The Variety reviews are reprinted by kind permission of Syd Silverman and Variety and those from Exceptional Photoplays are reprinted through the courtesy of the National Board of Review.

Anthony Slide

SELECTED FILM CRITICISM:
1912-1920

☐ THE ADVENTURES OF KATHLYN (Selig, 1914)

The remarkable series of photodramas under the title, The Adventures of Kathlyn, is based on Harold MacGrath's fictional work of that name, the photodramatic adaptation being made by Gilson Willets, also a well-known author and literary man. The entire series forms a serial story in thirteen sets. The first set, already released, took up three reels; each of those remaining comprises two reels, making twenty-seven reels in all. The sets will be released so that two weeks will intervene between any one and that immediately following, thus requiring twenty-six weeks for the showing of the entire series.

These films mark not only a new departure in production and in the method of treating a prolonged subject, but they will also establish a new standard for all who follow, in the domain of perilous adventure and thrilling photodramatic narrative. One thrill succeeds another so rapidly that the spectator is out of breath, mentally, in trying to keep abreast of them; and the atmosphere of Orientalism that prevails throughout adds a feeling of mysticism that reminds one of the days long ago, when the "Arabian Nights" transported us into a new heaven and a new earth.

Director F. J. Grandon has brought himself into the limelight by the art and skill shown in the action and settings of these photodramas. His task was arduous at all times, for the scenario demands the performance of big things and nice attention to detail. Massive exteriors and interiors, impressive spectacles and weird, grim ruins bear witness to this. The hoary, mouldering Parsee temple, with its lone, prowling lion, has a haunting influence on one's mind. The harem scene is finely set. The imposing durbar scene; the great concourse of people as they assemble to hear the final decision of the Council of Three on the fate of Allaha's unwilling queen; the fete-day scene, and the arena, where she confronts a host of hungry lions, and her rescue from the burning pyre by the ponderous elephant are some of the other striking spectacular features of sets number two and three.

In all these, Miss Kathlyn Williams, as the queen of Allaha, is the great compelling figure on which every eye is centered. She is the mainspring of the action and of interest; and she is so continuously beset by dangers and seemingly insurmountable odds that one unconsciously commiserates her on her fancied woes. But some of the dangers are not at all fanciful. It takes a stout heart and a fearless spirit to stand alone before twenty lions or more, not one of

3

which is the proverbial circus lion--"all gums and no teeth." Miss
Williams is fairly bewitching through it all. I don't think I have ever
seen her in pictures to finer advantage. She is always equal to the
demands of the occasion, and is always ready for other exploits.

Other principals in sets two and three are Charles Clary, as
Prince Umballah; William Carpenter, as Ramabai; Thomas Santschi,
as Bruce (the American hunter); Miss Goldie Coldwell, as Pundita,
and Hurri Tsingh (a native Hindoo), as the high priest. All are to
be commended for excellent acting, costuming and make-up.

The opening scene of set number two shows the durbar, where
the Council of Three decides that Kathlyn, on her refusal to become
the wife of Umballah, shall be given a week's respite. During the
week she rescues Ramabai from a false charge of murder made by
Umballah and also frees his wife, Pundita, appointing the latter her
lady-in-waiting, and Ramabai captain of her bodyguard. At the same
time Bruce, an American hunter of big game, arrives in Allaha and
proves a timely factor in the fortunes of Kathlyn.

Still refusing to wed Umballah, at the end of the fateful week,
the Council of Three decrees that Kathlyn must undergo two ordeals
with wild animals, which, if accomplished successfully, will entitle
her to remain a maiden queen. The first required that Kathlyn should
be human bait on a leopard's trap; the second, that she should be
cast into the arena with hungry lions. She escapes in both instances
by the aid of Bruce, whose aid has been secured by Pundita. In the
second test Bruce blows up the great arena by a hidden mine of powder,
which he had placed there. The final scene in set number two shows
Bruce rescuing Kathlyn from the arena.

Number three continues the rescue, showing Kathlyn and Bruce
fleeing through the forest on the backs of two elephants. Kathlyn's
mount takes fright at a baboon just as Bruce had alighted from his
beast to secure water. The frightened animal easily outdistanced that
ridden by Bruce and carried Kathlyn to a town in a neighboring state,
where she was immediately recognized by a high official and arrested.
This official condemned her to die on a funeral pyre, on the ground
that she had broken the laws of her own state by refusing to wed Umballah. Just in the nick of time she is saved by the arrival of her
elephant, which had heard her cries.

The elephant traveled all day, and at nightfall stopped at the
ruins of a great temple. There Kathlyn dismounted and sought refuge
in the ruins for the night. A huge lion, which made the temple his
home, approached her, but she escaped by hiding in a great sarcopha-
gus. In the morning she was discovered by the high priest of the
temple, who worshipped her as the high priestess. Food was brought
her and she was appointed to keep the sacred fire burning day and
night. The closing scene in number three shows Kathlyn fleeing for
her life from the lion of the temple.

                              --James S. McQuade in The Moving
                              Picture World, Vol. 19, No. 3
                              (January 17, 1914), page 266.

☐ AN AMERICAN CITIZEN (Famous Players, 1914)

There is an abundance of fine comedy as there are also many
strong dramatic situations in An American Citizen, adapted from the
play of Madeleine Lucette Ryley, which the Famous Players released
on January 10. It is a story in which the comedy apparently predominates until suddenly you discover the fun has been pulled out of a
situation and that you are looking on gray life. One of the more notable instances of this quick reversal is where John Barrymore deject-
edly faces a portrait of the Father of His Country on a table opposite
him. He is in financial difficulties; a partner has absconded and the
office rent is due. A wealthy relative in England has left him a
fortune contingent on marrying an Englishwoman and becoming a British subject. The only apparent chance of restoring to his trusting
clients the money they have left with him is to accept the terms im-
posed by his late uncle. There is a laugh as the screen shows him
sadly waving a hand to the first president and saying: "Good-bye, old
man!" But as he leans over and from the corner of the frame gently
removes an American flag there is an ominous hitch in the mirth.
When he presses to his lips the bit of cloth the change is complete.
If at home the act strikes deep, imagine the feelings of the expatriate
thousands of miles from home.

John Barrymore more than makes good on the screen. His
performance in the role of Beresford Cruger is unusual in that it is
different. It has rare quality. There are the attractiveness of youth,
the skill that comes by training, and the talent that is in his blood.
In the language of the screen, he always "registers." Evelyn Moore
plays Beatrice Carew, the cousin who has been disinherited in favor
of Cruger and with whom she makes a loveless marriage for the sake
of keeping the money in the family. Miss Moore has a charming
personality--and what is better, she has stage intelligence. There
are many delicate touches in her portrayal of the woman who is wife
in name only. We see the development of the affection from the first
meeting until she challenges her husband by standing under the mistletoe in the backroom of the little old bookshop in London on the snowy
Christmas eve.

The work of the cast is uniformly excellent. Peter Lang is
the whole-souled, jolly senior partner in the firm of Barbury, Brown
& Cruger, the firm friend of the junior member. Hal Clarendon is
Brown, the partner who takes the bonds from the large safe which is
also the refrigerator, and leaves for parts unknown. Howard Missimer, just back from a three months' rest on a farm, is his old self
again in the portrayal of the aristocratic Sir Humphry Bunn. Alexander Gaden is the persistent agent of town lots. Wellington A. Playter,
who was the gladiator in A Daughter of the Hills, as the giant English
valet makes a pronounced hit. Joe Short, as the office boy, contributes to the comedy, and Ernest Truex, as Mercury, the London news-
boy and later assistant in the bookstore, adds much to the effectiveness of the final act.

The settings are elaborate. One scene that would stand out
in any production is the representation of the House of Lords across
the Thames, with the higher buildings of the city showing in dimin-
ishing prominence in the background. There will be many who will
fail to realize that this is a studio triumph. Another notable setting
is the hotel front in Nice. Not the least effective are the scenes
about the office building elevator.

The story holds throughout. In the beginning there is straight
comedy until the partners discover that, instead of having no assets,
they have real liabilities--through the absconding of Brown. The situations in the hotel, when Cruger, through the excusable blunder of
a clerk, is assigned to his wife's room, are full of rollicking fun.
The episode of the stocking will upset any house. The best of all,
however, are in the last half reel. Barbury gets word that the opera house lot has advanced in price--worth a small fortune, in fact--
and seeks out Mrs. Cruger. He brings her to the little bookstore,
where Cruger has been busy hanging Christmas greens. As the
American sits by the blazing logs--they really are blazing--with his
tiny flag in one hand and a faded flower bearing memories of his
wife in the other, Mrs. Cruger steps in on him. Gradually she
edges her way to the mistletoe as Cruger backs against the wall.
When he realizes the situation the end is sudden--and dramatic.

    J. Searle Dawley is the producer.

                          --George Blaisdell in The Moving
                            Picture World, Vol. 19, No. 3
                            (January 17, 1914), page 292.

☐ ANNE OF GREEN GABLES (Realart/Paramount, 1919)

        Mary Miles Minter is a bit of established popularity. So are
L. M. Montgomery's Anne books. The combination, ergo, was a
well-advised one for the young star's debut on a new programme.
The same advised selection proceeded in the selection of Frances
Marion as the person who could best weld four tales into one string
for the celluloids. The result is no drama to speak of, but a more
or less biographic account of a little orphan girl who was alternately
pathetic and funny; and later, alternately fiercely tragic and meltingly
lovely. The high spots of the picture to me were Anne's black-and-
white chicken, the feeding of imprisoned Anne by the little boy,
Anne's innocent encounter with the mephitic polecat while hunting the
picnic, and--later--adolescent Anne's tribulations as the disciplinarian
of the village school. William D. Taylor's direction of the picture
is pleasantly adequate without being in any way original, and the best
work of the long cast is done by Marcia Harris, as Aunt Marilla.
                          --Julian Johnson in Photoplay,
                            Vol. 17, No. 3 (February 1920),
                            page 72.

☐ THE AVENGING CONSCIENCE

Griffith has absorbed the whole spirit of Edgar Allan Poe and reflected it in Avenging Conscience. Poe's remarkable genius, his rejection of customary forms, his crystalline imagery, his gloom, his grandeur, his abrupt transitions from scenes of exquisite beauty to those of ghastly horror, all the spell that transports us from the baseless fabric of a delicious dream to common and hideous reality, the marvels of his powers of contrast, dwelling one moment in a heaven of ideals and another in a hell of mental torture, are reproduced with marvelous fidelity on the screen. Griffith exhibits not only a sympathetic understanding of his subject from start to finish, but seems deeply sincere in his effort to perpetuate the genius of a man too harshly criticised because of his private errors, too little praised until this late day for his splendid public service.

"Through many a night of want and woe
His frenzied spirit wandered wild
Till kind disaster laid him low
And Heaven reclaimed its wayward child.

Through many a year his fame has grown--
Like midnight, vast, like starlight sweet,
Till now his genius fills a throne
And nations marvel at his feet. "

Eliminating from our minds the harsh opinions of what was the once popular conception of the man, one has only to look at portraits of Poe to feel that his dreamy soul was a sad one. His face is the embodiment of tragedy, with something of the dark fatalism in it that marked the countenance of Edwin Booth. His face is that of a poet, but drawn away from its mental sweetness by physical tendencies that are at once sensual, sorrowful and sepulchral.

It is so with Avenging Conscience. Delighting you with its flashes of exquisite beauty at one moment, the very essence of spiritual charm, it moves you at another to pity and then to horror.

I can very easily see how such a photodrama would baffle a critic whose knowledge of Poe's works was either vague or superficial, but it did not baffle the vast audience that sat spellbound at the Strand during an appropriate presentation of the work. I feared that my own interest might be entirely that of a playwright in watching the constructive methods, so I looked around and listened to the occasional comments. The audience sat enthralled. An old lady back of me did not wholly grasp the meaning of Walthall's masterly portrayals of terror, but her escort swiftly explained. A stout gentleman next to me betrayed emotion during the sorrows of sweet Blanche. There were words of praise to be heard here and there, but the general tribute was a silent one, that of close attention, until the crisis was over, and there was generous applause all over the house at the conclusion.

Poe's strange fascination seems to lie in his handling of a
primitive emotion, that of fear, which enlightenment has not wholly
eliminated from our hearts. He could translate his thrill prose and
he gave us a few exquisite examples of poetic genius. All that is in
Griffith's Avenging Conscience, --all that and more. There is something in the photodrama that Poe's own works seem to lack, "The
Message. " There is a message in Annabel Lee--

>"Our love was stronger far than the love
>Of those who were older than we--
>Of many far wiser than we. "

But this message is only tinkled in the poem--it rings out clear and
sweet in the screen story. And the big message, the grand theme
fairly thunders, like the Strand's organ, in portraying the terror of
them who usurp the privilege of Him who declared, "Vengeance is
Mine, " in the hollow of whose hand rests the sceptre which a certain plumed knight of Europe imagines belongs to him--to "Me und
Gott. "

Never has a play driven home the lesson "Thou shalt not
kill, " as has Avenging Conscience.

The story is "illustrative" and as such is eminently suited to
screen visualization. It is that of an uncle who has set his heart
on his nephew's literary success, who sees all his plans about to be
thwarted on the verge of success by that little tyrant "Love. " The
clash between intellection and natural emotion results in a hypothetical series of dramatic incidents which can not be given in detail
without spoiling the story for those who have yet in store the pleasure of seeing it. On that account, a synopsis of the action is omitted. The form and treatment are those of the screen alone, and
the acting raises all five principals, in proportion to their relative
importance, to a very high rank, that of veritable artists. Walthall
and Blanche Sweet have as far exceeded themselves as to deserve
the highest compliments on their work.

Poe professed to be an apostle of what was beautiful in art,
and Griffith has taken him at his word. He has not faltered at the
horrible, but he has more than balanced it with a long succession of
beautiful scenes and a spiritual ending, whose daintiness barely saves
it from being an anti-climax. Griffith depicts the horrible, but he
overthrows it with scenes of delight that charm the senses, and moments of delicate humor in contrast with tender sentiment. It is
such a tribute as any man of sympathetic appreciation would be glad
to pay to him.

>"Whose soul went down to death in loneliness
>A death too pitiful for aught save silence
>Too mournful in its wretchedness for tears.
>But not with death he dwells. Above his dust
>Time's slow impartial hand has made for him
>A shaft, memorial, builded of the stones

Which Hate and Envy cast upon his grave
He dwells not with the shadows. "

--Louis Reeves Harrison in The
Moving Picture World, Vol. 21,
No. 9 (August 15, 1914), page
936.

☐ BABY MINE (Goldwyn, 1917)

Margaret Mayo's celebrated farce comedy as made into a
picture by Goldwyn is bound to prove one of the most successful
farce comedies that the screen has ever seen. Baby Mine will
bring a twinkle to the eyes of the "man who never laughs" and make
the cynic forget himself. When it was shown to capacity houses at
the Strand theatre it called forth gale after gale of laughter that
swept the house. It is advertised as the "picture of a thousand
laughs" and the announcement does not exaggerate.

Baby Mine should prove even more successful as a film production than it was on the speaking stage, for the screen permits
a range of action that was not possible in the spoken form. And as
a picture there is none of the cleverness of the spoken word lost for
the titles are unusually clever. Practically every one of them
brought the quick response of laughter, it seemed, almost before
the audience had time to read them. Goldwyn has given the farce
a superb production. There are some splendid lighting effects and
the direction of John Stuart Robertson and Hugo Ballin is of the highest order.

Madge Kennedy, the star, promises to exceed her popularity
of the speaking stage. She screens perfectly. There is something
about her screen work that reminds one at once of Billie Burke and
of the Gish sisters at their cleverest best. She is a woman of unusual beauty and is able to grasp the comedy expressions perfectly.
And to that she adds the quick gracefulness of youth. John Cumberland, as Jimmie, has the chief male comedy role and shares with
the stars in the laughs. Frank Morgan as the husband, and all the
remaining members of the cast do splendid work. A bunch of babies
register pronounced hits.

--R. E. Pritchard in Motion Picture
News, Vol. 16, No. 15 (October
13, 1917), page 2581.

☐ BARBARY SHEEP (Paramount-Artcraft, 1917)

Elsie Ferguson's screen debut--in Barbary Sheep, which

crowded the Rialto to its capacity during its stay there--was a most
auspicious one.   Her beauty and charm, coupled with her ability to
act with restraint and feeling, will go far towards making her one
of filmland's--as well as stageland's--most popular stars.   Miss
Ferguson was very fortunate in obtaining Robert Hichens's colorful
novel for her first production, and through the splendid direction of
Maurice Tourneur none of the charm and atmosphere has been lost
through its transference.   All the romance and sensuousness of the
East were portrayed with remarkable realism, the desert beneath
the bright moon's rays and the Algerian street scenes being particularly fine products of Mr. Tourneur's imaginative art.

The story concerns the activities of Sir Claude and Lady
Wyverne, who have come to the East--Sir Claude to hunt Barbary
sheep and Lady Wyverne to satisfy her longing for romance.   While
her husband is hunting, Lady Wyverne, left to seek her own amuse-
ment, meets and almost falls victim to the fascinations of Benchaalal,
a seductive Arabian chief.   Under his guidance she sees the desert
under a glorious moon and hears soft native love music.   The vividness of it all attracts her and she dreams of what life might have
been like had she lived in the days of Oriental splendor and experienced the burning love of a son of the desert.   But while she is
only guilty in thought, Benchaalal plans to abduct her.   Sir Claude,
at a distant village, hears disturbing stories of the Algerian chief's
past career and, alarmed for his wife's safety, hurriedly returns.
He sees his wife and Benchaalal alone in the desert; he sees him
attack his wife and is about to shoot, when a mad marabout, recognizing Benchaalal as the man who robbed and murdered his sweetheart several years ago, steals upon the pair and stabs him.

Elsie Ferguson's acting throughout was a telling example of
her delicate artistry.   Pedro de Cordoba, whose every movement
suggested the fascination and mystery of the East, gave an admirable performance as Benchaalal, while Lumsden Hare played Sir
Claude with commendable naturalness.   Others who contributed splendid support were Macy Harlan, Alex Shannon and Maude Ford.

Exhibitors will find this an extremely artistic production, with
the valuable addition of Elsie Ferguson's name in the leading role.
                              --H. S. D. in The New York Dra-
                              matic Mirror, Vol. 77, No. 2022
                              (September 22, 1917), page 18.

                         *   *   *

It is difficult to determine between Elsie Ferguson's beauty
and talent or Maurice Tourneur's artistry and subtlety as being responsible for the superiority of Barbary Sheep.   It is, of course, a
combination of both star and director, but the acting of the former
and the fine hand of the latter vie with one another for first honors
throughout the picture.   Miss Ferguson's screen debut could not have
been made under more notable circumstances than those provided her
by the role of Lady Wyverne in the adaptation of Robert Hichens's

novel, Barbary Sheep. There is a continual conflict of emotions in the character and Miss Ferguson brings out both feelings with a skill that has seldom been approached by actresses used to the picture camera and its exhorbitant demands. Combined with her talent she has a beauty and charm that is altogether irresistible.

Mr. Hichens's novel has to do with the Far East and possesses an atmosphere that is constantly rich and exotic--the dangerous charm of the desert under the moon and stars--a theme upon which a composer of music might sing to his heart's content. The descriptive beauty of Mr. Hichens's book has by no means been lost in its migration to the screen. If anything, Mr. Tourneur has succeeded in bringing out the atmosphere in a still more subtle, more fascinating way. He has proven before that he is an artist. If he wasn't he couldn't have staged a scene between an English woman in evening dress and an Arab in picturesque robes on the Sahara desert and make it appear convincing. His fine direction is apparent in every scene, from the smallest detail to the largest, while settings, photography and light are excellent.

Barbary Sheep, shorn of its beautiful word pictures, left a rather bare and slim plot before the eyes of the adaptor, Charles Maigne. It presents in brief the old story of the busy husband, the neglected wife and the other man--this time a native of the desert. But he arranged his continuity so that the utmost suspense has been derived from it--which is no small amount. Particularly are the scenes leading to the climax, when Sir Claude begins to doubt his wife, able to thrill with a power far more than ordinary. But the story never gets to dragging even though the same plot, decorated with many more complications, has been seen time and again. It is the locale, the mystic third angle and the magnificent manner in which Mr. Tourneur has transferred the atmosphere of the descriptive passages in the novel to the screen that places Barbary Sheep in a class by itself.

Lumsden Hare as Sir Wyverne and Pedro de Cordoba as Benchaalal are well fitted to their respective parts and give excellent performances.

--Peter Milne in Motion Picture News, Vol. 16, No. 13 (September 29, 1917), page 2205.

☐ THE BARGAIN (Ince/Paramount, 1914)

Among the present-day directors and script writers of westerns, Thomas H. Ince, aided by William H. Clifford, has a very small number of equals. Whenever we hear the name of Ince it is involuntarily linked with the best of western dramas and melodramas. His wide experience and the wonderful equipment that the forces at Inceville offer are perhaps the best. So that his honors in producing this variety of pictures are well earned.

In The Bargain Mr. Ince and Mr. Clifford have produced a wonderfully strong western, which in its own particular class is very good.   It contains a typical western story, full of fast, thrilling action, some of which is most sensational.   One scene in particular warrants special mention.   William S. Hart, who plays the leading part, and his horse, which most certainly must be a trick animal, roll over and over down a steep embankment.

This act in itself is most wonderful, but it seems almost miraculous when we learn that neither of them was seriously injured. Mr. Hart, who plays the part of Bill Stokes, "The Two-Gun Man," is constantly exhibiting his prowess in the saddle throughout the picture.   The times when he is not astride his horse he is exhibiting his ability as an actor, and altogether gives an excellent account of himself.

J. Frank Burke is cast as the sheriff, Clara Williams as the girl, J. Barney Sherry as her father, and James Dawley appears in the small part of the traveling minister.   Photographically the picture is excellent.   Some remarkably extensive scenes have been obtained, and the film is clear in all parts.   As the picture was taken in the Grand Canyon of Arizona, scenes have been obtained which are not at all familiar, which give the picture an air of decided freshness.

The experiences and hair-breadth escapes of Stokes, the Two-Gun Man, consume the major portion of the picture.   Once he poses as an honest man and wins the heart of the daughter of a miner. Then he has to flee for his life.   Finally he is caught on the Mexican border, just as he is about to reform and send the money he robbed the mail of back to the government.

The sheriff locks him in a room, then repairs to the gambling hall, where he proves he is not such a competent sheriff after all, by losing all the money.   He bargains with his prisoner that if he will get the money back for him he will give him his freedom. This the bandit does in a very clever manner.   He returns for his bride, explains matters and the two set off for Mexico to live straight.

--Peter Milne in Motion Picture News, Vol. 10, No. 20 (November 21, 1914), page 41.

*   *   *

This is a weird spot on the Paramount program.   It is a bold, I might even say a reckless, attempt to revive a style of motion picture which we had hoped was a thing of the past.   Old-timers well remember the days when exchanges and newspapers cataloguing films divided them into "Drama," "Comic" and "Western."   In 1908 and 1909, and even later, "Western" dominated many programs. Nor will it be denied that in the heyday of the single reel many of these "Westerns" were splendid pictures, often portraying most

accurately and most pathetically and most picturesquely the life of
the early West. Indeed, the success of the early pictures soon
produced an excess of supply over demand and the public became
surfeited not to say nauseated with sheriffs, outlaws, bad Indians,
good Indians, Mexican villains, heroic outlaws, desperate halfbreeds,
etc.

  The Bargain is nothing more than an old-fashioned "Western."
I cannot truthfully say that it is one inch above the average of such
pictures. Its scenic background is superbly beautiful, but not more
so than that shown in many old single reels. Its plot follows the
old familiar lines: the outlaw, finely acted by William S. Hart,
robs the stage coach, wounding or killing at least one of the men
on the top of the coach, then he steals the money belonging to the
express company, and then, still following familiar lines, the bandit
falls in love with a good girl. He repents of his robbery and decides
to return the stolen money, but the sheriff gets him before he can
make restitution.

  Here comes a slight departure from conventional lines. While
in the old-fashioned pictures the sheriff is a rock of honesty, this
officeholder is tainted with a fatal weakness, and, taking the stolen
money from the bandit, loses it in the gambling hall. Now comes
The Bargain. The bandit proposes to the sheriff that he "turn him
loose," promising in return to get the lost money back. The bandit
is as good as his word, holds up a gang of gamblers, gets the money
and returns it to the sheriff. The latter, duly grateful, allows the
outlaw two hours to reach the "Mexican border." The outlaw escapes happily and something like six felonies committed by two men
go entirely unpunished.

  It is said that pictures of this sort are still popular in certain
sections of the country and that nickelodeons in many big cities still
yearn for them. This may be true, but it does not alter the fact
that pictures of this sort have in the past been the most dangerous
weapon in the hands of our enemies. There can be no doubt whatever that a picture of this kind has a bad influence on youthful minds.
I hear it has been passed by the Board of National Censors. If this
is true, the board have for the time suspended all the rules so nicely defined in their little pamphlet.

--W. Stephen Bush in The Moving
Picture World, Vol. 22, No. 10
(December 5, 1914), page 1390.

☐ THE BATTLE CRY OF PEACE (Vitagraph, 1915)

  The Battle Cry of Peace, the new Vitagraph feature, is to the
usual motion picture as the American football game to lawn tennis.
There is tremendous mass play, occasional brilliant sprinting of action, spectacular displays of gigantic forces at death grips; but there

is no romance, no constant presentation of leading players in a con-
secutive story.   In other words, it is cohesion of idea and not of
plot.   With all the insistence of the measured beating of tympani, it
repeats with every turn of the crank: "These terrible things may
happen to you, to your home, to your loved ones, if America does
not arouse herself from her lethargy and arm against (not for) war."

In the first part, Hudson Maxim is seen delivering a lecture,
the alternating scenes amplifying his statement of the defenselessness
of America, showing modern types of fighting machines with which
this country is so inadequately supplied.   John Harrison, a vigorous
American type, impressed with the argument, presents it to Mr.
Vandergriff, a multimillionaire railway owner and peace, or rather
disarmament advocate, but he has come under the influence of a
foreign spy, Mr. Emanon.   Incidentally Harrison loves Vandergriff's
daughter.   The spies are shown working secretly, preparing for an
invasion within the month.   This invasion comes in the second part,
bombardment of New York without warning causing tremendous destruction.   This is the spectacular division of the film, explosions,
flight of terrified thousands, conflagrations, and all manner of disaster being pictured with graphic intensity.   In part three the enemy
has landed.   Emanon betrays Harrison and Vandergriff into the hands
of the invaders, and they are placed in a squad which is mowed down
by a machine gun.   Miss Vandergriff kills Emanon, when he tries
to make forcible love to her, and with her mother, sister and brother, flies in an automobile.   They visit the place of execution and
discover that Harrison is not dead, but in trying to escape with him
they are captured, and Harrison is bayoneted when he strikes an officer of the invading forces who insults his sweetheart.   In the power
of the brutal officer, Mrs. Vandergriff kills her two daughters to
save them from the fate suggested, and herself goes insane.   Parts
four and five suggest general educational methods to be employed to
make such events impossible, and introduce real and allegorical
scenes calculated to inspire patriotism, and promote a revival of the
spirit of the G.A.R. and of '76.

At the opening projection at the Vitagraph Theater, New York,
a mistaken idea of producing realism by hammering the bass drum
for every cannon shot and bomb explosion, accompanied by a weird
assortment of other noises, even to the cries of the scurrying populace and groans of the wounded by a mob behind the screen, made
the general effect so confusing that it was impossible to concentrate
the mind upon the serious matter presented.   Still, two points stand
out.

First: The photography is magnificent throughout, and at
times transcendently beautiful.   The night scenes of Coney Island
and Times Square, showing the well known electric signs in full operation, are astonishing, even to those who know something of the
speed of the cinema's eye.

Second: The horrors attending the descent of a hostile force
upon a defenseless land are shown with a ruthlessness that makes

the message "register." This was the sole aim of the author, J.
Stuart Blackton. But the question now remains, whether or not argument can be regarded as entertainment. Granted the subject is
vital and timely, it seems, upon reflection, that fully one-third of
the film is reading matter, and necessarily so. Will the public pay
for propaganda, even if the propaganda is popular? That is the
question that The Battle Cry of Peace presents. If the answer is
"Yes," motion photography has reached another stage in its evolution.
                                    --Julian Johnson in Photoplay, Vol.
                                    8, No. 6 (November 1915), pages
                                    80-81.

☐ BEHIND THE DOOR (Ince/Paramount-Artcraft, 1920)

        This is the story of a strong man's revenge, woven with con-
summate skill and enacted by a cast of great types, headed by Hobart Bosworth, veteran of many a picture of the great outdoors and
who fits in the role of Captain Krug, a German American in command of a U.S. merchant marine ship during the war, as perhaps
no other actor of the whole profession might. As a foil for his
wonderful portrayal Mr. Bosworth has Wallace Beery, who plays the
part of the German submarine commander.

        The story begins on land, with Captain Krug suspected of be-
ing a German sympathizer. It ends on the high seas, with the war
of the world, so far as Krug is concerned, narrowed down to a personal conflict with the German who has outraged his wife beyond the
power of words to express it, and the inflicting upon him of the
most terrible vengeance that the strong mind of a man who hated to
the point of insanity could devise.

        You do not see what goes on "behind the door" except by
shadows, as the two giants of the human race struggle, but there is
no mistaking what is occurring. Even if the craftsmanship in film
construction and the acting of those whom the film purports are seeing had failed, which it does not, you would still know what had happened.

        Dramatically it is a great picture. Rough, even brutal and
horribly realistic, is the story which Irvin Willat has evolved from
Gouverneur Morris' story as published in Collier's, but it will not
soon be forgotten. And it marks Hobart Bosworth's return to the
screen. Both this fact and the production are events.
                                    --J.S. Dickerson in Motion Pic-
                                    ture News, Vol. 21, No. 4
                                    (January 17, 1920), page 915.

                        *   *   *

Only the other day we made a plea in Photoplay for tales of

the sea, not knowing at the time that out in the Thomas H. Ince studio they were making a grim and terrific drama of the ocean lanes,
Behind the Door, made by Luther Reed from the Gouverneur Morris
story. It is a drama of the sea in its most ferocious mood--the
period when it gave shelter to those pirates of civilization, the U-
Boats. At their mildest, the water prairies arouse all the fundamental emotions, strip them bare of pretence, and bring men and
women into grips with themselves. Lash this landscape into fury,
either with the storms of blustering Boreas, or the storms of human
passions gone awry and the result fairly wrenches the soul with
grandeur or with tragedy. It is such a tragedy that Hobart Bosworth, as captain of an American liner traveling the waters infested
by submarines, is called upon to portray in Behind the Door. It
took courage to make such a picture as this, for it is a "he-
picture," no pap for puling infants.

--Photoplay, Vol. 17, No. 4
(March 1920), page 111.

☐ BELLA DONNA (Famous Players-Lasky, 1915)

In Bella Donna, Pauline Frederick scored more heavily than
the producers. This tale of violet-scented villainy, of gold-plated
murder, was susceptible of more subtlety, of a keener-bladed thrill,
than it received. Gazing at Miss Frederick's performance of the iniquitous woman, I'll believe you'll say hers is the best dramatic assumption this modern Borgia has ever had. Certainly it was better
than Nazimova's upon the stage of the Empire Theatre, for Nazimova
was more snake than human being. There is no fault to find with
setting or material equipment; only, the direction as a whole did not
approach Miss Frederick's personal performance.

--Julian Johnson in Photoplay, Vol.
9, No. 3 (February 1916), page
105.

☐ THE BETTER 'OLE (Welsh-Pearson/World, 1919)*

There are several reasons why I am glad to see The Better
'Ole getting a general American welcome. For one thing, it is first-
hand information on the pathos and humor of the first black months
of war, such as could not possibly be possessed by any man not in-
timately concerned with it, as was the cartoonist-captain, Bruce
Bairnsfather. It is novel, and different. And last but far from

---

*Directed by George Pearson, The Better 'Ole was one of the first
major British films to be released in the U.S. It was remade in
1926 by Warner Bros.

least, it is a look through another man's camera. No matter how
perfect our own productions are, we'll fall into a rut of some kind
unless we have a chance to make foreign comparisons, even though
such comparisons seem heavily in our favor. Three actors whom
we do not know at all and may never see again play, respectively,
Old Bill, Bert and Alf: Charles Rock, Arthur Cleve, and Hugh E.
Wright. As fillers of the lines and shadows of Mr. Bairnsfather's
drawings, they are a combination of sadness and uproar. They are
human. The story is only a conventional little melo; the depictions,
incidents and subtitles are highly unconventional. The piece shows
the army of a real democracy, "grousing" at pomp and military
ceremony--plain duffers anxious to finish up their job of war and
get home again. And alas for the sensibilities of the arid--these
lads certainly did not return to a beerless England! Barks Old Bill:
"Alf, take yer feet out o' the water we got to sleep in!" There's
the cheerful irony of the whole thing.

> --Julian Johnson in Photoplay, Vol.
> 16, No. 1 (July 1919), pages
> 119-120.

☐ THE BIRTH OF A NATION (Epoch, 1915)

   And the greatest of these is D. W. Griffith, whose magnum
opus, The Birth of a Nation, was shown to specially assembled
spectators at the Liberty theatre, New York City, on Monday, March
1, two days before its public presentation in the same theatre.

   As a spectacle D'Annunzio's Cabiria will never be made to
appear foolish. Probably the strongest story yet seen on the screen
is that of Judith of Bethulia, taken from the Apocalypse, that part
of the Bible which appears between the Old and New Testaments in
old versions.

   But for a combination of spectacle and story (and emotional
appeal follows the latter as the night follows the day), The Birth
of a Nation has never been approached.

   An attempt to criticise The Birth of a Nation would be utter
folly. The word criticism is odious and is reserved for cub re-
porters with its implication of superior knowledge. A review of the
picture might be attempted. But the proper frame of mind in which
to attack the typewriter is the one adduced by seeing the picture and
that is appreciation and reverence.

   In the reviewer's mind, as he follows scene after scene of
this greatest of photo dramas, every one of the whole gamut of
screen essentials and possibilities is met and fulfilled. Historically
it is magnificent; it is a great, true, artistic photograph of the crisis of a great war. Educationally it takes rank with, and excels in
vital ways, our best war records.

True Greatness Is Its Emotional Appeal

In dramatic and photographic technique, it is beyond our present day criticism. These are surpassing accomplishments; but these are not all. The true greatness of this production lies in its emotional appeal, an appeal so forceful that it lifts you out of your seat and thrills you as the speaking stage never did and never will. This is the greatness of the motion picture, at last realized. And did any one of us ever believe it could be done--like this?

Griffith is the present day Homer of the motion picture industry. Remember what Kipling said about Homer?

When Homer smote his blooming lyre
"He made men sing by land and sea
"And what he thought he might require
"He went and took the same as me."

For The Birth of a Nation Griffith has taken Thomas Dixon's novel The Clansman as a foundation. On this foundation he has builded a structure bits of which are reminiscent of (and possibly suggested by) works of art and literature of many ages. These are woven together with masterful motion picture technique into a harmonious whole which is ninety per cent. Griffith and ten per cent. other great minds.

There are bits which remind one of Cabiria, such as the silhouette of the Ku Klux Klan crossing the brow of a hill in the moonlight as the camels did in Cabiria. There is a wonderful man-to-man encounter, plainly speaking, a fist fight, which overshadows the remarkable fight in The Spoilers. There is an allegorical scene which reminds one of the famous painting "War," which showed a giant horseman on an idiot steed riding rough-shod over grovelling human bodies. But the whole picture is Griffithian and Griffith is the master painter of the screen.

Historical Value of Scenes Is Marked

Too much stress can not be laid upon the value of the picture as a spectacle and on the historical value of such scenes as Lee's surrender and the assassination of Lincoln. Never before, on canvas, by photography, or by literature has the great grapple of the Civil War been so graphically visualized. The Civil War scenes of the first half of the picture, showing Sherman's march to the sea, the burning of Atlanta, the downfall of Petersburg, and the gathering of the Ku Klux Klan in the second half and the attack made by that organization to save the beleaguered whites are spectacles unsurpassed. The stage with its four brick walls could never begin to rival them. No pageant has ever been produced which bore the meaning and interest these scenes do. Nor have the scenes been surpassed by the spectacular element in any other motion picture.

At the conclusion of the performance cries for "Griffith" brought the producer before the curtain, for a little speech which ended in choking voice.

The theme of The Clansman, from which The Birth of a Nation is taken is a strong one.   Mr. Griffith has dealt with it along the lines of the old instructions on grasping a nettle.   He has handled the theme so strongly that its sting is crushed.   The Clansman dealt with the conflict between the whites and the negroes in the reconstruction period of the South.   The Birth of a Nation devotes its second half to that theme.   The first half deals with the Civil War itself.

It is entirely fair at this time to remember that the Civil War occurred some fifty years ago.   So, sub-titles accentuating memories of the past may not be relished by all.   It is hard for a New Englander accurately to predict what the attitude of the South will be toward the picture, especially as the views of several Southerners, who saw the picture, varied greatly.   It must be borne in mind that this paragraph deals in no way with the merits of the picture as a picture.   The scenes between Austin Stoneman and the mulatto girl are unnecessary, though well played.

Griffith's technique stands alone.   It has been carried further than ever in The Birth of a Nation.   Better than any other he understands the value of perspective, dramatic values, the use of photography and repressed yet forceful work by the players.   Time and time again in this picture the action in the big scenes stretches away and away in the distance as far as the eye can reach.   Time and again two parallel lines of fighters move slowly across the line of vision.

Combination of Spectacle and Story

The burning of Atlanta and the downfall of Petersburg, impressive and stirring scenes, are two instances of clever use of photography.   They are done in double exposure with the field of vision not cut straight across but cut on an irregular line with several indentations.   Above the spectator sees the burning city, flames shooting out of crumbling houses, while below are the fleeing inhabitants and the pursuing soldiery.

The Birth of a Nation is a most happy and strong combination of spectacle and story.   To do the spectacle justice is practically impossible.   It is a low down trick to think of dollars and cents when art is concerned, but just the same it is hard to see this picture and not think "Griffith certainly didn't care how he spent money when he put this on."   For many times the horses and men cover the screen in the battle scenes and the action depicted must cover several miles of ground.   Further, the main street of an ante-bellum Southern town was especially constructed as was an historically exact

replica of Ford's theatre, where Lincoln was shot. The scenes
around the president's assassination are as gripping as they could
be in any speaking production.

But spectacle is spectacle and never, per se, will grip the
heart and mind. So what really makes The Birth of a Nation a thing
to be remembered, what stamps it on the mind, what makes the
spectator think, is its theme, its story.

The Birth of a Nation is divided for exhibition purposes into
two acts, each of them about 5,500 feet long. Each is practically
complete, yet not quite so without the other. The first act is devoted to the struggle between the North and the South. In this act
comes the terrific battles of the Civil War, Sherman's march to the
sea, the burning of Atlanta, the downfall of Petersburg, Lee's surrender to Grant and the assassination of Lincoln.

The second half is devoted to the Clansman's story of the
reconstruction period. In this come the enfranchisement of the slaves
and the subsequent attempt by carpet-baggers to "crush the White
South under the heel of the Black South" and the answer of the White
South in the shape of the Ku Klux Klan. Closing the picture a few
well chosen allegorical scenes, carrying a preachment against war.

The main characters in the story are the members of two
families, one Southern and one Northern. Ralph Lewis plays Austin
Stoneman, the father of the Northern family, who later carpet-bags
it to the South and sets up his protege, Silas Lynch, a mulatto, as
lieutenant-governor. Stoneman's daughter, Elsie, is played by Lillian Gish. Spottiswoode Aitken and Mrs. Crowell play Mr. and Mrs.
Cameron, parents of the Southern family. Mae Marsh and Miriam
Cooper play the Southern girls, while Henry Walthall is Col. Ben
Cameron of the Confederate army. Robert Harron has a small part
as a Northern boy. George Siegmann plays Silas Lynch, the gigantic
mulatto.

Picture Is Excellently Cast

The picture is so excellently cast that it is unfair to single
any of the players out for especial praise. Without exception they
are competent. Still, if one must bow to custom, the most conspicuous are Henry Walthall, Mae Marsh and Miriam Cooper, whose
work elevates her to stellar ranks. Ralph Lewis and Mrs. Crowell
give the excellent work for which they may be trusted. George
Siegmann and Spottiswoode Aitken are not under as severe histrionic
demands, but do well what they have to do.

In the first half of the picture there is shown the friendship
between the Camerons and the Stonemans. Ben Cameron falls in
love with Elsie Stoneman's daguerreotype. Then comes the outbreak
of the war and the subsequent battle and historical scenes. Ben
Cameron, wounded and in the hospital, meets Elsie.

After the war comes the even more horrible reconstruction period with the racial conflicts. Cameron's sister (Mae Marsh) leaps to her death from a high cliff to escape the attentions of a degenerate negro. Ben organizes the Ku Klux Klan. His sister is avenged. But Ben's action in joining the Ku Klux earns him Elsie's refusal when he asks her to marry him.

Silas Lynch, mulatto, and protege of Stoneman, covets Elsie. The contrast between the coffee-colored brute and the lily-like white girl is striking. The Ku Klux Klan gather, in impressive scenes, and set out to disarm the negroes. Meanwhile the Camerons have been forced, with the exception of Ben, to flee. Elsie goes to Lynch's house to beg for mercy and thereby plays into his hands. He sees his chance and forcibly detains the girl. Her father, who comes to the house, is held off by other negroes.

Then comes the cleverly worked up quadruple climax. The actions flash back and forth from the gathering and riding to the res-cue of the Ku Klux Klan to the Camerons, besieged in a wooden cot-tage, to Elsie Stoneman's predicament and to the street fighting be-tween the whites and the blacks. The finale brought the spectators to their feet. The Ku Klux Klan rescues the Camerons and Elsie and disperse and disarm the blacks. Then follow the allegorical scenes and Ben and Elsie's happiness.

Stirring and strong as the action is, the little human and comedy touches, such as only Griffith can give, relieve the tension and make the atmosphere of the picture far from gloomy.

Now for the benediction. It is regrettable that the phrase "greatest picture ever produced" has been used so often that its strength has been abrogated through over-enthusiasm and over-eagerness to please. But, had that phrase never been used, now would be the time to use it. For The Birth of a Nation is the greatest picture yet produced. In fact, it is so great that it seems to be a photographic record of actual happenings, rather than the handiwork of the master producer.

--George D. Proctor in Motion
Picture News, Vol. 11, No. 10
(March 13, 1915), pages 49-50.

*   *   *

The scoffers came to see Cabiria, and left overwhelmed with admiration, but only half-converted. "It is a triumph of pictorial art," they said, "but its appeal is solely to the eye, and we have long granted that province to the motion picture."

They came again to see The Birth of a Nation. But this time found tongues stilled, minds stunned, as the last scene faded from the screen. Here was drama that wrung tears from a far-from-impressionable audience, spectacle worthy of panegyrics, a treat-ment of human problems that has furnished seed for endless discus-sion. And it is a motion picture.

One is sorely tempted to seek safety in bromides when setting out to review The Birth of a Nation. The pen falters in vain
search for means of expression, and collapses with "The greatest
picture ever produced." But this bromidic truth tells only half of
the story; it means comparison, and Griffith's greatest triumph in
The Birth of a Nation is in a field in which he is a pioneer. We
may compare the stupendous battle scenes with the spectacular Cabiria, the intense dramatic passages with moments in a half-score
of productions, but with its selection and treatment of a vital theme
the past offers nothing for comparison.

This is the summit of Griffith's achievement--he has created
thought and discussion. Perhaps he may not have moulded that
thought to his own ideas, the discussion may more often be disagreement, but that is the penalty of grappling with throbbing themes.
You may not approve of the reopening of old sores to furnish a
present-day thesis, but Griffith has presented his justification, for
you to accept or reject, in the introductory sub-title, "The viewpoint of the South on the great events of the Civil War and the Reconstruction period has never been impartially presented in the pages
of history."

That presentment Griffith sets out to give. He chose The
Clansman for his text, but dug deeper for his foundation. The Stonemans of the North, and the Camerons of Piedmont, N.C., furnish
the personal element. Austin Stoneman is a "power in Washington";
his children, Phil, Tod and Elsie, are friendly with the Camerons.
The sons' visit to Piedmont serves to introduce us to the placid
beauties of the South of 1860. A few deft touches paint it a contented and carefree South. Then we are whirled into the vortex of
the Civil War, and from here on Griffith mingles spectacle and story
with the hand of a genius, his eyes set always on the creation of a
single impression--that of sympathy, bordering on admiration, for
the South of the Reconstruction period, the South of the Ku Klux
Klan. His means to the end are twofold, firstly, a portrayal of the
bitterness engendered by the Civil War and the heavy hand of desola-
tion it laid upon the South; second, the painting, in broad, scarlet
strokes, of the negro granted equality, and the attempt of the radi-
cals of the North to "crush the White South under the heels of the
Black South."

The war scenes present the Griffith technique on a broader
scale than it has ever been seen. In that showing the burning of
Atlanta we look from an eminence across a plain dotted with the
figures of the fleeing populace and harassing troops. Tearful women, clinging to their helpless children, and wounded, stumbling
soldiers in gray pass before us. The high note is sounded with a
masterpiece of double exposure when the flaming city is shown above
the panic-stricken flight.

It is difficult to hope that any war scenes will soon surpass
those showing the Petersburg battle. For miles away the perspective
disclosed twisting lines of opposing trenches. Cannon and rifle belch,

and now and again serried lines of blue or gray surge forth to the
charge. Awe-inspiring panoramas are followed by nerve-gripping
close-up views of hand-to-hand fighting. The bombardment by night
and Sherman's march to the sea are only two of the many other war
views that deserve more lengthy mention than is possible here.

But Griffith has his purpose in view, and lest you be carried
away by the martial aspect of the conflict, he craftily interposes
views of the real sufferers, the "folks at home." From a pulse-
quickening charge you are transported to a heart-torn mother learning of the death of her sons. This portrayal of war is undoubtedly
one of the strongest of arguments for universal peace, though that
is a by-product of the picture, and not its underlying motive.

The close of the war finds Ben Cameron returning to a Piedmont that is in ruins. But the South is indomitable and sets out
hopefully to rebuild a shattered empire. Then the fanatical mind of
Booth removes the South's greatest friend. The scene showing the
assassination of Lincoln is a masterpiece of screen technique and
historical accuracy. It is real enough to shock.

The showing of events up to this tragedy has taken close to
six thousand feet of film. As presented at the Liberty Theatre this
forms the first act. The second half deals more particularly with
The Clansman and its terrible story of the suffering of the Reconstruction. Carpetbaggers flood the South, and under the leadership
of Stoneman they plan political domination through the control of the
enfranchised negro. Little instances of negro aggression, mounting
in importance, lead up to the producer's commanding justification
for the Ku Klux. Flora, Ben's younger sister, is forced to suicide
by jumping from a cliff to escape the attack of a crazed negro. The
Ku Klux, organized by Ben Cameron, as the result of an inspiration
most cleverly shown, avenges her. A night is chosen to disarm the
negroes.

We are now approaching scenes that, in their swift onrush of
action, surcharged with excitement, reach the pinnacle of intensity.
The blacks' answer to the Ku Klux is a night of terror for Piedmont.
While they overrun the stricken town, terrorizing the white populace,
the Ku Klux members are gathering at a distant point for the supreme effort. Dr. Cameron and his family have been forced to flee,
pursued by a hounding pack of negroes. Elsie Stoneman seeks aid
from Silas Lynch, a mulatto leader of the blacks. His reply is a
proposal of marriage; her indignant rejection is met with violence
and she is imprisoned, while preparations are made for an enforced
wedding. Flashes take us from this scene to various other parts of
the hell-ridden town, then to the Camerons besieged in a cabin surrounded by armed negroes, and finally to the Ku Klux Klan, silent,
spectral figures, gathering in the shadowed woods. Word is brought
of Elsie's peril and the mad race to the rescue is begun. There
seem to be hundreds upon hundreds of the white-clad figures, as
they stretch out in pale relief against the night's darkness.

The pitch is heightened by every device of the Griffithian art until the climax, with the conflict in the streets of Piedmont, the rescue of Elsie and later of the Camerons, and the day dawns with a Ku Klux triumphal parade.

The love story of the main characters is settled, and here the picture could well end. But "even Homer nods," and trite allegorical passages are dragged in to preach a universal peace moral. They seem weak in comparison with the wonders that have preceded, lame in their application to a story that in every other respect is developed with the hand of a master craftsman.

The acting is such as only Griffith can command. Henry Walthall's work is at all times impressive. His moment of agony on realizing that his pet sister is dead is a bit of histrionic art that will not be easily erased from the memory. Mae Marsh surpasses the fondest prophecies of her admirers as Flora Cameron. Her every move is carefully planned acting, yet so clever is the art that it is not acting. But why attempt to give due credit to such a cast? Lillian Gish, George Siegmann, Ralph Lewis, Josephine Crowell, Spottiswoode Aitken, Mary Alden, Jennie Lee, one and all, principals and minor characters, down even to the extras, seem to be players of ability. Miriam Cooper's work causes surprising disagreement. There are those who praise her repression, others who criticize the over-stress of placidity.

But the hand of Griffith overshadows all. Telling his story fearlessly and masterfully, at times he cuts deep beneath the skin, till one must question the brutality while praising the art. Times are when he seems more the skillful lawyer than the impartial historian, but never is he a boresome pleader. If there is to be a greater picture than The Birth of a Nation, may we live to see it.

--W. in The New York Dramatic
Mirror, Vol. 73, No. 1890
(March 10, 1915), page 28.

☐ THE BIRTH OF A RACE (Renco, 1919)

A few words will suffice to do justice to The Birth of a Race. Starting with the creation, it attempts to follow the development of mankind down to the present day, and throws in a disconnected war story for good measure. About everything has been applied to the production but common sense. There are numerous scenes from sacred history which employ mammoth sets, large mobs and the services of actors of established reputation. The Garden of Eden, the Tribes of Noah's Time, the Land of Egypt, Jerusalem at the time of Christ, and on down to the present are presented at an outlay of time, labor and money that are astonishing--and all to no artistic purpose. The structure is without form and is a striking example of what a photoplay should not be. The disconnected modern

story is no better than the biblical history in its handling. The producers have attempted to impress by bulk and have been overwhelmed
by their lack of skill.

The names of three men are given as the authors of the scenario. It will be a deed of charity not to reveal their identity nor
the names of the members of the cast. All have well earned reputations and are probably anxious to live down their connection with
the entire affair.

> --Edward Weitzel in The Moving
> Picture World, Vol. 40, No. 6
> (May 10, 1919), page 938.

☐ BLACK ORCHIDS (Bluebird/Universal, 1917)*

The author of Black Orchids, a five-reel romance produced
for the Bluebird by Rex Ingram, is a master of his profession--a
writer fit to rank with Guy de Maupassant or Edgar Allan Poe. The
story has all the unbridled passion of the French author's work and
several touches of the uncanny and horrible that is associated with
the creator of The Murder in the Rue Morgue. Love and lust, a
fatal duel, murder by poison, insane jealousy that ends in a horrible death for two more of the characters, and a father that succeeds
in supplanting his son in the affections of a notorious woman, are
the main incidents of a drama which deals almost exclusively with
open defiance of all moral law, but which nevertheless holds the
spectator's undivided attention to the end of the last reel.

The heroine of this carnival of crime is a beautiful woman,
a fortune teller who reads the destinies of others by the aid of crystal gazing, but fails to foresee her own finish. She becomes, successively, the mistress of three men, then doubles back to the first
of the trio--the young chap whose father has had him sent to the
front battle line so that he may not interfere with the elder man's
intrigue with the fascinating sibyl. The drama gets its title from a
wreath of black orchids which the woman has procured for the tomb
of her third lover, after the young soldier fights with and supposes
he has killed the gentleman--a wealthy marquis who has willed the
crystal gazer a larger fortune. Although fatally wounded, the noble-
man has sufficient strength to plan and execute a terrible revenge
on the woman and his rival. He succeeds in trapping them both in
an air-tight vault, and then dies upon the threshold, the fourth victim of a violent death.

It goes without saying that the one factor that could make such
a story acceptable to the greater portion of moving picture patrons
is a display of the highest artistic achievement in the drama's production.

---

*Rex Ingram remade Black Orchids in 1922 as Trifling Women.

Black Orchids has received just such treatment at the hands of the
director, the cameraman and the members of the cast. Rex Ingram
has been particularly successful with his part of the work. While
no points of the plot are glossed over or left in doubt, there is no
undue stress put upon any of the incidents, and the atmosphere which
surrounds the entire story belongs to it by right of birth. Artistic
settings and effects are of frequent occurrence, and Duke Hayward's
camera has lost none of their beauty or weird suggestion.

Cleo Madison plays the French Vampire, and Wedgewood
Nowell, Howard Crampton and Francis McDonald her trio of lovers.
All are excellent selections physically and show fine artistic perception. Black Orchids is a tale within a tale, a story written by a
celebrated French novelist and told to his capricious daughter, that
she may be warned of the harm which lies within the power of a
fickle woman. Heroic treatment, perhaps, but it effects a speedy
cure.

> --Edward Weitzel in The Moving
> Picture World, Vol. 31, No. 1
> (January 6, 1917), pages 98-99.

                              *   *   *

Among Universal's best pieces this month are Black Orchids,
a violent melodrama of considerable compulsion, and Polly, Put the
Kettle On. Black Orchids has a needlessly dirty note in its plot,
but if you wish a thrill of medieval horror to jar you out of placidity, have a look. No, we won't tell you what it is. Cleo Madison,
who in months has perpetrated nothing but matrimony to keep her
name in the papers, is the principal performess.

> --Julian Johnson in Photoplay, Vol.
> 11, No. 4 (March 1917), page
> 120.

☐ BLIND HUSBANDS (Universal, 1919)

Erich von Stroheim has always been a consummate actor.
He has proved his histrionic ability as the living symbol of Prussi-
anism in Hearts of the World, and The Heart of Humanity. We little
dreamed, however, that he is a master story teller and a very capable director as well. He has come forward as the sponsor of Blind
Husbands, a picture of the eternal triangle, and of all the subjects
which have been based upon this favorite theme, his creation looms
up as one of the best things ever conceived. Enacted against the
Alps, the pictorial appeal is no stronger than its drama. It throbs
with vitality and soars with tremendous sweep straight to its climax.
And it is always lifelike in plot and characterization.

Mr. Stroheim makes the "other man" unique. He does not
impress you as a moral leper or a despoiler of feminine virtue; he

only suggests a weakling, a youth irresponsible for his actions. But just as sure as his performance is the skill with which he has woven the dramatic threads together. There is no play for heroics, no bid for big climaxes. These come spontaneously without effort. And so the picture does not assume the aspect of a photoplay but resembles a slice from life. The action is intensity itself and the suspense is at times overpowering--especially when the husband and the lover make the ascent of the Pinnacle. One instinctively feels some impending tragedy.

The summit is reached after a perilous climb. And it surely is a dramatic spot for the climax. And after the lover has revealed his true colors he is left to perish. An uncanny touch depicts the shadows of vultures hovering about waiting for his death. The atmosphere and the details are correct. Nothing is missing to make this picture a greater achievement.

--Laurence Reid in Motion Picture
News, Vol. 20, No. 17 (October
18, 1919), page 3044.

*   *   *

Technically, Erich von Stroheim's photodrama, Blind Husbands, is a flashing thing--but it lacks soul and spirit. Von Stroheim will be remembered as the Hun villain of a number of wartime films. Blind Husbands, his own story produced by himself, relates the triangle of three people in the snow-capped Alps; a self-absorbed American doctor, his heart-lonely young wife and a young Austrian officer on sick leave. The dashing Austrian tries all Continental wiles upon the American girl, but he finally meets retribution in a fall down the snowy precipices of the Alps. Von Stroheim has told his story with remarkable directorial dexterity--but, in the end, it is just an adroitly presented silversheet melodrama. Von Stroheim's characters fall short of the breath of realism, despite the remarkable superficial excellence of his direction. He has, for instance, attained his Alpine effects in striking fashion.

--Frederick James Smith in Motion
Picture Classic, Vol. 9, No. 6
(February 1920), pages 48-49.

☐ THE BLUE BIRD (Paramount-Artcraft, 1918)

Here's to a flock of "Blue Birds"! We have it on the word of Maurice Maeterlinck that The Blue Bird brings happiness, and the screen version of the Belgian poet's beautiful fantasy is incontestible proof that his statement is true. The man who adds to the happiness of the world is entitled to a rich reward. And so the Famous Players-Lasky Corporation, that made the moving picture of one of the most human fairy stories ever written, should be repaid by achieving a financial success equal to the artistic merits of its pro-

duction. The scenario, by Charles Maigne, the direction, by Maurice Tourneur, and the acting by the members of the cast, all have
a share in shaping The Blue Bird into a screen poem of rare beauty.

The Maeterlinck masterpiece will appeal to every mind. It
has the simplicity of childhood and the wisdom of a deep but kindly
philosophy. It tells great truths and it teaches the folly of fear.
It dignifies the humble virtues and makes lovelier the graces of life.
It has delicious humor, and its note is always one of hope. The
lessons it teaches are for all ages. To sit under its spell is to receive an impulse for good that will never be effaced. It is a potent
argument in favor of the screen.

Technically considered, the closest scrutiny of the Artcraft
production finds but little that is not entitled to the highest praise.
Certain transformations could be quickened to advantage, and the
spell of weirdness is occasionally absent. For the most part the
desired effect is created with compelling power and the mood of the
poem is seldom lost. The first reel discloses a novel and amusing
bit of screencraft. The Rich Children are having a party at their
home across from the humble cottage where Tyltyl and Mytyl live.
The house is brilliant with lights, but the window shades are drawn.
Against the shades appear the grotesque silhouettes of the happy little dancers and the serious musicians, the latter blowing and sawing
and scraping away with untiring energy.

The list of weirdly impressive or rarely enchanting scenes
includes the Palace of Night, the graveyard at midnight, the Palace
of Luxuries, the Cavern of Miseries, the Cathedral of Happiness and
the Azure Palace. The last named is where the unborn children
remain until Time opens the gate and sends them to earth where
their mothers await them. Here the delicate, almost naive fancy of
Maeterlinck finds its most charming expression and Director Tourneur has reproduced the spirit of the episode with a poetic simplicity
that leaves nothing to be desired.

There is no need to recall in detail the story of the boy and
the girl who go in search of the Blue Bird of Happiness and return
to find that the object of their search dwells in their own home. The
mortals, fairies and the odd characters, Light, Night, Dog, Cat,
Fire, Water, Milk, Sugar and Bread that accompany the children on
their search are all excellently played. Robin Macdougall as Tyltyl
and Tula Belle as Mytyl are an uncommonly gifted pair of youngsters.
Little Miss Tula is the embodiment of naturalness, without missing
one of her points in the slightest degree. Emma Lowery as Mummy
Tyl, Katherine Bianchi as Berlingot's daughter, Charles Ascot as
Dog, Tom Corless as Cat and S. E. Popapovitch as Fire stand out
prominently. The Blue Bird is in six reels.

--Edward Weitzel in The Moving
Picture World, Vol. 36, No. 2
(April 13, 1918), page 283.

*   *   *

One of the countless moving-picture journals takes Life to task for not preferring the movie-picture play to the spoken drama by pointing out how much superior to The Copperhead is the film version of The Blue Bird. Of course our critic cannot demonstrate superiority in a comparison of two such entirely different things. There is an argument, however, in a comparison of the filmed The Blue Bird and the beautiful production of the Maeterlinck fairy play at the New Theatre. Life, having seen both, could ask for no fairer test of the artistic value of the two mediums. Even in one detail the comparison makes for laughter--the majestic sailing of the baby-laden ship in the stage version and the depiction of the same idea by the jerking of a toy-boat across a bit of smooth water before the movie camera.

--"Metcalfe" in Life, Vol. 71, No. 1854 (May 9, 1918), page 763.

*   *   *

There is no director of moving pictures with a keener sense of the beautiful than Maurice Tourneur, and his genius for creating scenes of exquisite loveliness comes to its full fruition in The Blue Bird, made from Maeterlinck's drama. It is so beautiful, from beginning to end, that it fairly stings the senses, awakening in the spectator esthetic emotions so long dormant, so seldom exercised, that the flashing light of the awakening is almost a surfeit of joy. Almost--only not entirely. For while this is an allegory, or dream picture, it is so closely bound to humanity in all its phases, that it goes deeper than the mere artistic observation, and appeals to the heart direct. I saw this wonderful picture in a small projection room, the lights flashing up between the reels, and yet a small company of staid editors and film folk were enchanted, and audible gasps could be heard from time to time as Tourneur's creation revealed some new, astonishing thing. It is Maeterlinck, himself--the Maeterlinck of the first decade of the twentieth century, after he had emerged from his decadence with a glorious understanding of the simplicity of existence.

The blue bird is the symbol of happiness. Two children go on a pilgrimage in search of this bird. All the common things of life--bread, milk, water, fire, the dog, the cat, and so on--are given souls and speech, and accompany them. They visit the Palace of Night, the graveyard, the home of children not yet born, and all sorts of mysterious places, finally discovering happiness to be just where they started. It is an idea that can be either platitudinous or illuminative, depending upon the treatment. I want to go on record as saying that the Tourneur interpretation is greater than the play as it existed in a book, and much greater than it was on the stage. This is because Tourneur has understood what Maeterlinck meant, and has added to the Belgian's masterpiece his own splendid imaginative powers. His selection of a cast was perfect, and I decline to praise any individual here, where there is not space to speak of all. Ben Carré superintended the construction of the marvelous sets, marvelous because they tell so much in such striking, simple manner.

This is one of the most important photodramas ever made.
It blazes a new trail in production. It is addressed to the keenest
and most critical audience. It defies the hypercritical. For the
vision to see the possibilities, the Artcraft executives deserve high
praise, scarcely second to that which must be accorded the genius
of the play himself--Tourneur.

--Randolph Bartlett in Photoplay,
Vol. 13, No. 6 (May 1918), p. 96.

☐ BLUE BLAZES RAWDEN (Ince/Paramount-Artcraft, 1918)

Laid in the Canadian Northwest, Blue Blazes Rawden, a five-
part Artcraft production written by J. G. Hawks, and featuring
William S. Hart, is strong on picturesque settings, and tells a human, if not particularly dramatic, story. The picture was directed
by the star, and supervised by Thomas H. Ince. It opens with the
promise of a struggle between two determined men for the possession of a woman, which is terminated in the second reel, when
"Blue Blazes" kills "Ladyfingers" Hilgard in a fair fight, the rest
of the story being devoted to the coming of the mother of Hilgard
and the remorse of Rawden when he realizes the grief he has caused
the sweet-faced old lady who thinks him her boy's best friend.

There are a few moments of real excitement when Babette
Du Fresne, the woman in the case, tells Hilgard's brother who it
was killed him, and the young chap takes the pistol thrust into his
hand and goes in search of "Blue Blazes." The lumber boss does
not deny his guilt or make any effort to defend himself, as the boy
raises the pistol and fires at his breast. Mortally wounded, he will
not permit young Hilgard to be harmed by his companions; nor will
he stay and allow Babette to care for his hurt. The mother of
"Ladyfingers" goes home without knowing the truth, and "Blue Blazes"
takes "the lone trail" into the wilderness to die.

There is a lively fist fight in the first half of the picture;
also a gripping pistol duel. For the most part, however, Blue
Blazes appeals more by the human side of its story than by the force
of its action, and a clean drive through to the end of the motive
which made Rawden, Hilgard, and Babette the central figures.

The local color is excellent, and the acting uniformly high
grade. William S. Hart portrays an entirely different nature from
that of his quiet and reserved badmen of the Southwest, and contrasts the open wildness of Rawden with his better feelings with much
skill. Maud George is vital and unconventional as Babette. Gertrude
Claire as Mrs. Hilgard, Robert McKim as "Ladyfingers," Hart
Hoxie as Joe La Barge, and Robert Gordon as Eric Hilgard complete the cast.

--Edward Weitzel in The Moving
Picture World, Vol. 35, No. 9
(March 2, 1918), page 1269.

*   *   *

In Blue Blazes Rawden William S. Hart gives the best exhibition of his acting ability that I have ever yet seen.   Rawden, a typical Hart terror, kills another "bad man" in a duel.   The dead man's
mother and young brother arrive and Rawden befriends them, re-
making his life to keep the mother from learning the character of
her son.   The story has no actual ending.   It is something of a
"slice of life."   Its interest lies in the struggle that goes on in the
heart of the naturally ferocious, brutal Rawden, turned gentle by
sheer determination.   Hart has tended, in recent pictures, toward
a certain immobility of countenance which is not acting.   It may be
realism, but it is not adapted to the screen.   In Blue Blazes Rawden he proves himself an actor of the first rank, for what is acting
but the projecting of an idea?   To my mind, Rawden is the best
thing Hart has ever done.   Maud George, who has seemed to be
waiting for nothing but an opportunity, finds it here in the role of
a half-breed girl, passionate and untamable.   She is hardly second
in interest to the star himself.

                              --Randolph Bartlett in Photoplay,
                              Vol. 13, No. 6 (May 1918), page
                              67.

☐   THE BRAT (Metro, 1919)

The Brat was a chorus girl.   She must have had an extremely
old-fashioned family, for "brat" went out of fashion as a colloquial-
ism about the time Roscoe Conkling came into prominence, and that
elegant and descriptive term "kid" entered the lingo Americana to
describe almost everything of that and many other sorts.   However,
the Brat was an exceptionally noble and unselfish chorus girl, so
perhaps she justified the antiquated appellation.   We find her entirely
ignorant, not devoid of an elfish charm, and so unwilling to make
use of the ordinary practices of her profession--that is to say, the
extraction of favors without return--that she is cast out in the rain,
against a wicked adventure, into the night court, and through it, into
her final happiness of home, comfort, plenty of eats, plenty of
clothes and a lot of kindness.   Maude Fulton wrote the original play,
produced by Oliver Morosco.   I don't know the impression that left,
because I didn't see it, but the photoplay leaves a blank expression
of unreality.   It is relieved only by the very fine acting of Nazimova
herself--she always manages to find some humanity even in her most
inhuman subjects--and the very fine and careful production which the
Rowland cohort supplied by the California studios.   Particularly an-
noying is that consummate ass, MacMillan Forrester, the chivalrous
writer-rescuer.   Seizing upon the Brat as copy, he brings her to
his house to be repeatedly insulted by his unreal and impossible
family, and, when moved by the ecstasies of composition, sits down,
grinning like an idiot or throwing some other spell which writers
are supposed to have when their pains take them, to embalm his
impressions in sentences.   His conduct and his household, and all

that it contains, are as inexcusable as the fairy-story of the play
itself.   As for me, I would have taken to heart that stately lady,
the scornful Angela, with fires no doubt beneath her icy exterior,
in preference to all the Brats the author could produce.   The subtitles are mainly stupid, but the performances of Frank Currier,
as a gluttonous cleric; of Bonnie Hill, as Angela; of Darrell Ross,
as Stephen, and, as we said before, of the exotic and artful Nazimova, as the Brat, are delightful.   Charles Bryant does not get off
well as the novelist.   Cursed with an asinine part, he contrives
only to make it worse.

> --Julian Johnson in Photoplay, Vol.
> 17, No. 1 (December 1919), page
> 73.

☐ BROKEN BLOSSOMS (Griffith/United Artists, 1919)

        If the celluloid prints of our day were destroyed by some
strange lover of gelatine among the moths and larvae there would
remain for the researchers of the next generation only the play-bills
and the press-notices.   And on viewing these I imagine they would
say, "This man Griffith certainly had his world by the tail--year
after year these laudations!   How tiresome!   Was there no one else
deserving the top of the column?"

        But at the risk of being called a mere D. Wark sycophant by
those that follow me, I must continue praising David W.   The immediate object of to-day's anthem is, as you probably surmise,
Broken Blossoms, a great photoplay of insignificant title.

        Let me say that Mr. Griffith's distinction lies not in the fact
that he writes fine narratives on the screen.   Other men do that.
The extraordinary part of Griffith is that he has never ceased to be
a pioneer.   He continues to advance.   He dares to present novelties
of form and novelties of material.   He does not always get away
with it, but he keeps right on pioneering.   He is a long ways from
dead, and already the Shakespeare-Bacon controversy has crawled
out of its narrow cell and taken a new form in the hexagonal debate
as to who invented the close-up.   People keep on appropriating his
notions, and he keeps on putting forth new notions.   He is like a
doctor who seldom troubles to make his nostrums proprietary--a
year or two after some Griffith knick-knack has been generally
adopted almost anybody can tell you that Griffith didn't invent it at
all--Harold Mike Bings did it first, in A Sight for the Gods.

        To come to a more intimate consideration of Broken Blossoms:
it is the first genuine tragedy of the movies.   An unhappy ending
doesn't constitute tragedy; tragedy seems fore-ordained; the drums
of doom are sounding from the first steps of the pageant.   So they
are for Lucy, the forlorn little thing without a last name, unwelcome
child of a Limehouse bruiser, idol of a half-crazy Oriental idealist.

Mr. Griffith's adaptation of Thomas Burke's grotesque red story,
"The Chink and the Child," is extraordinarily clever.   There the
Celestial was little more than a coolie--an old beast of the East in
whom, somehow, the forlorn little girl lit a queer late lambent
spark of immortality.   It would have been hard to make an Occi-
dental audience accept Burke's slant on this dirty, dried old citron;
sounds well enough in a book that you don't have to read aloud,
maybe, but in a show it would almost certainly be disgusting.   Especially to men, who sometimes reverence women more than women
reverence themselves.   So in making the Chinaman a splendid but
embittered and fallen young Buddhist, D. W. rose authorially in that
moment right alongside Mr. Burke.

For the rest, the tale runs as written except for the very
finish, with Lucy dragging out her cowering little life by the London
waterside, beaten into semi-imbecility by her accidental father,
picked up, reverenced, honored and enthroned by the lonely opium-
eater, and at length slain in a monstrous moment of mock-virtue by
the insensate chunk that caused her to come into the world.   Then
the beast dies before the Chinaman's gun, the Chinaman dies upon
his own knife, and the cycle is finished.   There is a satisfaction in
the death of all three that is an unconscious verification of both its
art and its truth.   Burrows the battler should not survive the weak
little thing he made and slew, and for the yellow man to go on living would have been a hideous hell.

The visualizing of this bitter-sweet story is, I have no hesi-
tancy in saying, the very finest expression of the screen so far.
There seems to be no setting or accessory which is not correct in
its finest details.   The composition is a painter's.   The photography
is not only perfect, but, with caution, is innovational, and approxi-
mates, in its larger lights and softnesses of close view, the details
of bright and dark upon the finest canvases in the Louvres of the
world.

Not content with driving his lens to a record of unexampled
recording, Mr. Griffith has added a revolutionary color touch by
the use of a Chinese blue, thrown, not by the projector or out of
the film, but independently, from the projection booth.   This is not
a tint and it does not give the impression of colored film.   It has
a dramatic value which can only be compared to the vital, living
blue of the incomparable scene-painter Urban.

Photographer Bitzer has done the best work of his career in
this picture.

The fated trio is played by Lillian Gish, as Lucy; Donald
Crisp, as Battling Burrows, and Richard Barthelmess, as the Yellow Man.   The piece is high tide for all of them.

Miss Gish has been allied with the delicate flowers upon
Griffith's tapestries for a long, long time, but here she is called
upon to play more than a delicate flower.   She must, and does,

characterize a little creature of infinite pathos. She has to be both
Lillian Gish and the Mae Marsh of old rolled into one sorrowful little
being, and her success in this strange combination of motives and
beings is absolute. Mr. Crisp as the ferocious Battler is more than
physically violent; he has, by many little side touches given intriguing,
even humorous little glimpses into the bovine mental processes, the
vast self-satisfactions of an ox such as Burrows would be. Mr.
Barthelmess as the Chinaman is lofty, exalted, immeasurably removed from a sordid world and its sordid passions, and a calm,
implacable dispenser of fate in the last phase. Edward Piel, George
Beranger and that delightful pugilistic thespian, Mr. Kid McCoy Sel-
by, perform small parts with admirable finish.

Only one part of this splendid essay is open to real criticism.
Mr. Griffith is not a title writer and his words most inadequately
garb his visions. The spoken titles are not so bad, but the descriptive phrases lean lamely upon crutches of sentimentality.
                              --Julian Johnson in Photoplay, Vol.
                              16, No. 3 (August 1919), pages
                              55-56.

                    *   *   *

It is trite, of course, to repeat that David Wark Griffith's
Broken Blossoms marks an epoch in the march of the photoplay.
Nearly every one has pronounced this verdict, but the fact must be
stated again.

Broken Blossoms reveals something of what will be the photoplay of the future. For the screen drama of tomorrow is to be a
blending of the art of the dramatist, the painter--and the poet.
Broken Blossoms is just this.

Since the first animated picture we have had the methods of
the stage applied to the screen. Bald stories they have been, in
the main, with here and there a flash of splendid dramatic suspense,
of fine spectacular effects and of superb beauty of photography. But
the thing that was to differentiate the stage and the screen has been
slow in coming. Distant flashes had appeared, it is true, but the
poetry of the camera has never been really plumbed.

Broken Blossoms reveals a lyric quality we have long dreamed
for the photoplay, but never discovered. There are other splendid
qualities to Broken Blossoms, but it is because of this alone that we
place the production as a milestone of the screen. Indeed, at moments Mr. Griffith makes the camera fairly sing.

So it is not because of its technical advances, its fine handling
of a relentless tragedy, its philosophy, indeed, its moving spiritual
vein, that we rate Broken Blossoms so highly. It is because Mr.
Griffith has at last revealed what the film camera will do--tomorrow
and in the days to come.

We have frequently lamented what we consider Mr. Griffith's

weakness--a lack of literary discrimination, which, it seemed to us, left his work without a real foundation. Broken Blossoms, however, has an excellent literary distinction. It is adapted from Thomas Burke's story, The Chink and the Child, of his book, Limehouse Nights. Mr. Burke is an able writer who has set out to paint the London of today as did Dickens of yesterday.

Limehouse is the slum of London, where "East meets West" and the Hindus, the Siamese, the Chinamen and the negro mingle with the Caucasian in the leveling gambling and drinking river-front dives where the swirling fogs of the Thames rise up to hide the hell of it all. To Limehouse has drifted the Yellow Man, a young China-man who, fired with zeal, some years before left his native land to bring the message of the Orient to the struggling, blood-mad white man. But the yellow idealist has reckoned without things as they are and his collision with sordid realities of Limehouse has left him dulled and sickened, but still hearing the old call of his temple bells of far-off China.

The Yellow Man keeps a little shop in Limehouse. One day the daughter of a brutal cockney prize-fighter falls in a faint across his threshold, fresh from a beating administered by her parent. Now the dreaming Yellow Man has long watched this waif of Lime-house from afar and, in his still idealistic eyes, she is something of a flower growing in the mire. So, all unmindful of consequences, he lifts the unconscious girl and carries her to a sanctuary above his shop. There he gently dresses her bruises, gives her gay Ori-ental robes, decks his room in honor of the visiting goddess and worships. Thru the little drudge's undeveloped mind runs derisive laughter, then a bit of fear and ultimately an acceptance of this sudden invasion of a quaint Eastern heaven. Finally she even comes to smile.

But her happiness is not for long, for the bully father, fresh from a triumph in the prize ring, hears that his daughter "has taken up with a Chink." He sets out to avenge his family and racial honor and rushes to the shop when, by chance, the Yellow Man is absent. He wrecks the rooms and drags away the girl. Once at home, he kills her in his wrath. Then returns the Oriental. He follows the brute to his lair, desperately resorts to the terrifying means of vengeance by which the beauty of his life had been destroyed, shoots the murderer and then carries the dead girl back to his shattered room. He rearranges the torn silken robes, sets up his smashed altar to Buddha--and kills himself. So Broken Blossoms ends with the police, the personification of misunderstanding materialism, just forcing their way into the Yellow Man's shop. But, in vague out-line, we see a mystic ship drifting eastward down the river of souls.

Critics have said that Broken Blossoms is brutal and even depressing. The note of brutality did not touch us, we must admit. To us the idealism and the spirituality of the theme far overtopped the mere physical side. It is, as some one has said, as a flower unfolding, as delicate as incense smoke. Only the beautiful and the

spiritual seem real; the slums and the brutality are as of an unreal
land of materialism.   Mr. Griffith has told Mr. Burke's story with
the lyric quality of the poet.   There are subtitles that are golden
gems of direct, finely conceived expression.   There are scenes that
are living paintings, in their light and shade and balance.

Broken Blossoms is the best acted photoplay we ever saw.
(A broad statement, but nevertheless true!)   Lillian Gish is the
waif of Limehouse.   At once vivid and gentle, pathetic and wistful,
Miss Gish gives a performance of the little girl "with age-old eyes"
that is unforgettable.   And--when she hides herself in the closet to
escape her father's final wrath--she presents a picture of passionate
fear realized so realistically that it tears at the heart like a hungry
wolf.   Richard Barthelmess is admirable as the Yellow Man--indeed,
superb in moments.   Here is the dreamer of the East almost broken
before the realities of life, painted with strokes of splendid subtlety
and restraint.   And Donald Crisp as the brute, Battling Burrows!
Smug, brutally degenerate, vainglorious, Crisp makes Battling a
hated figure, relentless in its power.

For the moment we have neglected to speak of the technical
advances of Broken Blossoms.   Mr. Griffith is making more extended use of the idealistic close-up of vague out-of-focus photography.   Here, it seems, is just what the close-up needed to rob it of
its material beaded eyelash and painted lip revelations.   Mr. Griffith resorts to it with tremendous effect in handling Miss Gish's
scenes where Battling breaks down the closet door to reach her.

Mr. Griffith is using living colors--palpitating blues, pale
bronzes, hot golds and a vivid rose--to aid the dramatic moods of
his photoplay.   And how singularly effective it is!   Who knows but
what mood colors may ultimately fill the void left by the human
voice?

We might go on endlessly talking of Broken Blossoms.   It is,
for instance, the initial production of the screen's first repertoire
season in New York and other cities.   It is the screen's first tragedy.   We have had stories with "unhappy endings," but Broken
Blossoms, with its inevitable tale of passions, clashing prejudices
and brutal forces, marches with the steady, inexorable tread of a
Greek tragedy.

--Frederick James Smith in Motion Picture Classic, Vol. 8,
No. 6 (August 1919), pages 46-
47 and 60.

☐ BUMPING INTO BROADWAY (Rolin/Pathé, 1919)

The reviewer saw two of the two-reel Lloyd comedies before
he viewed Bumping Into Broadway, which happened to be the first

scheduled for release.   They both registered heavily and this one
scores 100 per cent.

Mr. Lloyd has "Snub" Pollard and Bebe Daniels with him in
this one and it is elaborately mounted.   He is a refreshingly original
comedian who does not have to indulge in vulgarities or the slap
stick to get his stuff over.

The star appears in Bumping Into Broadway as a would-be
playwright and after being kicked out of the manager's office he
meets the chorus girl behind the scenes.

Later he sees the girl getting into a limousine with a man
and he rides with them by inserting himself on the extra tire at the
rear of the car.

Their destination is a swell gambling house and the comedian
somehow manages to get by the doorkeeper.   While standing outside
the circle of a group surrounding a roulette table, he finds a bill
on the floor and after trying in vain to pry his way into the crowd
to return the bill to its owner he tosses it over the heads of the
people and it lands on number 13.

Yes, number 13 wins and then repeats itself enough so that
the bank is "busted."   As the bales of money are forced on the
comedian the place is raided and from then on the fun is fast and
furious.

This is certainly an irresistibly funny comedy offering that
will score with the high brows as heavily as it will with the masses.
Many new pieces of comedy "business" are injected by Mr. Lloyd
which mark him as absolutely original.

--Tom Hamlin in Motion Picture
News, Vol. 20, No. 23 (November 29, 1919), page 3971.

☐ CABIRIA (Italia, 1914)

This is the day of the new masters.   We are witnessing a
new style in dramatic kinematography.   Within the last four weeks
there have been splendid manifestations of a new art on the screen.
The skill and the inspiration of the director, the skill and the patient
striving of the cameraman, a deep and conscientious study of screen
possibilities, a new school of actors who have fathomed the mysteries
of unspoken language--all these elements working toward the harmony
of the whole have in part been responsible for the new school, which
is opening the eyes of the world.   I have not mentioned the keystone
of the success of the new art in this hasty enumeration.   The keystone is the story written for the screen and for the screen alone.
The freest adaptation imposes restraints on the producer.   In the

novel we are confronted by the problem of what to leave out and
what to leave in, in the adaptation of the speaking stage we are still
in the bonds of tradition.   How different is the free untrammelled
flight of the Muse of the Screen.   She conquers every obstacle which
is unsurmountable to pen or stage.

In Cabiria a genius furnishes the theme--Gabriele d'Annunzio.
He wrote the story directly for the screen.   Nobly does the screen
respond to every touch of the gifted hand.   D'Annunzio is a very
wizard of description.   In this film-drama his thoughts and images
stand forth as vividly as the summer landscape in a prolonged flash
of lightning.   The tremendous moral of the play, the keenly dramatic and the broadly humorous, the historic facts--are all absorbed
in an incredibly short time.   Of course the spectacular features
help--with all due respect to its classic predecessors I must confess that in the portrayal of the spectacular this film creates new
records.   The torrent of fiery flakes, the mouth of the volcano a
veritable furnace of the Inferno, spewing forth unceasing sheets of
fire, the rush of the fugitives lit up by a ruddy glow which half conceals and half reveals, the temple of Moloch with its worshippers
and its fearful rites, the hero of Carthage passing over the Alps,
the siege of Carthage, the burning of the ships which the aged
Archimedes fought with the power of the sun, all these and a hundred other marvels of the spectacular make this feature pre-eminent
among the spectacular successes in all the history of spectacles.   It
is true that the classic theme always carries the spectacular element best, and this advantage the producer has pressed to the limit.

It would be a grave mistake, however, to emphasize the
spectacular in this film above the dramatic.   The spectacular is all
the more impressive because an artistic masterhand has subordinated
it to the dramatic and poetic moments of the play.

Cabiria is the name of the child whose strange salvation after
cruel perils forms the skeleton of the story.   The plot takes us to
the days when the dominion of Rome was threatened by the growing
power of Carthage.   To this day the site of Carthage has remained
more or less of a mystery.   We know that the plough of the Roman
conqueror passed over the site of the fated city, but no mortal even
in our day knows where the site is.   Carthage magnificiently situated
on the northern coast of Africa was sending her ships and her soldiers into every part of the world, her trade and the martial spirit
of her people made her a conquering nation.   At last she threw the
gauntlet down and challenged Rome.   Rome in later years achieved
a magnificence never equalled in the chronicles of man, but at no
time in her career was she as rugged, as noble and as brave as
in the third century before the Christian era, when the hordes of
Carthage set their foot on her sacred soil.   In the midst of this
struggle between two nations and two civilizations the little girl
Cabiria was born in Italy of noble parents.   The city in which her
parents lived was overwhelmed by a fearful eruption of a volcano,
and when the wretched survivors looked about themselves even as
Nature seemed at last to have tired of her anger, little Cabiria

could not be found.   She was believed to have perished in the general destruction.   Such, however, was not the case.   She and others were captured in their flight--Phoenician pirates brought them into the slave market at Carthage.   She was with her nurse, and the man who bought Cabiria also took the little girl's faithful nurse Croessa.   The sweetness and purity of the child attracted the notice of the High Priest of Moloch, the horrible idol to whom little children were sacrificed.   He places little Cabiria with the children in the temple where they are being prepared for sacrifice.   In spite of all the protests of Croessa little Cabiria is selected as a victim for the next day of sacrifice.   Croessa in despair looks about for means of rescuing the little child.   Fulvius, a Roman patrician, and his slave, a huge black named Maciste, are wandering about the outer temple when Croessa begs them to save Cabiria, giving the Roman a charm which she promises will never let him perish.

Just as in the midst of the worshippers in the temple little Cabiria is offered to Moloch the monster that glows and shines and devours, Fulvius and Maciste defy the priests by seizing the child in the moment of its supremest peril.   They flee, and the black slave escaping offers the child to the queen into whose protection Cabiria is now commended.   She grows up to be a beautiful young woman.   In the meantime the arms of Carthage have suffered defeat after defeat, the noble Scipio has risen up to grapple with the armies of Carthage, and the mighty Hannibal, the hero and the hope of Carthage, perishes.   The priests, seeking to divine the cause of the anger of the gods, discover that a victim has been hidden from Moloch, hence the impending destruction of Carthage and her people.   Cabiria is found and her sacrifice demanded by the priests.   How Cabiria is saved again and finally reunited to her parents and joined in wedlock to Fulvius who has dared so much for her is the theme of the last part.

I have only mentioned the more prominent parts of the story, which has many episodes too numerous for detailed recital here.   I must at least allude to the tragicomic part of Maciste and the wine-merchant in whose shop so many of the strange adventures of the knight and his servant took place.

Summing up, it may well be said that Cabiria ranks in the very first flight of the masterpieces of kinematographic art.   Nor must I omit a tribute to Italy, the country which has given us all our greatest classics in films.   Those of us who remember the Italia Company's first ambitious effort, The Fall of Troy, will be in a good position of judging of the giant's strides with which the art is approaching its summit.   The Fall of Troy was considered a new departure in 1910; four years later it is eclipsed by Cabiria. Who knows what the next four years may bring?

--W. Stephen Bush in The Moving
Picture World, Vol. 20, No. 8
(May 23, 1914), pages 1090-
1091.

*   *   *

Usually the announced cost of a theatrical spectacle is in in-
verse proportion to the press-agent's sense of humor. That "figures
do not lie" is an aphorism not applicable to chorus girls and bill-
boards.

"The Itala Film of Torino" declares that Cabiria cost $200,000,
and the most casual view of the production is an antidote for skepti-
cism. In point of fact, one marvels that certain scenes, such as
those showing the eruption of Mount Etna, could have been obtained
at any price. One can't walk up to a volcano, and say: "Here's
ten thousand dollars! Erupt!"

Mount Etna, which, of late, has confined its activities to the
advertisement of a certain life insurance company, performs heroic
service for "The Itala Film of Torino." One sees the mighty old
mountain vomiting--I believe vomiting is the proper word--smoke
and flame, the burning lava sky-rocketing to the heavens, descending, and rolling down the cone-side, while, in its fitful light, Sicilian
peasants, garbed in the dress of the third century before Christ,
drive their sheep, their goats and their donkeys ahead of them in a
long and panic-stricken procession. One sees the stricken city of
Catana fall into cinderous ruins, its marble columns and porticoes
crumbling beneath the weight of ashes, and tumbling upon the heads
of fleeing slaves and masters.

These pictures, part of the first episode of D'Annunzio's
picturesque and dramatic story of the Punic Wars, are not more
remarkable than a dozen that follow. The sacrificial ceremonies in
the Temple of Moloch, a structure as vast and apparently as solid
as St. Peter's, crowded by a worshiping throng thrown into relief
against the blazing altar fires, give way to illimitable stretches of
desert, with caravans of camels crossing in the moonlight, and to
glimpses of rocky walls rising out of the sea, from one of which
walls the Roman hero, Fulvius, leaps a good hundred feet into the
sea. Hannibal with his hordes is shown crossing the Alps, and
Syracuse, besieged, pours burning lead from its battlements, and
casts huge stones from ancient machines into the ranks of its enemies. Fulvius scales the walls of Carthage upon the shields of the
Romans, who mount, layer upon layer, one group supporting the
shields upon which another group stands, and, finally, the Greek,
Archimedes, focusing the rays of the sun upon the wooden vessels,
affords us the opportunity of seeing a battle fleet burning to the
water's edge.

D'Annunzio's story relates how the infant, Cabiria, daughter
of a Sicilian patrician, Batto, is carried from her volcano-ruined
home by her nurse, Croessa, only to be captured by Phoenician
pirates, sold in the slave market of Carthage, and offered up as a
sacrifice to Moloch. Fulvius, aided by his giant slave, Maciste--
the colored counterpart of Ursus in Quo Vadis?--rescues the little
girl, but Maciste, taken by the Carthaginians, is chained to a stone

mill, where he labors for ten years, until Fulvius inspires him to
use his great strength in bursting his chains. Meanwhile, Cabiria
has become the slave of Sophonisba, daughter of Hasdrubal, chief
of the Carthaginian Republic, and the fall of Carthage gives opportunity to the wicked priest, Karthalo, who declares that the girl, now
a young woman, once saved from Moloch, must be sacrificed to save
the Republic. Again condemned to death, Cabiria again is rescued
by Fulvius, who loves her and takes her to his heart in a scene of
marvelous beauty.

This epoch-making photo-play is acted with as much skill as
though it were a parlor comedy at the Lyceum. The film company,
after searching everywhere for a Hercules to perform the mighty
deeds of Maciste, hit upon a dock laborer, who, patiently trained,
not only looks the part, but, programmed Ernesto Pagani, acts it
amazingly. The other roles are equally well played, while the mobs,
literally numbering thousands, so vast that individual effort goes un-
noticed, give a conglomerate effect nothing short of remarkable.
The scenery, both natural and painted, is imposing; the costumes
and the hundreds of ponderous properties are accurate and convincing; and the spectacle, taken all in all, fairly surpasses belief.

Cabiria is more than the last word in motion pictures. It is
a woman's last word--which is the last word, and then some.
                              --Channing Pollock in The Green
                                Book Magazine, Vol. 12, No. 3
                                (September 1914), pages 495-496.

☐ THE CAPTIVE (Lasky/Paramount, 1915)

Blanche Sweet's second experience with the Lasky Company--
her first was in The Warrens of Virginia--is in every way satisfying, for in The Captive, a five-part picturization of a play by Cecil
B. DeMille and Jeanie MacPherson, she has a role of possibilities
well in keeping with her personality and histrionic method. This
time she is cast as Sonya Martinovitch, a Montenegrin peasant girl
of an elementary, subdued nature; but underneath the rather coarse
surface there lies a vein of feminine tenderness and plenty of fire
and passion, once they are aroused. It rests with Miss Sweet to
bring out the varied qualities of Sonya as she is influenced by the
handsome Turkish soldier, made a prisoner in the Balkan War and
detailed by the Montenegrin government to cultivate the farm occupied
by the peasant girl and her little brother. All the men of the family are fighting their country's battles.

Much of the interest in the picture centers in the expressive
by-play of Miss Sweet and House Peters, playing the Turk, a man
of noble birth who at the point of a pistol is forced to do the bidding
of an ignorant girl. The humor arising out of the odd situation is
natural, as is the gradual alteration in the attitude of Sonya toward

her prisoner. In numberless little ways she shows the growth of a
passion, the meaning of which she scarcely realizes at first, and
equally effective is her portrayal of the character under the stress
of a fully recognized emotion. The able acting of the two principal
players saves several scenes from the charge of being superfluous
in the development of the plot.

The story in itself is rather scant for five reels and suffers
at the end from an anti-climax and a fortuitous meeting that serves
to unite the lovers. But to counterbalance shortcomings there is the
excellent acting already mentioned, and the charm of picturesque
settings perfectly photographed. The atmosphere of the production
is out of the ordinary and of a fine artistic quality, due to a wise
choice of locations, care in the furnishing of interiors and painstaking direction. Theodore Roberts, Gerald Ward, Jeanie MacPherson,
Page Peters and Billy Elmer are in the cast.

                            --Lynde Denig in The Moving Pic-
                              ture World, Vol. 24, No. 5
                              (May 1, 1915), page 743.

☐ CARMEN (Lasky/Paramount, 1915)

No living woman has had greater stage triumphs than Geraldine Farrar; but whatever these triumphs have been her conquest in
the picture Carmen will be infinitely greater. Miss Farrar has
caused the New York Fire Commissioners to look anxiously at the
Metropolitan Operahouse when she played the cigarette girl within
its walls. But at most, only three or four thousand people heard
and saw her. When the new and immortalized Carmen is released,
tens, scores, even hundreds of thousands may see and acclaim her
at one time. And in the immemorial springtimes of the future,
when her lithe and passionate beauty is as much history as the wars
of yesterday, all the glory and splendor and fire of her impersonation may be rekindled, studied, analyzed, thrilled over. In perpetu-
ating the furnace-heat of this tropic, exotic characterization the
Carmen film will, in its own way, stand alongside The Birth of a
Nation as an epochmaker.

The history of this picture has been often told: how Miss
Farrar, induced to perpetuate several of her roles, went to California early in the summer, and played the parts before the Lasky
cameras at Hollywood. Of the releases this is the first; and whatever artistic importance the others may develop, this is unquestionably the photoplay of supreme public interest, as far as Miss Farrar is concerned.

In making the scenario William DeMille followed the large
outlines of Prosper Merimee's story, though, unfortunately, he de-
viated from it in some particulars of Carmen's character as will
be noted later.

Carmen, a Seville cigarette maker, is the able coadjutor of
Pastia, innkeeper and smuggler. Carmen exercises her fascination
upon Don Jose, a corporal of dragoons, and takes him away from
his nightly post at a breach in the ruined city wall. While Don Jose
is enjoying his Delilah's society Pastia's cohort evades the customs
with a vast lot of plunder. Later on, Carmen gets into a terrific
fight with another cigarette girl, and Don Jose is sent to arrest her.
She pleads with him to be permitted to speak to Pastia a moment on
her way to prison. Although such permission is a breach of discipline, Don Jose indulges her. Scarcely have they entered Pastia's
tavern when Morales, a sneering officer of dragoons whom Don Jose
particularly dislikes, makes, out loud, the obvious comment of an
enemy upon such a situation. Don Jose and Morales close, there
is a terrific struggle in which Carmen takes no small part, and at
length, in a breathing spell, Don Jose discovers that his final grip
upon Morales' scrawny neck has strangled him. Carmen bars the
doors to other dragoons, indicates a way of escape, and says, coolly,
that the debt is cancelled between them: he helped her, she has
helped him--they are quits. Dazed, Don Jose exits safely, but more
at the instance of Pastia than at her bidding. Now an outlaw, the
corporal who gave all for the wanton's love endeavors desperately
to keep her for himself. She, with her mountain band of brigands,
has formed a violent fancy, more ambition than passion, for Escamillo, toreador of Granada who is the talk of all Spain. Escamillo
desires her much as Don Jose did and still does, though more com-
posedly, and she accompanies him to Seville, where the greatest of
his fights is to take place. Don Jose summons her from the box at
the side of the bull ring, and, upon her refusal to go with him into
the outland, stabs her. She dies with her satiric smile on her lips;
he does a Japanese finish with the same knife over her body.

Cecil DeMille must have enthusiastic mention for his direction of this photoplay, and Alvin Wycoff for his photography. The
artistry of both is beyond criticism.

It is of course with Farrar's assumption of the gypsy that
people are mainly concerned. All else--plot, players and produc-
tion--are of secondary importance when judged by public curiosity.

And be it said that Farrar has never so played Carmen, perhaps never will again enact her with such brilliance of movement,
such drama of facial expression and gesture, such sheer physical
power, such sunlit splendor of primitive ferocity, such selfish and
intoxicating joy of living. The horror of the tragedy is not the disaster of Jose the Basque--as it should be; it is the appalling and
dreadful anticipation of the end of this embodied orgy of flesh which
seems so swift and vital and potent that it cannot die.

Thais and the rest of the Alexandriennes had nothing on this
Carmen as a maker of writheful love. There is nothing in this pic-
ture which does not belong to the lusty Spanish wench, but the local
Simon Pures and their censorial shears may have busy days.

The DeMilles, as well as Miss Farrar, evidently left no
rocks of research unturned in seeking accuracy of attire and constructive investiture.   Only at Seville's bull-ring does the gypsy
wear the fine mantilla and fan-comb and other habiliments known
conventionally as the "Carmen costume." Otherwise she is either
in or out--mostly out of the chemisy bodice of an Andalusian female
of the people; her muscular but lovely arms playing like swords,
naked to their shoulder-hilts.

No women of the screen have ever indulged in so ferocious
and unrelenting an encounter as that battle between Carmen and the
other Bull Durham maiden in the cigarette factory. Farrar begins
the fight by pulling the unfortunate across a table with one hand, a
neat bit of derricking which divests her of most of her apparel above
the waist. The encounter thus begun ends in a cat-session of biting
and nail tearing which for reality can only be compared to that immortal mill in The Spoilers, in which Bill Farnum and Tom Santschi
actually demolished each other to make a celluloid holiday.

Young Wally Reid rose to the big occasion of Don Jose to a
great primadonna's Carmen. He is ideal in the role. If he had a
tenor voice, down and out would go imperturbable Giovanni Marti-
nelli at the Metropolitan!

Pedro de Cordoba is a matador by name and nature as well
as job. He brings to the assignment the hauteur, the silent fervor
and that subtle, inordinate conceit without which no bull-fighter
graduates.

Horace Carpenter as Pastia, William Elmer as Morales,
Jeanie MacPherson as Frasquita and Milton Brown as Garcia complete a flawless cast.

Here is the fault of DeMille's scenario: he has made Carmen sincere at no point. Carmen's affection for Don Jose, though
brief, was very real.

"I believe I love you a little bit," says Carmen (of the novel)
to Jose, even after they are quits on their service to each other.
"I should like to be your romi" (wife in Romany). And later: "It
must be that I love you ... since you left me I don't know what's
the matter with me."

Yet at no moment in the DeMille play does she love anybody.
Hence her tigerish and exhausting passion as she gasps and droops
upon the corporal in the first scenes seems, at length, a bit theatrical. With Farrar's tremendous impersonation and Cecil DeMille's
fine directing it needed only reality of motive to make the character
herself real as daylight. Did not the operatic Carmen slap Don
Jose with a cassia-blossom long before there was any necessity for
him to connive at her escape?

Some of the captions are needlessly stupid. A moment's

thought should have told the caption-maker that smuggled goods should not be "goods"--uninterestingly impersonal--but as the things they were.

Dramatically, the piece is strongest--in point of speed and suspense at least--in its first part.

> --Julian Johnson in Photoplay, Vol.
> 8, No. 6 (November 1915), pages
> 77-80.

☐ THE CHARGE OF THE LIGHT BRIGADE (Edison, 1912)

J. Searle Dawley deserves much credit for his direction of the pictorial presentation of this famous poem.   The difficulties to be overcome in presenting scenes appropriate to the noble lines were many, and it is a feather in the cap of the Edison Company that they have been met so successfully.   The picture opens with a touch of sentiment when two of the gallant six hundred say good-by to their wives and join the brigade.   Thereafter the film depicts scenes in camp preparatory to the charge and the battle itself, showing the men being mowed down by the rain of shots from the enemy's cannon.   The mad excitement, the horror and the sadness of a battlefield have been truthfully suggested.

> --Reviews of Licensed Films in
> The New York Dramatic Mirror,
> Vol. 68, No. 1765 (October 16,
> 1912), page 30.

☐ THE CHEAT (Lasky/Paramount, 1915)

Features like this one put the whole industry under obligations to the Lasky company.   On every conceivable test this picture shows a hundred per cent.   Indeed, the feature is of such extraordinary merit as to call for the highest term of praise.

The plot is simple.   This always constitutes special merit in a film story.   It is worked out rapidly with that rise of interest which is the mark of every successful dramatic composition.   The climax is overpowering.   As one of the men that sat behind me in the Strand Theater said, "I would like to be in that mob. "

Like all really strong stories, that of The Cheat can be told in a few words.   A young, extravagant wife, a social butterfly, is playing with fire.   In her craze for fine clothes she gambles with money entrusted to her by a Red Cross society.   She loses the money.   Her husband knows nothing of the desperate plight of his wife.   Even if he knew, however, he would not have been able to

help her. His investments had stripped him of ready cash. With
visions of horrible disgrace haunting her mind, she is offered help
from a strange and dangerous quarter. A rich Japanese who has
found entree into the social set, and who has paid much attention to
the young wife in the absence of the busy husband, comes forward
and says he will give her the money and ward off the impending exposure "upon conditions." In her despair the young wife gives an
almost unconscious and quite mechanical consent, and in the daze
that has seized her she takes the check from the Japanese. Here
Fate intervenes. The troubled wife learns from her husband that
he had been successful in his operations and that he is now rich.

"Does that mean I can have ten thousand dollars right now?"
asks the agonized wife in a frenzy of joy mixed with fear. She gets
the money and then goes to the Jap's home to return his treacherous
gift. And now the beastliness in the Oriental's nature leaps forth.
Not only will he not release her from her bargain, but he means to
be paid at once. I shall not attempt to describe what follows--words
seem altogether too feeble for that. In the struggle the Jap sears
the woman's shoulder with a red-hot iron to mark her as his own
by right of bargain and purchase. Lying on the floor and steeling
herself for the next attack and still writhing under the pain of the
burning flesh, the woman seizes a revolver and fires it at her tor-
turer. The bullet hits him and he falls. The woman escapes. A
moment later the husband enters and finds the Jap, covered with
blood, gripping convulsively a hank of hair. He sees other proof of
his wife's visit. The police are alarmed. The Jap is asked who
shot him, but before he can open his mouth the husband accuses
himself of the crime.

The wife hastens to the cell of her husband and confesses all.
He forbids her to speak. Now follows the trial. Never before have
I seen a more gripping climax. It is built up with exquisite skill.
The accused husband and the guilty wife sit side by side. The court
room is crowded with spectators, following with feverish interest
every new turn in the trial. We see the jury, thoughtful, tense,
nervous. The Jap takes the stand, impassive, mysterious, but convincing. The verdict is guilty. The trembling wife is no longer
able to restrain herself. Her passion rising superior to all the
form and severity of court procedure, she leaps upon the witness
stand, a fearful and unconquerable resolve in her eyes. The next
two minutes the audience is as spellbound as the men and women
in the court room. She tells far more by her looks and gestures
than by words of what has happened between her and the Oriental,
and when the audience seems on the verge of hysteria the woman
tears the dress from the seared spot on her shoulder. It was like
the spark thrown into a keg of powder. The wrath of the audience
bursts forth with elemental fury and there ensues a scene that for
tenseness and excitement has never been matched on stage or screen.

Space bids me be brief. I cannot, however, omit words of
unqualified praise for Fanny Ward, whose impersonation of the social butterfly with the singed wings was a masterly performance.

The lighting effects must be mentioned, too.   They are beyond all
praise in their art, their daring and their originality.   There are
those deft and subtle touches that we find all the Lasky pictures
possess--only here they crowd upon one another.   What a delicate
but powerful effect was the omission of the bars in the prison scene.
The shadow of the bars, the sombre light, the bent head of the
prisoner silhouetted against the bare wall--this is but one of the
numerous happy touches.   The Cheat is worth advertising to the
limit.   It is one feature in a hundred.

--W. Stephen Bush in The Moving
Picture World, Vol. 26, No. 14
(December 25, 1915), page 2384.

☐   THE CHRISTIAN (Vitagraph, 1914)

        Manhattan Opera House, home of Salome and Mary Garden,
was well filled by a fashionable audience at the first presentation of
an eight-reel Vitagraph release adapted from The Christian, by Hall
Caine.   This daring invasion is probably made in the nature of an
experiment, and it has its own revelations, among them the fact
that intermissions, such as occur between the acts of a stage play,
operate as a source of relief without breaking continuity of interest.
It is also indicated that an instrument of varied musical effects,
such as that in use at the Vitagraph Theater, is better suited than
a church organ to accompanying screen presentations.   There was
variety of selection, from Chaminade's "Autumn" to the pizzicati
and valse lente of Delibe's "Sylvie Ballet," at the showing of The
Christian, but it could be felt that the charm of contrast was absent.

        The eight-reel feature was chiefly remarkable for beauty and
accuracy of treatment, for discriminating judgment and fine selective
taste in all that pertains to the visualization of a story.   The cast,
with one exception, was nicely balanced and the acting of a superior
character, rising to moments of intensity in the concluding scenes
between Earle Williams and Edith Storey.   At the end came one of
Mr. Blackton's poetic touches, one of those spiritual appeals to the
imagination which he developed as belonging to the art of picture
production and no other medium of expression.

        There is some spirited action here and there in the story,
but the general atmosphere is one of gloom, the characters are shaped
by that all-of-a-sudden process which entails constant readjustment,
and the novel is so obviously a makeshift of construction on a subject of no particular concern to Americans that it met with complete
failure in this country in spite of a lot of blatant publicity.   What
is the meaning of The Christian?   Is there soundness of purpose or
stability of character in the book?

        John Storm is the son of a man of position and wealth.   The
father plans a very natural career for his son and lays bare his

plans in manly fashion. John fluctuates. He has a natural inclination to marry the girl of his choice, but it alternates for no visible
reason with an inclination to become a monastic recluse. A normal
man in love with a girl and not refused by her--would he give a
moment's thought to turning monk? John is really distracted from
his natural purpose by Father Lamplugh. Then he recants and re-
vokes, an apostate in sentiment throughout the story.

    Glory Quayle is the girl, and she is in revolt against her
narrow environment. She falls into perilous company, Lord Robert,
Polly Love, a hospital nurse, and Horatio Drake, music hall manager, out in the country on an excursion. Glory leaves home with
this bunch, goes to London and becomes in succession a hospital
nurse and concert-hall singer. Lord Robert wobbles between Polly
Love, to whom a baby is later born, and an heiress, Vera MacCrae,
and attains temporary equilibrium by marrying the heiress. She
finds out all about him through the instrumentality of John Storm,
who has now quit the brotherhood and returned to the outer world,
when Polly dies. Vera takes the baby and dismisses Lord Robert.
Through all this vacillation and backsliding we reach an arbitrary
situation. Glory Quayle is singing at a concert-hall managed by
Lord Robert's friend Drake. Next door, placed there by the author
rather than by any good reason, is a large hall which erratic John
Storm has converted into a sort of club house for working people.

    John Storm has inherited money through the death of his
father and is devoting it to good works, becoming the supposed idol
of the people. He is an unstable idol. Lord Robert, of vagrant
fortunes, easily upsets all the good John has done, acquiring by no
perceptible means such an influence over "the people" that they turn
against their friend and benefactor. Like the rest of the characters,
they seem to suffer from an utter lack of stability. Lord Robert is
nowhere pictured as a man of enough ability to fool London newspapers or to powerfully influence "the people," but, presto! he
causes them to skip from one side to the other, because he says
that John Storm has predicted the destruction of London on Derby
Day. How easy! People who have been through a bitter experience
and have found some relief from it in what Storm has to offer re-
linquish that good and their common sense at the same time because
of a rumor circulated by Lord Robert and denied by John Storm.

    Now that the mob has turned a pirouette and landed on the
side of Lord Robert, and now that John Storm's club house for the
people is located next to the concert-hall in which his former sweetheart, Glory Quayle, is singing, over which Lord Robert's dastardly
influence is made to extend, we reach "the dramatic situation."
Glory participates in the general inconstancy of purpose--she tires
of her brilliant success in the concert-hall--and goes over to the
side of John Storm. Drake learns of this and gets possession of
John's lease. Drake wants to marry Glory Quayle. She goes to
John and tells him that she is about to forsake her career for his
sake. John wakes up and takes her into his arms. At this oppor-
tune moment, the people mob their own club house and hoot their

benefactor. Drake asks Glory to become his wife, showing that he
has a deed of possession to John's club house. Glory refuses him
because she loves John. Drake immediately changes about and gives
the deed to John as a gift from him to Glory. As John now has
both the deed and the girl, the story ends.

If any such method of construction will serve in a play, what
does it serve? Is there a single and supreme thought in all this
shifting about of motives and characteristics? Is there anything in
Caine's story that compels the spectator to imagine and to realize
some truth of life? Is there anything in the story to broaden our
potential range of sympathy? Has the author tried to tell us something new? Is he in deep earnest, or has he simply combined a lot
of old materials for the sake of a transitory thrill? The author's
technical dexterity might be assumed, but it seems to me that there
is a continual surrender of the plausible and the convincing in this
story's methods because there is no great big sincerity of purpose
behind it all.

If The Christian as produced in photodrama meets with popular success, it will not only be a triumph for the Vitagraph Company, but for the whole art of visualization over that of literature.
                              --Louis Reeves Harrison in The
                              Moving Picture World, Vol. 19,
                              No. 13 (March 3, 1914), pages
                              1656-1657.

☐ CINDERELLA (Famous Players/Paramount, 1915)

It seems almost useless to state that Mary Pickford is un-
surpassably well suited to the role of Cinderella. All those who
have seen the little star in previous releases of the Famous Players' company need not be told of this. If there is an exhibitor in
the country who has never seen Mary Pickford, he can cut this out
and paste it in his hat, that if he advertises Mary Pickford in Cinderella he will fill his house to the doors.

While the old tale of Cinderella was written primarily to
amuse the children, none of you will deny that you enjoyed it again
when you read it to your own little girl or boy. But, to use a
somewhat base but fully expressive phrase, the picture "has it all
over" the story, and "then some."

Grown-ups will enjoy the picture just as heartily and just as
sincerely as children, because the former will be apt to take note
of its more serious and pathetic side, as well as the more humorous moments.

Need it be said that it is to Mary Pickford that the credit
for this pathetic and human interest side of the production should

go? You all remember her delightful characterizations in <u>Such a</u>
<u>Little Queen</u> and <u>Behind the Scenes</u>, both pictures that were officially
termed comedies, but you all remember that all the way through
these productions there was an underlying touch of pathos in both
her portrayals. In <u>Cinderella</u> it is the same story, only here she
is Cinderella and in the others she was distinctly someone else.

Although Mary Pickford is by all means the most conspicuous
figure in the picture, credit should go to James Kirkwood, the director. In staging the production he has shown that he is a master
in putting on a fairy tale in an effective manner. Scenes laid in the
palace are gorgeous, offering a striking contrast with those in the
house of Cinderella's stepmother, particularly with those in the little
girl's dingy room.

The transformation of the pumpkin, rats and mice into the
coach, ponies and attendants is prettily effected by fadeouts, followed
by fadeins. The photography is beautiful in all scenes, and some
excellent light effects have been obtained.

Playing opposite Miss Pickford in the role of Prince Charming is Owen Moore. Georgia Wilson and Lucille Carney are the
stepsisters and Isabel Vernon is the mother. W. N. Cone is cast
as the king and appears in but a few scenes.

All in all <u>Cinderella</u> cannot help but be a success, for reasons which are too obvious to repeat.
--Peter Milne in <u>Motion Picture
News</u>, Vol. 11, No. 1 (January
9, 1915), page 47.

☐ CIVILIZATION (Ince, 1916)

With the arrival of the gentle month of June there descended
upon Longacre Square, New York, such a deluge of blood as would
have flooded all the trenches of Europe. Two days before the mur-
derous exploits of Macbeth were exposed at the Rialto, the Ince engines of destruction began their work of wholesale slaughter at the
Criterion, and two days after the Shakespearean orgy of death, the
Thomas Dixon massacres were confessed at the Liberty. It is more
than a coincidence that Ince projected his peace fantasia, <u>Civiliza-
tion</u> in the same theater which had housed Blackton's <u>Battle Cry of
Peace</u> about a year earlier, and that <u>The Fall of a Nation</u> was
focused upon the same screen which for a year carried <u>The Birth
of a Nation</u>. This is more than coincidence, it is challenge, and
even if one were not inclined to employ comparative criticism, such
circumstances make it practically unavoidable. To state the case,
arbitrarily therefore, the order of merit of these four war spectacles must be awarded in the following gradation: <u>The Birth of a
Nation</u>, <u>Civilization</u>, <u>The Battle Cry of Peace</u>, <u>The Fall of a Nation</u>.

And to make the statement complete, it must be added that an un-
assuming little five-reeler from the Fine Arts Studio, now several
months old, The Flying Torpedo, should be remembered, and given
third place.

The strength of Civilization lies in a remarkable achievement
by Thomas H. Ince, who has not permitted his story to be cheapened
by the introduction of a trivial romance.   The moment a titanic struggle such as is depicted in any of these creations is pushed aside to
make way for personal romance, there is a long, hard drop.   Mr.
Ince has used just what story was necessary to knit his reels into a
unified whole, and no more.   The King of Wredpryd has become involved in a war for which there is no justification but conquest.
Count Ferdinand, commander of a submarine, is influenced by a
vast organization of women, through the girl he loves, to refuse to
carry out an order to sink a liner, and in the mutiny of his men
which results, he is badly wounded.   Hovering between life and
death he meets the Christus in a vision, and the Divine Man says:
"In your body my spirit shall return to the world of realities and
spread the gospel of peace."   Urged on by this spirit, Count Ferdinand, upon his recovery, makes his appeal, which finally touches
the king and converts him.   That is the entire story.   Upon this
slender but all sufficient thread, the theme is woven, showing first
the beauties of pastoral life, then the calamity of war, and finally
the return to peace.   That universal appeal, absolutely necessary to
the success of any art work, known as "human interest," is provided,
not through a portrayal of the joys and sorrows of one little group
of persons, but in a great series of bereavements and reunions.
Thus there is not one "heart punch" but a score.

Here, then, is the grip of Civilization, in that before Mr.
Ince rolls on his heavy artillery, his 42-centimeter guns, his submarines, his bomb-dropping aeroplanes, he has created a deep and
enduring interest in the army against which these engines of death
are operating.   In the background are the deserted forge, the invalid
mother, the tearful children, the shepherdless flocks, swiftly and
graphically suggested in such juxtaposition that when the crash and
flame of explosions leave the field strewn with bodies, there is a
personal interest in the fate of the army, not weakened by futile
guesses as to whether or not some handsome hero will stagger off
the field to clasp to his bosom a beauteous damsel, but an interest
which embraces all these men, compelled by the war power to abandon all that makes life lovely to engage in the business of destroying
life.

The thrill of the spectacle must ever be secondary to the
thrill of emotion, since it appeals to the brain instead of to the
heart.   Mr. Ince's spectacle is tremendous, its mechanical equipment a revelation, save in one respect.   His air fleet is numerically
strong, but battle planes are not to be had for the asking in this
country.   His aeroplanes are mere sky runabouts and roadsters,
bearing about the same relation to a war plane as the familiar De-
troit road-obstructor to the latest eight-cylinder go-devil.   On sea

and land, however, the eye is satisfied. Devastation is not represented merely by shattering a rickety shed, and then showing a
horde of people rushing pell mell out of a tenement. Nor has Mr.
Ince indulged in that popular banality of showing soldiers pursuing
and slaying civilians. He has endeavored to approximate, as closely
as possible, actual war conditions, and has not attempted to lend
spurious aid to his argument by introducing incidents of doubtful au-
thenticity.

When the film was first shown to the supersensitive and hy-
permoral critics on the Pacific Coast, it is reported that a shrill
protest arose to the effect that in portraying the Christus Mr. Ince
had committed sacrilege. Despite the fact that Jesus was a historically real man, there is an absurd tradition which has fastened itself upon the stage, that He must not be impersonated. Writers,
painters, sculptors, and all other artists, are free to present their
visualizations of the Man of Sorrows, but the actor has been barred.
There is no good reason why, if the spirit of Christ is one which
should be brought before men, any method of achieving this end
should be rejected. We believe that if Jesus were on earth today
He would gladly employ this far-reaching influence. In Civilization
He is seen moving sadly but majestically about the scenes of car-
nage, for the purpose of leading men to higher ideals than power.
It is a symbolism which appeals to both the artistic and the ethical
senses.

What, then, keeps this from being a Master Film? Simply
its absence of intimacy. These people are not our people, this king
not our king, this war not our war, this flag not our flag. It is a
myth of the imagination. True, it all might happen to us, or to any
other nation, but to realize this the audience must pause and trans-
pose its allegory into American terms. Note the difference in The
Birth of a Nation. Here was a struggle that meant something definite
to every American, revived ancient passions and flung us back headlong into that maelstrom of the Civil War. Its scenes left us riven
in every emotion and gasping for breath. It struck deep into the
consciousness of every spectator as a visualization of something
through which men he had seen in G. A. R. parades had passed.
Civilization is addressed to the mentality, and even in its most emotional moments never touches the core of our lives. Yet it stands
head and shoulders above any other picture drama which has grown
out of this war era. The scenario is by C. Gardner Sullivan, with
more than a slight suggestion that he has read or seen the Beulah
Dix piece, Across the Border. The acting is secondary. Howard
Hickman of the noble brow is a consistent Count Ferdinand, Herschell
Mayall an impressive king, and George Fisher a truly reverent
Christus. Civilization was more than a year in making. In one
scene the U.S. navy co-operated.

--Julian Johnson in Photoplay, Vol.
10, No. 3 (August 1916), pages
135-137.

*   *   *

All hail to Thomas H. Ince as a master producer of filmdom.
His work in visualizing Civilization compares with anything yet attempted in that line.   But he was handicapped by the limitations of
C. Gardner Sullivan's scenario, which is designed as a strong protest against the horrors of war, and to show the utter selfishness
of a monarch who plunges his people into such a dreadful situation.
The entertainment opens with a pantomime, with scenic and musical
accompaniment, showing a nation at peace, suddenly plunged headlong into war by its king, due wholly to his selfish desire for conquest.   He is dependent for success upon Count Ferdinand, who has
invented a submarine calculated to destroy the enemy's fleet, thus
insuring victory.   The Count is in love with Katheryn, "a woman of
the people. "   Katheryn belongs to a secret society, which is opposed
to war.   She takes him to one of the meetings and he becomes a
convert.   When the Count puts to sea and receives a wireless to
blow up an enemy vessel carrying innocent passengers, he refuses
to obey orders and as his own crew attacks him, opens the valve
which sinks his own vessel and deliberately drowns himself and crew
as a sacrifice to humanity.   His body is picked up and brought to
land and the king sends for his scientists to restore life in order
to secure the secrets of the death-dealing submarine.   But it is only
the Count's body with the soul of Christ who resolves to return to
earth to teach the message of Love and not Hate.   The "Count, "
in his reincarnation, has decided not to build any more submarines.
He is stoned and sentenced to death.   When the king enters his cell
he finds only the body of the Count.   As he gazes at it the figure
of Christ materializes from it and the monarch is treated to a vision
of the horrors of war.   The king declares the war at an end and
begins the restoration of peace and happiness to his devastated land.
While the "foreword" in the program announces the spectacle as a
pure allegory, the mythical kingdom is palpably German, the king,
the Count, the soldiers and many of the others being unmistakably
Teutonic types, their hair brushed back, with various mannerisms
and other indications tending to create that impression.   When a
casualty list is flashed, the names thereon are undeniably German.
The scenes showing Christ and the visualizing of Purgatory smacks
strongly of Catholicism.   There is very little opportunity to criticize Mr. Ince's magnificent effort, but Mr. Sullivan's captions are
altogether too preachy.   In his efforts to project pathos he slops
over to bathos.   Many similar situations in the plea for Preparedness in The Battle Cry of Peace were much more effectively brought
home by the aid of calm, argumentative captions.   A revision of
many of the titles might be worth while and would be a comparatively
easy task.   Then again, the pantomimic prolog and epilog might be
dispensed with.   They contribute little or nothing to the entertainment and are merely corporeal repetitions of scenes flashed upon
the screen.   With the exception of Enid Markey the cast is uniformly
excellent.   Most of the time she seemed unable to keep her eyes
open, as if she was blinded by the sun's rays.   Her conception of
"a woman of the people" smacked throughout of a modern society
woman playing a part in an amateur theatrical performance.   The
musical score by Victor Schertzinger contributes materially to the
generally fine impression.   Many of its strains are reminiscent of

Victor Herbert's Algeria.   All told, Civilization ranks with the
world's greatest cinema productions.

                              --Jolo (Joshua Lowe) in Variety,
                                Vol. 43, No. 2 (June 9, 1916),
                                page 23.

☐ CLEOPATRA (Fox, 1917)

There have been many mimic Cleopatras since the birth of
the drama but never before has a feigned "Serpent of the Nile" been
given such a massive and artistic setting as one furnished by William
Fox for the ten-part production in which Theda Bara acts the Egyptian vampire.   The scope of the story embraces many of the historical facts used by Shakespeare in writing both Julius Caesar and
Antony and Cleopatra, and it is evident that Adrian Johnson, the
author of the scenario, has gone to the English poet for most of his
incidents, rather than to Plutarch.   The author has furnished some
original material, however, and has also borrowed a character and
a striking scene from Sardou's drama on the same subject.   Several
of the subtitles are from Shakespeare.

The result of this literary patchwork is a lucid and fairly authentic account of the love affair between Cleopatra and Julius
Caesar, and the Egyptian queen's overmastering passion for Mark
Antony.   The scenes shift from Alexandria to Imperial Rome, and
several historical moments that have been immortalized by the brush
of some famous artist, are reproduced with impressive fidelity.   The
most important of these are the murder of Julius Caesar in The
Capitol, the first meeting between Cleopatra and Caesar, and the
triumphant return of the enchantress in her barge with Antony a
willing captive.

Opening with the lady's conquest of Caesar and his return to
Rome, the action busies itself with a fictitious love affair between
Cleopatra and a gentleman of the house of Pharaoh, while fate is
disposing of Julius and setting the stage for the entry of Mark Antony into the life of the Egyptian.   The meeting between the two,
the sudden and violent love engendered in both, Antony's return to
Rome, his marriage with Octavia, the weary waiting of Cleopatra,
the reuniting of the lovers, the interference of Octavius Caesar in
behalf of his sister, the battle against the forces of Antony and Cleopatra by those belonging to Octavius, the sea fight at Actium and the
deaths of the Egyptian queen and her Roman, all these historical
situations are thrown on the screen with an accuracy that necessitated
the employing of one of the largest forces of actors, extra people
and other essential workers ever used in a photo-spectacle, and the
building of a correspondingly large number of edifices of ancient
Rome and Egypt, with streets, waterways and interiors that truthfully reflect the period.

J. Gordon Edwards, who directed the production, has held

his work well in hand and brought out a series of rapidly shifting pictures that tell the story with a force in keeping with the subject and the ambitious attempt to make it live on the screen.   Toward the end the action would be strengthened by condensing it, the move-ment up to this point having been firm and engrossing.

The cast is exceptionally able.   Theda Bara as Cleopatra is always satisfactory to the eye, save that a certain grade of spec-tators will criticise unfavorably the very frank display of her physi-cal charms and some of the seductive wiles she uses to ensnare her lovers.   Technically her acting commands respect without ever reaching any great tragic outburst, and she is best in the lighter scenes of the part.   Her dressing of the Egyptian is remarkable for the variety and beauty of the garments employed.

A gratifying feature appertaining to the male members of the cast is their ability to wear the costume demanded by the time. This is notably so in the case of Fritz Leiber, who plays Julius Caesar, and of Thurston Hall, the Antony; of Herschel Mayall, the Ventidus, and of Henri De Vries, the Octavius Caesar.   All four are to be credited with impersonations of the first rank.   Albert Roscoe, Dorothy Drake, Dell Duncan, Genevieve Blinn, Hector V. Sarno and Art Acord are useful members of the cast.   The camera-men were Rail Schellinger and John W. Boyle.

--Edward Weitzel in The Moving
                    Picture World, Vol. 34, No. 5
                    (November 3, 1917), page 708.

☐   THE CLODHOPPER (Ince/Triangle, 1917)

Score two for author [Monte] Katterjohn: while The Clodhop-per, his recent writing for Charles Ray, does not possess the power of The Flame of the Yukon, it has that which most photoplays lack: a fresh, even if not novel viewpoint.   The clodhopper is the chore-boy son of a country banker.   As father's safe swells his fists grow tighter, and at length the boy, having no desire to become the man with the hoe, beats it to "the city."   The first job that stares him in the face is a janitorship in a theatre; and here the stage manager, struck with his humorous possibilities, injects him into the frou-frou entertainment.   His success proves him no clodhopper.

--Julian Johnson in Photoplay, Vol.
                    12, No. 4 (September 1917),
                    page 105.

                    *   *   *

It is Charles Ray and a wonderful supporting cast that make The Clodhopper an excellent comedy-drama.   Mr. Ray has another of his "boob" parts, in which he reigns supreme.   There are vari-ous episodes of the picture that might be singled out as particularly

striking examples of the star's ability.   When he receives his new
suit, when he goes to the Fourth of July picnic with his best girl,
and when he makes a hit with his clodhopper dance on a cabaret
stage, these are truly wonderful pieces of humor tempered with
pathos.   One can go into paroxysms of laughter at the picture time
and again and at the same time there are so many human touches
that a laugh is never forced.

Monte Katterjohn has treated his rather slight story with much
colorful incident and one never tires of it as a result.   Every one
of his characters is drawn carefully and each one has its part in the
development of the story.   In the person of Mrs. Nelson much of the
pathos of the story is centered and Lydia Knott in this role contributes
a mighty fine character.   Charles K. French further adds to his
many laurels in his interpretation of Isaac Nelson, the mercenary
president of the village bank.   Margery Wilson is the girl and does
an admirable bit of work.

Victor Schertzinger has scored another success in the direction of The Clodhopper.   He has already made a name for himself
in the "upper few" of directors.   There is many a touch of his that
hugely benefits the picture and never a one of them is artificial.   The
setting collectively and the scenes individually are excellent.

--Peter Milne in Motion Picture
News, Vol. 16, No. 1 (July 7,
1917), page 114.

☐   CONRAD IN QUEST OF HIS YOUTH (Paramount-Artcraft, 1920)

It is a feather in William de Mille's cap that he has been
able to enrich Leonard Merrick's delightful story, Conrad in Quest
of His Youth, and visualize it to such an extent that the characters
actually seem to live and the sentiment and humor colored with reality.   The book is a charming, sentimental journey of a man approaching forty who would search for the happiness of his youth.
William de Mille has kept it a narrative, emphasizing its salient
points, and the result is that the Merrick readers will find in the
screen edition a humanization of Conrad and the other characters.

It will never enter the mind of the spectator that the picture
is episodic because the scenes build so evenly.   There is no rush
of action, nor climactic development.   This picture gives the lie to
those who maintain that the screen must needs be a medium of
rugged conflict and vivid characterization.   One becomes thoroughly
engrossed in the man who would renew his youth because it brings
back memories to those who would turn back the pages of yesterday.
Merrick is artist enough to keep his tale from being unduly sentimental and de Mille has proven himself an artist by constructing
his picture with the utmost sympathy for the charm of the author's
style.   It is a straightforward little story well adapted by Olga

Printzlau, who has kept in mind that Conrad's youthful amours must provide the interest. Of course the development of these romances could not be incorporated for feature length.

The sponsors have presented them at their full blossoming period with just enough emphasis placed upon the pangs of disillusionment and pathos to touch the spectator. Conrad is disillusioned to discover that Time will not turn backward in its flight. His cousins lack his poetic nature; the first love, Mary Page, is a distinct shock with her constant cackling. But does Conrad brood over it all? His great sense of humor saves him according to Merrick and de Mille has painted him correctly. A delightful touch is the attempt to renew his first great passion. Conrad goes to Italy in search of her and finds her still good-looking but very absent-minded. Then, when he would keep an appointment identical with one of his youth he falls asleep which is another shock to his memories. Not until he actually falls in love with a charming widow of the present does he realize that he has found his youth. The picture is William de Mille's best without a doubt. His piloting of the players, his well arranged episodes set in scenes of charming atmosphere--these touches spell a picture which resembles a rare tapestry. Thomas Meighan and his company give well modulated performances and have seemingly stepped from the pages of the book.

--Laurence Reid in Motion Picture News, Vol. 22, No. 22 (November 20, 1920), page 3989.

☐ THE COUNTESS CHARMING (Paramount-Artcraft, 1917)

The Countess Charming is bound to charm, and in that respect it stands unique among the class of production known as a "vehicle," principally because it rises out of the vehicle class at times, and because of the remarkable personality of Julian Eltinge. It was a happy thought to utilize this accomplished actor on the screen. He is an artist outside of his specialty. In that specialty he is a high comedian to the finger tips, one of the most interesting characters shown on the screen recently, though that is hardly a compliment. He has an individuality all his own in the guise of his sex, and he is highly refined in his sex-transformation, very much such an interesting human creature as woman would be if she grew up the way she ought to her normal status, physically speaking, mentally perhaps, and morally maybe.

Not because he is a clever impersonator, but through those innate qualities, both obvious and subtle, which combine to make the true artist, Eltinge completely dominates The Countess Charming, but there is a happy union of other essentials to success. The story is original and told with high constructive skill. The settings are admirably chosen and photographed; the types are all good; the handling that of fine craftsmanship, and the subtitles fairly sparkle

at times--"laughter and applause" went to the lines in the presentation before a large audience.   The story relates to a social snub
given to a bright young man not in an exclusive set and his amusing
method of turning the tables on snobbery, but it is screamingly funny
at times, particularly when he is compelled to die in his assumed
identity.   The story, direction and acting form one of those nice
blends which interest all classes of people and constitute a decided
contribution of merit to the motion picture art.

> --Louis Reeves Harrison in The
> Moving Picture World, Vol. 34,
> No. 1 (October 6, 1917), page
> 70.

* * *

Enter Julian Eltinge, female impersonator, as they miscall
him in vodeveel, taking a short cut from the fact--impersonator of
women.   There is nothing female about Eltinge, and in these later
days he is now barely able to appear the grand dame, whereas not
many years ago he could do you an ingenue that you would find yourself making eyes at.   But his picture, The Countess Charming, is
great fun.   The story is not especially important, the entertainment
consisting in the swift transitions from masculine to feminine and
back again.   Here Eltinge has an opportunity that the stage denied
him, and it is too bad that he failed to realize it until he had lost
his girlish beauty.   The film gives an instantaneous change of costume in a flash-back; a similar change in a stage performance would
occupy so much time that the value of the juxtaposition would be lost.
Florence Vidor, Edythe Chapman, Tully Marshall and Mr. and Mrs.
George Kuwa provide more than common support.

> --Randolph Bartlett in Photoplay,
> Vol. 13, No. 1 (December 1917),
> page 66.

☐   THE COWARD (Kay-Bee/Triangle, 1915)

Charles Ray is an able challenger of Frank Keenan for first
honors in The Coward, an Ince play.   Not since William Elliott's
remarkable but hardly appreciated study of a weak boy in A Grand
Army Man have I seen so carefully developed, so sincere a depiction
as young Ray's.   Ince wrote this scenario, and the psychological
side of this lad is the subtlest and biggest thing about the picture.
Here is a character on whom a great big play could be written--a
gentle, kindly lad to whom war is a fearful thing; whose spirit is
willing, but whose flesh is weak; one who, in overcoming his weak
flesh, becomes a hero of gigantic proportions.

Keenan, as the father who takes his cowardly son's place in
the ranks, has a part of tremendous force, and he plays it--oh, ye
aloof gods of the masque, how he does play it!   Keenan still has

some screen mechanics unlearned.   In "registering" he winds up his
intensity as laboriously as an ancient grandfather's clock.

The denouement is a bit sudden; the defi of the self-
saved lad a bit grotesque in its implausibility ... he might have
gotten his battle plans less improbably, but ... the play is a whirlwind of power with some breath-catching moments.

This drama is Ince.

> --Julian Johnson in Photoplay, Vol.
> 9, No. 1 (December 1915), page
> 84.

☐   THE CRISIS (Selig, 1916)

Little need be said about the great popularity of The Crisis
in book form.   It was first published in May, 1901, and since then
no [fewer] than thirty-two reprints of the edition have been made to
satisfy the demand.   In addition, two reprints of a special edition
issued in 1904 have been required to meet the wishes of certain
readers.

Just as the play is the thing in a dramatic success, so in a
photodramatic success the story is the all important factor; and as
we have in The Crisis a great story, one that is well suited to the
requirements of visualization, we naturally expect to find a great
photoplay in the Selig production.

In this, I am bold to predict, no one will be disappointed.
For myself, the oftener I viewed the films the stronger this conviction became.   I refer, of course, to critical viewing and not to
viewing for entertainment only.

Colin Campbell's adaptation of the Churchill novel shows a
comprehensive grasp of its possibilities for moving pictures.   He
has used from the book, with a few exceptions, all that contributes
to the interest of the spectator, and he has furnished him the very
atmosphere in which the story develops.   In this connection I except
the lack of greater prominence to the fine character of Captain Lige
Brent, whom Colonel Carvel esteemed so highly that at one time he
considered him worthy to become the husband of his beloved daughter,
Virginia.   On the other hand, Mr. Campbell has changed the story
of the book for the better, where he affords the spectator a view of
the scene in which the gallant Colonel receives his death wound.   Mr.
Churchill, to the disappointment and even grief of many readers, lets
him pass out of the story without giving any definite knowledge of his
fate.

I can see no good reason for changing the book story where
Colonel Carvel steals through the Union lines to see his daughter

Jinny, as he endearingly calls Virginia.   In the film story, Mr.
Campbell makes it appear that through the reading of an item in a
St. Louis paper, which told of the serious illness of Judge Whipple,
the Colonel had made the dangerous journey to see his old friend.
And the film shows where a brother officer gives him the greatcoat
and the hat of a Union officer to serve as a disguise, as he leaves
the Confederate camp.   In this greatcoat we see him as he stands
by the deathbed of his friend, Silas Whipple.

On page 454 of the fifty-cent edition of The Crisis the Colonel
answers Virginia's question, "Why did you come to St. Louis at all?"
by saying, "I came to see you, Jinny, I reckon."   And on the same
page the following description is given of him as he looked at that
time: "His hair was nearly white and his face seared.   But he was
a fine, erect figure of a man, despite the shabby clothes he wore,
and the mud-bespattered boots. "   It seems to me that in these "shabby clothes" and "mud-bespattered boots" Colonel Carvel would have
been a much more affecting figure than he is in the disguise of a
Union officer.

In the production of The Crisis, Mr. Campbell has given us,
undoubtedly, the finest effort of his career as a director.   In the
opening scenes he reveals at a glance the underlying burden of the
story--the abolition of slavery and the throes suffered by the nation
in its accomplishment.   In the posed picture showing Abraham Lincoln freeing the slaves, the spectator will marvel at the almost perfect resemblance of Sam D. Drane (now deceased), in face, mien
and stature, to the martyred president.

Viewing the numerous exteriors and interiors used in the production, the intelligent spectator will be amazed at the outlay and
labor involved, never to speak of the imagination, knowledge, art,
skill and painstaking required for the successful accomplishment of
such a task.   The battle of Vicksburg, in which the most spectacular scenes of the production are shown, was filmed on the historic
ground where the grave men in blue and gray fought and died over
fifty years ago.   Thousands of men of the National Guard of Missis-
sippi participated in the filmed battle, and Admiral Porter's fleet is
also represented by the rain of shells that light up the beleaguered
city by night as they explode.

The entire Selig company was there, and Thomas Santschi
and Tom Mix are seen in thrilling action.   The former is seen
charging up the heights with his command, and the color bearer
falls by the explosion of a shell at his feet.   As Stephen Brice, Mr.
Santschi seizes the colors in one hand and the wounded man in the
other and dashes up the slope followed by his impetuous men.

On the slope of another hill we see an officer on horseback.
A shell explodes deep in the sand beneath the horse, and we see
horse and rider fall and roll over and over, until the bottom of the
hill is reached.   That man was Tom Mix, and the horse is one of
his favorite mounts, which has already been seen in various astound-

ing stunts, in Wild West pictures.   William N. Selig brought master
and horse all the way from California to perform this one spectacular feat.

The procession at night, in Freeport, Ill., where Abraham
Lincoln and the "Little Giant" met in one of their most important
debates, is another memorable exterior.   The marching throngs in
the streets, which are lit by the sputtering flare from old-time transparent banners that bear the names of Lincoln and Douglas, will be
viewed with more than passing interest.   The night scene showing
the great outdoor assemblage listening to the two leading Americans
of their day will create a sense of sacredness that only lovers of
Lincoln's memory can know.

But it is impossible from a space viewpoint to dwell on the
many other deserving scenes of this finely filmed story, so I shall
confine myself to the replica of the well-known engraving showing
Lincoln and his cabinet, on the signing of the declaration of force
against the seceding States, as made under the direction of Mr.
Campbell.   Compare the original engraving with its imitation on the
screen.   The latter was made in the Selig studio, with actors and
a room specially built, and the furniture and the other essentials.
Is it not a wonderful likeness of the original, so far as President
Lincoln and the members of the cabinet are concerned, and in other
particulars?

If you look closely enough, you will see a small deep box on
the large table.   That box has great historic value.   It is the box
that Lincoln used (when he did not use his hat) for his private dis-
patches and papers, when on his stumping rounds.   Mr. Selig was
fortunate enough to secure it for this scene.   He has been just as
careful, to a nicety, in other important scenes in his filmed story
of The Crisis.

To the assignment of the characters of the story, Mr. Selig
devoted careful attention and a wide knowledge of actors and their
special abilities.   In this he was ably assisted by Director Campbell,
whose judgment on fitness and ability for a part is almost a second
nature.   The result of their joint efforts and judgment is a cast that,
for fine ensemble acting, has been rarely surpassed.   True, I think
the assignment of certain characters might have been still more
happily made; but that is only a one man's opinion.

George Fawcett's Silas Whipple is one of the finest heavy
characters I have ever seen presented on the stage or the screen.
A perfect study of the man as he is revealed in the book, is evident in Mr. Fawcett's admirable impersonation.   And no better opposite could have been chosen than Matt B. Snyder for the role of
Colonel Comyn Carvel.   To watch them in their wordy passages at
arms has nearly always a grim humor and begets a real fear of
disaster to their lifelong friendship in the mind of the spectator.

Judge Whipple is a man of granite in the book, and Mr.

Fawcett's art makes him still more so on the screen.   Inflexible in
will and purpose, fearless for the right as he sees it and easily
moved to anger in its defense, strong in friendship unto death, soft
of heart beneath a rugged exterior and readily susceptible to the gentle influence and direction of his women friends, Mr. Fawcett's
Silas Whipple will appeal to every spectator as a man of real flesh
and blood--a great, unusual type of man.

     The scene showing the death of Judge Whipple will go down
as a classic in moving picture art.   When I think of the millions of
people that will be moved to tears by the powerfully affecting spectacle of this strong-souled man going out fearlessly into the Beyond,
as the melody of "Lead Kindly Light" falls on his enraptured ears,
I am amazed in contemplating the power of the moving picture to
sway mankind.

     Mr. Snyder's conception of Colonel Carvel and its expression
are most happy.   He brings out mirthfully at times the almost boyish roguishness of this old Southern gentleman, whom Time has
failed to tame.   Take, for example, the scene at Glencoe, where
one of the disputes between the old friends is caused by the Colonel's
aggressiveness.   You cannot fail to smile at the roguish look on his
face, as Virginia leads him by the ear from the room.   His quick-
ness with the pistol is a proverb among his friends, and we see it
illustrated twice on the premises of Carvel & Co., but without blood-
shed.

     Without Virginia Carvel in the many amusing and exciting
scenes between the Colonel and the Judge, they would fall exceedingly flat, and Miss Bessie Eyton's Virginia is always a joy, and
sometimes much of a puzzle as well.   Miss Eyton's characterization
of the Southern belle is the best effort she has made in moving pictures up to the present time.   The happy ease with which she shows
the changing moods of Virginia impresses one that she is actually
living the part.

     How delicately and with what exquisite fineness she overcomes
the scruples of Judge Whipple and induces him to make up and be
friends on several occasions.   And what a peacemaker she is between
the two friends.   In the Carvel home she assumes the air of mistress
without effort.   In her early contact with Stephen Brice she more than
once touches the quick of that polished young Bostonian by her haughty
Southern manner and pointed retort; and poor Clarence Colfax, who
has loved her since they both were children, with all his patrician
arrogance, lowers his colors when she takes him to task and shows
him what he must do to be a real man.   In short, Miss Eyton is not
only clever and artistic in her impersonation of Virginia, but she
looks beautiful and captivating as well.

     Thomas Santschi is somewhat old to look the part of Stephen
Brice when a student in Judge Whipple's office, but his acting is up
to the mark.   As a lieutenant in Union uniform Mr. Santschi is a
fine, strapping figure of a man, and the dashing charge he makes
with his men at the battle of Vicksburg has been referred to already.

Miss Eugenie Besserer's Mrs. Brice is a splendid characterization.   One is always pleased to see her on the screen.   As
Clarence Colfax, Marshall Neilan is seen in several brilliant exploits
during the civil war.   In the part of Eliphalet Hopper Frank Weed
gives a faithful depiction of that mole-like creature, and Will Machin
is a likeable type of man in the character of Captain Lige Brent.

Sam D. Drane's impersonation of Abraham Lincoln is really
remarkable in my eyes.   It cannot fail to delight millions of others.
How sad to think that Mr. Drane was called by the final summons
before he ever saw himself in the pictures!   I believe that his Abraham Lincoln in The Crisis will be a lasting monument to his memory.

The photography of The Crisis will add to the pleasure of
viewing it.   The subtitles are set in artistic, pictorial panels and
appear bold and clear.

The Crisis is shown on the screen in three acts, the entire
length being a little over ten reels.

The first showing of The Crisis in New York was at the
Strand Theatre on the morning of September 29, a large number being present as the guests of H. S. Sherman, president of Sherman-
Elliott, Inc. , the owners of the fine Selig production.   Among these
were Winston Churchill, the author of the book from which the story
was taken, and Booth Tarkington.   Mr. Churchill declared he was
delighted with the work of the Selig company.   There seems to be
no doubt in the minds of those who gave expression to their opinions
that the treatment of the subject had been marked by the highest of
intelligence--in adaptation, in direction and in acting--that The Crisis was a really great photoplay.

--James S. McQuade in The Moving Picture World, Vol. 30, No.
2 (October 14, 1916), pages 218-
219.

☐ DADDY-LONG-LEGS (Pickford/First National, 1919)

There is no man working in the sunlight medium who has a
greater mastery of human touches--whimsical, gay, tender or eye-
filling--than that Marshall Neilan who is never Marshall, but always
"Mickey. " Those touches are the keynote, the big success, the
whole value of Daddy-Long-Legs, a screening of the play made popular by Ruth Chatterton.   As an architect of drama, Mickey has not
yet arrived.   Considering his plays as plays he rather flounders
through, but an ability to reflect humanity is much nearer genius
than the practiced, acquired craftsmanship of making four or five
mechanically perfect acts.   If Mickey could now build plays that
satisfied us as to their technique, yet left us cold, I would say that
he would never be able to rise above mediocrity.   As it is, he

makes us laugh, and sometimes cry, and always enjoy ourselves--
and falls into some haphazard and usually hasty conclusion. So he
is in the position of a young singer of glorious voice and no great
skill in its use, rather than one who can execute a flawless cadenza
--in a sound that is windy and cold. The gift of holding the mirror
up to nature, which is Mickey's, is heaven-sent; I am confident that
he will acquire the upper mathematics of his profession. Daddy-
Long-Legs, is, indeed, a better thing constructively than his other
efforts. It is deeper, too, in thought. When the forlorn little girl
in the orphanage looked up at her foster-mother, Mary Pickford, and
asked "What is a mamma?" ... I don't know what to say about that
moment. I can only tell you that tears came into my eyes; and it
has been years since I wept at a picture or a play. On the other
hand--Mary, Wes' Barry, the little dog, and the jug of hard cider--
ten minutes of positive uproar. Pathos and laughter are near allies,
but it takes genius to interweave them as deftly and inextricably as
they are interwoven here. Miss Pickford plays the little girl of the
orphanage with all the zest of a beginner--as if she were indeed an
awkward little girl in a horrible union suit, and not the greatest lady
in the book of screen peeresses. It is this ability to put the utmost
of herself, the best of herself, so completely and wholly into everything she does, that keeps Mary Pickford at the top of the vast feminine heap. She has never done a thing more wholeheartedly in her
life, and, as parts go, she has never done anything better in her
life. That perfect combination of freckles and warts, Mr. Barry,
is an admirable side-kick and Mahlon Hamilton plays Daddy Long-
Legs with sincerity and repose. Daddy-Long-Legs is universal entertainment. Take your grandma, your girl, your four-year-old,
your mother, your minister or your (late) bar-tender; it is an hour
and a half of perfect enjoyment for all.

--Julian Johnson in Photoplay, Vol.
16, No. 3 (August 1919), page
56.

*   *   *

Mary Pickford has probably contributed nothing to the screen
which will be more popular than her adaptation of Jean Webster's
story, Daddy-Long-Legs, of the quaint orphanage foundling who becomes the ward and finally the bride of a wealthy chap. Ruth Chatterton played it upon the stage in an entirely different key, sounding
the pathos of the character. Miss Pickford makes Judy Abbott a
figure of comedy--and boisterous comedy at that. Judy even innocently collides with a hard cider jug. Mahlon Hamilton makes a distinguished Daddy-Long-Legs, and Mickey Neilan, who directed the
picture, himself plays the chubby Jimmie McBride. From a technical viewpoint, Daddy-Long-Legs is of too choppy continuity development. But Miss Pickford has jammed in the laughs at any cost.

--Frederick James Smith in
Motion Picture Classic, Vol.
8, No. 6 (August 1919), page
60.

☐   A DAUGHTER OF THE GODS (Fox, 1916)

        The great and growing gallery of American screen classics
has been enriched by a new production, which ranks with the very
best.   Enthusiastic as this may sound, it is still far from anything
like a full appreciation of A Daughter of the Gods.   The play with
this singularly happy and strikingly appropriate title was presented
to an invited audience at the Lyric Theater on the night of October
17.

        Of all the great film spectacles now appealing to popular favor
few will enjoy greater and, I think, longer popularity than A Daughter
of the Gods.   To begin with, the subject is the most cheerful and
the most charming of any of the big features.   Every man, woman
and child that goes to the theater wants to be delighted and entertained
first of all.   Now, here is a spectacle which fills us with genuine wonder.   No nursery was ever hushed into more attentive silence than
the audience which followed the marvelous succession of scenes of
supreme beauty unfolding themselves on the screen.   I would as soon
think of testing Grimm's fairy tales for syllogisms or dramatic sequence as applying ordinary standards to this clever and most delightful flattery of the human eye.   No need for the title-builder to urge
a return to the days of our childhood.   The spirit of this happiest
time in our lives grips us before the film is fairly under way.   We
are beguiled, we are bewitched, we lose the perception of time and
we get back to the naked realities of life like one who is waking from
a lovely dream.

        Beauty is the keynote of the film.   Beauty and symmetry of
the female form, grace, suppleness, strength, glowing health, modesty are but single items in this catalogue of human beauty.   Added
to this are natural beauties which overpower the most blasé of critics and knock his best epithets and adjectives into smithereens.
Even the colorful word-painting of such a master as Lafcadio Hearn
could not translate into language the ineffable majesty of this sea
and must fail to portray its moods which are in turn calm and alluring, tempestuous and terrifying, now wooing with gentle waves the
favor of the sweet and elusive mermaids, now tossing its angriest
billows against "the daughter of the Gods. "   And the glowing beauties
of the shore.   The one scene where Miss Kellermann, in obedience
to the Good Fairy's command, begins to arm her troops of gnomes
and elves, is one of ravishing beauty.   Not that this scene is in any
way more glorious than any other; there are no blanks anywhere in
this production as far as art and beauty go.   The dive from the high
tower, the race with the expert swimmers, the battle with the treacherous surf and the jagged rocks, the dance of the mermaids on the
shore, the play of the mermaids, their sweet sleep in the water, the
marvelous performance of Miss Kellermann in the rapids and in the
falls of unexcelled beauty, the crystal clearness of the ocean, whose
waters for a depth of many feet allow free access to the camera,
the splendors of the Oriental City, the glories of the Sultan's palace,

the great and agitated masses, the exquisite charm of the children, the ingenious uses of the animal creation, the miracles of sunrise and sunset on the waters on whose brow "time writes no wrinkles," the dashing movement of mounted troops in full gallop, the burning of a city, the tragedy of the slave market, the clash of arms, the hosts of gnomes and elves and their strange homes and habits--all these are but a few leaves from this animated album of beauty. In all my experience as a film critic I have never seen such a fascinating and gripping prologue. It must have taxed the patience and the ingenuity of the director to carry out his very subtle and very appealing conception. To make the illusion of these early scenes perfect and win the spectator's heart without a moment's delay he not only had to have a real "picture mind," but he must have given infinite pains to all the details. His success here was complete. The spell works from the very rising of the curtain and it is most cunningly sustained to the last. I, for one, kept no track of the reels, nor cared to keep track; all I know is that I was sorry when it was over.

A Fairy Tale--this much I have concluded--is the screen's own favorite expression; the master of the screen most revels in his task when he can tell all his story in pictures.

Miss Kellermann, aside from her daring feats, acted with great skill and gave a most creditable impersonation. Little fault can be found with the acting of the old Sultan (Hal de Forest). The rest of the cast was good enough with the exception of the Prince (William E. Shay), and Zarrah (Violet Horner). Outside of the principal these two were the only persons who had a chance to show histrionic talent, but neither succeeded in showing it. I cannot say that the title builder is entitled to congratulations. He had a puzzling task, for there is no sense or sequence to the story, no more than there is logic in Arabian Nights, but he might have smoothed the path by not obtruding himself and avoiding verbiage.

Much must be said in praise of the music, which fitted the picture and every part thereof like a glove. Here and there I recognized a Wagnerian motif handled with uncommon skill and well adapted to the tale on the screen.

Summing up I might say that there was a touch of Cabiria, a touch of The Last Days of Pompeii, a touch of The Birth of a Nation, but that not one of these touches was at all plagiaristic. Then I will say that this magnificent production has one great merit of its own, not to be found in any part of our screen literature: the magic and dazzling spell of the Southern Sea and greater than even this-- the irresistible "eternal feminine."

It is a feature which seems destined to add to the prestige of the screen by exciting new wonder and admiration for the art of the camera--it is a feature which will particularly delight the children.
                                        --W. Stephen Bush in The Moving
                                          Picture World, Vol. 30, No. 5
                                          (November 4, 1916), page 673.

*   *   *

We weary of every earthly thing--save the sea. The echoes of its first mysterious call have not ceased to sound through the ages, and it has kept a lure for every man who has been on, in or about it, from the first argonautic Greek to the latest commander of a U-boat. It was the sea which Herbert Brenon chose as canvas and ruling tint for his first heroic camera painting, Neptune's Daughter, and half a year ago, when he took the fabrics and arms of another Damascus, ten tribes of players, a seraglio of beauty, the edificers of a capital city, a day's steel from Bethlehem, the building materials of a new Jerusalem and the world's champion wet woman--he took them back to the sea. It was toward Jamaica that he steered the celluloid armada of William Fox, some time in the autumn of 1915; and it is from Jamaica that he comes in the early summer of 1916, with a great photographic ultramarine still wearing its prop handle--the sort they give unborn plays for convenience sake--The Daughter of the Gods. Miss Annette Kellermann, sweetly lustrous fish in Neptune's Daughter, is the finny queen of the new expression.

It is not upon a scene of grandeur or voluptuousness that this curtain of shadow rises, but upon a little girl who sorrows because her caged canary pines for freedom. She releases it to join a frolicsome sparrow which parades its liberty in a nearby wood. But a dog--alas!--uses the sparrow as an entree, and the canary, finding free loneliness more terrible than solitary confinement, flies out over the sea, and flies, and flies, and flies until it falls. The lonely little royal child, pining like the lonely little free canary, soon sends its wee spirit winging out over the ocean of eternity. And there is a king's son, too, who finds a coracle on the crystal beach of the palace keep, and, as his guard slumbers, paddles out, and out, and out--and over he goes.

Enter tailed water-sprites whom Brenon learned to call by name three years ago. It is theirs to reincarnate the water-killed children; and, reincarnated and matured, this pair of will-o'-the-wisp fortune is personated by Annette Kellermann and William Shay.

There's the pretty prologue to as grand a tale of nereids and necromancy, villains and voluptuaries, coryphees and combats as was ever wrought outside the Burton edition of The Thousand and One Nights.

If a cataloguer were sent to describe the articles in Captain Kidd's fabled treasure he wouldn't know what gold monastic cup or Aztec jewel on which to begin. I don't believe in writing a tale in a review, yet I don't know whether to jump in the middle of Brenon's picture and drill my way out with a hard pencil, or knock off specimen assays from its edges.

Seldom has any photoplay been conceived with such a wealth of varied material, with thrills so interspersed between moments of quaintness and closeup bits of expressive pantomime.

For sheer material size of spectacle, The Daughter of the
Gods outdoes anything yet seen. The mighty plain across which
white and black armies charge makes one wonder at finding so much
dry Atlantic island outside Cuba. The crowds of citizens and sol-
diers--countless, almost--which surcharge the great squares beneath
Brenon's long shots make one involuntarily applaud the discipline and
military technique which made this picture possible. There are
wall-battles with all the impedimenta of ancient verduning, outdoing
anything in epic Cabiria. The gnome village--a nation of miniature
men--comes toward that Somewhere in Arabia hundreds strong, jog-
ging absurdly on its score after score of donkeys; the reigning demoiselle of the fairies conducts the air with her demoniac baton--
instantly it is a crusade, a mighty convoy of crossed and galloping
white knights. There's the thrill of double exposure!

Architecturally, The Daughter of the Gods is another Troy.
Not merely a fortress, a wall and a palace were erected for its
taking pleasures; a whole city rose, with streets and armies for
shooting, and, afterwards, for fiery destruction beneath an omnivo-
rous lens which sometimes likes its fodder cooked.

Miss Kellermann does little acting, but much effective posing,
and feat upon feat of daring which leaves no margin for further exploits. If she passes her water-valor here, she dies. I doubt if
ever again will she undertake to swim in such a storm over such
infernal rocks as those she is horribly tossed upon in one of these
scenes. Nor will she do a more spectacular dive than her hundred-
foot leap from one of the Brenon-built towers.

Nor will any more of Miss Kellermann be seen, for she performs the most of her finny duties with no adornment save an over-
plus of artificial hair.

From time to time producers have used nakedness as diversion or attraction, but Brenon has made a perfectly logical use, not
of nakedness, but of nudity. One doesn't suppose that the belles of
an oriental hammam wore Hickson swimming suits; the Persian poets
don't suggest it, and Alma-Tadema, for instance, doesn't portray it.
Mr. Brenon's exquisite galaxy of hammamettes quite properly wear--
nothing. And you are not shocked. There is far more indecency,
you know, in a paraded bit of gauze than in the natural, absolute
unclothed.

This is not a perfect picture. One wishes that there were
more flashes of comedy to bind people and episodes together in
warmer humanness. Occasionally Miss Kellermann cavorts like an
H$_2$O primadonna, getting quite out of the play to sing an optic cadenza of splash. And again one longs for the dramatic value of
closer, more contrasty photography.

But what has been perfect since the Greeks finished their big
house on the Acropolian hill? Here is a stunning photoplay which is
a marvel of its kind, and the proclaimer of its author-maker as a

master-director of first order.   For every fault it has a dozen excellencies.

Mr. Shay is his sufficient self, and Jane Lee has an awful
race for her honors as First Little Kid of Photoplay with her artless sister, Katherine.   But it is Marcelle Hontabat, a tinily intense French girl, who pirouettes away with all the acting honors.
                                        --Julian Johnson in Photoplay, Vol.
                                        10, No. 3 (August 1916), pages
                                        133-135.

☐   THE DELHI DURBAR (Kinemacolor, 1912)*

Kinemacolor has outdone itself in much the same manner that
a champion athlete sometimes beats his own record.   The first presentation of the Delhi Durbar ceremonies in Kinemacolor took place
on Monday evening, February 19, at the New York Theater, New
York City.   A large, fashionable and representative gathering filled
the theater to its utmost.   It was a full dress affair and resembled
a night at the opera.   Many noted New Yorkers were among the
number, and also men of progress in the motion picture industry.
A large proportion of the audience had not as yet witnessed any of
the previous Kinemacolor presentations and accordingly were not
prepared for the great surprise that the evening had in store for
them.   Others who had seen former presentations, such as the Coronation pictures, gravitated there, but for the most part could not
bring themselves to believe that it was possible to surpass the Coronation pictures.   There was a surprise in store for them as well
as for the uninitiated.

The Durbar in Kinemacolor is a great success; probably the
greatest success that moving pictures have ever scored at any time
or place.   After observing this spectacle one does not feel so sorry
at not being a millionaire with a millionaire's opportunities for visiting foreign lands and foreign events.   There in their seats the audience began to realize, perhaps for the first time, that it will be no
longer necessary to undergo long and tedious journeys in order to
witness ceremonials in obedience to deep-seated longings of the
heart.   They learned also that they can see more of such things by
staying at home than they could by being on the spot.   It is much
easier to sit in a comfortable orchestra chair and get a close view
of the principals than it is to be an ordinary mortal hanging on the
fringe of a hot and dusty crowd and half of a mile away from the
stage, in a far distant land.   It is quite probable that most of the
persons who actually witnessed the Delhi Durbar will see more of it
afterwards through the medium of Kinemacolor than they did in the
city of Delhi, to say nothing of the expense and fatigue they went to.

---

*The Delhi Durbar was the first major film shot in Kinemacolor.

According to the picture, if one did not happen to be a British soldier, there was not a chance of getting within gunshot of the Imperial
Marque, and only a very favored section of the army got anywhere
near it at that.

The exhibition was remarkably smooth; it had been carefully
rehearsed and much praise is deserved by those who supervised the
details of it. Two projection machines were used. One picked up
where the other left off with such nice precision that the pictures
were thought by many to be one long continuous film. The light was
brilliant and the film, with all its color, was perfect. It is more
easy to imagine than to describe the riot of color at an Oriental
ceremony, but Kinemacolor is better than imagination and it can be
truthfully said that none of the colors have been lost in this truly
great record. The predominance of red in the British army uniform
is well calculated to produce a brilliant effect and has much to do
with the success of the Durbar pictures. In detail the program is
as follows:

The landing of their Imperial Majesties.

Preparation for the Coronation Durbar--A series of animated
snapshots of native workmen and the cosmopolitan population busily
preparing for the great event. These were of great interest as side
lights and furnished a very good idea of native customs and types,
as well as being an exposition of queer vehicles and methods of
transportation.

Arrival of their Majesties--Life size view of the King and
Queen and members of the Royal Court.

State Entry into Delhi, December 17, 1911--Showing the arrival of the Royal train on the East India railway; an immaculate
white palace on wheels. Also showing the ostentatious reception by
various dignitaries, military and civil.

The scene then changes to Calcutta, furnishing one of the
most enjoyable parts of the entertainment, that of the natives preparing for the coming of the King to their city. In this picture we
observe the elephants, camels, sacred cattle and Oriental vehicles
of state being prepared for the festivities. In this view the colors
run riot, the like of which it has been given to but few Americans
to witness in their native country. The profusion of rich and multi-
colored silks and other fabrics is positively amazing and the audience
was duly amazed. If P. T. Barnum could ever arise from his tomb
and witness some of these processional scenes, he might be glad to
hie himself back again, with all haste, at finding himself so far outdone.

After an intermission the Coronation ceremonies are taken
up. Beginning the parade with the mutiny veterans, there is a constant exposition of immense military maneuvers. Time after time
the audience burst into applause as the various well-drilled regiments

put in appearance.   Much of the second part was occupied by the
procession of various detachments through the Elephant Gate at Delhi.
In the opinion of many of those present, this was prolonged a trifle
too much and it would be well if other scenes were substituted for
the sake of variety.

The Coronation ceremonies at the throne are seen at close
range; also the native chiefs swearing allegiance to the crown.   Interspersed in the second half are numerous camp scenes about Delhi
and Calcutta, showing many interesting details incident to the occasion.   A magnificent and impressive part is the review by King
George of 50,000 of his most select troops, regiments and batteries.
Also a panoramic view of the great throng assembled on the day of
the Coronation.   Spontaneous applause punctuated the pictures at frequent intervals.   It is estimated that 150,000 people surrounded the
Imperial canopy, of which the camera could record but one-quarter
at a time.   A spirited polo match was well received, but the scenes
within the elephant stockade at Calcutta pleased the audience as well
as anything in the entire evening's exhibition.

The stage was beautifully arranged for the presentation with
a splendid piece of work by the well-known scenic artist, Ernest
Albert.   It is a representation of the beautiful Taj Mahal at Agra.
At the close of the exhibition congratulations were many for those
interested in Kinemacolor presentation.   Automobiles by the score
rolled away the departing guests, profuse in their praises of what
the Kinemacolor people, and others, are disposed to consider the
eighth wonder of the world.

--H. F. H. in <u>The Moving Picture</u>
<u>World</u>, Vol. 11, No. 9 (March
2, 1912), page 774.

☐   THE DEVIL'S PASS-KEY (Universal, 1920)

Universal has a good picture in Erich von Stroheim's <u>The</u>
<u>Devil's Pass-Key</u>, which misses being a great picture by reason of
that little matter of foundation building of which we were speaking.
The idea is original and interesting and the pictorial background
richly effective.   "A playwright of moderate income" living like a
prince in Paris, flocking with the haut monde, is trying to write and
sell highbrow dramas.   The directors of the Comedie refuse his
work, passing him the kindly word of advice that what they are looking for is plays of real life, dramas of the street and of the people.

Meantime his extravagant and beautiful wife is running up bills
at the shop of a wicked coutourier.   When she can't pay, the shop
lady suggests that she borrow the money from a certain rich gentleman.   Madame, being innocent, agrees, meets the gentleman, who
happens to be an American army officer, and though by appealing to
his better self she retains her wifely virtue, she gets herself talked
about.

The story is printed in a scandal sheet.   The playwright husband sees it, recognizes the possibilities of the plot, writes a play around it and has it accepted and produced before he learns that he has written the story of his own wife's escapade, a discovery he makes the night of the play's sensational success.   He is then intent upon shooting holes through the army officer, but is convinced finally that both he and the wife are innocent.

Here, as said, is a plot with a clever twist; a fine bit of ironic criticism of life in New York, London, Paris and points east and west.   But the gifted von Stroheim fails to convince me that these people of his are real; that they were living as he pictures them living in Paris and still pressed by need of funds as he suggests; that being so pressed the wife would have acted as she did, or that, having so acted, would have set all Paris agog.   Paris does not become agog en masse over members of the American Colony. Pictorially, however, and constructively The Devil's Pass-Key is easily one of the best screen exhibits of the month, and is splendidly acted by Una Trevelyn, Clyde Fillmore and Sam De Grasse as the points of the triangle, and by Maude George and Mae Bush as attractive natives of the French capital.

--Burns Mantle in Photoplay, Vol. 18, No. 2 (July 1920), pages 71-72.

☐ DR. JEKYLL AND MR. HYDE (Thanhouser, 1912)

There have been several other pictures of Stevenson's great novel.   It offers one of the most attractive themes to picture makers, because of the effectiveness with which the substitution of Jekyll for Hyde and vice versa can be accomplished.   This is a remarkable portrayal of the situation.   It is played very acceptably and gives a heart-gripping feeling of wonder as we see the picture alternate between terror and romance, romance that is wild with all regret and terror that reaches the depths in our knowledge of evil.   The picture is more effective, in its own way, than any of the others that this reviewer has seen; because its idea seems to be merely to bring this fearful contrast.   It doesn't tell so much of the story as the others.   Exhibitors will make no mistake in using this as a special attraction and in advertising it as an unusually strong production.

--The Moving Picture World, Vol. 11, No. 4 (January 27, 1912), page 305.

☐ DR. JEKYLL AND MR. HYDE (Famous Players-Lasky/Paramount, 1920)

I have a friend, a wise little friend, who insists that John

Barrymore's Dr. Jekyll and Mr. Hyde will be numbered with the classic productions of the screen and, years and years from now, be regularly taken from its tin boxes to be run before the astonished eyes of students of the pictured drama as a perfect sample, not only of what once was accomplished by a great actor before the camera, but of what all actors of even that advanced time should strive to achieve.   That is one popular opinion.

I have another friend, not so little and it may be not so wise, who insists as strenuously that Dr. Jekyll and Mr. Hyde gave her a most terrific attack of the movie blues, from which she has not yet recovered, nor expects ever fully to recover.   Its very excellences as an acted horror, says she, have set her advising all the mothers she knows to keep their children away from it and to guard themselves accordingly as their condition and belief in pre-natal influences may suggest.

My own reaction to this cinematographic tour de force strikes somewhere between these two.   I left the picture cold, not to say clammy, but eager to sing the praises of J. Barrymore and his sincere and quite amazing performance in this famous dual role, by which he reaches the peak of his screen achievements.   Eager also to declare it to be the finest bit of directing John Stewart Robertson has ever done, and a job that places him with the first half dozen intelligent directors in the field.

But I felt a lot like the friend who would keep her children away from it and suffer nary a pang of disappointment if I were told I should never look upon its like again.   Frankly I do not care for horrors, either on screen or stage.   If they possess a soul-purging virtue that does us good it must work subconsciously in my case, for never a satisfying thrill do I get from them, nor more than a fleeting suggestion of entertainment.   Invariably I am so very conscious of the actor's acting that I become much more interested in the facility with which he achieves effects than in the effects themselves.   Or in the spiritual significance involved.

A physician once told me that medical men never see a person as ordinary people see him; as a good looking, or homely, or thin, or fat, or short, or tall human being, but always as a physical specimen; as one whose features are perfectly assembled or slightly scattered; whose shoulders are evenly squared or curiously twisted; whose legs are sympathetically aligned or humorously mismated.

In somewhat the same way I see actors playing abnormal humans.   Sometimes they succeed in stirring my imagination, often they hold my interest, but usually to analyze these emotions is to discover that they are inspired by something commonplace, something plausible, something suggestive of a reasonable human action in the story they are illustrating rather than in the perfect pictures of abnormality they are creating.

So much for Dr. Jekyll and Mr. Hyde.   It will easily become

the most talked of picture of the time.   A door and two windows
were broken by the crowds that tried to see it on its first showing
in New York.   It may tour the country to the tune of similar crashes.
Unquestionably it has lifted young Mr. Barrymore to the leadership
of his contemporaries of the screen, as his Richard III. had put him
in the forefront of the advancing actors.   The curiosity to see it will
be great.   But as to its continuing popularity I have my doubts.

The story of the good Dr. Jekyll who, believing that the way
to be rid of a temptation was to yield to it, and who succeeded in
concocting a drug by means of which he could transform himself into
the brutal and loathsome Mr. Hyde, in which state he was free to
revel in all manner of bestial excesses, is too well known to bear
repetition.   The screen version takes a few more liberties with the
Stevenson original than did the Mansfield acting version, but does
not overstep cinema license.   Hyde is a little more brutal than he
was on the stage, Jekyll far more handsome and soulful (pictorially)
than any other actor of our time could make him.   The cast is
chosen with rare good judgment and includes Martha Mansfield.
                                    --Burns Mantle in Photoplay, Vol.
                                    18, No. 1 (June 1920), pages
                                    66-67.

☐ DON QUIXOTE (Fine Arts/Triangle, 1916)

Don Quixote was the greatest disappointment which has issued
from the Fine Arts studio.   Here was a chance for active photography to demonstrate all its arch-magic of mechanics.   Years ago the
wonderfully imaginative drawings of Gustave Dore paved the way.
Don Quixote should have been a permanent film, but this thing can
never be.   It was directed without imagination, and the ecstatic
vision of the Don--that vision which should have transformed the
episode of Dulcinea's stocking into a passage as glorious as King
Cophetua's transfiguration of the beggar-maid--never appears.   Here
Dulcinea is made into a female Charley [sic] Chaplin, when she
should have resembled Lady Godiva.   The comedy as a whole is not
so much reminiscent of Cervantes as of Mutt & Jeff.   For Dulcinea
herself, I have nothing but praise; Fay Tincher's performance is
little short of wonderful.   All things considered, she surpasses Hopper.   A young woman who can do this sort of thing deserves stardom.
Never, for the Don, will there be a man more perfectly endowed by
nature and acquirements than DeWolf Hopper.   His own performance
is all that his direction permits--even more.   Consider the pathos
of the death scene.
                                    --Julian Johnson in Photoplay,
                                    Vol. 9, No. 4 (March 1916),
                                    page 110.

☐ DON'T CHANGE YOUR HUSBAND (Famous Players/Paramount, 1919)

In a way, this is the opposite of Old Wives for New. And, like that picture, it is a masterpiece of artistic direction. Its story is that of a beautiful and spoiled woman, married to a wealthy man, who lets his business and his personal comfort interfere with his attentions to his wife. Another man, a dandy, affords a contrast that she is not proof against, and when this other man shows up the carelessness and slovenly ways of her husband, Leila decides to get a divorce and marry the newcomer. But Porter loved her truly, even if he did kiss her after he had eaten green onions, and Van Sutphen wanted only her money. After a good deal of unhappiness, Leila is freed from Van Sutphen and is reunited with Porter, while a fresh understanding is reached.

Gloria Swanson, in the part of Leila Porter, is exceedingly beautiful in a wild, exotic way. Her affectation of Oriental wearing apparel is a little exaggerated; while her consciousness of the effect she is creating is more obvious than is quite consistent with the best results. However, Miss Swanson contrives to give character to Leila, and if the desire is to satisfy the eye, she can most surely accomplish that desire.

> --Chester A. Blythe in The Photo-
> Play World, Vol. 2, No. 7 (May
> 1919), page 36.

☐ THE DUMB GIRL OF PORTICI (Universal, 1916)*

The adroit, imaginative and indefatigable Lois Weber-Smalley has done it again with her Pavlova photoplay, The Dumb Girl of Portici. Here was that bane of stage managers, a "costume play," coupled with the delicacy of handling a great European artist whose name was supposed to bring home the golden bacon, whose dancing had to be thoroughly exploited, and who had to be effectively placed in a real drama. Happily Mrs. Smalley's native ingenuity and Pavlova's theatric sense amalgamated without explosion to produce a swift, vital play.

The scene is the Italian coast; time, the middle of the Seventeenth century; subject-matter, one of the innumerable local revolutions of semi-barbaric Italy emerging from the long night of the Middle Ages, and in such localities as this untouched by the exalting white fire of Renaissance.

---

*The Dumb Girl of Portici was Pavlova's only feature-length film appearance.

Not since the production of The Birth of a Nation has a director faced such problems in the handling of masses of people. In many of these scenes not only were there populace, and soldiery, and other two-legged what-not, but the able corps of Pavlova's Ballet Russe for effective disposition, with dancing so adroitly conducted that all should synchronize, exactly, with the performances of future theatrical orchestras.

The tale itself follows the general trend of its parent inspiration, the opera-ballet "Masaniello," which spins along harmoniously on the dark strand of Fenella's piteous existence to its tragic close.

The brilliance, splendor and melodramatic power of these scenes are testimonials to the finest female imagination in filmland; the comprehensiveness and material quality of the surroundings attest an unusually opulent production.

Rupert Julian as Masaniello, Douglas Gerrard as Alphonso, and Wadsworth Harris as the Spanish Viceroy are three of a splendid regiment of interpreters.

It would be well if every screen performer could see and study Pavlova's indescribable pantomime. With two hands and two seconds of time she writes half a novel on the air.

This scenario, as is usual with her productions, is Lois Weber's own.

--Julian Johnson in Photoplay, Vol. 9, No. 5 (April 1916), pages 102-104.

*   *   *

Anna Pavlova, the Incomparable, has made her debut on the screen, but made it in a production of such magnitude, that her art and her personality, which it had been hoped would be given to the millions through this vehicle, is entirely lost. It is not the Pavlova of the ballet that flits about before the camera but an entirely different Pavlova, one whom it is safe to say never would achieve the title of the Incomparable. She does not possess what is known as a screen face and it is for this reason largely that her work is not as pleasing or as impressive as her reputation would lead one to believe.

The production was a great disappointment in so far that it gave the star so little opportunity to dance. She was only seen in one short length of film dancing in the deep sand of a beach, and we defy any one, even with the reputation of the Incomparable, to be graceful under such conditions. For all of the dancing which Pavlova did in the picture any tyro of the ballet would have done just as well. With Pavlova playing the star part in a production one naturally expects to see her dance. The fact that she does not is a keen disappointment.

As a spectacle the picture may be called an artistic success although there are several features that could be improved upon. Nearly all of the first reel could be eliminated, for the action is merely a picturization of the introductory sub-titles which preceded it. We believe also that more action could have been compassed within several of the succeeding reels, for they were filled to over-flowing with scenes which were incorporated merely for the purpose of establishing atmosphere, the manners and customs of the people at that time, and the economic burdens under which they la-bored.

Naturally it was necessary to establish these features, but it could have been done in much less footage. The rioting and the scenes showing the revolution of the populace against oppression were extremely well handled, the mob effects being especially im-pressive, although there was difficulty at times in distinguishing which body it was leading the fighting, whether the mob or the sol-diers of the Duke. The licentious scenes following the success of the revolution contained some very effective moments and served to show the utter abandon of a mob drunk with power.

The photography throughout was most excellent, clear, dis-tinct and with many soft artistic effects. Many of the scenes had unusual focal depth, those characters in the far background being almost as distinct as those in the near foreground. Nothing but praise can be given for the manner in which the production was dressed. The settings were both elaborate and beautiful with detailed attention paid to the demands of realism. The costuming was true to the period and the gowns of the women of the Duke's household particularly beautiful.

In a spectacle of this kind little can be said of the individual acting. Rupert Julian pleased as Masaniello but gave a trifle too much dignity to the character of a peasant fisherman of this period. Douglas Gerrard scored as Alphonso, while Edna Maison gave a dig-nified and human portrayal of the Princess Elvira. William Wolbert did a good bit of character work as Pietro. The balance of the cast was consistently good.

Little need be said of the story. It is as tragic as many of those forming the basis for opera and in the end brings about the death of all the principal characters. It is big enough, however, to serve as a reason for all of the spectacular effects. It is what is known as a picture story and as such it fulfills its purpose.

Taken all in all, The Dumb Girl of Portici is a good spectacle, not as good as some that have been shown but still good enough to make its production well worth while.

--E. in The New York Dramatic Mirror, Vol. 75, No.
1947 (April 15, 1916), page
28.

☐ EASY STREET (Mutual, 1917)

In Easy Street, Charlie Chaplin's latest and best, if we may
venture to obtrude so decided an opinion, an original key has been
struck.   At any rate, it is Chaplin at his funniest; and nothing much
more entertaining, by way of comedy, could be imagined than his
adventures with the street bully, when on occasion he has been placed
on patrol duty in wild and woolly Easy street, after having changed
his profession from tramp to policeman.   It is useless to try to describe the antics of the little policeman and the giant bully, whose
superior strength made the rubbing of the nose of a lamppost on the
ground appear but a mere trifle.   And it would be equally useless to
try to picture the turn of the tables when the bully, overcome by the
gas turned on him by the little policeman as a finale to his post-
twisting demonstrations, lies unconscious in the street, and the law-
less throngs, now in awe of the policeman instead of the bully, disappear as by magic at the flaunt of his coattail.

With all this excellence of entertaining quality the picture presented a couple of points which would require elimination.   One of
these occurs in the suggestive handling of an overturned baby's bot-
tle in one of the scenes in the Easy street mission, and the other
where the dope fiend makes a too free use of the needle in one of
the East street tenements.

                                          --Margaret I. MacDonald in The
                                          Moving Picture World, Vol. 31,
                                          No. 7 (February 17, 1917), page
                                          1037.

                          *   *   *

Mr. Chaplin again.   He has not only the floor, but a street,
and four floors on each side of the street.   Here he becomes a
policeman, is assigned to a terrible district named by the title of
our story, and is elected to abate Mr. Eric Campbell, public nui-
sance but an undoubted Samson.   Playing little David to this Goliath
Mr. Chaplin gets the Campbellian head fast in the bones of a street-
lamp, and turns on the gas.   Anon, he drops a cook stove upon his
enemy, from the third story.

These diversions make for a merry evening, although the
opening scene, burlesquing a rescue mission, is not in high taste.
La Purviance is again the lily in this bouquet of garlic, neither
toiling nor spinning, but sufficient.
                                          --Julian Johnson in Photoplay, Vol.
                                          11, No. 5 (April 1917), page 172.

☐ ENOCH ARDEN (Majestic/Mutual, 1915)

The story of Enoch Arden, as visualized by William Christy

Cabanne, is a splendid composite of imagery and illustration, just
what the distinguished poet intended it should be. The very simplicity of the story is artfully preserved. That simplicity, however, is
not in atmosphere, feeling and humanity. In its avoidance of sensation and false sentiment, it is all the more impressive and more in
accord with the author's own mood when he wrote it. The pictured
version, in fact, becomes a formidable rival to the poem, instead
of a poor and inadequate reflection, as are most transformations
from literature to the screen.

Because of its background it is manifestly impossible to present this story of other days without resort to studio costumes and
settings, but these do not jar by their artificiality. They are overlooked because of the evident sincerity of the producer. He has
taken infinite pains in the small details of household equipment, and
has even attempted, though less successfully, to "plant" a tropical
island.   Mr. Cabanne has made an effort that deserves high praise
because he has absorbed his subject and given to it the soul and
feeling of a genuine artist.

A strong factor in the success of Enoch Arden as offered by
the Majestic Company is Lillian Gish as Annie Lee.   I feared at the
outset that she could not respond to the exactions of the role, but
she gathers strength as the story goes on, and her slight figure
gradually becomes the center of sympathetic attention.   She has
caught the idea of mental revelation without effort--her face is very
expressive--but she still adheres to a painful eccentricity of Griffith's pupils, that of bent elbows and clutching hands.   What is done
with hands and arms depends entirely upon the character to be depicted, and to repeat a peculiarity under all circumstances gives a
sameness to characterization.

Miss Lillian is admirably supported by Alfred Paget and Wallace Reid. Both men act with convincing sincerity and dignity.
These three fine interpreters complete and round out what I have
already designated "a splendid composite of imagery and illustration."
--Louis Reeves Harrison in The
Moving Picture World, Vol. 24,
No. 4 (April 24, 1915), page
568.

☐ THE ESCAPE (Reliance-Majestic/Mutual, 1914)

Griffith's adaptation from the stage version by Armstrong is
characteristic in embellishing the story whenever and wherever an
opportunity is afforded, intensifying it by methods of character contrast, and giving it new charm, but the director has gone further
and endowed a rather morbid and commonplace play with some nobility of purpose. He takes pains to make his underworld scenes
such strong ones that they are realistic in effect, terribly so at
moments, but the true charm of his method is only revealed when

he can appeal to the imagination, where beauty is a logical part of
the picturing.

Within a few years--perhaps in a few months--we will look
back upon this period of adaptation, very much as we look back upon
periods in the evolution of "pictura," with more relief than tolerance.
We are adapting because of the uncertainty about original screen
plays and because producers feel a greater sense of security when
putting out something that has been on the stage, even if it failed.
Hence adapters of ability are simply using old and crude material
for reconstructive purposes, rather than for any actual renewal of
stage plays.   Some of the old material is good enough for a foundation, and it had better be kept there--out of sight.   On this, a new
structure, bearing the old title, may be raised by those who are
gradually establishing methods for the new art.

Griffith is one of these.   He has simply used The Escape for
a ground plan and cellar walls, thereafter raising his own structure
with the skill of a really great architect.   When he comes to treat
a big story to be built from the ground up for screen presentation,
the same methods will serve with a vast amount of intrinsic structural beauty and strength added.   As usual, he handles a small
group, enough to be numbered on the fingers of one hand--the first
five in the cast--and brings others on the screen for supporting or
reactive purposes.   Of this small group, Blanche Sweet carries off
the honors, with Mae Marsh a close second in consistency and intelligent interpretation.   Harron does some fine acting; Crisp is a perfect type, and Owen Moore does all that a perfect gentleman is permitted to do under the circumstances.   The cast is nicely balanced,
and the policemen shine as never before in the underworld plays.
They look and act like the real thing.   Miss Sweet is growing in
subtlety, in refinement of interpretation, but her personality is, in
itself, an effective contribution.   She has caught the idea of discovering the combined childishness, wondrous cunning, and intense natural longings of womankind in a very charming way.

The story is that of the effect of improved environment.   It
shows, within certain limitations, that we could, if we always knew
how, so enrich the soil in which the human plant grows, and cultivate it by proper nutrition, sunshine and care into finished results
that would consign criminal courts and prisoners to the ash-heap.
But this showing is only a whisper.   Sociological plays are new, and
it is no easy matter to make them so entertaining that the purpose
will be felt, rather than unpleasantly obvious.   Mr. Griffith is pursuing such a straight path in the right direction that what is worthy
of approval in his plays overweighs his occasional mistakes to the
extent of disarming adverse criticism.   There is a ring of sincerity
in his work and in the work of many others adapting stage plays that
was never particularly conspicuous in the plays themselves.

One can almost number sincere American dramatists on the
fingers of one hand--surely on two hands--who have exhibited craftsmanship to rise into established place.   Men like Bronson Howard,

James A. Herne, David Belasco, Augustus Thomas, Percy Mackaye, William Gillette and Clyde Fitch, are all too rare. The stage has been given over to so much greed, slush and general inanity that people of intelligence rushed to the picture shows for relief. The Escape of their lives was made possible to millions, was made possible by the wordless drama that swept the country like a flood and caught most of the stage pretenders up in its swirl. Many who were simply clever enough to squeeze the old lemon dry in an effort to get all the juice there was in it are now profiting by revivals of their ancient fruit on the screen, and it must stagger them into a sense of pseudo-propriety to witness the artistic dressing of their past performances.

The Escape is being shown at the Cort Theater to very appropriate music, and constitutes a dignified contribution to the line of feature adaptations now in vogue.

--Louis Reeves Harrison in The Moving Picture World, Vol. 20, No. 11 (June 13, 1914), page 1515.

☐   THE ETERNAL CITY (Famous Players, 1915)

There has not been a picture produced in the past year, and only one or two that we can think of since the birth of the motion picture, that so fully illustrates the familiar phrase: "The field of the motion picture is unlimited. " It is a short and easy sentence to quote, but the Famous Players company has proved it so in a manner which has never been equaled. Nothing would be more ridiculous than to compare The Eternal City with any other picture. It stands in a class by itself, in a class which others may be placed in the future, but not in the present.

When a picture is so perfect in every degree, when there is really not a point which deserves severe criticism or any uncomplimentary words at all for that matter, it is very hard to find words adequate enough to express our true opinion concerning such a marvelous offering.

The Eternal City is a visualization of Hall Caine's novel of the same name. The story as presented in the picture is so powerful, so wonderfully constructed, is so replete with powerful situations, that if there are any who will not appreciate it they have no sense of the artistic whatsoever. It is eight reels in length, longer than the average picture, yet it is gripping, absorbing and tense all the way through, and each individual scene contains a little grip all its own.

Here's another point, and a very big one, in favor of the picture, a point that practically doubles the quality of the story. The

scenes laid in Rome and London were actually filmed in Rome and
London.   Such magnificent scenes as are shown have seldom been
equaled on the film.   The Piazza before St. Peter's on the day of
the Pope's jubilee, the Castle of St. Angelo, the Coliseum, the
Forum, the beautiful Villa D'Est and scenes in the gardens of the
Vatican, besides countless other smaller but no less effective scenes,
are laid as backgrounds to the story.   The mobs before St. Peter's
and in the Vatican were obviously handled by a master hand.

In all these scenes none but the best photography prevails.
The lighting is most magnificent, and is more noticeably artistic in
the Coliseum scene, and again among the buildings of the Villa D'Est.
If the photography had been below the high standard of the Famous
Players it would have lowered the picture's value, but the photography throughout the eight reels sets a mark which will be very difficult to live up to.

On a par, and perhaps even more important than the story
and the scenic effects is the cast, which is headed by Pauline Frederick.   As Donna Roma, the principal role in The Eternal City, Miss
Frederick makes her first screen appearance.   There are many difficult scenes in which Miss Frederick is seen to splendid advantage.
Her manner in interpreting her role is so wonderfully clear, so expressive, that it is hard to believe that heretofore all her efforts
had been consigned to the stage.

In the opposite part is Thomas Holding as David Leone.   As
a leader of the people he does excellent work.   In the heavy, emotional scenes his acting is finished and powerful.   Frank Losee as
Baron Bonelli is such a thoroughly efficient heavy that he transforms
an unsympathetic part into a telling and rather pathetic role.   John
Clulow as Bruno Rocco is another capable member of the cast.   He
is the right-hand man of David and a real, living exponent of the
Italian people.   Ciquel Lanoe as Charles Minghelli is another heavy,
and Fuller Mellish interprets the role of Pope Pius XI.   The rest
of the large cast ought to be mentioned as they all do uncommonly
excellent work.

It is to Edwin S. Porter and Hugh Ford that the credit for
producing the picture should go.   This is by all odds the best picture that they have turned out while working together.   The atmosphere, the construction, and all the other significant and insignificant points in the picture are the results of their untiring work, but
it is work that will be immensely appreciated when the production is
viewed.

A condensed idea of the story may be obtained from the following paragraphs.   David Leone is left alone in the world after his
mother has sought oblivion, because she thought her husband had
deserted her.   The husband, overcome by grief, joins the church
and many years later becomes Pope Pius XI.   David, after being
sheltered by Roselli and learning his teachings, becomes an ardent
socialist.   The death of Roselli is caused by the scheming machina-

tions of Bonelli, who later becomes the Prime Minister of Italy.
Roma, the daughter of Roselli, is brought up by Bonelli, and when
he reaches his high position she becomes his mistress.

It is David's burning desire to avenge his benefactor's death,
find Roma, and also lead his political party to triumph.   How he discovers Roma, marries her despite her character, how he kills the
infamous Baron and how he learns his father's identity, makes such
a powerful series of events that unless seen their full power cannot
be appreciated.   Suffice it to say the story is one of the most dramatically powerful ever seen on the screen, and as said before made
doubly more so by the backgrounds afforded and the exceptionally
expressive interpretations rendered by the cast, especially Pauline
Frederick.

A word concerning the premier presentation of The Eternal
City at the Lyceum Theatre, New York, on the evening of Sunday,
December 27.   Mr. Rothapfel, of the Strand Theatre, arranged the
music and conducted the orchestra.   The results he attained with
his music, and also with a number of men to imitate the mobs, were
most satisfactory.   There never was a better chance to play music
to the picture as there is given here, and it is to be hoped that everyone who can will grasp the opportunity.

A number of prominent motion picture and theatrical person-
ages attended the first showing of the film, among whom were Charles
Frohman, Channing Pollock, James K. Hackett, John Mason, John
Barrymore, A. H. Woods, F. P. Adams, William Collier, Robert
Hilliard, J. Stuart Blackton, Joe Weber, Louis Joseph Vance, Burns
Mantle, Jane Cowl, Gail Kane, Margaret Illington and Oliver Morosco.
                          --Peter Milne in Motion Picture
                          News, Vol. 11, No. 1 (January
                          9, 1915), page 45.

☐ EVANGELINE (Fox, 1919)

Longfellow's immortal poem, Evangeline, has been wonderfully humanized upon the screen by William Fox.   The sublime and
tragic love story told so beautifully in the poet's word pictures is
translated into a photoplay with remarkable fidelity.   The result is
it remains faithful to one's own conception.   Such treatment is important in a work of this character.   It makes the subject vital,
truthful and lifelike.   Raoul Walsh is a director who can draw a
canvas with the utmost appreciation of the author.

As drama goes it carries no appeal.   But that is not important.   What is important is the spark of the poem which is caught
and carried onward--the spark, the inspiration of his beautiful song
of faith and love.   The picture introduces a prologue which reveals
a lover's quarrel.   And the poem is read and visualized to point an

object lesson in faith and devotion.   And the spectator is drawn into
the canvas and follows the lovers with the keenest sympathy from
the time they plight their troth in youth only to be torn apart, to
the day in a far-off land when they meet in the autumn of their lives.

Excerpts from the poem are used in the subtitles and they
contribute in giving it beauty.   It is spectacular and rich in atmosphere.   And acted with fine understanding and feeling by Miriam
Cooper as Evangeline, and Albert Roscoe as Gabriel.   Some of their
scenes are heartrending, and a deep running note of pathos is felt
throughout the visualized reading.

                              --Laurence Reid in Motion Picture
                              News, Vol. 20, No. 9 (August
                              23, 1919), page 1697.

☐ EXCUSE MY DUST (Paramount-Artcraft, 1920)

I liked Wallace Reid's Excuse My Dust, first, because it is
a good short story, attractively screened, and second, because its
creators have not tried to make it anything more than that.   One of
the eleven or fourteen things we all find to object to in pictures is
the obvious effort of scenarioist and director, the one usually abetting
the other, to build a mansion out of the material laid down for a
bungalow.   When the thing is finished the foundation is fairly solid,
but the superstructure is so very wobbly and thin you can plainly
see through it.

Excuse My Dust relates a plausible and interesting incident in
the life of "Toodles" Walden, erstwhile demon driver of the good old
Darco bus that won the Los Angeles-San Francisco road race in
Speed Up.

No sex stuff here, and no suave young villain.   Just a good,
interesting, at times exciting, and always well told short story.   The
ingratiating Reid is as cheering a screen hero as usual, Theodore
Roberts is excellent as the blustering "J. D. ," and Ann Little is a
lovable wife.

                              --Burns Mantle in Photoplay, Vol.
                              18, No. 1 (June 1920), page 68.

☐ THE EXPLOITS OF ELAINE (Pathé-Hearst, 1914)

Following on the success of The Perils of Pauline, the new
Pathé-Hearst Serial, The Exploits of Elaine from the pen of Arthur
B. Reeve and picturized by Chas. L. Goddard, bids fair to surpass
in popularity its predecessor, judging from the briskness with which
the first two-reel instalment, entitled "The Clutched Hand," strikes
the imagination.

In this first instalment the audience is given just enough daylight on the mysterious forms and happenings which characterize the
story to arouse the most rabid interest as to what is to follow.
From the mysterious death of Mr. Dodge, the wealthy president of
an insurance company, and which, as the audience is shown, is
brought about by the agent of "The Clutched Hand," through some
mysterious use of an electric current and the fumes of a certain
chemical diffused into the room above, where Dodge is in the act
of using the telephone, by means of a connection with the heating
register, the clever scientific detective work of "Craig Kennedy" is
brought into play, when he discovers with astonishment that the
finger-prints on the safe and articles handled by the murderer are
an exact duplicate of his own.

At this point of the story our curiosity is suspended on to the
next instalment, when the hope of solving the mystery will no doubt
be deferred for several succeeding releases, the first of which is
expected to make its bow to the public on Monday, December 28th.
Fourteen weekly episodes of two reels each compile the series.

The mystery to be solved by "Craig Kennedy" is, "What, or
who is the Clutched Hand that so surely descends and crushes life
from the unfortunate individual who ignores its warning?"

Arnold Daly plays the role of "Craig Kennedy," Pearl White,
that of Elaine, whose exploits will be followed with intense interest.
William Riley is seen to advantage in the short-lived role of President Dodge. Other well-known names appearing in the cast are Sheldon Lewis, Raymond Owens, and Robin Towney. Director Wharton
is engaged in the work of guiding this excellent cast through the in-
tricate paths of the big serial.

> --Margaret I. MacDonald in The
> Moving Picture World, Vol. 23,
> No. 1 (January 2, 1915), page
> 80.

☐ EYES OF YOUTH (Equity, 1919)

Marjorie Rambeau created a dramatic furore in the stage version of Eyes of Youth. Clara Kimball Young does the same thing in
her umbrageous translation. Not since the good old days have we
seen Clara so gloriously gowned, so well photographed or so powerfully emotional. I feel that in making the Oriental seer who shows
the young heroine what would happen should she choose the path of
duty, wealth, fame, or love, a philanthropist who savors of an effort to mimic the altruism of the chink in Broken Blossoms and The
Miracle Man, the director has made a mistake. For the character
is neither subtly nor poetically played and adds nothing to the effectiveness of the picture. Miss Young was most sympathetic as the
woman grown old doing her duty, and most gloriously realistic as
the opera singer in the fame episode. Her depiction of the drug

addict savored simply of theatricalisms and grease-paint. Eyes of
Youth is a decidedly well produced picture. Every girl cannot help
wishing that she, too, might have a crystal in which to see the results of her choice at the "crossroads of life." I found Edmund Lowe
good to look upon as the hero and Milton Sills smugly correct in a
minor role. *

--Hazel Simpson Naylor in Motion
Picture Magazine, Vol. 19, No.
4 (April-May, 1920), page 75.

☐   THE FALL OF A NATION (National Drama Corporation, 1916)

Firmly grasping the parachute, we now descend to a consideration of the Thomas Dixon confection, The Fall of a Nation. Here
we have our friend of last summer, The Battle Cry of Peace, with
the punch taken out and low comedy substituted, and Hoyt's A Milk
White Flag resurrected as a serious finale. Here we have the Pil-
grim Fathers taking possession of New England to the caption, "First
they fell upon their knees, then upon the aborigines." Here we have
a caption stating that Carl Schurz and his followers escape to America, followed by a picture of six men crawling through some shrub-
bery. Here we have a sweet young girl of about eighteen elected as
leader of a sort of vast Federation of Women's clubs. Here we have
plotters openly unloading guns from a truck in a city street in broad
daylight. Here we have people taking seriously headlines in a yellow
journal. Here we have a producer the limit of whose imagination in
ridiculing the peace movement is repeating Commodore Blackton's
lampoon of W. J. Bryan, tiresome even a year ago. Here we have,
once more, the spectacle of high commanders of an invading army
dropping everything to force their attentions upon sugarplum ingenues.
And so on, until, as a climax of pure, triple distilled saccharine to
top this pyramid of glucose, we have the loyal Americans regaining
control of their country by the simple and direct method of a great
organization of 1,200,000 delectable young females in natty white
suits, winning the love of the soldiers of the army of occupation and
persuading them to desert to the American forces, with their heavy
artillery and side-arms. Oh joy! Oh cataclysms of bliss!

The fable itself is not worth repeating, for it is familiar to
many as the plot of The Battle Cry of Peace, with the sole difference that instead of saying, at the close, "This never happened," it
shows the Americans regaining, in the bloodless fashion described,
control of their land. The celluloid is described by its author as
"A story of the origin and destiny of our republic by one who believes the time has come for a revival of the principles upon which
it was founded." With the propaganda feature of this film, as with

_____
*It is interesting to note that Ms. Naylor makes no mention of Ru-
dolph Valentino in the role of the professional corespondent.

that of Civilization, we have nothing to do.   In these days of preparedness parades and political debates that can be safely left to the
reviews which deal with such matters.   We are concerned solely
with the question of whether or not this is good entertainment, regardless of the sincerity of the author's patriotic motives.   And it
is not good entertainment because it is neither original nor spectacular.   At this writing, twelve hours after witnessing the display, it
is impossible to recall one battle scene.

Yet the picture contains some of the finest acting, and offers
some of the finest types, ever projected upon the patient white sheet,
and the photography could not well be improved.   Lorraine Huling,
as generalissimo of the flapper army, is a delightful personality,
despite the handicap of her silly role.   Flora MacDonald as an Italian
woman and Phillip Gastrock as her husband are perfect cameos of
characterization.   Numerous other types of minor importance are
marvels of detail.   But it cannot be said that these are of sufficient
interest to redeem, even in a measure, the utter failure of the piece
as a whole.

The advertising heralded this as "the first grand opera cinema. "   To our stubbornly literal mind, grand opera suggests, for
some reason or other, a considerable amount of singing.   In the entire evening no voice was raised in lay, aria, recitative, chorus,
cavatina, glee, cadenza or madrigal, save that of Mr. Dixon, who
came before the curtain (when the audience called for Victor Herbert) to say how glad he was we all liked his piece, when it was for
Victor we were all rooting.   Symphony-cinema it might be called,
or better, a symphony with pictorial fetters.   In the opening episodes, where the picture prelude was leading up to the founding of
the American republic, Mr. Herbert displayed true Beethoven genius,
introducing faint suggestions of the themes of the various American
national airs, and in the battle scenes the jargon and dissonance was
so masterful that it almost hypnotized the audience into the belief
that the picture was thrilling.   It was the music which thrilled and
awakened the flagging interest.   It was not surprising, nor without
significance, that the calls in the intermissions at the opening performance were all for the composer, nor was it surprising that Mr.
Herbert did not care to appear in person.   The question is, what
will become of this splendid composition when the picture succumbs.
--Julian Johnson in Photoplay, Vol.
10, No. 3 (August 1916), pages
138-139.

*   *   *

The Fall of a Nation, Thomas Dixon's sequel to his Birth of
a Nation, with Victor Herbert's original operatic score expressly
composed for it, had its metropolitan premiere Tuesday evening at
the Liberty.   In this instance Dr. Dixon's film is a plea for preparedness, surrounded by a simple love story, some comedy and a
series of spectacular battle scenes.   It is in three acts and a prolog, the first showing the origin of our republic; Act 1, a nation

falls; Act 2, the heel of the conqueror, and Act 3, the uprising two
years later.   There is a wealth of fine filming, so much so that the
main criticism is its abundance.   Much of it might be deleted.   The
simplest way would seem to be to abandon entirely the prolog which,
while all right, is not essential to story, being a recapitulation of the
history of the United States dating from its invasion by the white man.
The story proper shows Charles Waldron, an American millionaire,
in love with Virginia Holland, a leader of suffragists pledged to peace.
She is also loved by John Vassar, a Congressman, who has a bill
providing for a large American army.   Waldron is secretly at the
head of a plot to capture America, backed by Germany.   Twenty
thousand followers rise and capture New York from the National
Guard, and in a series of battles, aided by a powerful fleet bringing
150,000 invaders with Krupp guns and other modern war devices,
Washington, Philadelphia, Boston, Chicago and St. Louis are occupied.   Waldron is appointed Viceroy, with the title of Prince.   The
horrors of invasion are vividly depicted, with rape and rapine ram-
pant, it all being brought home forcibly to Miss Holland when it
touches directly her own family.   With characteristic femininity she
pretends loyalty to the new regime and is entrusted by Waldron with
the organizing of the Imperial Legion of Honor among American women.   She secretly organizes The Daughters of Jael, a million girls
and women pledged to the overthrow of the foreign usurpers.   Employing their feminine wiles upon the foreign soldiers, the guns are
captured and at given signals, with some spirited night-riding by both
men and women, America is once more recovered and John Vassar
claims Virginia for his own.   Considerable comedy is created by the
introduction of William Jennings Bryan and Henry Ford as pacifists,
poorly "disguised" under the names of Plato Barker and Cuthbert
Pike.   The big battle scenes were remarkably well staged, calling
forth volumes of tremendous applause at the premiere.   Victor Herbert's interpretative music aided materially to the general effectiveness.

                                        --Jolo (Joshua Lowe) in Variety,
                                         Vol. 43, No. 2 (June 9, 1916),
                                         page 23.

☐ THE FALL OF THE ROMANOFFS (Herbert Brenon, 1917)

        Among the many excellences to be found in The Fall of the
Romanoffs, Herbert Brenon's eight-part picture novel, based on the
Russian Revolution, one attribute stands out in bold relief--the swift
onrush of events.   Realizing that the multiplicity of amazing happenings which have taken place since Rasputin, the Sacred Devil of
Russia, came in contact with the unhappy ruler and his family, offered an embarrassment of historical facts, Austin Strong and George
Edwardes-Hall, the writers of the scenario, and producer Brenon,
have hurried the action from one salient episode to another and dispensed with the minor detail generally found in works of fiction.   In
this way the historical events of several years have been compressed

into an eight-part picture, and its effect on the beholder is as if he himself were an actor in the scenes that have but recently been added to the pages of history.

It is hardly necessary to outline the plot of The Fall of the Romanoffs. Rasputin, the illiterate sled driver who rose to power on the ladder of religious superstition, is the dominant figure of the novel. Other characters from life are Nicholas II, the Czarina, the German Emperor, Grand Duke Nicholas, Alexander Kerensky, and Iliodor, the Siberian monk who attempted to overthrow Rasputin, and was himself obliged to flee from Russia. The fictitious characters and events that have been introduced to assist in telling the story fit in admirably with the selection of material from the actual course of affairs. In tracing the rise and fall of Rasputin, the self-styled prophet, the overthrow of the Romanoffs is also shown; and the amazing power commanded by this drunken, licentious mountebank fascinates the spectator, despite his better judgment. Rasputin's effect upon the fate of a great nation when ruled by a man whose only qualification is one of birth, offers a potent argument in favor of democracy. The spectacle of the Czar and Czarina listening to this charlatan as to one inspired and allowing him to direct matters of state as well as their private lives, strengthening the conviction that absolute monarchs are no longer needed on this war-rent world.

To Herbert Brenon belongs a large share of the credit for putting The Fall of the Romanoffs before the public in an able and impressive manner. The reproduction of the scenes, episodes, characters, and all that goes to make up the life of the country, has been accomplished with convincing skill. Palace and hut, noble and peasant, the lone figure of the Czar or the rabble in the streets clamoring for freedom--the director has placed them on the screen in exact counterpart and made them do his bidding in an absorbing story which he wisely classifies as a picture novel. One touch of theatricalism mars his work. In the banquet scene, which ends with the killing of Rasputin, a soldier enters the room on horseback and rides his mount down the length of the long table. A very good circus trick, but out of place in this scene.

The cast could hardly be bettered. Edward Connelly as Rasputin gave a character study, based upon actual knowledge of the man, that was finely conceived and adroitly executed. Charles Craig's performance of the Grand Duke Nicholas was equally meritorious, and Conway Tearle as Prince Felix, Nance O'Neil as the Czarina, Alfred Hickman as the Czar, R. Payton Gibbs as Baron Frederick, Mlle. Ketty Galanta as Anna, Pauline Curley as Princess Irena, Mlle. Marcelle as Sonia, William E. Shay as Theofan, George Denueburg as Wilhelm II., Master Lawrence Johnson as the Czarevitch, and W. Francis Chapin as Alexander Kerensky, sustained their roles with commendable ability. Iliodor, the Russian monk, appeared in person and was surprisingly excellent before the camera.

--Edward Weitzel in The Moving Picture World, Vol. 13, No. 33 (September 22, 1917), page 1859.

☐ FATTY AND MABEL ADRIFT (Keystone/Mutual, 1916)

     Fatty and Mabel Adrift was the month's best Keystone. It
was ingenious, it was acrobatic to a degree, it was sensational, it
was clean, and it was always funny.   Through it ran the prevalent
Keystone notion of burlesque, glorified to the thirty-third degree by
Al St. John, Signorina Normand and the well-known Monsieur Arbuckle.   Undermining your enemy's house and floating him, his wife
and all their chattels out to sea is a new notion for the professors
of revenge.   Try it some time.   I presume you've seen this picture.
Did you notice the coy way in which Mabel's bed floated around
through the house to pay a comforting visit to Roscoe's bed, the
morning after the voyage began?
                              --Julian Johnson in Photoplay, Vol.
                              9, No. 5 (April 1916), page 148.

☐ FLIRTING WITH FATE (Fine Arts/Triangle, 1916)

     Superior in many respects to any vehicle Fairbanks has had,
Flirting with Fate introduces a comical element of fear which would
enable the story to stand on its own merits in open competition,
whether interpreted by Mr. Fairbanks or not.   Of course, he brings
to it an element of intense personality which materially helps where
there is structural strength and enlivens in moments of weakness,
but Flirting with Fate comes nearer being a true story than any of
those in which he has recently appeared, and it contains opportunity
for other members of his company, those who ordinarily support
him as merely negative members of a chorus with one active principal.   This greater story breadth is of high value in sustaining interest.

     Mr. Fairbanks impersonates a poor artist in love with a girl
of high society, one of unusual beauty, and he is driven to despair
by a combination of misfortunes, including the loss of a much-
cherished portrait he has painted of her and, as he believes, the
girl herself.   He fails in all attempts to commit suicide and hires
a professional assassin, Automatic Joe, admirably impersonated by
George Beranger, to kill him on sight.   The characterization of the
professional killer, with his peculiar scruples, constitutes a large
enough comedy element in itself to carry over the play.   Having received fifty dollars to do the job, Automatic Joe is determined to
earn the money, though it be the last act of its kind in his life.   His
mother's death and the efforts of a Salvation Army officer induce Joe
to reform, but he will not let his past reputation suffer, he, the
greatest of his kind.

     Through overwhelming good fortune the poor artist is nearly
driven crazy.   The stolen portrait is recovered; a friend lends him
ready money; the misunderstanding with his sweetheart is adjusted

and he is left great wealth. In spite of it all he must die. He cannot find Automatic Joe, and the great killer has never been known
to swerve from duty. He has a hundred disguises, may be any one
of the people the artist meets, and he may deal death by pistol,
dagger, bomb or poison. The artist engages a correspondence-
school detective to guard him and flees from his own employee when
he sees him in disguise. His agony of mind grows more and more
intense, until he runs at the sight of any one who might be Automatic
Joe in disguise. He is finally married, but he is only fairly started
on his honeymoon when he is chased by Automatic Joe in the guise
of a Salvation Army recruit, and he is finally treed, only to learn
that Joe has completely reformed and only wanted to return the fifty
dollars.

The story is a winner straight through, admirably constructed,
capably handled and interpreted by a notable cast.

--Louis Reeves Harrison in The
Moving Picture World, Vol. 29,
No. 2 (July 8, 1916), page 263.

☐ A FOOL THERE WAS (Fox/Box Office Attractions, 1915)

Perhaps the highest word of praise that can be cited concerning this picture is that it is powerfully absorbing in all its parts.
No six-reel picture witnessed by the writer has surpassed it in its
gripping and tenacious qualities, which it may be judged is no mean
comparison.

Based on Rudyard Kipling's great poem, "The Vampire," the
picture's greatest appeal lies in the terrible weakness of the man
and the fateful fascination and relentless heart of the woman--the
Vampire.

As a play A Fool There Was enjoyed a tremendous success
on Broadway, with Robert Hilliard in the role of the Fool. Edward
Jose, who takes this part in the film version, is practically sure of
making the same tremendous hit, as the manner in which he grasps
the many heavily dramatic opportunities which his part has presented
him, stamp him as one of the greatest character actors which the
screen boasts of.

Theda Bara, in the opposite principal part of the Vampire,
has an equally important part, which she plays with great skill. As
she appears on the screen hardly a better personality could be found
for the role. The rest of the cast is equal to any occasion that presented itself; their acting is as finished as that of the two leads, and
without their able assistance the picture would lose much of its dramatic value.

Frank Powell directed the picture, which is his second for

the Box Office Attraction Company. In this he has made just as big
a success as he has with Samson. The work is of a totally different
nature, and by his success in both of the works, he has shown himself a master of screen direction, if that fact has never been established before.

The photography is good in all scenes, and the lighting is appropriate at all times. The scenes in which the Fool is seen hope-
lessly dragging himself about on the floor of his once gorgeous house,
drivveling with drink and lust are tinted a dim red, and materially
enhance the dramatic effect.

In the beginning of the first reel we see the man who is later
the Fool, in the midst of a very happy family. He is rich and influential, beloved by all who know him and respected by the entire
country. Because of his popularity and ability he is commissioned
to go abroad on a mission for his nation. Circumstances prevent
his wife and girl from accompanying him. On board ship he meets
the Vampire, who has been responsible for the ruination of a score
of men, and who has set her heart on procuring the man for her
plaything. She accomplishes her desire (on the screen) by the profuse use of kisses and the absence of the accustomed styles in women's fashions.

Thereafter the Fool becomes her slave. Back in America his
friend comes to take him home--he will not go. His wife comes,
but when he has about decided to depart with her, the temptress appears. The Fool's decision is immediately changed by being taken
in a warm embrace and feeling the woman's lips pressed against his
own.

And the story ends with the man dead on the floor, with the
Vampire kneeling by him, gloating and smiling.

Aside from the fact that it will do the very young little good,
and perhaps harm, to witness the film, it is exceedingly excellent.
It will practically absorb all classes; it is convincingly and powerfully acted; bears the marks of excellent direction, and is photographed well, and little more could be asked.
                              --Peter Milne in Motion Picture
                                News, Vol. 11, No. 3 (January
                                23, 1915), page 47.

                    *   *   *

The ball that Kipling set rolling in his immortal poem, known
as "The Vampire," hit here and there on the high spots, and was
perused more or less by the thinking public. The stage version by
Porter Emerson Browne, which served for several seasons as a
starring vehicle for Robert Hilliard, trickled into a few more crev-
ices of the great human machine. It remains, however, for the film
version to penetrate with the baldness of its nauseating truths the
depths of the human tide where the language of a poetic oration is
non-understandable.

A Fool There Was, as presented by William Fox, hits its
mark squarely. The first exhibition of this splendid production for
the benefit of representatives of the press, and a few other fortunate
ones, was aided largely in its effect by the good offices of Mr.
Rothapfel of the Strand Theater, where the exhibition was given at
10 a.m. on Tuesday. Following the well-applauded rendering of a
medley of national airs by the Strand orchestra, the Kipling poem
was given a fine oral interpretation, presumably by Edouard Jose,
who appears as the "Fool" in the pictureplay. And then the ghastly
theme following in the wake of a ghastly blue glare from the footlights, which aided largely in preparing the mind to receive it,
started on its way through the six splendid reels of its development
accompanied by appropriate music from the Strand orchestra.

Frank Powell has directed the picture, the scenario of which
was prepared by Roy L. McCardell. The "Vampire" has been given
an inimitable interpretation by Theda Bara, leading woman at the
Theater Antoine, Paris. Little Runa Hodges, as the child of the
"Fool," brings a wealth of childish sunlight into a production which,
but for the interpolation of a few beautiful and realistic bits of home
life, reeks with the foulness, the sorrow, and the horrible consequences of the life wasted in the toils of a human vampire.

The degeneration of the man, or the "fool," as Kipling has
chosen to call him, as interpreted by Edouard Jose, formerly leading man with Sara Bernhardt, leaves little, if anything, to be desired; and at the end of the fifth reel he has reached the fearful
climax in his career where he discovers at last that "she never
knew why, and did not understand." Here his exploitation of the
dramatic art is perhaps more complete than at any other point of
the play.

Others of the cast who have done splendid work are Clifford
Bruce, Victor Benoit, May Allison and Mabel Fremyear.

There are moments in the first and second reels when there
seems to be some little tendency toward padding; but even this as
a possible fault in the production is altogether a matter of opinion;
and it is even possible that some suspense and a better understanding of the main theme are created thereby.

There is also noticeable, beside the fine photographic results
achieved, a marvelous attention to the smallest human detail, all of
which tends toward the realism of the picture. And again perhaps
what strikes one most is the splendid contrast drawn between the
two walks of life.

The production is a successful artistic effort in every respect.
True, there has been made no attempt to get under cover; moral
truths have been given in all their nudity, and "sin" has been presented in its most revolting aspect.

--Margaret I. MacDonald in The
Moving Picture World, Vol. 23,
No. 5 (January 30, 1915), page
677.

*   *   *

When shown before an invited audience at the Strand Theater
this picture was preceded by a recitation of Kipling's poem, "The
Vampire," the inspiration for Porter Emerson Browne's drama, and,
in turn, for Frank Powell's photoplay. Exhibitors using this film
might well adopt the idea, for the tragic verses place an audience
in the mood for what is to follow:

> A fool there was and he made his prayer
>   (Even as you and I!)
> To a rag and a bone and a hank of hair
>   (We called her the woman who did not care)
> But the fool he called her his lady fair
>   (Even as you and I!)

After hearing the poem recited to the bitter end, one is rather
anxious to know more about this Fool and his "rag and a bone and a
hank of hair." They suggest an interesting couple. We would like
to see just what sort of a mess they made out of life and the picture
is here to show us--to show us, in fact, quite graphically.

It is bold and relentless; it is filled with passion and tragedy;
it is right in harmony with the poem. For a few moments during
the last reel we had fearful premonitions of the approach of a happy
ending--the Fool turned into a repentant wise man--but fortunately
there is no such inartistic claptrap. He is a wreck, he dies and the
Vampire continues on her path, red with the blood of men. The
film, then, remains true to its theme, for which the producers are
to be thanked.

The people are of to-day, with the interests of modern business and social life; but the veneer amounts to nothing when shot
through by the lightning bolt of sex. The Vampire is a neurotic woman gone mad. She has enough sex attraction to supply a town full
of normally pleasing women, and she uses it with prodigal freedom.
To come in contact with her is like touching the third rail, and all
along the track we see, or hear about her victims. Some are dead,
others are beggars tramping the streets, still others complete her
work with a bullet through the brain. Such is the end of the youth
who is deserted in favor of John Schuyler.

The affair with Schuyler starts on an ocean liner, and is continued abroad under the warm sun of Italy. Alternating with languor-
ous tableaux and intense kisses, with which the Vampire holds her
latest Fool, are scenes showing Schuyler's wife and child at home
in America, the simple pathos and comedy relief in the picture being
supplied by the little girl. In passing, it may be remarked that the
scenes introducing the child are human and appealing; but the appeal
is overworked and one incident, at least, that of the child, her doll
and the butler might better be omitted.

Completely dominated by the woman, Schuyler returns with her to New York, where his physical and moral degeneration continue, despite efforts of his wife and friends to drag him out of the quicksand of the Vampire's lips. "So some of him lived, but the most of him died (Even as you and I)."

Director Powell has used enough secondary characters to fill out an adequate plot, and they are well played; but the real acting in the picture, the kind of acting that is interesting every moment, is supplied by Edward Jose as the Fool and Theda Bara as the Vampire. During his decline from a strong, self-reliant man of affairs to a spineless weakling, fit only for the alcoholic ward of a hospital, Mr. Jose undergoes a remarkable change that affects every expression of his personality. Miss Bara misses no chance for sensuous appeal in her portrayal of the Vampire, a horribly fascinating woman, vicious to the core and cruel. When she says, "Kiss me, my fool," the Fool is generally ready to obey and enjoy a prolonged moment, irrespective of the less enjoyable ones to follow.

The physical side of the production has been well looked after, with many attractive settings and clear photography that includes several pleasing light effects.

--D. in The New York Dramatic
Mirror, Vol. 73, No. 1883 (January 20, 1915), page 31.

☐ THE FORBIDDEN CITY (Select, 1918)

Personally, I consider this production a masterpiece. There are three factors in it that make me come to this conclusion. One of them is the most realistic Chinese atmosphere, accomplished by the use of elaborate settings, impressing the mind as being an exact reproduction of originals, and the real Chinese costuming, the kind worn by wealthy Mandarins and other Chinamen. The second is, the interesting story, barring two points on which there might be a difference of opinion. The third one is, the almost unequaled emotional acting of the star, including that of the capable supporting players who impersonate the Chinese Emperor and the Mandarins in the most convincing manner ever attempted on the screen by players of the white race. You can't tell them from real Chinamen.

The story is divided in two sections. In both of them the leading parts are played by Norma Talmadge. In the one she is the mother, while in the other, the daughter. It starts in Peking, China, introducing the heroine as a young girl, the daughter of a Mandarin, who has fallen from the grace of the Emperor. She meets the assistant secretary to the American representative, and they fall in love.

To win back the Emperor's grace, the father promises him the hand of his beautiful daughter. At the presentation it becomes known that she has a child, the result of the union with the American. The Emperor orders the execution of the father and the lancing of the daughter. The baby is kept to be brought up in scorn. The lover, unable to communicate with his sweetheart, comes to the conclusion that she has been done away with. Just then he is transferred to another post.

In the other section, which takes place eighteen years later, the daughter, aided by a Chinaman, escapes to Manila. There she becomes a nurse, meets her father, who is the Governor General, and marries his ward.

The points that may cause difference of opinion are the following. It is not made clear whether there was any legal marriage performed between the hero and the heroine, in the first part of the picture. The impression left is that the child is the result of pure love.

It should be a known fact to the producers by this time that a number of you, limited though it may be, will not play a picture that exhibits an illegitimate baby. It is not wise, therefore, to leave this point ambiguous, thus embarrassing such among you and doing harm to your business, when a few words in one of the subtitles could make it clear whichever way it should be preferred.

The other point is the death of the heroine, at the end of the first section. The Emperor's guards, hidden behind curtains, thrust lances into her body, killing her. Such a scene will undoubtedly be considered too horrible by a great many picture patrons. There are more than one close up scenes showing the dead body, where one would suffice to produce the dramatic effect. Both of the above referred to points could be easily remedied.

This picture will undoubtedly please all picturegoers, excepting those who, on account of racial prejudices, are prevented from rendering the right verdict, based solely on its merits. The employment of several Chinese children, used as companions to the heroine, is quite amusing.

--P.S. Harrison in Motion Picture
News, Vol. 18, No. 16 (October
19, 1918), page 2607.

☐ FROM THE MANGER TO THE CROSS (Kalem, 1912)

The titles of this production to be classed as the greatest achievement in cinematography are many, but chief among them is the realism of it all. It is not a Passion Play; it is the very story of the Passion and of many incidents recorded by the evangelists. It is indeed a cinematographic gospel. Because of this sublime work it will be easier than it was before to "go forth and teach all nations."

There are only two standards of comparison which I can find: The Passion Play of Oberammergau and the Pathés' Life of Christ. The Passion Play in the Bavarian mountains lasts an entire summer's day, it has behind it the pious endeavors of more than seven generations and it has had the benefit of expert biblical study in even the minutest points. Its dramatic machinery is complete in every detail. The work of its actors is world-famous for its sincerity and its compelling power. In spite of this, if I had to choose between the loss of these films and the abolition of the Passion Play I would with little hesitation decide in favor of the films.

The Oberammergau Play is in the main nothing more than a dramatic recital, while the films reverently avoid any distinctly dramatic display; the Oberammergau exhibition seeks to portray events which happened in places thousands of miles away from Bavaria and which occurred in an environment, which no skill or art of man could re-create, while the films bring before our eyes not only the events and characters of the sacred records, but show them to us in the very places where they occurred. The reels show us the real Lake of Tiberias and the very type of nets in which Peter and the other fishermen of Galilee pursued their ancient calling; they show us the very road on which Joseph, Mary and the boy Jesus returned out of Egypt into their own beloved Nazareth; they show us some glimpses at least of the glorious temple of Solomon, as reconstructed by archeologists; they make the tragedy of the Crucifixion stand out in plain but rigidly historic relief, using as far as this is humanly possible, the very ground on which it was enacted; they follow in the journey to Golgotha, the Way of Sorrows (Via Dolorosa), trodden by Christian pilgrims even to this day in honor of a very old and authentic tradition; they show us as it existed nineteen centuries ago the barren and desolate regions about the Dead Sea, where The Voice in the Wilderness was heard; we see the real Bethany, parts of the ancient road that led north out of Jerusalem in the direction of Galilee and along which Mary and Joseph had been travelling, when they became alarmed about the absence of their child; we are led to the very spot where the shepherds tended their flocks and where the first glad tidings were heard.

It would far exceed the limits of this article to enumerate more instances. I can only pause to commend the fine reverent spirit of the master hand which directed this production. In this respect the producers have consciously or unconsciously followed the Oberammergau school. A chaste decorum characterizes every scene. Treading on ground which was full of pitfalls they have not made one single misstep. The treatment of the "Childhood of Jesus" is typical of this rare judgment and perfect discrimination. The records of the childhood of Christ, as they are now accepted by the Christian churches, are very meagre. There are, however, a number of apocryphal or pseudo-gospel, which attempt to elaborate the plain and concise details of the authentic writers. In the miracle plays of the past some of the crude and improbable stories of Christ's childhood were often portrayed. The films show four exquisite scenes, one taken from the recorded events and the others either

taken from old traditions or constructed out of the probabilities of
the known events.   The scenes in and about the home at Nazareth
are beautifully conceived and full of a sweet and pathetic naturalness.
In taking into the films an ancient Christian belief, that Joseph, Mary
and the Divine Child were during part of their sojourn in Egypt near
Babylon, the producers have added a charming and instructive scene,
which will be new and most interesting to many audiences.

In selecting the actors and the costumes the producers have
followed the best Christian traditions, as they have in the course of
the centuries become embodied in a thousand paintings and statues.
To conclude the comparison with the Pathé production it must be
said that while there is more of a dramatic sequence in the Pathé
pictures, the Kalem reels have the infinite advantage of giving us
the real scenes and the real people of the east.

The exhibition in Wanamaker's Auditorium was attended by
many clergymen.   This expression was frequently heard at the end
of the performance: "We hope they won't put this in the picture
houses."   With all due respect to these ladies and gentlemen we
hope it will be put in every motion picture theater in this and every
other country of the world.   What story is fitter for human eyes to
see than the story of Jesus of Nazareth?   To whom did He address
Himself more often than to the plain people?   To whom did He
preach on the shores of Gennesaret?   Very much to the same people, who gather nightly by the millions in the motion picture theaters.   His religion was for all the people at all times.   Where is
the missionary spirit of our Christian ministers and priests and
churches?   These men are indeed hard to please.   When the motion
picture gave stories of life, not failing to show the seamy side,
these good people denounced it for being sensational and corrupting
and what not.   Now when the noble art of cinematography has produced its greatest triumph and has put itself to the loftiest possible
use, there are ministers and pious ladies who raise their hands in
horror at the thought of such "glorious pictures being shown in common picture houses."   To some it seemed "shocking" that these pictures should be exhibited for money.   Is this any more shocking
than the payment of money to ministers for their services?   An extreme willingness to take money for good and pious purposes has
always struck me as a characteristic of most churches.   If there
are any benevolent and wealthy persons who cannot bear the thought
of seeing people pay for witnessing these reels I suppose there is
nothing to hinder them to rent a set and exhibit it free of charge.
If their religious convictions take shape in that manner they are entitled to respect, otherwise their ideas are purely ornamental.

When five years ago the Pathés brought out their Passion Play
conditions in the industry were chaotic and the personnel of the exhibitors was by no means imposing.   In spite of this the Passion
Play was treated with the utmost reverence everywhere and I cannot
recollect any instance where the religious sensibilities of the audiences were outraged or offended.   Conditions have vastly improved
since that time and the personnel of the American exhibitor to-day

compares favorably with that of men in any walk of either commer-
cial or professional life. It may be assumed for a certainty that
exhibitors will rise to the occasion and give these wonderful reels
a worthy and appropriate setting. A musical program has been com-
piled which has some merit. It is, however, by no means the last
word in musical accompaniment. A little Gregorian chant and music
interspersed with classic music of a religious tinge would seem to
be at least as fully effective as the singing of a number of hymns.
The works of Gounod, Handel and Bach will be found full of good
popular suitable music. The pictures tell their own story and a
lecture is scarcely needed. All the quotations from Holy Writ that
are used in connection with the titles on the screen have been selected with great judgment and sufficiently elucidate every single
scene.

The character of the subject will evoke reverence in every
human mind. The work of the producers will increase this reverence.

--W. Stephen Bush in The Moving
Picture World, Vol. 14, No. 4
(October 26, 1912), page 324.

*   *   *

Even the most optimistic of moving picture companies can
hardly hope that, no matter how reverently so difficult a subject is
handled, some one will not be offended. As soon as this picture is
exhibited to the general public at a fixed admission price, the Kalem
Company must look for criticism which will range all the way from
clever satire to Billingsgate invective. With the best intentions in
the world, the company cannot wholly disarm criticism. Now it is
scarcely our function to discuss the question whether, in the first
place, such a picture ought ever to have been made. It is only our
business to examine how successful is the picture, once it has been
made, from an artistic point of view. And at the outset it is pleasant to record the emotional power, the impressiveness and the general artistic excellence of this picture. Only a very few times did
faults of technique of defects of interpretive insight mar the silent
depiction of a life, every moment of which is so deeply impressed
upon the religious imagination of millions of human beings. Only
once did the mechanical difficulties give an impression of stage
trickery and consequent cheapness. That was when Christ was shown
walking on the waves--it was painfully obvious that two trick pictures
had been awkwardly combined. With this exception, the story of
Jesus's life flowed by with a naturalness and simplicity that arrested
and enthralled.

The film is divided into five parts, the first two dealing with
the Annunciation, the birth and childhood of Jesus, the last three
with the Ministry and Passion. Rather curiously, the cast describes
the protagonist as Jesus, the Man so that it was to be expected that
the Resurrection would not be shown. As scene after scene flashed
before us on the canvas, we received a peculiar kind of intuition of

the inwardness of the life of all prophets. Almost all the actions of the story of Christ seemed to center in the people that surrounded Him. Action, as it were, impinged upon Him. We saw Him drive the money changers from the temple; again we saw Him staggering under the weight of the cross on the Via Dolorosa--but oftenest He stood almost idly by while people around him adored or reviled or pressed upon His head the crown of thorns. Hence the immense value of pageantry and mob scenes, which were handled, as it fortunately happened, with consummate skill. There was one picture of Christ as He entered Jerusalem, the multitude waving palms and strewing flowers in His path, which was singularly moving. Christ before Pilate and Herod were also excellent scenes. And the scenes depicting Christ performing miracles were played without a trace of cheapness. Most charming, moreover, were the scenes showing the Annunciation, Joseph's flight into Egypt and a scene in the house of Mary and Martha. As it was shown recently at Wanamaker's Auditorium to an invited audience, the film closes with the Crucifixion and Jesus on the Cross--a scene almost too ghastly in its strict realism.

Evidently the Kalem Company has spared neither trouble nor expense to make the picture artistically perfect. The flight into Egypt, for example, is shown with the Sphinx for a background. The temple scenes were built and carried out entirely in accordance with the great works of Dr. Schick, while the garb was reproduced from the paintings of M. Tissot, the French artist. As nearly as possible the scenes were shown in authentic locations, which obviously necessitated much arduous travel. Whatever criticism can be brought against the picture, certainly no one can accuse the Kalem Company of undertaking their work in anything but the right spirit.

Photographically, the film is a masterpiece of its kind. The bright sunlight and the white reflecting sands of Palestine materially aided the purely mechanical part of the picture-taking. Hardly an expression or gesture was obscured. Then, too, the acting was unusually good. R. Henderson Bland, who represented Christ, never attempted to be theatrical. He handled a tremendously difficult role with delicacy and discrimination. Alice Hollister, who represented Mary Magdalene, had not only beauty of face but a peculiarly appealing gesture of supplication which was unusually appropriate. Others in the capable cast were: Samuel Morgan, as Pilate; James D. Ainsley, as John the Baptist; Robert G. Vignola, as Judas; Gene Gauntier, as Mary, and George Kellog, as Herod.

Purely as an artistic entertainment, the picture needs to be shown under as favorable auspices as those which surrounded it at Wanamaker's Auditorium. It would be both bad taste and artistically ineffective to sandwich the picture between a juggler's act and a Broadway song and dance, just as it would be absurdly out of place to read Milton's poems in the subway. At the recent exhibition, appropriate quotations from the Bible explained the course of the story, while between the portrayals of different sections of the film hymns and organ music created an atmosphere of solemnity. We are not

arguing here for solemnity or organ music per se, but to attempt to
show this picture in surroundings which are much less than solemn
will merely result in a quick failure of the whole enterprise.   And
this, as we have pointed out, will not be so much because of moral
or religious reasons as because of artistic ones.   To make a moving picture of the life of Christ just an ordinary headliner in an ordinary moving picture house is bad art, and in the long run bad art
is financially unsuccessful.   This picture must be kept rigidly above
a certain level or it will fall immeasurably below it.

--S. in The New York Dramatic
Mirror, Vol. 68, No. 1766 (Oc-
tober 23, 1912), page 28.

☐ THE GARDEN OF ALLAH (Selig, 1917)

Robert Hichens' famous story has always been synonymous
with something stupendous.   The story itself was.   The first dramatization of it on the speaking stage was, and now, after the Selig
Polyscope Company has at great labor, time and expense filmed this
wonderful Oriental romance, it is stupendous plus.   I have enjoyed
it on the screen more than the stage.   The possibilities for visualizing the story are more and just now at the Colonial in Chicago,
where it is getting its initial showing, it is attracting record-
breaking attendances--even with record-breaking torrid weather ex-
isting.   It is being shown there under the direction of the Edmund
Allen Film Corporation, who have purchased the rights for it in
eight states.

Not an opportunity was lost by the Selig Company, its director and technical department, to take advantage of making this as
much and even more of a classic on the screen than it has ever
been in any other manner of presentation.   It is faithful to the nth
degree in all its detail and Colin Campbell, who directed it, has
reared a foundation for his fame and craft that will hold him aloft
for many a day.

Thomas Santschi and Helen Ware in the lead roles have likewise shoved their previous high reputations as screen artists up
many more notches.   As Boris Androvsky, the monk who wandered
from his vows, Santschi stands out with a scintillation that lights
the whole picture.   Miss Ware's delineation of Domini Enfilden,
seeking and lusting peace, is colorful and self-supporting.

The other great charm of the picture, aside from its story,
the work of the cast, etc., and one that dare not be passed over
here is its beauty of color and scene.   Picturesque becomes a feeble
word even though a well used one in raving over Oriental splendor.
For here is Oriental splendor multiplied.   The desert and its hot
and still nights, sandstorms, Moorish mosques, bazaars, baksheesh
and beggars; the wild dashing spectre-like Bedouins, the scene in

the Garden and a score and one of other high lights so naturally and
realistically reproduced that it cannot help rival the popularity of
the original play.

Mr. Santschi and Miss Ware, however luminary they are in
this picture, have their satellites, and worthy ones, too. There is
Will Machin as Captain Crevignac; James Bradbury as the Sand Di-
viner; Harry Lonsdale as Father Roubier; Matt Snyder as Count
Anteoni and others. Accompanying the picture at the Colonial is an
augmented orchestra of ability who add to the charm of the whole
with music that has been especially composed to garnish the picture.

--William J. McGrath in Motion
Picture News, Vol. 16, No. 7
(August 18, 1917), page 1150.

☐ THE GIRL WHO STAYED AT HOME (Paramount-Artcraft, 1919)

At last! David Griffith has contributed something to the
screen which deserves its meed of praise and which--at moments--
flashes to brilliant humanness. It is The Girl Who Stayed at Home
which is, at basis, just another war story.

This time Griffith takes two love themes, first the story of
a typical, healthy young American and his French sweetheart, and,
secondly, of the chap's weak, lounge-lizard brother and his cabaret
light o' love. It is in this second theme--in its showing how war
regenerates the two--that Griffith touches his heights. But the director must have his war, and we are shown how the two brothers
rescue the little French girl, undergoing the usual embrace from
the usual dastardly Hun officer.

There are two or three remarkable scenes in The Girl Who
Stayed at Home--bits of life showing the director's uncanny insight
into femininity. It may sound odd to mention a little moment where
the cabaret girl--who but Griffith would dare to call her Cutie Beautiful?--cuddles into a huge chair and whispers nothings into a telephone. But the blinding flash of greatness is here. Again, in a
moment where the lonely girl half sobs, half dances as her phono-
graph grinds out a rollicking war ditty. It is here that Clarine Seymour stands out so brilliantly. Griffith has a genuine discovery in
Miss Seymour, whose playing is vivid in every detail. And Cutie
Beautiful's fascinating "shimmie walk"! The screen has had nothing
like it since Dorothy Gish's little disturber came gliding across the
silver-sheet with piquant boisterousness.

In one other thing Griffith's The Girl Who Stayed at Home
stands out. He has dared to present a kindly German soldier, even
to showing the man leaving his old mother in the fatherland. Yet
shortsighted critics have condemned this broadmindedness.

It is in these few flashes that Griffith rather restores our faith in his leadership. If only he had literary discernment! The Girl Who Stayed at Home, credited to a mysterious S. E. V. Taylor, is banal stuff, another variation of the old Biograph chase.

Miss Seymour overtops every one in the production, altho Bobbie Harron indicates the regeneration of the weakling with broad strokes, Richard Barthelmess is commendable as the brother and Carol Dempster satisfactory as the Parisian sweetheart.
> --Frederick James Smith in Motion Picture Classic, Vol. 8, No. 4 (June 1919), pages 46-47.

☐ A GIRL'S FOLLY (Paragon, 1917)

The inside workings of a moving picture studio are thrown open to public gaze in A Girl's Folly, a five-reel Paragon screen drama starring Doris Kenyon and Robert Warwick. This is the novel feature of the picture, and its chief merit. The plot is rather slight, but the director, Maurice Tourneur, who is also part author of the scenario, has gone to considerable trouble and expense in adding humorous incidents of studio life and also of amusing happenings on a farm.

Mary Baker, a pretty country girl, longs to get away from her humdrum existence. A moving picture company takes pictures near her home, and a chance meeting with the leading man gives her the desired opportunity. She goes back to the city with him. Everyone is taken with her beauty, but she fails to register in her trial picture and, rather than return home, consents to let the leading man take care of her. Before matters have gone too far, Mary's mother arrives and the girl goes back home and marries her country sweetheart.

This plot, which does not reflect any too much credit upon the moving picture actor, is assisted materially by its comedy situations and by the care given the production. The cast is of unusual strength. Doris Kenyon is charming in the role of the country girl, and Robert Warwick plays the moving picture man as if entirely familiar with the role. June Elvidge and Jane Adair are two other names that insure high-grade impersonations, and Johnny Hines and Chester Barnett have the remaining important roles.
> --Edward Weitzel in The Moving Picture World, Vol. 31, No. 9 (March 3, 1917), page 1369.

☐   A GOOD LITTLE DEVIL (Famous Players, 1914)*

     On the evening of July 10, the Famous Players' Company did
its part in entertaining the delegates to the Third National Convention of the Moving Picture Exhibitors' League, giving a reception in
its studio, 213 West 26th street, New York City.   Considerably over
two thousand people called during the evening, and among them one
noticed many men and women of importance on the legitimate stage
as well as in motion picturedom.   The main floor of the studio is
unusually large; but there was not room enough to accommodate all
comfortably.

     The lighting of the room was subdued and pleasant.   Over a
part of the floor, railed off for dancing, electric lamps under the
ceiling were curtained by filmy blue cloth bordered with gold fringe
with the effect as of a fairy tent under which, after the four reels
of Belasco's production, dealing with fairies and happy children, the
guests followed the invitation of music to the exercise that seems to
give wings to human feet.   Another part of the floor was set with
tables on which refreshments were served and along one side there
was arranged a theater.   The stage of this was a beautiful scene
from The Good Little Devil, showing the garden of the blind girl's
home with its gates opening toward a mysterious country with a
castle perched high on a mountain top and full of suggestions of
"Magic casements opening on the foam of perilous seas in fairy lands
forlorn."   At one side of the little house stood the old tree with a
hollow heart from which the fairies came when called forth to meet
us.

     Mr. Daniel Frohman formally welcomed the guests, after
which Ernest Truex, the "Good Little Devil," delivered the play's
prologue, and then a scene was enacted just as before the camera.
The little blind girl, Mary Pickford, came from the house with her
collie dog and opened the gates for her playmate.   To see this scene
as played and then to see it shortly afterward as pictured, was a
great treat to most of the spectators, for it gave them a chance to
get an insight into motion picture making that few are fortunate
enough to have.   It was educational, too, as pointing out the difference between a scene on a stage and a picture on the screen.

     When this had been enacted--and, by the way, Mary Pickford
won in it tremendous applause from the audience--a screen was
swung out from the side and the complete picture thrown upon it.
The conditions, both in the way of comfort of the spectators and in
the projection, were not ideal, though fair.   The room was warm

---

*Although A Good Little Devil was the first Mary Pickford feature
to be filmed--it was based on a stage play in which Pickford had
also appeared--the film was not released until 1914, by which time
Miss Pickford was already a major star in the Famous Players
company.

and overcrowded and many had to crane their necks to see it all.
Some who applauded very enthusiastically stood up through the whole
of its four reels.   That the audience watched it so closely and was
so markedly pleased with it is a good indication that it will go very
strongly in the regular picture houses.   One heard such comments
as, "What a lovely picture!" and "Isn't it delightful?" and such expressions were heard from all over the house.

It is, indeed, a most artistic production, full of beautiful
scenes and backgrounds, and full, too, of pleasant sentiments and
of human situations and characters.   There is hardly an artistic
flaw in it through all its four thousand feet and, from first to last,
a master's hand in its making is plain.   If there have been stories
more surely adaptable to the peculiar illustration that motion pictures can give, the shortcoming, in considering it as an offering to
the public, is more than made up by the play's popularity.   That it
is one of Mr. Belasco's big successes is, alone, enough to make
people want to see it.   We think it as good, almost, as any fairy
picture could be and, in the past, fairy pictures have been very
popular, especially with children and their mothers.

The opening scene presents David Belasco in his study, before an open fire, visualizing a scene of the play.   While he sits
the fairies come in around him and with them the little blind girl.
This is remarkably effective.   In it the fairies surely "get over"--
in a poet's dream.   It seems, in its strength, to contrast a little
with some of the fairy scenes in the play itself, but the contrast
will be more noticeable to grown folks than to children, or to such
as can easily give themselves to the spirit of such a piece.   The
picture will invite such and carry them into the realms of dreams;
but it will compel none, unless they are eager to be led; yet it is
full of things that will please the many.

The story is well known.   Its hero is a little aristocrat, left
an orphan.   His grandfather, the old lord, sends him to a queer,
ogre-like aunt who treats him brutally; but he finds a friend, a
neighbor's child, a little blind girl whom he helps and who becomes
his playmate.   The children believe in fairies and live in a fairy
realm and are helped by the light-winged, dream-folk in their difficulties with the old aunt and, at length, after the Good Little Devil
has been educated above the blind girl and has come back a bad little
devil, it is they who give the girl her sight and also recall the Good
Little Devil into the boy's breast and make him her sweetheart once
more.

The aunt, the ogre, played by Will Norris, stands sharply
out in the picture as furnishing the darker contrast against which
the child-like sweetness of the love story, set forth by Mary Pickford and Ernest Truex, is brought out, and both of these elements
are clearly and effectively drawn, so that, in the very heart of the
picture, there is a quality with a strong appeal that is sure to make
the offering widely popular.   The old woman is played to give most
truthfully and half humorously the fairy tale atmosphere--the ugly

facial expression, the almost bloodthirsty cruelty, the fear-inspiring
walk, all these things are just what they should be. Then, Mary
Pickford has a role suited to her genius for delicate sympathies and
as delicate pathos. She is wholly lovely and is well supported by
Ernest Truex, who is a sort of Peter Pan at heart. We mustn't
forget the blind girl's dog, a frollicking, friendly dog, full of antics,
though it must have been warm playing the role in all that fur. And
the picture is also beautifully photographed with some exquisitely
lovely scenes. It is an offering that will excite enthusiasm and fulfill the promises of the exhibitor, who may pave the way for it with
extensive and strong advertising.

> --Hanford C. Judson in The Mov-
> ing Picture World, Vol. 17, No.
> 4 (July 26, 1913), page 407.

☐ THE GREAT LOVE (Paramount-Artcraft, 1918)

P. S.--We've just caught David Griffith's latest, The Great
Love. Griffith credits a British army captain as the author, just
as he named M. Gaston de Tolignac as the creator of Hearts of the
World. But, in both cases, we suspect Griffith's own hand in the
writing.* Jim Young, an American, goes to England in 1914 and
enlists on the side of democracy at the start of the great war. Jim
meets and comes to love a young Australian girl living near the big
training camp. But a youthful tiff and a sudden shift of Jim's regiment to the front, cause the sweetheart to waver and finally marry
a titled Englishman, who is not only a rake, with a cast-off favorite
and the inevitable baby waiting on his doorstep, but a traitor as
well. But she never really becomes his wife and, when hubby com-
mits suicide on facing exposure, she tumbles into Jim's khaki arms.
No, it isn't much of a story. It is ahead of the average feature in
handling but it isn't anything to add to the Griffith laurels. The director is at his best in the idyllic early love scenes between Jim
and Sue, at his worst in trying to achieve a height of suspense in
the Zeppelin invasion of England. Here Jim upsets the Hun signals
and causes the aircraft to blow up an empty field instead of Britain's
biggest munition storehouse. This is entirely too long drawn out.

The Great Love is merely a modern story of the war told in
the terms of the old Biograph melodrama. Lillian Gish overdoes
the kittenish tricks of Sue but she has several really poignant moments. Robert Harron is--Robert Harron, while Henry Walthall
makes the very villainous villain at least subtle. But Walthall isn't
at his best here.

> --Frederick James Smith in Motion
> Picture Classic, Vol. 7, No. 2
> (October 1918), page 77.

---

*Smith's suspicion was correct.

☐ THE GREATEST QUESTION (Griffith/First National, 1919)

I was still hoping that Mr. Griffith had seen the light when I went to see The Greatest Question. Here, I said, is a fine theme, and a big one. Here will be a story of that mystical never never land with which the world is just now trying to establish communication. And it will be a clean and wholesome picture with a sweep of sympathetic drama such as always surrounds the theme. But, I was wrong. There again was the beating of Lillian Gish by the degenerate old woman so well played by Josephine Crowell that you wanted to throw an orchestra chair at her. There was another attempted assault upon a young girl by a vicious, licentious, ugly old man, and a brutal murder to top off the excess of violence.

Why, in the name of all things reasonable? Why? If the story was to be based on that boundless love between sympathetic souls on earth that cannot be broken by death, as apparently it was the original intention to base it, why not let it be the logical development of that theme through the experiences of the young man who, called to war, still kept in touch spiritually with his mother and returned to her in the spirit after he had been swept into the sea from the deck of a submerging submarine?

The brute redeemed did not necessarily have to be the particular type of brute that preys upon innocence. His character would have been much more logical, much more convincing if he were just an easily recognizable kind of everyday brute, cruel and hard, selfish and ignorant. But, no, Mr. Griffith, with this obsession for scenes of assault and beating, must needs take both him and his degenerate wife out of character and exaggerate them out of all semblance to any but mentally unsound patients of a psychopathic ward in a hospital.

Dramatically, too, I believe this leading director is on the wrong track. He is shooting birdshot in place of bullets. And as a result he is scattering his dramas so full of incidental scenes that he loses all contact with his main story. The only connection between theme and title in The Greatest Question is found in the brief reappearance in the spirit of the dead boy, with whom the audience is not permitted to become sufficiently acquainted to feel more than a passing interest in whether he lives or dies.

Otherwise, it is the story of a little girl who, reared by gypsies, was witness to the murder of a young woman "who trusted too much." Grown up, she is adopted by poor but worthy people, seeks work in a neighboring farm house that she may earn something to help her benefactors, discovers in her new employers the brutal pair before mentioned, and finally recognizes in them the perpetrators of the deed that had been stamped upon her infantile mind.

Now, having that much off my heaving chest, I can say some nice things. The pictures themselves, as pictures, are beautiful.

There is a fine sense of location in the Griffith equipment. He
finds the truest backgrounds for his scenes of any director with
whose work I am familiar, and once they are found, the admirable
G. W. Bitzer, his camera man extraordinary, employs them to
perfect advantage. The countryside pictured in The Greatest Question, the gypsy camp, the tumble-down farms, are intelligently
chosen locations, and in composition the pictures are charmingly atmospheric. There is a real thrill, too, in the submerging submarine that leaves a man in the sea. Griffith also has an impressive sense of character (which is probably one reason I dislike his
brutal types so heartily) and each individual is convincingly visioned
on the screen. Even his exaggerations of character have point, in
that they carry home to dull minds what he intends they should.
Lillian Gish is again a charmingly wholesome innocent, Robert Harron an upstanding boyish hero, and Eugene Besserer, Josephine
Crowell, George Fawcett and Tom Wilson all splendidly vivid.

> --Burns Mantle in Photoplay, Vol.
> 17, No. 4 (March 1920), page
> 64.

☐ THE GREATEST THING IN LIFE (Paramount-Artcraft, 1918)

We confess our disappointment in The Greatest Thing in Life.
At heart it is the old Griffith chase. It reveals just one thing new,
a sort of idealized close-up--with hazy, dreamy outlines, singularly
suited to Lillian Gish, who plays the heroine. Her role is a sort
of tomboy character, to which this particular Gish, to our way of
thinking, isn't suited. Please, Mr. Griffith, let Dorothy do the
comedy of the Gish family and leave Lillian a dream idyll. We
liked Bobby Harron as the regenerated American. Griffith, by the
way, has endeavored to duplicate his Monsieur Cuckoo of Hearts of
the World with an almost similar character, the stolid, humorous,
garlic-eating Mons. Le Bebe. But there is a vast difference between
Robert Anderson's Cuckoo and David Butler's Le Bebe. One is
spontaneous, the other imitation.

> --Frederick James Smith in Motion
> Picture Classic, Vol. 8, No. 1
> (March 1919), page 76.

☐ THE GULF BETWEEN (Technicolor, 1917)*

The Gulf Between is unquestionably the finest natural color
picture ever produced. The process over which C. A. Willat has
labored so long results in the absence of all "fringe," absence of

_____

*The Gulf Between was the first Technicolor subject.

eye strain and produces colors that are really natural. The green
is natural, so is the blue, the yellow, the pink, the red--every
color. The invitation audience at Aeolian Hall where the picture
received its first showing was moved time and again to burst into
applause of the sort that lasted long. The final shot, showing the
sun setting over the water is beautiful--mindful of a Japanese painting.

     Naturally Mr. Willat wanted to show off his natural colors to
the greatest possible extent in his first picture. It is a perfectly
just pride that he takes in a work so pretentious and really--epoch
creating. But if he releases the subject for the exhibitor, which
he probably will do, it is to be hoped that he eliminates some of
the footage in the last two reels. Here the story is very obviously
drawn out. This might be excused providing some startling color
effects were displayed, but the nation repeats itself through the same
scenes and a cutting would benefit the story and consequently make
the color stuff more enjoyable. The subtitles should be rewritten
as well.

     But these faults can readily be erased and The Gulf Between
will then not only offer a novelty but an entertaining story as well.
Anthony P. Kelly did not draw upon very original material for his
plot and yet he has filled it full of clean, wholesome comedy and
pathos that brings tears. It is laid on and around the water and
pleasant homely scenes furnish a delightful background.

     Wray Physioc has done good work as director. The camera
work--the all important angle of production in this case--is all
O. K. with the exception that in quite a number of the scenes it
lacks definition. There is a perceptible haze, ever so slight, but
still perceptible, which however, comes far from spoiling the picture. Grace Darmond is a charming heroine. Certainly natural
color photography will come as a great boon to actresses as pretty
as she. Niles Welch is a pleasing juvenile and Herbert Fortier a
stalwart old sea captain.

                              --Peter Milne in Motion Picture
                              News, Vol. 16, No. 14 (October
                              6, 1917), pages 2391-2392.

☐ THE HEART OF HUMANITY (Jewel/Universal, 1919)

     A year or two ago the name of a certain young director ap-
peared occasionally among the one and two-reel subjects being made
by the Universal Company. The name was Allen Holubar, and every
time it appeared it was attached to a picture that stood out in a
promising way from the general run of things. Last Friday night,
at the Broadway Theatre, Mr. Holubar appeared personally with a
nine-reel vehicle featuring Dorothy Phillips which amply redeemed
this promise. Mr. Holubar has been reaching for the moon, as the

saying goes, and if he has not entirely got hold of it, he has at least found a very conspicuous "place in the sun."

This production, The Heart of Humanity, is one of the biggest and most satisfying stories that have come out of the great war. It may be late from the point of stimulating morale, but it is never too late to see a story such as this--wonderfully mounted, splendidly acted, altogether beautifully done. We have seen nothing recently that has quite so successful a blend of scenic beauty, humor and human tenderness. The director has an almost unerring faculty for selecting vital and pertinent situations, and his whole production is "on the key." The close of the subject leaves one with only two minor critical suggestions worth recording, the question of whether a few of the battle scenes might not be spared, and whether the struggle between the girl and the Hun--splendidly as it has been acted--does not occupy too much space.

This story, which was written jointly by Olga Scholl and Mr. Holubar, and to which the latter has given seven months in the making, is a great war epic of Canada, a pictorial poem of exquisite feeling and sentiment. The story is so well made that it might well be presented officially by our Government to the Government of Canada as a tribute to her splendid spirit of sacrifice. The sufferings of the Widow Patricia, who sends her five sons and sees but one of them return, typify the sufferings of all Canadian mothers, whose Spartan courage has until now received but little recognition.

The settings of the story are its first claim to special merit, at least first in order, for by the time the plot itself gets to moving and the actors get their chance the observer has already succumbed to the charm of lake and timber and the Canadian out-of-doors. The introduction of the widow and her sons--John, Paul, Jules, Maurice and Louis, is something that will linger in the memory. All love the girl, Nanette, but she marries John, and it is on the very day of the wedding ceremony that the news of war comes in dramatic fashion.

Dorothy Phillips is seen here at the height of her abilities as a screen performer. This means a great deal for, to the writer's way of thinking, she is one of the most natural and effective artists we have. She plays here with assurance and fine emotional effect, and even though we favor cutting somewhat the struggle scene at the close, for the sake of proportion, we have never seen this situation more admirably acted. It threatens to run away with the whole story as it stands. Much of the credit for this also goes to Erich von Stroheim, a most hatable Hun, who has previously appeared in The Unbeliever and The Hun Within.

Margaret Mann, as the Widow Patricia, carries the sympathies every moment; she visualizes perfectly the sufferings of the mother which are only soothed by the glory she later feels in the sacrifice made by her sons. In the latter roles appear William

Stowell, Robert Anderson, Frank Braidwood, George Hackathorne
and Walt Whitman.

The battle scenes are stupendous and compel the closest attention every moment they are on the screen.   Tanks, aeroplanes,
flame-throwers, and all of the paraphernalia of modern warfare,
are employed.   We think this will stand cutting, though it is a pity
to see it go, for it has been astonishingly well produced.   As it
stands the offering is a great success.
                    --Robert C. McElravy in The Mov-
                        ing Picture World, Vol. 34, No.
                        1 (January 4, 1919), page 113.

                    *   *   *

We are genuinely sorry that Allen Holubar's The Heart of
Humanity, starring the vivid Dorothy Phillips, arrived after the end
of the war, because it deserves its measure of success, and we
fear that nobody wants war drama now.   With all its palpable imitation, The Heart of Humanity stamps Holubar as a director of promise.   For it is reminiscent, in handling and flashes of story, of
Griffith's Hearts of the World, DeMille's When I Come Back to
You and even Chaplin's Shoulder Arms.   Oddly, Holubar has done
a whole lot of these imitation things better than the originals.   We
went to see The Heart of Humanity at a private midnight showing,
intending to remain but a short time.   And we stayed until the final
scene at about 2 A. M.

Briefly, it is the tale of four brothers who join the allied
forces from the wilds of Canada.   One has just married, and much
of the story deals with her experiences "over there" as a nurse and
her rescue from the Huns by her husband.   Robert Anderson, Griffith's M. Cuckoo, plays one of the brothers, a somewhat similar
character, and stands out strongly.   We are not particularly interested anywhere with William Stowell as the hero, but Erich von
Stroheim's handling of the unscrupulous German deserves its meed
of praise.   And Miss Phillips!   Here is an actress of singular vividness.   Her fight with a brutal Hun officer and her sudden loss of
mind are done in a mighty strong way, flashing to a big height for
a second.
                    --Frederick James Smith in Mo-
                        tion Picture Classic, Vol. 8,
                        No. 1 (March 1919), page 76.

☐ THE HEART OF TEXAS RYAN (Selig/K-E-S-E, 1917)

The Heart of Texas Ryan is a story of the great Southwest,
in the Texas borderland, in which Colonel Ryan (George Fawcett)
owns a ranch of thousands of acres, over which many more thousands
of cattle roam.   Texas Ryan (Bessie Eyton), the only child of the

grim, old Colonel, arrives at the old ranch home early in the story, after completing her education in an Eastern College.

Jack Parker (Tom Mix), a devil-may-care cowpuncher, a stranger from nowhere, is the ablest hand on Colonel Ryan's cowboy force, and always gets into a scrape when he visits the nearest town--too much whiskey and a fondness for using his shooting iron being the prevailing causes. That was before Texas Ryan came home for good; but when Jack discovered that she was the original "dream girl," whose photograph he had worshipped for months without knowing that such a beautiful creature as Texas Ryan lived, he became a changed man, and the thrilling adventures in which he figures later are confined to the protection of his employer's interests and to the safety of his daughter, Texas.

Tom Mix is the most picturesque cowboy impersonator in America. His magnificent, reckless riding; the realism of his brawling encounters; his neck-risking feats in a roundup, in addition to all the other qualities that combine to make a true knight of the plains, always delight or thrill the spectator.

Was there ever a more realistic encounter of its kind than the saloon fight which is forced on Jack Parker by the former road agent, "Dice" McAllister (Frank Campeau), who at the time of the fight is marshal of the Texas village of Red Eye? The finish is made still more impressive by being conducted behind closed doors--in the poker room, into which the bad man has been shoved by the crowd in the barroom. Although both men were supposed to have entered without firearms, a shot is heard, and one of the listening crowd at the door has his face creased by a bullet. A few minutes later, when Colonel Ryan unlocks the door from the outside, the crowd stands aghast at the sight. McAllister is an inanimate heap on the floor, while over him stands Jack (greatly disfigured but still in the ring), holding aloft the spurred boot of the defeated man, whom he had pounded into insensibility after he had shot to kill Jack with a concealed weapon.

Jack Parker's celebration of Independence Day, in the village of Red Eye, impresses me as being exceedingly humorous. He is positively laden down with fireworks of all kinds, from giant firecrackers to skyrockets. The village constable has warned Jack to keep off the main street; so, to conform with the law, he climbs up forty feet to the small platform over the open water tank, which supplies the village with water, and there begins his bombardment. Owing to his libations he is careless and sets off the whole fireworks. To save himself, he drops into the tank, many feet below; but even there he is almost blown out of the water by the explosion of giant crackers, which have fallen from the platform just in time to go off as they strike the surface.

Jack's brave stand across the borderline, in Mexico, against a band of cowrustlers, among whom are two of his old enemies, will bring another thrill.

George Fawcett's Colonel Ryan is a fine characterization, as
is the McAllister of Frank Campeau. Bessie Eyton as Texas Ryan
will please her large following of admirers. She takes full advantage of the demands of the part to display her ability as an accomplished equestrienne.

--James S. McQuade in The Moving Picture World, Vol. 31, No.
9 (March 3, 1917), page 1369.

☐ HEARTS OF THE WORLD (Griffith/Paramount-Artcraft, 1918)

At last we have something mightily worth while to record,
for David Wark Griffith has revealed his third big screen drama,
Hearts of the World.

Hearts of the World deals with the world war, and yet it
isn't a spectacle. Griffith calls it "the story of a village." The
vigor of Hearts of the World lies in its simplicity. Some one has
said that the big screen plays will come when producers discover
the value of the simple. Griffith realized that truth in this romance
of the world's tragedy. Thru the maelstrom of battle smoke he
never loses sight of his principal characters. Personifying any man
and any woman, they bring the war home with crashing directness.

Hearts of the World gives a new realization of modern war.
Griffith has centered his story in a little village of northern France.
Here the Boy, son of an American painter, and the Girl, daughter
of a French artist, meet, love and plight their troth. Then comes
1914. The village throbs with the coming of war. The gray German hordes descend upon France. The battle-line skirts the little
village and finally engulfs it. The Boy is now a soldier of France
and the Girl a prisoner within the Teuton lines. The Boy casts his
life into the balance as a spy and finds his sweetheart just as he
is discovered. The two seek refuge in an old inn tower. German
soldiers surround the place and are battering the doors down when
the French recapture the village and save them.

Subordinate to the romance of the Boy and the Girl is the
story of a little street singer, the debonair and piquantly brazen
Little Disturber, who looks upon the Boy with longing eyes and,
realizing that "if you can't get what you want, then want what you
can get," takes a boisterous French peasant lad to her heart.

This is the simple theme. Back of it sweep fleet aircraft,
lumbering tanks, thousands upon thousands of soldiers, masses of
artillery, fleeing throngs of terrified refugees, all the triumphs and
tragedies of modern war. Barrage fire, curtain fire, poison gas,
shrapnel, huge shells, all play their grim parts. Griffith, by permission of the Allied governments, obtained many scenes on the
actual battlefields of Europe. Others he created in the peaceful

fields of California. But we defy you to tell where the real moments end and the make-believe ones start.

It is the very simplicity of Hearts of the World that drives the grimness of war home. Griffith shows war's reaction upon the life of a small community much as Wells did in Mr. Britling Sees It Thru. We do not say that Hearts of the World has a story which deserves recognition as dramatic literature. It is frequently trite, as the scene in which the Huns hammer upon the inn doors and the Boy stands within with his revolver, holding just two cartridges, pressed against his sweetheart's breast.

You and I, seeing life as something more than the moonlight-tinted study of an ingênue listening to a serenade in a garden, will feel that the screen drama of the future is to be something more vital and searching than this. But Griffith has taken the familiar film ingredients and vivified them with hundreds of human touches.

We were disappointed in Hearts of the World in the sense that Griffith revealed nothing technically new. He uses all the old screen resources--and uses them better than they have ever been utilized before--but he fails to open up a new avenue of advance. Intolerance, which failed because of its half-baked philosophy and lack of the simple human note, at least presented Griffith as a man experimenting with his materials. Intolerance was an effort to utilize the cut-back to present a story much as the human mind thinks.

Hearts of the World is developed in the same way that Griffith did his one-reelers in the old Biograph days six years ago. The alternating flashes of the prisoners within the inn tower, of the pursuers battering the doors outside and the French soldiers coming to the rescue are examples of the old Griffith method of attaining cumulative suspense. Here, too, the climax is delayed too long. The tension is over-strained and the punch is deadened.

Not that we do not look upon Griffith as the one leader of the photodrama. No one else can humanize a story in the way Griffith does it. There are many moments to go to the spectator's heart, as, for instance, the hero-worship and jealousy of the Boy's youngest brother.

Hearts of the World has many remarkable instances of direction and photography. There are the scenes in the trenches during a driving rainstorm. There is a before-the-war long-shot of singular beauty, depicting the lovers strolling thru the gardens of the Girl's home at night. Flashes of Grey and Viviani addressing their respective parliaments in the memorable days of August, 1914, are superbly handled.

The acting--which, of course, reflects Griffith in every minute phase--is wholly excellent. Lillian Gish lends a note of wistful poetry to the role of the Girl. Dorothy Gish portrays the Little

Disturber, gamin of circumstances and something of a philosopher, with insouciance and piquant humor. Robert Harron gives human directness to the Boy. And Robert Anderson, as the boisterous Monsieur Cuckoo, George Fawcett as the good-hearted village carpenter, and little Ben Alexander as the littlest brother stand out as presenting splendid characterizations.

Hearts of the World has temporary emotional appeal of a high order--it sways and carries your interest. On the whole, we congratulate Mr. Griffith.

--Frederick James Smith in Motion
Picture Classic, Vol. 6, No. 5
(July 1918), pages 18-19.

*   *   *

Here the camera drama demonstrates possibilities at its command that are impossibilities to the theatrical stage. The latter can only present imitations of the great things which the photographic lens reproduces literally. Many of the war pictures shown in Hearts of the World were taken at the actual front and under fire of the enemy's guns. With remarkable skill they have been woven into the warp of the play, so that it is difficult to distinguish real scenes from the manufactured ones.

Mr. Griffith's big undertaking uses the moving-picture in its most splendid capacities, but it also demonstrates all the old defects. It gives us the mugging "close-ups" in all their absurdity, it is full of exasperating "cut-backs" or "cut-in," or whatever they are called in the jargon of the movie trade, and sickly sentimentality receives the usual emphasis. Mr. Griffith is doubtless not to blame for these things so much as are the demands of the public to which he has to cater. He evidently has full appreciation of the value of what is best in his picture, and gives full scope to its patriotic inspiration of hatred for the Hun and Prussian methods of waging war.

Everyone should see Hearts of the World. It is the moving-picture play with many of its defects and also with its greatest possibilities. It is the war brought to our very doors.

--"Metcalfe" in Life, Vol. 71, No.
1851 (April 18, 1918), page 642.

*   *   *

No motion-picture production under any auspices, with any star, would prove a superior first-night attraction to a premier by the celebrated gentleman whom Potash and Perlmutter refer to as "Mr. Grifficks." Notwithstanding few recent appearances in the squared circle of the silver-sheet, David Wark Griffith is still heavyweight champ of the movies, and Spring's largest single interest is undoubtedly his new war play, Hearts of the World, first publicly presented at the Auditorium, Los Angeles, in March and viewed by many Allied notables.

Hearts of the World is, as the programme states, the story of a village. I suspect that there is considerable camouflage in the accredited authorship. Screen and programme allege that the scenario was written by one Gaston de Tolignac, and translated by Captain Victor Marier. Why give Mr. Griffith two extra names?

The camera provides a full evening's occupation, first unrolling the intimacies of a French village in time of peace, and then displaying the lurid scroll of its destruction, occupation by and final recovery from its rabid northern neighbors, the Huns. As an apotheosis, the triumphant Frenchmen, holding a festival of reunion with their wives, sweethearts and children, behold the first of Pershing's columns swinging into the end of the long street. You may imagine that this epilogue of Americana, and what follows, causes the audience to resemble nothing but an old-fashioned Fourth of July celebration before we became safe and sane.

There is no name, real or imaginary, to suggest any particular sector along the warfront. While large masses of troops and famous leaders are introduced from time to time, the story concerns no part of the great conflict but those phases which have to do with the little town. This is characteristic Griffith simplicity, in fine contradistinction to the screeching ambitions and booming platitudes of those ruthless kings and people's leaders chucked lavishly about in the average war fillum. As a drop of water epitomizes the ocean, so one of her little towns epitomizes France, and the happiness or sorrow of a single family, the joy or tragedy of one pair of sweethearts, sums up the tranquilities of peace or the terrors of tyranny.

While Hearts of the World covers great areas and contains large scenes and many people it is not, primarily, a spectacle, as was Intolerance. It is not even as much of a spectacle as The Birth of a Nation. It has not the irresistible dramatic unity and power of The Birth of a Nation--that perfect picture!--nor the splendor of imagination and bewildering variety introduced in that noble mystery, Intolerance. But it has warm humanities, great sincerity and sweetness, those delectable touches of intermingled laughter and tears which are the hallmark of genuine art, and--as we have indicated-- subject-matter which comes rousingly home to every man on earth who has not been mechanically deprived of his virility or born with his foot under the neck of an infallible monarch.

I think the main secret of Griffith's clutch at people's hearts is his patient preliminary exposition of every detail of his characters' lives. It doesn't jar you to read that private 'arry 'opkins, of the New Zealand Fusileers, has been gassed to a horrible death in Flanders. You don't know 'arry and you recognize only that he died for the sake of liberty and to uphold the government which sent him there. But Charlie Smith, the enthusiastic college boy who lived next door, and sat on your front porch to read the Sunday paper, and whittled your kiddie a wooden dog, and brought his girl around so your wife could pass on her--Charlie loses a couple of fingers in a little skirmish on the Chemin des Dames, and, somehow, it breaks you all up and you hope they'll invalid him home right away.

So in our little French village we see Douglas Hamilton, an artist who has adopted France as his home, in the varied channels of his life and occupation; we see also Marie Stephenson, chasing her stray gosling into Hamilton's backyard--and in that funny meeting altering the lives of both of them; Hamilton's father and mother, comfortable folk accepted in the village as though they had always lived there; the girl's mother and her placid old grandfather, unswerving in his childlike faith that nothing can harm France; the gay-ferocious M'sieur Cuckoo, village clown, yet something finer than that; the Little Disturber, demoiselle whose practical philosophy is that if she can't get what she wants to want what she can get; the village-carpenter, a lovable Gallic rube; the idolizing wee brother of Douglas.

When the horde of the Potsdam Attila strikes, it is with throat a bit tightened that we see Marie put away the wedding clothes she had "sewed with white thread and whiter thoughts"; observe the grotesque ends of the girl's mother and grandfather, and Hamilton's father; witness the enslaving of Marie; the decline and pitiful death of Douglas' mother; the destruction of the village we have learned to love, and the all-but-death of Douglas Hamilton himself. When the French retake these stone-heaps--once homes in which we saw love and laughter--it is as personal as if someone had saved the relics of our own home town after a German uprising.

The two most significant portrayals are Robert Harron's, as Douglas Hamilton; and Dorothy Gish's, as "The Little Disturber." Young Mr. Harron has come to mature stature in acting without losing a whit of his lovable, boyish personality. He makes Hamilton the prototype of the liberty-loving young man of the world today --gentle, tender, yet an implacable and ferocious soldier when his loved ones are menaced. Dorothy Gish, as a little twelve-o'clock girl in a nine-o'clock town, jumps clear out of all Gish tradition. Saucy and startling, bewitching inspite of her pertness, she and her swing-walk (descendant of the Mountain Girl's stride?) are to be seen rather than described. Lillian Gish, as Marie, is called upon for possibly the hardest and most continuous work of the piece, and, for the first time in her career, is drafted for the most extreme emotions. The intelligence and sincerity she manifests throughout remark her misfortune in not having the magnetic personality of her younger sister--who gets much bigger effects with a minimum of endeavor. Robert Andersen seems to be the Griffith find of the year, playing that glorious fool, M'sieur Cuckoo, the town boob of comic love and grand heroism. Smaller parts fall to that jewel among actors, George Fawcett, playing the carpenter; to George Siegmann, as Von Strohm; to Ben Alexander, playing a most lovable little boy.

The portentous moment of the picture (to me, at least) was that episode in which Hamilton's mother, a delicate woman forced into the hardest sort of service by the German occupation, fails and finally dies in the cellar she and her three little boys inhabit. Whereupon the little fellows, sprung from babyhood to manhood in

a day by the fearful elixir of war, resolutely dig her grave in the
floor of their one-room habitation and lay her where they can be
sure no Saxon ghoul will disturb her rest.   This scene, simply
written, realistically acted and directed by the hand of genius, is
Tolstoy literature.

Hearts of the World is the most timely photoplay that could
possibly be devised.   It should be a tremendous box-office attraction
in every country in the world--save one.

> --Julian Johnson in Photoplay, Vol.
> 14, No. 1 (June 1918), pages
> 48 and 111.

☐ HELL'S HINGES (Kay-Bee/Triangle, 1916)

In this subject, William A. Hart still further clinches his
position as one of the foremost "western" actors on the screen.
His work in a difficult part is most finished, and his mastery of
the situations marked.

Mr. Hart has been assisted by a capable company, and,
moreover, by capable direction.   Scenic effects have been added to
the thrills, and these culminate in the burning of a church, and
eventually by the burning of a whole village.

As Blaze Tracy Mr. Hart is one of the leading citizens of
Hell's Hinges, a western hamlet which has richly earned its name.
When the young preacher and his sister arrive and try a little reform work, he falls in love with Faith, the sister, and consequently
is of the greatest assistance to the preacher.   The flock grows, and
soon enough money is raised to build a little church.

The spread of religion annoys Silk Miller, proprietor of the
notorious saloon and dance hall, and he sets about the ruin of the
minister.   This he does by getting one of the dance girls to work
her wiles, and the young man falls.   He is found by his congrega-
tion, the next morning, helplessly intoxicated.

In an endeavor to save him, Blaze rides to the next town for
a doctor.   In the meantime, the preacher, wandering delirious, gets
back into the saloon, and is plied with liquor until he is again under
the influence.   Then the whole crowd starts out to burn the church,
with the intoxicated preacher in the front ranks.

There is a gun fight in front of the church, and several of
both parties are killed, including the minister; then the church is
fired.   When Blaze returns with the doctor, he finds Faith weeping
over the body of her brother, stretched on the church lawn.

Enraged, he makes his way, pistols in hand, to the saloon;

there he holds up the whole crowd, shoots a couple, and by shooting
the lamps to the floor, sets the place afire. While the terrorized
habitues flee, the whole town goes up in flames. Blaze and Faith
make their way off together into a new and better life.

The scenes of the fires, taken from considerable distances,
are immense in their sweep of atmosphere and realism. Conviction
is the key-note of the entire production, and the dramatic work presented is of the highest order.

Louise Glaum, as the dancing girl, and Clara Williams as
Faith, give excellent characterizations. Jack Standing, Alfred Hol-
lingsworth, Robert McKim, J. Frank Burke are also members of
the cast.

> --Harvey F. Thew in Motion Pic-
> ture News, Vol. 13, No. 7
> (February 19, 1916), page 1029.

☐ HIS MAJESTY, THE AMERICAN (Fairbanks/United Artists, 1919)

Here goes picture number one, of the Big Four output.
Knowing the Big Four, and reading that title, it is almost superfluous to say that his majesty is Douglas Fairbanks. He is, indeed. The piece reminds me, very directly, of the popular romances of a decade or two decades ago, which were strung around
the reading world in the years following Hope's ten-strike with The
Prisoner of Zenda. The Hollywood acrobatic hero is introduced as
an adventure-lover in his own small village of New York, where,
with few excitements on tap, he has his house fitted out like a fire-
station, with gongs, sliding-poles and other get-there-quick whatnot,
and he has a pretty time with the police and fire departments until
a reform quiets things down, whereupon he goes to Mexico for his
thrills--and thence to the mythical kingdom of Alaine, where he
straightens out a nation, rescues a princess and marries her, and
does many other particularly Fairbankian things by way of incidental
diversion and civic excitement. The piece is simply a good-humored
diversion in which no one, including the star, seems to take things
or himself too seriously. It is a most ordinary story to begin with,
lifted up a bit by rapid and unconventional treatment, devoid of bunk
or bombast, and peppered with colloquial titles throughout. The
treatment and settings have been generous, and one of the latter, a
masked-in piece of modern scenic trickery representing the valley
of Alaine lying at the foot of Alp-like mountains, is quite striking
though it would be palpably paint and canvas if it were left more
than a moment, each time, in the spectator's eyes. Mr. Fairbanks,
alert and brisk as usual, is assisted very cleverly by Sam Sothern,
Frank Campeau, Lillian Langdon, and that sweet child, Margery Daw.

> --Julian Johnson in Photoplay, Vol.
> 17, No. 1 (December 1919), page
> 117.

* * *

His Majesty, the American is another routine Douglas Fairbanks celluline cyclone. Doug gymnastics as a young New Yorker
who gets involved in a middle Europe revolution and turns out to be
the heir apparent to the throne. The star dashes from mantel to
balcony and from housetop to window-ledge with his customary dramatic power. In other words, His Majesty, the American is just
another Fairbanks comedy of the usual sort.

--Frederick James Smith in Motion Picture Classic, Vol. 9,
No. 5 (January 1920), page 57.

☐ HIS ROYAL SLYNESS (Rolin/Pathê, 1920)

This is the most pretentious of all the Harold Lloyd comedies, but I don't think you are going to like it as well as his first
ones: Bumping into Broadway or From Hand to Mouth. It only
goes to prove that Lloyd himself is the whole show and as long as
he is provided with a reasonable situation or two, an involved story
isn't necessary. This is another mythical kingdom story--my word,
where will it ever end? The film producers seem to be as keen
about mythical kingdoms as the legit. is for China. Lloyd makes
the most of everything that comes his way, from a beautiful princess to a lot of bolshevik bombs. His new little leading woman,
Mildred Davis, is an appealing child--but not, alas, a Bebe Daniels.
Snub Pollard is one of the genuinely funny grotesque comedians in
films. We have Mr. Lloyd's brother here, too; he is a ringer for
resemblance but he is fortunately not called upon to be funny.

--Photoplay, Vol. 17, No. 5 (April
1920), page 109.

☐ HOME, SWEET HOME (Reliance-Majestic/Mutual, 1914)

A photodrama of beautiful motive, of exquisite treatment, and
of exposition imbued with the personality of brilliant Griffith, Home,
Sweet Home, ranks among the highest screen productions--"masterpiece" has been so indiscriminately used that it has lost all dignity,
if not significance. One does not have to state that there is a "beautiful motive" and leave it to the imagination. The immortal works
of man make him akin to God, partaking of and participating in the
divine purpose so far as the world is concerned. The splendid motive is sounded in the biographical sketch of Payne, as idealized by
Griffith, and leading up to the composition of the imperishable song:

"It is something too strange to understand,
How all the chords on the instrument,

> Whether sorrowful, blithe, or grand,
> Under the touch of your master hand
> Were into one melody blent. "

> "And now, though I live for a thousand years,
> On no new chord can a new hand fall.
> The chords of sorrow, of pain, of tears,
> The chords of raptures and hopes and fears,
> I say you have struck them all;
> And all the meaning put into each strain
> By the Great Composer, you have made plain. "

The poem of Miss Wilcox seems so appropriate that it might have been written of Payne and his imperishable song, and it is, like the photoplay, an appreciation of genius by genius, though offered in general rather than individual tribute. Mr. Griffith portrays Payne in the natural and sympathetic character of man, as we know him, mortal in his weaknesses, divine only in an occasional expression of all that is fine in his personality. The composer's story is that of a man who wandered away from his home and from the sweet-true-hearted girl to whom he was engaged, to end his days in foreign lands, after yielding quite as much to vagrant impulses as to noble inspirations.

He broke his mother's heart--she deemed him an unworthy son--and the girl who waited for him on earth died, constant in her love to the erring man of her choice. He was only a man, and the nearer our hearts for all that. In extenuation, he created what has come down to us through uncounted sources, that will go on in the countless centuries to come, softening other hearts as it has sweetened ours.

From the moment that the biography starts with the raising of a window upon the domestic life of Payne and his mother, to the pathetic end of this part of the play, the vast audience at "The Strand" sat spellbound. The dramaturgic skill of the director, enabling him to utilize the histrionic skill of the actors, brought out an enthralling performance, the honors going to Harry Walthall as Payne, and Lillian Gish as his sweetheart, with some dainty touches by Dorothy Gish.

The first episode offered a delightful comedy relief and gave opportunity to one of the best comediennes ever seen in photodrama, Mae Marsh as "Apple Pie Mary. " She fascinated the audience as completely as if she had been before them in person, the thousands present laughing at her delicately-conveyed mental processes. She has the art of picturing thought to a degree that argues her own intensity and intelligent grasp of all she is required to convey, going even beyond that into spontaneous delineations of her own.

The story of "Apple Pie Mary" is in illustration of the power exerted by the song, Home, Sweet Home. So also is the episode in which James Kirkwood and Donald Crisp do some forceful acting, as

two brothers of lifetime hatred, driving their mother insane by a
double tragedy, from which condition she is restored to the remaining child by the song. So also is the third episode, in which three
stars of the first magnitude, Blanche Sweet, Owen Moore and Court-
ney Foote, present a version of the indispensable triangle, one with
a happy termination through the all-pervading influence of one man's
contribution to human enlightenment.

     The allegory is a spiritual phrase of great beauty, and a fit-
ting termination to what will undoubtedly be an enduring work. The
spirit of the whole play, as well as its theme and treatment, is so
imaginative and artistic, while appealing to the purest sensibilities,
that "poetic drama" seems to designate the production. This is
meant in high praise. Drama of noble purpose that is poetic in
spirit and artistic in presentation, tends to make life lovely and
wonderful, to give it that stimulus which leads to progress. Home,
Sweet Home is an enchantment of the screen.

> And nothing that ever was born or evolved,
>   Nothing created by light or force,
> But deep in its system there lies dissolved
>   A shining drop from the Great Love Source;
>   A shining drop that shall live for aye--
>   Though kingdoms may perish and stars decay."
>   --Louis Reeves Harrison in The
>   Moving Picture World, Vol. 20,
>   No. 9 (May 30, 1914), pages
>   1234-1235.

☐ THE HONOR SYSTEM (Fox, 1917)

     There is so much that is admirable in The Honor System,
the screen drama written and directed by R. A. Walsh and produced
by the Fox Company, that it seems almost ungracious not to mark
one hundred per cent, for each of its ten reels. As presented at
the Lyric theater, New York, at its first public showing, it was divided into three acts, the first two, in point of construction, being
practically without a flaw--unless one objects to some humorous incidents that do not advance the story but are human as well as
amusing.

     The Honor System is founded upon a story by Henry Christeen
Warnack and relates of a young man who kills a ruffian in self-
defense while protecting a Western dance hall girl, is convicted of
murder and sent to the Arizona State Prison for life. The second
act is taken up with revealing Joseph Stanton's experience while in
prison and the terrible conditions under which the institution was
conducted. This is told in uncompromising detail, the Arizona State
Prison itself having been used by permission of Governor George W.
P. Hunt, who was instrumental in putting an end to the disgrace. In

the drama the prisoner, Joseph Stanton, is the means of bringing
the matter to the attention of the Governor, and at the end of the
second act Stanton, who is suffering from his experiences under the
old system, cannot obtain a pardon, as that lies within the power
of a man he has antagonized.

The last reel is devoted to the freeing of Stanton and the
happy termination of his love for the daughter of the new warden.
There is no fault to be found with such an ending, the moral lesson
is driven home with sufficient force without the death of the innocent man, but the act is too long drawn out. Matters to be cleared
up are few, and the sooner this is done, the better.

The one and only test to put to a drama of this nature is not
whether the protagonist proves his contention, but if the subject
makes good entertainment regardless of its standing on moral reform. The Honor System meets every demand of such a test. On
its artistic side, it reveals an extensive and correctly mounted production filled with striking scenes, much quick action and based upon
a human appeal that will find a ready response from every true man
and worthy woman.

Splendid judgment has been shown in the selection of the cast.
Milton Sills is superlatively fine as Joseph Stanton. Without pose,
or one touch of theatricalism, he showed a man who suffered deeply
and bore his sufferings with a strength of mind and heart worthy all
praise. The screen never saw a more touching display of emotion
than the moment when Stanton stands face to face with the Governor
and realizes that his wrongs and the wrongs of his fellow prisoners
are about to be righted.

Gladys Rockwell was another member of the cast who gave a
flawless performance, and of uncommon merit were the impersonations to which are attached the names of Mrs. Cora Drew, James
A. Marcus, Arthur Mackley, Miriam Cooper, George Walsh, Charles
Clary, Roy Rice, P. J. Cannon and Johnny Reese. Photographer
George Benoit and Title Editor Hettie Gray Baker are also to be
felicitated. S. L. Rothapfel staged the production and arranged the
incidental music. His work adds to the merit of the entertainment.
                        --Edward Weitzel in The Moving
                          Picture World, Vol. 31, No. 9
                          (March 3, 1917), page 1370.

☐ HOODOO ANN (Fine Arts/Triangle, 1916)

Here is Mae Marsh in her first Triangle play, fully justify-
ing all predictions of her eminent fitness to be starred in pictures.
She has been provided with a typical Fine Arts story, a first rate
supporting cast, and superior direction.

Even if Miss Marsh were not surrounded with these, we believe she could not fail to gain a personal success. For, without shadow of a doubt, she was born to the camera.

But Granville Warwick's* story makes possible her creation of a real character--Hoodoo Ann, drudge of the orphanage; heroine of a fire; central figure in a mystery, and finally Mrs. Jimmie Vance. All Miss Marsh's gifts of expression and pantomime are called into play. She does not act Hoodoo Ann; she is Hoodoo Ann. There you have summed up in four words the whole story, so far as Miss Marsh is concerned.

It may be well to tell you also that this picture will delight not merely your adult patrons, but children as well. It has as universal an appeal as any picture we have ever seen.

Robert Harron, as Jimmie Vance, is Miss Marsh's able first assistant, and is perfectly at home in his role. It is superfluous to talk about Harron's screen ability, or his work in a particular picture. He is always good. Others in the cast--they all do well-- are William H. Brown, Wilbur Higby, Loyola O'Connor, Mildred Harris, Pearl Elmore, Anna Hernandez, Charles Lee, Elmo Lincoln and Robert Lawler.

Lloyd Ingraham, the director, and Granville Warwick, the author, lavished cleverness on this production. It is filled with those little human touches for which Fine Arts pictures are famous. This applies to the subtitles also. A neat surprise is gained by the introduction of a character who has nothing to do with the story. This is a clever trick which needs to be seen to be appreciated. Suffice it to say, it supplies a very novel ending.

Another fine stroke is the introduction of a moving picture show which Harron and Miss Marsh attend. They see there an old style Western "mellerdrammer." The picture they see is, of course, really a burlesque on the old school of pictures, but it also is necessary to the plot.

Finally, Hoodoo Ann has a high degree of suspense, as well as a high degree of heart interest and humor. The management of the "murder" mystery at the end is exceedingly ingenious. There is no murder, but until the mystery is cleared up, the spectator is anxious for the safety of little Hoodoo Ann. There are other notable things about this subject, but they all point the same moral: it is a real photoplay.

--Oscar Cooper in Motion Picture
News, Vol. 13, No. 15 (April
15, 1916), page 2212.

---

*Granville Warwick was, of course, a pseudonym of D. W. Griffith.

☐ HYPOCRITES (Bosworth, 1914)

     Hypocrites is a Bosworth four-reeler that will probably be
placed independently. Although the Bosworth company releases usually through the Paramount, it would not be surprising, after seeing
this film, that the maker should decide to present it as a special
picture show. In a way Hypocrites is daring, but only because no-
one else has attempted as much or has gone as far. Lois Weber
wrote the scenario and directed the film. After seeing it you can't
forget the name of Lois Weber, though it be well known already in
and out of the trade. To get right to the sensation of this four-reel
picture, it is the figure of a naked girl, about 18 years of age,
probably designated on the program as "The Naked Truth" walking
and flitting through the woods. Even the most fastidious can find
nothing offensive in this to carp at, it has been so well handled.
Although a couple of times the young woman walks directly toward
the camera, there is no false modesty exhibited, and a shadowy
trick by the camera does not permit of the nude figure too long in
sight at any time. The nakedness comes about through the destruction of a statue, erected by a priest, who is stoned to death by a
mob at its unveiling. Incarnated as the young woman, the story
works out to its conclusion. Some doubt seemed to exist as to the
limit of the feature, when it was first shown at the Strand some
weeks ago for a private review, but there is nothing in this picture
at all that should stop its public presentation. There is no other
picture like it, there has been no other, and it will attract anywhere,
for it is a pretty idyllic pastoral picture of faultless taste. The
title, Hypocrites, is faithfully carried out for the theme. As a
moving picture, in the manner Miss Weber has done this film, it
could be truthfully proclaimed as the essence of sweetness in purity,
but you will have to see the picture before realizing that. It is
quite remarkable from every angle of the picture art.
--Sime (Sime Silverman) in Variety,
Vol. 36, No. 10 (November 7,
1914), page 23.

☐ THE IDOL DANCER (Griffith/First National, 1920)

     David Wark Griffith still has his whip in The Idol Dancer,
but he uses it sparingly and only on a slave person who probably
was used to it. Many of my confreres report this a disappointing
picture, but I suspect if anyone else had made it they would have
considered it very good. You can't help expecting a lot from D. G.
Merely because he is D. G. I quarrel with him as frequently as
any gent whose business it is to comment upon the work he does,
but between ourselves the quarreling is largely inspired by the hope
that it may make him so doggone mad some day he will take it seriously and double back to the time when he was at once the leader

and the promise of the screen. He went all the way to the Bahamas
for the local color needed for The Idol Dancer and brought precious
little back that he could not have ordered in his Westchester studio,
or found in Florida. Unless it be the native canoe in which the men
of the threatened village paddle umteen miles in umteen minutes to
save Clarine Seymour and Richard Barthelmess and the other worth-
saving persons of the cast from manhandling, arson and sudden
death. However, better a real background that seems a waste of
money than an imitation that could be recognized.

The only really disappointing feature of The Idol Dancer to
me is the commonplace and familiar story--familiar in the sense
that it is the old complication of the lost sinner and the hopeful
saint with their horns locked in a battle for the girl. It has a little
new color in this instance because one boy is a beach-comber, an
atheistical youth who is willing to let the faithful worship what god
they will so long as they leave him his gin and room on the sand
to sleep off his excesses, and the other a New Englander with weak
lungs who comes suddenly upon the beauteous Seymour dancing the
hula-hula and straightway wants to live. For which neither you nor
I could blame him. The Seymour herself is a native girl adopted
by an old English salt, to excuse her speaking English titles, and
renamed Mary. She wears not so very much in front and a little
less than 'alf of that be'ind, as the gifted Rudyard phrased it, and
she is a beauty bright from the bells on her toes to the permanent
wave in her hair (a wave she never learned to do in the South Sea
Islands). Moreover she not only negotiates the hula with considerable grace, but she plays the dramatic scenes with enough fire and
sincerity almost to convince you that she is what she pretends to be,
a dusky island belle. Richard Barthelmess is the heavy-eyed beach-
comber, a youngish youth to carry his philosophy of life, but handsome and a good screen actor, with personal appeal plus.

--Burns Mantle in Photoplay, Vol.
18, No. 1 (June 1920), page 67.

☐ THE IMMIGRANT (Mutual, 1917)

In The Immigrant Charlie Chaplin comes across with about
five big, spontaneous splashes of laughter and a tidal wave of gig-
gles. In the latest Mutual-Chaplin we get a new, and, if possible,
funnier idea of the famous Chaplin walk. This happens when the boat
rolls. In fact, the rolling of the boat furnishes Charlie with opportunities for laughmaking all during the first reel. There is some up-
roariously funny stuff pulled when the bunch of immigrants go to the
messroom for eats. During the trip over Charlie meets a beautiful
girl--Edna Purviance. He also wins a little money at cards and
craps, but soon after landing is broke.

The fact that he is broke leads him into some fine complications in a restaurant, where he once more meets the girl. After

many vicissitudes and tribulations Charlie drags the girl to the marriage license bureau.

All during the piece Charlie is pulling Chaplinesque business
which cannot be adequately described.   It should be enough commendation for any film to say that it is almost two thousand feet of
Chaplin.

--Ben H. Grimm in The Moving
Picture World, Vol. 32, No. 13
(June 30, 1917), page 2115.

☐ IN THE BISHOP'S CARRIAGE (Famous Players, 1913)

It is several months since picture lovers have seen on the
screen Mary Pickford in a new film.   In this refined melodrama they
will see Little Mary in a new light.   In the Bishop's Carriage, from
the book of Miriam Michelson, is a crook play; nevertheless its
treatment is so artistic, so delicate, so finished, that it will please
every division of society.   In its delineation of the character of the
charity girl who falls out of the clutches of the virago in the charity
house into the hands of the thief--out of the frying pan into the fire,
as it were--and then under the influence of a man animated by honest motives, the picture is more than interesting; it is instructive.
Nance's attempts to reform, her failures, and her final triumph over
wrong will be followed with the closest attention.   Dave Wall, as
Tom Dorgan, the crook, gives a splendid performance.   His work
is restrained at times, yet showing, when the occasion justifies it,
every ounce of force necessary to carry over a situation.   He has
much to do, and it is all well done.

House Peters, in the role of Obermuller, the theatrical man,
makes his debut on the screen in this picture.   He makes good.   It
is a popular part, one that will carry all the way the sympathy of
the observer.   Mr. Peters is tall, of good figure, and altogether of
pleasing personality.   John Steppling plays Mr. Ramsey, the bibulous
husband who is robbed of jewels belonging to his wife.   This versa-
tile actor's work is always finished and always good to see.   Grace
Henderson, who will be recognized by screen followers, plays well
the role of Mrs. Ramsey.   Mme. Dalberg is the star actress who
leaves temptation in the way of Nance, the former companion of the
crook, given a chance on the stage.   Her delineation is effective,
convincing.   George Moss as the bishop will be enjoyed.   His con-
sternation at the discovery of a pretty young woman in his carriage
makes a delightful bit of comedy.   Howard Missimer is the plain-
clothesman.   What little he has to do is well done, as it is bound
to be.

In the Bishop's Carriage cannot be described as a love story.
There are two scenes in it, though, where the affection of the girl
whose life has been such a rough one comes to the surface.   The

first, where Nance, after her successful debut on the stage, is surprised in her room by the entrance of Dorgan as she is contemplating the bouquet thrown to her by an admirer, will stir the heart.
The escaped convict, demanding that Nance return to him, is in
turn surprised by the entrance of Obermuller.   Nance flies to him
for protection.   It is the awakening of the good in a heart that has
been trained to evil.   The second is where Obermuller and Nance,
on the waterfront, watch the departure of a tramp steamer bound
for India, bearing on board Dorgan.   If the love element is lacking
its absence is atoned for by the presence of the note of suspense--
in continuity.   Thrilling situations abound; situations legitimately
thrilling, made so by the art of the author and the skill of the director and the fine acting of the players.

     The interest is established in the first scene, where Nance
is beaten by the matron.   Her escape and pursuit by the police and
the finding of shelter and protection in the rooms of Dorgan mark
the beginning of a train of adventures the number of which precludes
description.   It is just one after another.   One scene deserves special mention.   Nance visiting the star actress has seen jewels.   The
force of habit is too strong.   She fights against her inclination to
steal--and falls.   No sooner has she taken them, however, than she
repents and rushes to the room of Obermuller.   She throws them
on his desk.   "I stole them," she confesses; and then pleads: "Why
can't you keep temptation out of my way?"   The action of the theatrical man will recall the nobility of the fine old bishop when the
gendarmes brought in Jean Valjean.

     The play is almost entirely of interiors.   The settings are
skillfully and tastefully constructed.   One that will stand out is the
theater scene on the occasion of Nance's debut as an actress.
Among the outdoor views are those of a hotel roof garden and fine
residential neighborhoods.   The photography is excellent.   In the
Bishop's Carriage is a strong picture.

--George Blaisdell in The Moving
Picture World, Vol. 17, No. 12
(September 20, 1913), page 1266.

*   *   *

     When Miriam Michelson wrote In the Bishop's Carriage he
unwittingly supplied first-class material for motion pictures.   With
due respect for Mr. Michelson we imagine many people who found
little of consequence in the author's book will enjoy watching Mary
Pickford and her co-workers of the Famous Players' Film Company
in their four-reel adaptation of the novel.   It excels in every element that goes to make a good picture.   Ben Schulberg, who wrote
the scenario based his plot entirely on the book, not the play, and
each reel is crammed full of action, some of it much out of the
ordinary.   The development is plausible, the acting of a uniformly
high order, and the photography excellent.   The photography, in fact,
deserves more than the conventional word of praise, for it has been
made a notable feature of the production.   Some of the interior night

effects reveal extraordinary camera work even in this day of photographic achievement.

And more than all else we have "Little Mary" at her best, which in itself would be reason enough for wanting to see the picture. She is on the screen most of the time and scoring points with every move in a part that pretty nearly runs the gamut of girlish emotions. For after all, Nance Olden is scarcely more than a child, ill-treated, susceptible to evil influences, but a charming and naturally good-hearted little person at bottom. So much we gather from watching Miss Pickford's beautifully varied performance. At no time does she fail to hold both sympathy and interest, whether as a poor waif fleeing from the Charity Home, the active partner of a pickpocket, or a troubled girl tempted almost beyond her strength. An actress who can suggest feeling with so little apparent effort is indeed a rarity.

The story follows the many adventures of Nance after she escapes from an institution and by chance finds refuge in the room of Tom Dorgan, a pickpocket, who decides to make use of his new acquaintance. Their partnership progresses profitably until, to elude the police after stealing valuable jewels, Nance enters "the bishop's carriage." Complications follow thick and fast until the girl finds herself in the home of Obermuller, a theatrical manager, who influences her to attempt an honest life. Nance goes to Dorgan without the jewels and in a powerfully acted scene is compelled to return with him to Obermuller's house. They are captured, Dorgan is sent to Sing Sing, and Nance is launched as an actress. Temptation returns, but always the sympathetic theatrical manager is ready to assist his protege, and in the end they rest contentedly in each other's arms while Dorgan sails away never to return. This is but a bare outline of the story, that contains quantities of adventure, sufficient heart interest, and creditable character drawing.

Second only to the performance given by Miss Pickford comes that of David Wall in the part of Dorgan. He is an actor of much virility and discrimination. It is difficult to believe that in this production House Peters, playing the role of Obermuller, is making his first appearance as a motion picture actor. Evidently his stage training made it a simple matter for him to play before the camera. He has a fine presence and displays a forceful dignity in his acting of a role that offers many opportunities. Others of less importance in the cast are Grace Henderson, George Moss, Howard Missimer, and Madame Dalberg. Edwin S. Porter and J. Searle Dawley directed the picture.

> --D. in The New York Dramatic
> Mirror, Vol. 70, No. 1813 (September 17, 1913), page 28.

☐ IN THE DAYS OF THE THUNDERING HERD (Selig, 1914)

About twelve months ago Colin Campbell and Tom Mix paid a

visit to Chicago and went over the story of In the Days of the Thundering Herd with Gilson Willetts, which had been written with the
object of giving an accurate glimpse of life as it was lived in the
far middle west in the years around '49, when gold was first discovered in California.

I was favored by being present at some of these "talks," and
was impressed by the decision arrived at, on the suggestion of Mr.
Selig, that strict attention should be paid to historical correctness,
both in incidents and detail, in the production. In other words, the
Indians of those days and the plainsmen, their manner of living,
their camps, their hunting expeditions, their fierce and sanguinary
engagements, etc., should be visualized as nearly to the life as
possible. To bring back the days of the buffalo chase realistically,
it had already been arranged at the time that that 7,000-acre buffalo
ranch of Pawnee Bill, at Pawnee, Oklahoma, with the largest herd
of buffalo in the world, should be used in the hunting scenes. A
large force of native indians had been secured among the tribes in
Oklahoma and a carload of tepees had been manufactured in Chicago,
on the order of Mr. Selig, to furnish the pictures a typical Indian
village. How well the plans and preparations have succeeded remains for each spectator to judge for himself.

From my viewpoint, after viewing the picture twice, I can
say fearlessly that the five reels teem with action and radiate with
atmosphere of the old days with a vividness that can be felt. One
is translated from the wonders of modern days to the old Santa Fe
trail and the long, winding lane of "prairie schooners" headed towards the setting sun. We see them making camp for the night,
and watch the stealthy approach of the Indian girl, who soon makes
known to her people the presence of the white men.

Then comes the attack by the red devils, who gallop swiftly
around their victims, discharging their muskets as they circle, until only two of the whites--the hero and the heroine of the story--
are left alive. Next follow the thwarted torturing of the man and
his escape with the white girl, only to be pursued and recaptured,
and their next get-away which is successful. This time they come
upon a band of white hunters, and this camp is, in turn, attacked
by the same tribe of Indians. A running fight takes place, in which
the white men are pocketed in the hills and are saved from annihila-
tion by the timely arrival of another group of white hunters.

This battle, which results in the defeat of the redskins and
in the death of their chief is a most exciting spectacle, and may
well be termed the last word in a scene of this kind.

The reader naturally concludes that where there are so many
hunters there must be an abundance of big game, and he is not disappointed. We watch both the Indians and the white men as they
kill the buffalo, the former bringing down the animals with bow and
arrow just as skillfully as do the white men with musket or old-
time rifle. The big herd is shown many times in the pictures, under

varying conditions, and some of these scenes are strangely impressive. It is to be regretted that still pictures of these remarkable scenes, which can never again be taken, were not included among those snapped for the occasion.

Tom Mix is pre-eminently the "big chief" in the photoplay, and this is no reflection on the admirable work of Wheeler Oakman in the role of Chief Swift Wind. Tom is Tom Mingle, the pony express man, and afterwards the leader of the white men in their fierce fights with the Indians. He is the sweetheart of Sally Madison, for whom he forsakes the pony express business to accompany her on the journey to join her father in the state of the Golden West. The amazing equestrian feats performed by Mr. Mix, as the pony express man, will probably never be repeated again in moving pictures. Seen one hundred years from now, they will cause men to open their eyes in wonder. In the Indian fighting scenes, Tom holds the eye with the same magic spell.

Miss Bessie Eyton is a worthy companion for Tom Mingle in the part of Sally Madison. I never suspected that she was such a daredevil on horseback. After that terrific fall, when she is swept from the saddle by the low hanging bough of a tree, I surely thought she had suffered broken bones, if not insensibility. But no; she was up again, after a moment of careful feeling, hastily making her way to a tree, in whose branches she sought safety from the stampeded herd of buffalo. Here's to you Miss Eyton, for wonderful horseback riding and just as convincing acting.

Wheeler Oakman so cleverly disguises himself in the part of Indian, Chief Swift Wind, both in make-up and impersonation, that one is often impressed with the belief that he is a real redskin. The final contest between him and Tom Mix is a most realistic struggle.

The poetic role of Starlight has been sustained most creditably by Red Wing, the full-blooded daughter of the Indian chief. In a very subtle way, almost imperceptibly, she shows that she is in love with Tom Mingle and that her love is hopeless.

It is needless to emphasize, after what has been written, that the production has been worthily made by Colin Campbell. I will just direct attention to the closing scene, in which Tom Mingle, Sally Madison and Starlight are shown as they set out for the land of promise. As we pathetically gaze at it, new vistas rise out of the saffron west, and we rub our eyes to find out whether or not we are dreaming.

--James S. McQuade in The Moving Picture World, Vol. 22, No. 11 (December 12, 1914), page 1506.

☐ INTOLERANCE (Wark, 1916)

The metropolitan critics who preceded me in learned discourse upon Mr. Griffith's sun-play, Intolerance, shot away all the
superlatives which were our common property. Thus deprived of
the communal ammunition I must lay about me with a week-day set
of words and present facts garnished neither with rhapsody nor rail-
lery.

Intolerance is a collective story of the penalties paid through
the centuries to those "who do not believe as we believe." It occupied its maker's entire attention for at least a year and a half.
Both the notion and the generalship are his. Intolerance is more
than the world's biggest photoplay. In size and scope it is the biggest art-work of any description in a decade.

Here is a joy-ride through history; a Cook's tour of the ages;
a college education crammed into a night. It is the most incredible
experiment in story-telling that has ever been tried. Its uniqueness
lies not in a single yarn, but in the way its whole skein of yarns is
plaited.

Its distinct periods are four: Babylon, at the end of the re-
gency of Prince Belshazzar; Judea, in the time of Christ; France
under the inquisitorial high tide of St. Bartholomew's; and the American Now, with the intolerances of capital, labor, and the courts.
None of these tales runs straightaway. You stand in medieval France
and slip on the banana-peel of retrogression to Chaldea. You are
sure America has you--a wink has aviated you back to Palestine. It
is much like listening to a quartette of excellent elocutionists simultaneously reading novels by Arnold Bennett, Victor Hugo, Nathaniel
Hawthorne and Elinor Glyn.

Any of these carnivorous legends would fang you emotionally
if you were left long enough in its cage. But just as it is about to
bite, out you come, slam goes the door, and you are thrust among
the raveners of another century.

There has never been such scenery, anywhere, as the edifices
reared for the Babylonian episode.

Pictorially, the greatest filmings are the Judean scenes, perfect in composition, ideal in lighting, every one in effect a Tissot
painting of the time of Christ.

The Chaldean visions will teach history to college professors.

Altogether, the accuracy and authority of Intolerance's historic information is stupendous.

The finest individual acting accomplishments are Mae Marsh's.
The unique figure is Constance Talmadge, as The Mountain Girl; the

most poignantly beautiful, Seena Owen, as Attarea, favorite of Belshazzar. But there are no male assumptions even approaching the chief portrayals in The Birth of a Nation.

Mr. Bitzer's photography, devoid of anything sensational, flows like the transparent, limpid style of a finished writer. It is without tricks, and without imperfections.

An attempt to assimilate the mountainous lore of this sun-play at a sitting results in positive mental exhaustion. The universally-heard comment from the highbrow or nobrow who has tried to get it all in an evening: "I am so tired!"

Profoundest of symbols is the Rocking Cradle--"uniter of here and hereafter"--which joins the episodes. This mysterious ark of life, the stuff of a dream in the dimness of its great shadowed room, almost belongs to infinity. Lillian Gish is the brooding mother.

The music is sadly inefficient--the most inefficient music a big picture ever had.

Thousands upon thousands of feet of this photoplay never will be seen by the public. In the taking, this story rambled in every direction, and D. W. G. relentlessly and recklessly pursued each ramble to its end. At least half a dozen complete minor stories were cut off before the picture was shown at all.

In all probability, Intolerance will never attain the popularity of The Birth of a Nation. It has not that drama's single, sweeping story. It appeals more to the head, less to the heart.

Babylon is the foundation-stone, and seems to have been the original inspiration, of this visual Babel. Its mighty walls, its crowds, its army, have won many long-drawn "Ahs!" of sky-rocket admiration. But these were not essentially Griffith--anyone with money can pile up mobs and scenery. Mr. Griffith's original talent appears in recreating the passions, the ambitions, the veritable daily life of a great people so remote that their every monument is dust, their every artwork lost, their very language forgotten. This is more than talent; it is genius.

You were taught that the Jewish Jehovah traced destruction's warning in letters of fire on the wall of Belshazzar's palace; and that Cyrus, to get in, drained the Euphrates river and walked on its bed under Babylon's gates. See this picture and get the facts. Babylon was peacefully betrayed by the priests of Marduk long after it had successfully withstood as frenzied a siege as the Persian conqueror could bring.

Not content with rearing the vast barriers and marvelous gates you have seen illustratively reproduced in these pages, the California necromancer showed life as it ran its slender course

among the poor more than twenty-five centuries ago. Always of this
undercurrent is The Mountain Girl, a wild, wonderful little creature,
to be followed from semi-slavery through the civic courts to the
marriage market, where she is released by an impress from the
roll-seal Belshazzar has strapped upon his wrist.   Thereafter she
is, to the death, a sweet Amazon in the service of her great Sar.
The camp of Cyrus, with the "Institution" of the Medes and Persians,
is as instructive as a West-Asiatic history.   The attack upon Babylon, with its terrible towers, its demoniac "tank" of Greek fire--
flaming prophecy of the Somme juggernauts!--its ferocious personal
encounters, is unparalleled in battle spectacles.   Behold the vivid
though perhaps dubious realism of gushy close-ups on sword-thrusts.
Heads literally fly off above shearing swords, hot lead sears, rocks
crush, arrows pierce horridly--and withal there is the unconquerable
animation and fury of ultimate conflict.

     Otherwheres, the sensuous glory of the Chaldean court.   No
brush-master has painted more Oriental splendors than those boasted
by the golden bungalow of Nabonidus, quaint father of the virile'vo-
luptuary, Belshazzar.   Beauty blooms in wildest luxuriance in this
New York of the Euphrates.   The dances of Tammuz, god of spring-
time, flash forth in breath-taking nudity and rhythm as frank as
meaningful.   They are flashes, only; that is why they remain in the
picture.   One cannot imagine a more beautiful thing than Seena
Owen as Attarea--veritable star of the East.   The tiny battle-chariot
with its cargo of a great white rose, drawn down the table to Attarea's Belshazzar by two white doves, chances to remain the only
untouched thing in the palace of death which Cyrus enters.   There
is pathos!   Tully Marshall as the High Priest of Bel, Elmer Clifton
as the Rhapsode, George Siegmann as Cyrus--three players who are
especially redoubtable.

     The magical David pounds his points home by contrast.   From
the solemn grandeur of Ishtar's high altar, with its costly burnt offering of propitiation, he flashes to an aged widow offering her all
to the same deity--three turnips and a carrot, covered with a little
oil.

     The France which our film-etcher rears for the massacre of
St. Bartholomew is as fine a France as Stanley Weyman pictured in
words.   Griffith spares neither exactness nor feeling.   With delicate
touches he builds up keen interest in the home of Brown Eyes--then
slaughters the whole family.   Wonderful characters here are Josephine Crowell's Catherine de Medici; and Charles IX, as played by
Frank Bennett.

     Much has been taken from the Judean scenes, but so much
remains to hail as optic poetry that the loss is negligible.   I can
think of nothing finer in the handling of light, nor in the massing
and moving of figures, than the "marriage in Cana."   More education!   The complete wedding rite, with its odd observances according to Hebrew tradition, is a transcription from Minor Asia such as
one cannot find outside the pages of Josephus.   Stirringly dramatic,

yet faithful to the letter of the gospels, is the scene in which Jesus faces those who would stone the woman taken in adultery.   There is a scene of The Christ laughing, conversing, supping, interchanging views--a man among men.   And there is the Via Dolorosa.

The modern story is, among other things and preachments, an attack upon the arrogance of "Foundations," and that tyranny of some organized charities which makes their favored more victims than beneficiaries.   In its essence, the modern tale seems to me a dull, commonplace movie melodrama.   In it Mr. Griffith seems to lose his perspective of character.   He makes commonplace types and personifications, not his usual creatures: thinking, feeling men and women.

Mae Marsh and Robert Harron portray victims of poverty, lack of education and evil surrounding.   Both are driven from the home town by strike participation.   The boy turns cadet--eventually reforms to marry Mae.   His underworld master, "The Musketeer of the Slums," frames him criminally for this desertion, and, in the language of the caption, he is "intolerated away for awhile."   In the interim, the Musketeer endeavors to "make" the boy's wife, who has lost her baby to intolerant uplifters.   In the grand encounter of Musketeer, Musketeer's girl, boy and wife, the monster is shot, the boy is blamed though the mistress did it, and the capital sentence is carried out--nearly, but not quite--in the perfect gallows-technique of San Quentin penitentiary.

Best in the modern spectacle are not the dull details of things that happen, but the lifelike performances of those to whom they happen.   Mae Marsh's flirtation in court with her husband as the jury deliberates his life away--she a scared, drab little figure of piteous noncomprehension--here is a twittering smile more tragic than the orotund despairs of Bernhardt.   Miriam Cooper, as the Musketeer's mistress, gives an overwhelming pastel of jealousy and remorse.   All actresses who honestly provide for home and baby by the business of vamping and gunning, would do well to observe Miss Cooper's expressions and gestures.   Miss Cooper is police dock--she is blotter transcript.   Her face is what you really see some nights under the green lamps.   Harron is ideal as the boy, and Walter Long, as the Musketeer, approaches but does not equal his performance of Gus, in The Birth of a Nation.

Spades are not once termed garden implements in this sector, nor are the kisses paternal or platonic.

In this stupendous chaos of history and romance the lack of a virile musical score is the chief tragedy.   Proper melody would have bound the far provinces of this loose empire of mighty imagination into a strong, central kingdom.

I wish Mr. Griffith had worked out a whole evening of his great Babylonian story.   Sticking to this alone, he would have added an art-product to literature as enduring as Flaubert's Salammbo.

If I may predict: he will never again tell a story in this
manner. Nor will anyone else. The blue sea is pretty much where
it was when the sails of the Argonauts bellied tight in the winds of a
morning world, and so are the people who live in the world. Still
we wish to follow, undisturbed, the adventures of a single set of
characters, or to thrill with a single pair of lovers. Verily, when
the game is hearts two's company, and the lovers of four ages an
awful crowd.

> --Julian Johnson in Photoplay, Vol.
> 11, No. 1 (December 1916),
> pages 77-81.

*   *   *

It is easy enough, as you catch your breath at the conclusion
of Intolerance, to indulge in trite superlatives. Film reviewing has
been over superlatived. But this new Griffith spectacle marks a
milepost in the progress of the film. It reveals something of the
future of the spectacle, something of its power to create pictures of
tremendous and sweeping beauty, drama, and imagination. The future
will come when the great writer unites with the great producer.

Intolerance, of course, instantly challenges comparison, by
reason of its creator, with The Birth of a Nation. One is the dramatization of a novel, a gripping, even thrilling visualization of a
story dealing with a theme of national interest--our own Civil War.
On the other hand, Intolerance is the screening of an idea. That
alone places it as an advance.

The Screening of an Idea

Mr. Griffith sought a theme which has traced itself through
history. He advances the proposition that humanity's lack of tolerance of opinion and speech has brought about the world's woes.
Taking four periods of history, he traces the working out of this
idea. We have, perhaps, come to assume that our own age is one
of singular meddling and busy-bodyism. But Mr. Griffith points out
that the thing has been the same through the ages.

Briefly, the periods depicted revolve around the fall of Babylon in 538 B. C., the coming of the Nazarene and the birth of the
Christian era, the massacre of St. Bartholomew's day in France
during the reign of Charles IX, and the present day. Mr. Griffith,
of course, handles his four plots at one time. The threads are
interwoven. The moments dealing with the life of Christ, it may
be noted here, are brief, being in reality rich tableaux of the persecution of the Saviour. Griffith has endeavored to humanize Christ.
These moments are handled with reverence, dignity, and beauty of
picture. Indeed, there are moments worthy of Tissot. Once, oddly,
the director attains a singular effect of a shadow cross upon the
figure of Christ.

The modern theme of Intolerance has a Western town as its locale. The owner of a factory reduces wages that he may make extended--and widely heralded--contributions to charity. A strike devastates the town and the workers are forced to move away. The boy and the girl of the story, now married in the city, still remain the playthings of intolerance. The boy is sent to prison for a crime he never committed. In his absence the baby is taken away from the mother by a charitable society. The boy, on returning, becomes innocently involved in a murder and, through his criminal record, is convicted. The story finally races to a climax when, as the execution is about to take place, the wife, aided by a kindly policeman, hurries to the governor with the confession of the real murderer. They miss the executive, who has taken a train. The policeman commandeers a racing car and they speed after the express. The execution is stopped just as the death trap is to be sprung.

Spectacle's Appeal Lies in Babylonian Story

The principal appeal of Intolerance, however, lies in the Babylonian story. Here we see Belshazzar ruling Babylon with his father, Nabonidus. He is a kindly, generous monarch--as kings in those days went--but the high priest of Bel resents his religious tolerance. So, when Cyrus, king of the Medes and Persians, attacks the walled city, the priest betrays Babylon. So the city falls, after a mighty battle such as never before had been conceived in mimicry.

Mr. Griffith has reconstructed the city of Babylon--according to authentic records and researches, we are told by the programme and we may well believe. The city, with its great walls, three hundred feet high and big enough on top for two war chariots to pass, its temples, its lofty halls, its slave marts, and its streets, lives again, seething with life. The attack upon Babylon is handled on a tremendous scale. We are shown Cyrus's camp in the desert sands. Then we see his cohorts, his barbarians from distant lands, his war chariots, his elephants, his great moving towers, advance upon Babylon. Great catapults hurl rocks upon the defenders. Moulten lead is thrown from the walls. Showers of arrows fall. One great siege tower, black with fighting men, is toppled over and goes crashing to the ground. Ladders, manned by warriors, are flung down. So the battle goes a day and a night. Treason finally gives over Babylon, in the midst of a great bacchanial feast of victory.

This theme is unfolded with Mr. Griffith's fine skill in handling hundreds and thousands of men. There is a certain personal note in the spectacle. Belshazzar, his favorite, Attarea, the boisterous little mountain girl who loves the king from afar, and the crafty priest of Bel are finely humanized. The tremendous applause at Intolerance's premiere, occasioned when Babylon first fought off the invaders, was a vital compliment to the skill of the producer.

One forgot that, with the fall of the city, fell the Semitic race, and that ever afterwards the Aryan people controlled the affairs of civilization.

Huguenot Theme Least Compelling

The final, and least compelling, theme deals with Catherine de Medici and her instigation of the massacre of the Huguenots in Paris in 1572 under the cloak of religion. The personal side of the story deals with two Huguenot lovers, victims of the cruel religious persecution. This theme has been carefully staged, in the bigness of its court interiors, the depth of its street scenes, and its handling of the ruthless massacre.

The defense of Babylon brings the first half of Intolerance to a big climax, while the last portion is largely given over to the climax of the modern plot thread. Finally, we are shown the idealistic future, with two armies racing to meet each other, only to throw down their arms and clasp hands. This is banal, of course, but Mr. Griffith intends it to weave the themes together and point to the future, when tolerance will make war and all evils impossible.

A certain symbolical note is touched by frequent, half shadowy, glimpses of a woman rocking a cradle. Mr. Griffith gives programme explanation of the symbolism: "Through all these ages Time brings forth the same passions, the same joys and sorrows, the same hopes and anxieties--symbolized by the cradle 'endlessly rocking.'"

The Construction of the Four Plot Threads

Intolerance, let us sum up once more, stands at the outpost of the cinema's advance. It has an idea. It has a purpose. From a structural standpoint, the handling and weaving of four plots are revolutionary. There is never a moment's lack of clarity. Each story sweeps to its climax. Since the interest is divided, it would be reasonable to assume that the dramatic interest might, too, be divided. But the grip of Intolerance, to our way of thinking, surpasses The Birth of a Nation. Power, punch, and real thrills are there--thrills to equal the preceding Griffith spectacle. Its themes are overtopped by spectacular trappings, dwarfing them in a measure. The modern story, in its melodramatic present dayedness, seems a bit below the key of the historical divisions. It is lurid, even conventional, in its final working out. But, in its early moments, it points a caustic finger upon certain phases of modern charity, particularly upon the salaried uplifter. And it is the one vigorous story of the spectacle.

Griffith makes his point in Intolerance. There are obvious moments, moments a bit overdone, lapses to banality, but, on the whole, Intolerance is a mighty thing. Its spectacular appeal is certain.

The musical arrangement of Joseph Carl Breil has impressive moments. There is no strain, however, to equal the barbaric African theme, which ran through The Birth of a Nation.

The production has been awaited for new methods of plot handling and production. The mingling of four themes of different periods, told in parallel form, has not been tried before. It was a daring experiment. The method of blending the plots, switching from one to the other, is adroitly done. It will have its effect upon coming productions.

The Production

The spectacle, a number of times reveals close-ups of characters' faces which occupy the whole screen. Sometimes these advance in the camera eye to full screen size. It is an effective way of driving home the dramatic mood of the scene.

We find Griffith making his usual frequent and effective use of detail, as in the flashes of the doves in the shadows of the house as Christ passes, the close-ups of the Hebrews in the Judean streets, the page boy half asleep in French court, and the modern girl tending her pitiful little geranium in her tenement room.

Skillful use is made of camera tricks in handling the seeming hurling of soldiers from the Babylonian walls. We apparently see them strike the ground in front of the camera.

Care has been taken with the sub-titles. The bombastic captions of The Birth of a Nation are absent. Some humor and much historical information are to be found in the sub-captions of Intolerance.

The camera work everywhere is beautifully artistic. We recall, for instance, nothing in screen production more striking than the episode of Christ and the woman taken in adultery.

Cast of Intolerance Long and Able

The cast of principals is long and able. Mae Marsh stands pre-eminent for her touching playing of the girl of the modern story. Seena Owen makes a striking and unforgettable figure as Attarea, the favorite of Belshazzar. She lends genuine appeal to the picturesque role. Constance Talmadge gives buoyancy and spirit to the mountain girl. Miriam Cooper sounds a certain poignant note as a modern girl wrecked on the wheel of sordid city life. Margery Wilson has opportunity to reveal little more than prettiness as the Huguenot heroine.

Robert Harron makes the most of his role of the boy of the modern story, almost a victim on the altar of modern intolerance.

Alfred Paget's playing of Belshazzar has nobility and humanness. Tully Marshall makes the High Priest of Bel sinister and clean cut.

There are scores of slender roles well done. Prominent among these is the huge faithful warrior of Elmo Lincoln, who dies fighting for his king against hopeless odds. The kindly policeman of the modern story, done by Tom Wilson, stands out. Louis Romaine gives realism to the prison chaplain.

All in all, Intolerance is a stupendous production. It has the romance of four civilizations.

> --Frederick James Smith in The New York Dramatic Mirror, Vol. 76, No. 1969 (September 16, 1916), page 22.

☐ THE ITALIAN (Ince/Paramount, 1915)

In the character of Beppo Donetti, George Beban gives a masterly example of what an actor who is alive to his role and can feel his part, can do in the way of holding an audience in sustained tension.

By facial expression and the natural gestures with the hands he is capable of depicting so many different phases, so many different emotions, that though the action is only on the screen, we wonder why it is said that the screen has its limitations. It is nothing less than wonderful.

Coupled with good clear photography, well-chosen interior settings, and a few startling innovations, such as hanging on the running-board of a rapidly-moving automobile, being thrown off by a kick in the face, and so on, the acting of Beban makes a rather pleasing and interesting production out of a story whose plot is nothing out of the ordinary.

The story of the immigrant toiling in a foreign land to earn enough to bring his prospective bride to his side from their native land, and their subsequent struggles to subsist on the barest living wage, has been used over and over again.

But with the help of about 1,500 feet of film devoted to scenes in the native Italy, and the introduction of the political boss in the city of the land of the free, a rather novel twist is given to the story, and it is made a better one than the average.

On his release from prison, where he has been sent for trying to get milk for his dying child, Beppo learns of the girl's death and holds the political boss indirectly responsible. Remembering past favors rendered by him to the boss, he had expected help from that quarter only to be literally thrown in the gutter.

Learning of the illness of the boss' baby, a few days later Beppo, by impersonating a peddler, secures entrance to the house. He hears the doctor tell the father that the slightest sound or shock will prove fatal to the child, and when the child is left alone for a moment, Beppo attains the side of the crib. Raising aloft the glass shade of a lamp, he is about to dash it to the floor, when a slight movement of the child's arm brings to mind that his own child was wont to make the same gesture. Gently lowering the shade, Beppo steals away.

Altogether the scenes in the last thousand feet are heart-rending, and the pathos as expressed on the face of Beppo and his wife, Annette (Clara Williams) is enough to move the average audience to tears. The story interests, is well told, and it should be well received by any appreciative audience.

--H. S. Fuld in <u>Motion Picture
News</u>, Vol. 10, No. 26 (January
2, 1915), page 81.

☐ JOAN THE WOMAN (DeMille-Lasky/Cardinal, 1916)

Occupants of thrones are generally less interesting than the gentlemen or ladies behind them; Joan, the clair-audient wool-grower of Orleans, is merely the figurehead of a great spectacular enterprise behind which moves one Cecil DeMille, a sun-painter who makes her embattled, renowned, and eventually a steak at a stake. Which is to say that Geraldine Farrar, in Joan the Woman is not the whole show, as she was in Carmen. Carmen was the peculiar personal medium of this cosmopolitan witch. Joan the Woman is an historic materialization in which she plays a leading part with characteristic energy and effect, but which, as a spectacular photoplay, is no more dependent upon the substantial prima-donna than upon any of its other leading principals. Edith Storey, for instance, would have recreated Arc's fanatic virgin to much the same effect-- perhaps with even greater exaltation.

Though it is not faultless, Joan the Woman is the best sun-spectacle since The Birth of a Nation, and in the opinion of the writer only that sweeping review of arms and hearts has excelled it. The Birth of a Nation trumps all the picture spectacles yet made for its insistent humanity; its irresistible combination of power and simplicity, tempest and tenderness. Mechanically as well as photographically Joan equals but does not surpass Civilization, that photographic and mechanic milestone of flivver story; in legend and development of dramatic interest it would be absurd to mention Civilization in this connection. Mr. Griffith's radiant crazy-quilt, Intolerance, is also put by.

Miss Jeanie MacPherson is credited with the book of this opera for the eyes. She begins with Eric Trent, of the English expeditionary force in Northern France. Trent is in a trench at night,

and, finding a projecting bit of rusty iron, pulls and digs until he
has extracted the remnant of a sword of the period of Charles VII.
In his vision, as he sleeps, Joan appears. The story of the shepherdess begins.

Trent in a previous incarnation was of the English who occupied Burgundy. France lies in anemic disarray before a powerful
invader and behind a wretched king. Trent is of a pillaging foray
who drive the laggard soldiery of Charles from town and field.
Joan, the farmer's daughter, he regards as his special prize, but
Joan's purity has purity's frequent way: it disarms the conqueror,
turning his lust to love. Traitorously wounded by a Frenchman, he
is nursed back to health in a hayloft by the maid.

But the romance comes to no fulfillment. When Trent's
youthful blood is again coursing healthily, Joan is hearing things.
Her day of romance and dream is over. Mailed Anglo-Saxon hands
are beating down the traditions and the hopes of France, and, willy-
nilly, the militant shepherdess gets to the court of the clownish
monarch, still without a sceptre. The same fury that sped her
from hovel to hall puts her at the head of the army, despite the opposition of La Tremouille, silken spider of England in the court of
Charles. The mercenaries are vanquished, sieges are raised, English generals retire precipitately, French blood leaps and boils as
it always does when Gaul is endangered. At length united France,
with shout and paean, repair to Rheims' immemorial pile, and the
crown is pushed down on the narrow forehead of Charles with exu-
berant sanctity.

Bishop Cauchon, a ward-heeler of the church, spy of London
and general minority leader, has no part in the new and exultant
order. A creature of La Tremouille, it is his task to rid the land
of its girl David, or decline from luxury to actual clerical labor--
perhaps to the block or the assassin's thrust. The ready resort of
the day is superstition. People who take no baths are apt to believe anything, and the commentators of custom assure us that folk
of that day were suspicious as they were encrusted. In politics, too,
it is hail today and hell tomorrow, and Joan was in arch-politics.
Obtaining her from her English captor--Trent, her one-time lover,
betrayed her--Cauchon has little difficulty in indicting as a witch
one who received her ideals of leadership in trances. The canonical
trial is characteristically absurd and blasphemous. Charles keeps
his hand out through belief that Joan aspired to overthrow him.

Nevertheless, Joan holds to her faith and protests her innocence. The red fires of the inquisitor shake her body into submission; her flesh, not her soul, consents; she signs what she is asked
to sign. She is a witch, by her own confession--a traitor, a schem-
er, an agitator. The last chapter is staged in a square, and in a
pillar of fire Joan's soul goes to heaven, while the repentant Trent
and even the malicious monk who served Cauchon plead her forgive-
ness--as Cauchon himself, shaken by the horridity of her burning,
stumbles hastily from his ringside seat.

Trent, in the modern trenches, awakens. He is chosen from a number of other volunteers to bomb a Teuton salient before attack. His hazard is successful, but he stops a German bullet, and before he dies Joan again comes to him; in this Englishman's death for France he has expiated his sin of the centuries against her.

In the welter of magnificent impersonations let us seize upon the Charles VII of Raymond Hatton as a sterling example. Here is a screen-made actor whose study possesses the finest subtleties, the most adroit effects, absolute verity to human nature. It is an old saying that great parts make great actors, but of all flip quips, this is the most histrionically unjust. Charles VII is a great part, but in all the range of photographic and speaking performances I can think of no one who would--to me, at least--put this characterization across so thoroughly. The petulance and the weakness and the vanity of Charles, Hatton manages to express without a single bodily movement. His face is at once a drama and a novel. He has such fine bits of business; for instance, the scene after the palace revel in which he thrusts merely the tips of his fingers, absentmindedly, down the back of a drunken woman's dress to caress her shoulder. Here, without lewdness, is the complete expression of an orgy!

Those who object to Miss Farrar's Joan because she is rising to battle-cruiser weight had best turn to their histories. Joan is described as broad, short, heavy. But Joan had a peasant's face, placid except for wonderful eyes. One of Farrar's eyes reflects Riverside Drive, the other, Fifth Avenue, and her mouth seems to be saying "Broadway." This is perhaps quibbling, but the prima-donna's Joan is a bit too sophisticated in appearance. In Carmen she was Carmen; in Joan the Woman she is an accomplished and clever actress, possessed of enormous physical valor, dramatic re-source in gesture which is at moments thrilling, and great personal appeal. Her appetite for punishment and abuse has been paralleled only by the heroisms of Mabel Normand when Keystone prolapsed to dress suits and stellar names.

Theodore Roberts as Cauchon makes the churchly devil of the Middle Ages a grim reality. Hobart Bosworth plays the common soldier Le Hire--and makes of him a grand figure, figuratively as well as literally the plumed knight of the play. Charles Clary as the icy Tremouille is very fine; Tully Marshall as the wicked monk is a graphic figure; James Neill has a human bit. The whole inter-pretative resource of Laskyville has been deftly drawn upon.

To me, the great moment of Joan the Woman was the episode in Charles' shabby court where Joan pleads for soldiers to save France. As she talks the dim and shadowy figures of great knights in armor, on battle-chargers which would have upborne the Norse gods, plunge over them all, through the hall. This is more than double photography; it is handling a camera as Michelangelo handled his chisel--it is Michelangeloing the sunshine. This is the first time that the psychic force of active photography has been turned on an audience along lines fully demonstrated by the late Hugo Munster-berg--and completely neglected by all directors.

The material side of the picture is splendidly taken care of.
The reduction of a feudal fortress, the sweep of a great field of
knights to the charge are big incidents.   The flash to mouth of a
hundred brass trumpets, the glitter of five times as many pennanted
lances, the arching of what seem a thousand great swords demonstrate overwhelmingly the drama of arms in the mailed centuries.

William Furst's musical score is a pleasant one, and while
it rises to no particular merit, it never angers by its complete in-
efficiency--as does the Intolerance orchestration.   Those who criticise Mr. Furst for his large use of the "Marseillaise" on the ground
that it was not composed until hundreds of years after the winds had
scattered Joan's ashes, have no imagination.   The "Marseillaise" is
not a localized tune; it is a melodic expression of the spirit of
France.

Mr. DeMille has not Mr. Griffith's almost demoniac faculty
of making even an extra do in a picture just what he would do in
life.   Joan the Woman could stand a bit more humanity here and
there.   Nevertheless, it is a big and splendid thing.

--Julian Johnson in Photoplay, Vol.
11, No. 4 (March 1917), pages
113-116.

☐ JOHN BARLEYCORN (Bosworth, 1914)

When it comes to delineating the struggles of the soul Jack
London writes with an X-ray concealed in his pen.   The psychological
details of the ancient fight between Reason in Man and The Evil Spirit
in Alcohol have never been portrayed with greater pathos and with
greater truthfulness than in his famous story of John Barleycorn.
All the stages of the struggle from aversion and reluctance to half-
hearted acceptance and to final slavery are described with unrivaled
fidelity to truth and fact.

That such a story has lost nothing in its convincing power
when told on the screen will easily be believed.   The settings are
with perhaps two or three exceptions taken from Nature directly.
This is one of the greatest charms of this feature.   The tale is one
of the sea in great measure, and we can almost smell the salt air
and hear the murmurs of the waves--so much is there of realistic
atmosphere all through the six parts.   The underworld of sea-faring
men is brought before us in most faithful depiction; not always a
pleasant spectacle by any means, but well justified by the scope of
the story, which aims to show the dehumanizing effects of strong
drink on the frame and the soul of man.   I cannot bestow enough
praise on the selection of the types; even in these improved days we
rarely see such fine and subtle characterization.   Such figures as
"Scratch Nelson, " or as the old saloonkeeper or the parents of the
man who struggles with John Barleycorn or the old colored nurse are

absolutely convincing. The same fine characterization, no doubt in
large measure the result of thoughtful and painstaking direction, will
be found in every one of the minor parts in the films.

The leading part was taken by Elmer Clifton. His was no
easy task, but he proved fully equal to what was asked of him. He
enlists our sympathy from the first and skillfully sustains and stim-
ulates it, ending with a strong and impressive climax. The work
of the children, notably that of little Matty Roubert, was faultless.
Viola Barry was a trifle cold and seemed to lack sympathy.

John Barleycorn is not a drama, unless we choose to see a
drama in the lonely heart struggle of the individual. John Barleycorn is a biography, roughly and somewhat loosely scattered through
the leaves of a diary. It is a record of personal experiences, profoundly interesting and pathetic, but lacking dramatic construction
and not overrich in dramatic elements. It is the most powerful
moral lesson ever conveyed in films. Viewed as a graphic description it cannot be blamed for a certain diffuseness and a most minute
elaboration of details. In the drama proper such diffuseness and
such protracted lingering over details would be inexcusable.

Of Mr. Bosworth and his superb head and figure we get but
a fleeting glimpse in the last scene, more's the pity.

The photography shows the advantages of the California light.
These advantages, however, are sometimes balanced by the difficulty
in handling such rich light.

> --W. Stephen Bush in The Moving
> Picture World, Vol. 21, No. 3
> (July 18, 1914), page 406.

☐ JUBILO (Goldwyn, 1919)

In one of the most charming photoplays we have seen in a
long time Will Rogers thoroughly establishes himself as a screen
star of the first magnitude. This picture just naturally reaches out
and takes hold of your heart strings. And it keeps you enchanted
to the very end. A well balanced cast of perfect types artistically
portray the various roles.

The story is a simple one of humor and pathos. In spite of
the train robbery, the shooting, and two rattling good fights, it could
never be truthfully branded a melodrama. The suspense, the quaint
characterization of the roving hobo, the neat little love element, the
clever sub-titles, all contribute in planting the strong sympathetic
appeal in this picture.

A hobo asks a rancher for a meal and is told he must work
for it. After seeing the pretty daughter making an appetizing pie he

voluntarily breaks the habit of a lifetime and performs his first
manual labor.   And he stays on the job and becomes a producer
until the rancher is safely out of his difficulties, and then marries
the girl.   It sounds simple, and it is simple, --but it's great.   Direction and continuity are above par.

                                        --Tom Hamlin in Motion Picture
                                          News, Vol. 20, No. 26 (Decem-
                                          ber 20, 1919), page 4529.

☐ JUDITH OF BETHULIA (American Biograph, 1914)

        It is not easy to confess one's self unequal to a given task,
but to pen an adequate description of the Biograph's production of
Judith of Bethulia is, to say the least, a full grown man's job.   It
is in four-and-a-half reels, founded of course upon the biblical tale,
with the captions probably culled from the poem of Thomas Bailey
Aldrich.   A curious point of coincidence is that the picture should
be first shown in New York at the Fifth Avenue Theatre where Lawrence Marsden, * who staged it, for a long time held forth as stage
director for the once famous Fifth Avenue dramatic stock company.
Nothing that Marsden has done for the stage in the past, either as
playwright or producer, entitles him to the praise that rightfully is
his by virtue of his work in putting before the moving picture world
Judith of Bethulia as a genuine masterpiece of craftsmanship.   In
spite of the undoubtedly vast sum expended for architectural and other
"props" to conform to the period in which the story is laid, Marsden
did not deem it necessary to recruit a cast of star players with
names illustrious in the legitimate dramatic world.   It is to his
credit he succeeded in utilizing the services of competent ones in
the regular Biograph company.   For the name part he selected
Blanche Sweet; Henry Walthall for Holofernes; Robert Harron for
Nathan; J. Jiquel Lanoe for the Chief Eunuch; Harry Carey for the
traitor and so on.   There are really but two parts that stand out--
Judith far beyond all the others, with Holofernes a safe second.   Fine
as is the acting of the principals, the chief thing to commend is the
totally wonderful handling of the mobs and the seriousness with which
each super performed his individual task.   Among them must have
been planted a number of acrobats and horsemen.   No ordinary moving picture super could have done the things depicted in the hand-to-
hand battles that were shown.   And the marvellous lighting effects!
And the general detail!   Really you must see it all for yourself in
order to get any comprehensive idea of the presentment.   The
strength of the heart interest comes with Judith's vision and her
determination to sacrifice herself to Holofernes, if necessary, to
save her people from starvation.   From that moment her facial ex-

---

*It is perhaps an indication of D.W. Griffith's lack of importance
that Variety should persist in identifying the director of Judith of
Bethulia as Lawrence Marsden.

pression is an inspired piece of pantomime. "Hear me and I will
do a thing which shall go through all generations." She clothes herself in sackcloth and ashes and while scorifying herself her face is
streaked with tears.   Then she attires herself alluringly and goes
forth to captivate Holofernes with her beauty of face and figure.
"And his heart was ravished"--"Then Judith wrestled with her heart
for Holofernes now seemed noble in her eyes." This facial transi-
tion is worthy of Bernhardt.   Again "She struggled to cast away the
sinful passion." Eventually Holofernes sends for her to come before him and she lures him on.   He pleads with her: "Let me be
thy hand-maid alone for tonight" and she lures him on, playfully,
all the time plying him with drink, until he falls on the couch in a
drunken stupor.   When helpless her impulse is to decapitate him
and she takes up his sword.   Wavering between passion for the man
and duty to her people is magnificently depicted pantomimically.
Comes a vision of her people perishing from hunger and thirst and
the famous historical beheading is done, followed by the carrying of
the head to her people and their eventual victory over the Assyrian
army.   The whole thing is simply "magniloquent." It sounds almost sacrilegious to mention anything that might be construed as a
flaw, but dear old Larry Marsden, why was Mr. Harron, who played
Nathan, permitted to sport a modern moustache?   Forgive the inter-
rogation, please.

> --Jolo (Joshua Lowe) in Variety, Vol.
> 34, No. 4 (March 27, 1914), p. 20.

*   *   *

   A fascinating work of high artistry, Judith of Bethulia, will
not only rank as an achievement in this country, but will make foreign producers sit up and take notice.   It has a signal and imperative message, and the technique displayed throughout an infinity of
detail, embracing even the delicate film tinting and toning, marks
an encouraging step in the development of the new art.   Ancient in
story and settings, it is modern in penetrative interpretation--it is
a vivid history of one phase of the time it concerns, and is redemp-
tive as well as revelative, a lesson from one of those vital struggles that made and unmade nations as well as individuals, yet it is
not without that inspiring influence that appeals powerfully to human
sense of justice.

   The entire vigorous action of the play works up to the personal sacrifice of Judith of Bethulia, a perilous chance she takes
for the sake of the lives and happiness of her people.   She dares
expose herself to overwhelming humiliation and dishonor in a challenge of beauty to strength, struggles through a conversion of sentiment that makes the high crisis more acute, and sets at defiance the
"better-death-than-dishonor" platitude, escaping both through that all-
conquering combination in a woman, great physical beauty joined to
lofty intelligence.   She enters upon a relation of constant peril--only
delicate treatment saves the situation at times--abandons her native
purity of conduct and dares her own undoing, yet the noble end justifies the dangerous means and she emerges idealized by her people,
an apotheosis of splendid womanhood.

Bethulia is a fortified town of Judea, guarding a hill pass
through which an invading Assyrian army must march in order to
enter Judea.   In the town lives Judith, a devout young woman of
lofty character and remarkable beauty, when the place is stormed
by Holofernes at the head of a large army.   The fighting before the
gate brings into action an enormous number of soldiers on both
sides, and those engines of war, such as the battering ram and
catapult, which were used by the fighting male of other days under
close conditions of furious combat.   One desperate assault after
another is repelled, scaling ladders are thrown down, great rocks
are showered upon the invaders, and the wonder is that they keep
at it.   The reason is that Holofernes has a way of torturing and
killing unsuccessful captains.   An officer had better die in the thick
of battle than return with a confession of defeat.   Holofernes is as
merciless as nature to all who fail.

The great leader's brutality to his captains when they do not
succeed in carrying the fortress by storm indicates what the inhabitants of Bethulia may expect in the event of capture and serves to
intensify the clash of character later on--it adds peril to the undertaking of Judith when she resolves to sacrifice herself for her people.   Holofernes, after making a horrible example of defeated captains by frightful torture, resorts to strategy.   His soldiers have
seized the wells from which the inhabitants of Bethulia obtained their
water supply, and their leader adopts waiting tactics, diverting himself with dancing girls to break the tedium.   Bethulia is on the verge
of famine, and the besieged are almost ready to surrender the fortress and all Judea to the spoilers, when Judith goes forth in her
finest raiment, accompanied only by her maid, enters the Assyrian
camp and obtains an interview with the merciless Holofernes.
Against his formidable strength, his brutal ferocity and cunning, his
absolute power, are matched her fascinating personality directed by
intelligence and hidden purpose.   She is willing to carry "her fault
on her shoulders like a coronation mantle."

The dangerous and difficult situation from this point to Judith's
terrible triumph and the defeat of the invading Assyrians is pictured
without loss of force or charm by extreme delicacy of treatment.
Beauty is constantly asserted by almost reckless prodigality in the
matter of costume, and by the appeal of delightful acting.   The feminine sweetness and shyness of the lovely Judith are intensified by
her advances and retreats in measuring her sex attractions against
his formidable power.   She is weakened at the critical moment by
a sudden flame of passion and compassion aroused in her breast,
but self-control returns at a thought of all that is at stake, the safety
and happiness of thousands of her people, and she dares be all and do
all that revolts her finer nature from a deep hatred of injustice and
wrong meted out to her peace-loving kindred and friends, from a noble
desire to preserve her country and the destinies of her race.

--Louis Reeves Harrison in The
Moving Picture World, Vol. 19,
No. 10 (March 7, 1914), page
1242.

☐   THE JUGGERNAUT (Vitagraph/V-L-S-E, 1915)

One of the biggest sensations ever offered in pictures is to
be found in The Juggernaut, a five-reel Vitagraph feature released
under the Vitagraph-Lubin-Selig-Essanay banner.   Photographed in
such a way as to make one feel that he is at one end of a high
trestle, the spectator sees rushing towards him a passenger train,
made up of an engine and three coaches.   Just as it reaches the
middle of the trestle the rotted ties give way, plunging engine, cars
and passengers into the river below.

From the time that the train becomes an important factor in
the story until it reaches the wooden span the suspense, by means
of close-ups and flash-backs, is worked up to the point where a
person attempts to conjecture just what is going to happen to the
speeding train when it reaches that weak spot in the trestle--or if,
after all, the man hurrying to get to the bridge to flag the train,
will make it in time.   Good judgment is used here in cutting the
picture, so that the anxiety thus aroused does not change to impa-
tience or become irksome.

This thrill forms the core of a perfectly good, sound story.
The latter without the train wreck would be a forceful, attractive
drama.   It has an excellent cast, and has as its background artistic
interior settings and well-chosen outdoor locations.   Character portrayal and the atmosphere suggested by the environment count for a
good deal in the filming, as the action in the main part of the story
transpires twenty years after its beginning and in much different
surroundings.

William Dunn's characterization of the railroad magnate,
Philip Hardin, stands out as a strong example of the type of man
whom the author must have had in mind in writing the theme.   Earle
Williams makes an impressive district attorney as John Ballard, and
Anita Stewart gives charm and personality to the roles of the rail-
road president's wife, Viola Ruskin, and Anita, his daughter.   Julia
Swayne Gordon, Paul Scardon, Frank Currier, Eulalie Jensen and
Jack Brawn complete the cast.

Briefly, the story deals with the relations between John Ballard and Philip Hardin.   First, they are enemies at college, then
chums, later rivals for the hand of Viola Ruskin, and after gradua-
tion and Philip's marriage to Viola, they part friends; Ballard, following his pursuit of law, and Philip, taking up his father's work,
railroading.

Twenty years later they are brought together again.   Viola is
now dead, and her daughter, Anita, is an attractive girl of eighteen.
District Attorney Ballard begs railroad president Hardin to lessen
the cost of life on his road by having its deficiencies properly attended to.   Hardin refuses, and Ballard leaves, threatening to prosecute him.   The night before the day which Ballard has set for the
exposé, the district attorney receives a visit from Hardin, who

reminds him of a murder committed back in their college days of
which Ballard believes himself guilty.

The district attorney postpones his prosecution.   The next day
a train on Hardin's road plunges through a faulty trestle into a river.
Hardin's daughter is one of the passengers.   The railroad president
witnesses the accident, and dies of heart failure on the river bank.
Ballard, who has since learned that the man whom he thought he had
killed at college in protecting Philip was merely stunned, attempts
to rescue Anita, but she dies before he can pick her out of the de-
bris.

--Charles R. Condon in Motography, Vol. 13, No. 19 (May 8,
1915), pages 745-746.

☐ THE JUNGLE (All-Star Feature Corporation, 1914)

A somewhat daring and powerful story is exploited before the
general public, particularly at the psychological moment when the
author is so active in the socialistic field (see daily newspapers).
Nothing has been spared by the producing company in the way of
cost in this picturization to make it equal to the novel itself, or to
the dramatic version which was so universally popular at the time
of its production.

Owing to the fact that The Jungle enjoys a world-wide recognition and has been read by the majority of humanity, a description
of the plot seems to be almost superfluous.   The novel enjoys the
unprecedented distinction of having been translated and printed in
seventeen different languages, in each of which it had a record sale.

To overcome the decided opposition of those interested in the
packing business, so vividly described in the book, many difficulties
and obstacles were encountered.   The producers were compelled to
purchase machinery, install it in their own studios and lease stock-
yards, etc., to get the true atmosphere.   The All-Star Feature Corporation secured an exceptionally strong cast to depict the story,
composed of prominent Broadway players.   George Nash, star of
The Gamblers, Officer 666 and Panthea has the powerful role of
Jurgis, the head of an immigrant family, a part which seems to
have been created for him.   Miss Gail Kane, of Seven Keys to Baldpate reputation, essays the part of Ona, his sweetheart in Lithuria,
and later his wife in America.   Incidentally, Mr. Nash and Miss
Kane will co-star the coming season in the New York production of
The Miracle Man.   Among the supporting company of The Jungle appear such well-known people as Robert Cumming, Clarence Handy-
side, R. Payton Gibbs, Maxine Hodges, Alice Marc, Julia Hurley,
May McCabe, Ernest Evers, and Nickelas Sinnerella.

All the salient points of the story have been distinctly and

cleverly portrayed. The vivid distinction shown between the employer and the employed and the wide and bridgeless chasm that
yawns beneath the selfish and arrogant rich and the dependent poor
contains much that is of human interest.

The careless and unsanitary methods utilized in the manufacture of canned meats which are sold to the public, is clearly
demonstrated and, if true, are diabolical and criminal. The plot
is very simple to demonstrate so much, and could be easily followed
and understood without sub-titles. The vicissitudes encountered by
the struggling immigrant family for a mere existence, beset by persecution and disparagements at all angles, is but an illustration of
numberless others in the same condition. Many gripping scenes obtain, especially where Jurgis, after a desperate struggle, flings the
foreman into the cattle run of the stock yard. The mob scenes during the strike against a reduction of 20 per cent. in wages, ordered
by the packing house magnate, on account of the extravagance of his
family, are cleverly directed and extremely realistic.

Mr. Sinclair, the author, appears in the cast in the last
reel and is easily recognized. The finale of the story is gratifying.
Taken as a whole, the picture contains much that is wholesome.
The photography is excellent, and the acting and direction are above
criticism.

The Jungle has drawn and pleased capacity houses at the De
Kalb Theater, Brooklyn, the past week and can be seen in a Broadway theater in New York City this week when Upton Sinclair, the
author, will appear in person at each performance.
                                        --H. W. De Long in The Moving
                                        Picture World, Vol. 20, No. 12
                                        (June 20, 1914), page 1675.

☐ JUST PALS (Fox, 1920)

Buck Jones' last three or four pictures preceding this one
have been just one shoot-'em-up Western after another. He has
made good in them because he rode, fought, and protected the
abused lady in the case in fine fashion, and now he should do just
as well in a story of a widely different type. Just Pals is a human,
interesting and appealing story, with interpolations of good audience
incidents, and flavored with a bit of romance and, in the end, with
action that suggests his former pictures.

The star has new responsibilities in Just Pals, for he is
cast as the village good-for-nothing. Deprived of his guns, his
bucking broncho and a villain to pommel, he is called upon to act,
and he does it. Sharing his responsibility is little Duke Lee, who
plays "Bill," the little ragamuffin who becomes the pal of the good-
for-nothing. Together they "bum" about the little village until the

pretty school teacher, with whom the star is in love, demands that
"Bill" attend school. The youngster defends the good name of
"Bim" (the star) with his fists. "They said you were not fit to live
with pigs," he explains. "But, gosh, I said you were!"

There is a succession of good incident, some of it really
human and humorous, and some of it strained. The latter is the case
when "Bim" is so kind-hearted that he cannot bear to kill some
poultry to earn a meal. Melodrama develops when the school teacher loses the town's money entrusted to her care, and "Bim" brings
it back, taking the blame for its disappearance. He is driven out
of town, but returns to thwart a gang of robbers who are pillaging
the express office. Again, because of his bad name, he is accused
of the robbery and is about to be lynched when his little pal saves
him. The story becomes just a bit complicated in the end, with the
introduction of another kidnapped child and the collection of the reward by the star for his recovery.

But it is the human touches, both of comedy and pathos; the
well created atmosphere of the small Montana town; the very natural
dialogue; and the picturesque character of "Bim," that will win favor
for this picture. It is well directed throughout. Helen Ferguson is
the leading lady.

--Matthew A. Taylor in Motion
Picture News, Vol. 22, No. 23
(November 27, 1920), page 4163.

☐ THE KAISER, THE BEAST OF BERLIN (Renowned Pictures Corporation, 1918)

Rupert Julian and E. J. Clawson have welded together a series
of dramatic episodes from the life of the Kaiser in an offering of
seven reels, which have all the fascination of a narrative. There is
no definite plot, except that the events in stricken Belgium center
about a blacksmith and his family. The main intent of the producers, and they have adhered to it admirably, was to give the observer a look at the private and public life of this human monster whose
vanity and arrogance led him to undertake to dominate the entire
world.

The undertaking was a gigantic one, and has been carried out
with a surprising degree of success considering how close we at this
time are to the actual events drawn upon. Such a picture will not
only bring the situation confronting the world home to spectators of
the present time, when we are still fighting to put down Hohenzoll-
lern pretensions, but will be of value and, we think, increasing interest to future generations.

Mr. Julian's personal delineation of the Kaiser is a splendid
bit of acting all told. It reflects the tremendous vanity and arro-

gance of the monarch, his cruel, bloodless methods, his utter lack
of human sentiment, and his ruthless disregard of everything save
military prestige.   Mr. Julian not only succeeds in looking the part,
but he acts it intelligently and with conviction.   The study is based
on historical facts and incidents, with some recourse to dramatic
license, and the authors have been wise in their choice of "high
lights" in the career of this despicable ruler.   The picture is one
that will intensify the hatred of right-minded people for Hohenzoller-
nism.

There are any number of bold and vigorous characterizations
in the piece.   Most of them will strike only an interesting average
of merit, but several of them stand out in the memory.   Among the
latter are N. De Brullier as Captain Von Neigle, whom the Kaiser
decorates for sinking the Lusitania; Lon Chaney as Admiral Von
Tirpitz, Harry Carter as General Von Gluck, Harry Von Mater as
Captain Von Hancke, Joseph Girard as Ambassador Gerard, H. Bar-
rows as General Pershing, and Harry Holden as General Joffre.
Credit must also be extended in full measure to Elmo Lincoln, whose
Marcas, the blacksmith, is a gigantic and dominating figure in the
scenes following the destruction of Louvain.

The pastoral scenes in Belgium at the beginning are beautiful,
and furnish a strong contrast with what is to follow.   The scenes at
the German court, picturing the Kaiser, surrounded by his men of
"blood and iron," have every appearance of actuality.   The episode
of the young German captain who lost his life for striking and knock-
ing down the Kaiser is dramatically staged.

The picture closes with the advent of America into the war,
and shows the Allied forces entering and taking Berlin.   The Kaiser,
now haunted by his own guilty soul, is pictured as a life prisoner
turned over to King Albert of Belgium for safe keeping.   In the absence of a real ending for the Kaiser based upon actual facts this
close has a satisfactory ironical touch.

The women of the cast all appear in the Belgium scenes, and
include Ruth Clifford, Betty Carpenter, Ruby Lafayette, Gretchen
Lederer, and Zoe Rae.
                              --Robert C. McElravy in The Mov-
                              ing Picture World, Vol. 35, No.
                              12 (March 23, 1918), page 1704.

                        *   *   *

The Kaiser is less a photoplay than a dramatic presentation
of the crimes of Germany dominated by the Satanic sneer of her
leader.   It shows the invasion of Belgium, the wreck of the Lusitania and the attempted drive toward Paris all guided by a fiend in
a royal helmet and spiked moustache who does everything but snort
fire.   Rupert Julian impersonates this master-villain so successfully
that his entrance is greeted with spontaneous hisses.
                              --Photoplay, Vol. 14, No. 1 (June
                              1918), page 94.

☐ THE KERRY GOW (Kalem, 1912)

          The Kerry Gow, that romantic--should we say stirring--melo-
drama, rife with the jovial Irish spirit and Irish humor, that was
played on many stages in the dim past, has been made the theme of
the recent, three-reel special Kalem release. The company has
done admirably. Past experience in witnessing efforts on the part
of other companies to bring to the screen either books or plays has
convinced us that it is one of the most difficult of tasks--a task that
is usually rewarded with a flat product. This reviewer has often
seen the play and enjoyed it as one could enjoy at one time the ancient melodrama, and he is willing to assert that the present dramatization for the screen is equal in every respect, in a comparative
way, to the original. There are numerous characters, and, of
course, the spectator is expected to be alert, if he desires to grasp
the premises and fasten the characters and their relation to the action in his mind. There was only one difficulty to meet in this respect, and that was in discovering who Dan's brother is. Without
any introduction, he is brought into the picture just prior to his
contemplation of entering his horse in the Derby race. There is
the old father, the heroine, his daughter, the hero, and the final
victory of "our good people" in the play and the subjection of the
"bad man." As an added feature--one that we do not have in the
play--we are shown a genuine Derby race wherein the horse wins
that saves the old father's farm, and we must not forget the scene,
famous in the play, of the carrier pigeons. The director, Sidney
Olcott, has manipulated this in a realistic way. It is all a rare
bit of Irish drama that will undoubtedly spring into favor.
                              --G. in The New York Dramatic
                                Mirror, Vol. 68, No. 1771 (No-
                                vember 27, 1912), page 28.

☐ KISMET (Robertson-Cole, 1920)

          The long heralded production of Kismet, with Otis Skinner
making his screen debut in what is considered his greatest role,
certainly lives up to one's expectations. This play by Edward Knob-
lock which visualizes Bagdad of a thousand and one years ago offered
picture possibilities through its rich backgrounds, its array of colorful characters, its genuinely dramatic conflict and its compelling action which rises with a crescendo through bizarre and intimate
scenes, and these possibilities have been fully realized through a
perfect adaptation and direction marked for its atmosphere and de-
tail--values which truly transport the spectator and make him feel
an actual participant.

          The play depicts a single day's adventure in the hectic life of
Hajj, the beggar, one of the most vivid and interesting characters
ever presented on screen and stage. Certainly Skinner gives it life

through a perfect adaptability which combined with his superb skill
at pantomime makes the part stand out like a cameo--one of the
richest portrayals that ever graced the silver sheet. He should continue to lend his personality to a screen which is in need of an artist of his capabilities. And his assistants have caught some of his
magnetism, so enthusiastically do they play their parts.

Kismet offers a complicated story of Oriental cunning and intrigue, but one which is easily followed because of the clearly defined characterization. Hajj rises to high estate and sinks to his
level between dawn and sunset. Though he struts and poses and
steals and uses his wit to serve his whims, he never forgets that
he is a beggar. He is used as an instrument of intrigue by con-
nivers for the throne, but the wit born from begging stands him in
good stead. And when the day has vanished, there sits Hajj, contented as he was in the beginning--to beg alms "for the love of Allah." A picturesque philosopher, a fatalist, a humorist and play-
boy. Counterplots furnish contrast to the main narrative. Space
forbids detailing the individual scenes, but suffice to say that the
majority of them are rich in dramatic values. The prayers to Allah by the multitude, the harem scenes, the street episodes--these
are all faithfully caught.

The director has not departed from his narrative for the sake
of supplying irrelevant touches. And the opportunity was offered to
make it a spectacle. A tale of a beggar, he keeps it a tale throughout. The exteriors have an air of solidarity about them. Some of
the walls and steps are creviced and marked as if time itself had
carved its impressions. The interiors are thoroughly in harmony,
bizarre, lavish and Oriental. But for a back-drop showing a panoramic shot of Bagdad, there isn't a flaw in the production. The picture moves a trifle slowly at the start because of the introduction
of a long list of characters, but it hits its stride soon after and
maintains its interest to the conclusion. Kismet is Robertson-Cole's
biggest achievement--a truly artistic production and one which is a
credit to motion pictures.

--Laurence Reid in Motion Picture
News, Vol. 22, No. 20 (November 6, 1920), page 3621.

☐ THE LAMB (Fine Arts/Triangle, 1915)

Typewriter drivers should be licensed, like chauffeurs. One
reckless unlicensee declared that the cavalry charge in The Lamb--
feature offering of the first Triangle bill--surpassed the terrific ride
of the clans, in The Birth of a Nation. Others acclaimed the play
a worthy second to the Griffith drama.

Here's what The Lamb really is, it seems to me: a rollicking, typically American melodrama, presenting Douglas Fairbanks,
one of America's best known, best liked and most continually agree-

able stage personalities. Improbable--quite, and to one who knows
the desert, just a little bit absurd when one is asked to believe it.
Comparing The Birth of a Nation and The Lamb is like comparing
Balzac and one of our popular story-writers of today; it's so unfair
to today's man.

Gatling-gun fire is not the essence of thrill, any more than
gunfire on the bass-drum is the essence of dramatic emotion.

>   --Julian Johnson in Photoplay, Vol.
>   9, No. 1 (December 1915), pages
>   85-86.

*   *   *

A new star has appeared in the motion-picture constellation,
a comedian who wins through interesting personality and delightful
characterization, a decided relief from the raw crudities of acrobatic clowns. Whether or not he will continue to shine as he does
in The Lamb, Douglas Fairbanks has scored one decided hit--he
suits the role quite as well as the role suits him, and it seems to
have been especially created to display advantageously his striking
peculiarities. He holds the eye so strongly, and without apparent
effort, that he is the whole play from beginning to end. This is
not to the detriment of the story. It is a snappy and highly finished
product--the Griffith supervision assures that--it has an appetizing
dash of bitters from Christy Cabanne, and the subtitles are marvels
--they sound very much like the scintillations of a certain photo-
playwright who graduated from the highest ranks of criticism.

The entire product is the result of a unified effort by many
bright minds, a product trimmed smooth in careful revision. It
scores with the audience as soon as it is well under way and grows
in strength until it approaches intense drama, but it is always delightful comedy, clean, wholesome, not catering to low tastes at the
risk of nauseating minds not primitive. There is nothing that could
be called startling about The Lamb, but it has a quiet strength all
its own, a certain humanness that warms one to the story and to its
leading character. It belongs to a class of moving pictures which
firmly established the new art in popular favor, a story to charm
all who watch it unfold on the screen.

>   --The Moving Picture World, Vol.
>   26, No. 2 (October 9, 1915),
>   pages 235-236.

☐ THE LAST OF THE MOHICANS (Tourneur/Associated Producers,
   1920)

Maurice Tourneur's first picture* for Associated Producers,

---

*Clarence Brown was also heavily involved in the direction of this film.

The Last of the Mohicans, a visualization of J. Fenimore Cooper's
American classic, will certainly earn him a tribute. It cannot be
disputed that it is his greatest achievement--a picture which will be
talked about as a masterpiece of its kind. He has kept faith with
the author's memory by humanizing the characters and visualizing
scenes just as they are depicted in the book. We approached this
picture rather skeptical fearing that Tourneur would be unable to
make anything out of its descriptive passages. But he has taken the
salient episodes and dramatized them with stark reality. As for the
atmosphere which follows every paragraph and which makes the
reader catch the odor of the woods and makes him tense with ex-
citement--well the picture is saturated with it.

We knew Tourneur would not fail with the production--that
every detail would be complete--that expert photography and tinting
and suggestive backgrounds would be evident throughout. There are
moments which are simply breath-taking and the suspense of the
book becomes overwhelmingly acute as one follows the fortunes of
the white stragglers and the efforts of the faithful Uncas to rescue
them from the Hurons in general and Magua in particular. The action moves against marvelous backgrounds--backgrounds which are
rather awe-inspiring and give one an eerie feeling. The scene of
the Fort William Henry massacre is stark in its realism, and
Tourneur has kept faith again. It is not a scene for the under
hearted. Why you can almost catch the sound of the screaming
women and children as they are tortured by the blood-thirsty redskins.

This is Cooper to the life. And with true dramatic instinct
Tourneur switches to the sentimental side. He shows considerable
knowledge of Indian customs. Magua has captured the two white
girls. The brunette offers to go with him so that the little Yellow
Hair may be spared. And the Delawares permit him to go according to Indian justice. But Uncas, who loves the dark-haired girl
and whose affection is reciprocated, follows the trail. And far up
on a rocky ledge he fights with the Huron. The girl had threatened
to jump off if the vicious redskins approached. But with Indian patience he waited. He pushes the girl to her death and the fight with
Uncas is a thriller as the two men grapple and tumble down a mountain side, over rapids where the Mohican is stabbed to death. The
Indian burial is poignant and impressive. The acting is close to
perfection. Wallace Beery as Magua presents a study in cunning,
malicious devilishness that is quite as Cooper painted it. Albert
Roscoe is good as Uncas and Theodore Lerch makes a splendid
type as Chingachgook. Barbara Bedford's beauty and her acting
ability are thoroughly appealing. There is not a false touch in the
picture. The Indians have their heads shaven and are costumed
correctly. The camera work is exceptionally good. It's the greatest Indian picture ever shown.

--Laurence Reid in Motion Picture News, Vol. 22, No. 24
(December 4, 1920), page
4343.

☐ LES MISERABLES (Fox, 1917)

    The unforgettable story of Jean Valjean is once more before
us, in extremely elaborate form, and no effort has been spared to
render it intelligible. Les Miserables is a difficult story to drama-
tize. It is so crowded with incident that the dramatist discovers an
embarras de richesses in which he will flounder helplessly unless
he happens to be singularly adroit. Jean Valjean has foiled many
valiant attempts to achieve dramatic perfection. The present adaptation by Frank Lloyd is frequently meritorious. In the early episodes, the story emerges admirably and poignantly. For several
reels the attention is gripped successfully. The misery of the
wretched victim of hypocritical justice is a wonderfully pathetic picture of abject terror.

    The picture is at its best in the scenes dealing with Valjean's
visit to the old bishop, a rôle exquisitely played by George Moss.
The bishop's peaceful home, with the veracious French atmosphere,
the old housekeeper, and the odor of godliness is beautifully shown.
The episode in which he delivers over to Valjean the precious candlesticks, and adjures him with the words: "Jean Valjean, you no
longer belong to evil, but to God. Remember I have bought your
soul of you, and have given it to God." This episode is tremendously appealing, and is charmingly portrayed. Later, when Valjean
is the mayor of the small French town, the interest continues. It
is all most dramatically cumulative, and never for a moment re-
linquishes its grip. We are introduced to Fantine and Cosette, and
we already know the Nemesis of Jean Valjean--the iniquitous Javert.
There is no "villain" in any modern drama to compare with Javert.
He is the personification of vindictiveness and relentless hatred.
The discovery by Javert of Valjean's identity is remarkably well
shown.

    Those who are unfamiliar with Les Miserables will readily
understand all this, which is so cleverly intelligible that no single
incident goes astray. Later on, when we get to other events, such
as the matter dealing with Cosette and Marius, the coherence of
the picture tumbles. We lose the sequence. While the real significance of Les Miserables begins and ends with Jean Valjean, we are
asked to digress. Of course, in a book we are accustomed to digressions. In a volume of such mighty proportions as this Victor
Hugo, digressions are inevitable. Somehow or other, however, in
a picture we cannot quite enjoy such digressions.

    The vital episodes at the beginning of Les Miserables are so
excellent that when the digression comes it seems as though it were
a "let-down." However, the "let-down" is not insistent. There are
a few reels that I think could be advantageously eliminated--and I
am speaking of my own personal interest in the story. The Revolution scenes, of course, must be there. They are the excuse for
photography, and they are exceedingly well done. Valjean's trip
through the sewers of Paris is another praiseworthy piece of work,

and the final dealing with Javert quite rediscovers the main interest.
Javert--he would compel the attention of any villain student.

William Farnum covers himself with glory in his portrayal
of Jean Valjean.   It is undoubtedly the best thing he has done.
There is vigor and there is strength and there is fine dramatic appeal and there is poignant pathos in his impersonation.   This Jean
Valjean is worthy to live amid the many Jean Valjeans that we have
seen.   Mr. Farnum may take off his hat to himself.   In this picture he has stamped himself as an artist.   I was profoundly impressed by the Farnum acting.   It was a capital cast throughout,
without an exception.   The Javert of Hardee Kirkland was splendid
in its unerring message.   I have already spoken of the bishop, of
George Moss.   To that portrayal must be accorded second honors.
Harry Spingler, as Marius; Mina Rose, as Madame Thenardier;
Sonia Markova, as Fantine; Edward Elkas, as Thenardier, and
Jewel Carmen, as Cosette, were selected by a master selecter.
In fact, it is by all means the best and most skillfully chosen cast
that I have noted in any recent picture.

The prolixity of the picture is its only defect.
                              --Alan Dale* in Picture-Play Mag-
                                azine, Vol. 7, No. 6 (February
                                1918), pages 275-276.

                         *   *   *

The William Fox Company has made a truly admirable production of Victor Hugo's Les Miserables.   Frank Lloyd, in adapting
and directing the film, has approached the book with reverence and
respect and has created a picture that ranks with the dozen really
big feature productions in the film world.   Indeed, the presentation
places him in a class with Griffith, Ince, Brenon and DeMille,
showing him to be a man of intelligence and imagination and with
care for details.   The work will do more to convince the skeptical
that justice can be done in the films to the adaptation of great novels
than all the propaganda printed by film publicity men.   The spirit
of Hugo's masterpiece has been faithfully caught and conveyed.   One
senses keenly man's instinct for cruelty that the French novelist
depicted.

The tragic figure of Jean Valjean, the victim of vicious judi-
cial system, was characterized superbly by William Farnum.   The
brutishness, the stupidity, the development of criminal instincts in
the place of sympathy and a feeling for humanity were all brought
out with telling force.   And later, as the man reborn, he added to
the performance that is surely the best he has contributed to the
screen.

---

*Alan Dale was one of the most influential theatre critics of his
time.   He succeeded Peter Milne as film critic for Picture-Play,
but his tenure with the magazine was short-lived, for, as one may
readily observe, his style is not suited to a fan magazine.

The picturization follows the book closely and begins with
Jean Valjean's career as a criminal, when he is sentenced to years
of hard labor for having stolen a loaf of bread to save his family
from starvation.   He is later shown as the man-brute, hardened
and without conscience, and then we follow his regeneration through
the kindness of the Bishop.   Next we see him successful as a manufacturer and see him pursued by his nemesis, Javert.   Then come
his years of happiness in caring for Cosette, an orphan.   We see
him take part in France's great Revolution--in which autocracy is
overthrown.   We see his beloved Cosette married to Marius, and
finally we see the spirit of Jean Valjean pass from the weary body.
And so the life of that wonderful character is ended and Jean Valjean is at peace--at last.

The entire cast was notable for excellent acting, but those
whose performances stood out were: George Moss, as the Bishop;
Hardee Kirkland, as Javert; Sonia Markova, as Fantine; Kittens
Reichert, as the child Cosette; and Jewel Carmen, as the grown
Cosette; Harry Spingler, as Marius, and Dorothy Bernard, Anthony
Phelps, Edward Ellis and Mina Ross, as the Thenardier family.

Exhibitors who book this film will have capacity audiences as
a result.

--H. D. R. in The New York Dramatic Mirror, Vol. 77, No. 2034
(December 15, 1917), page 18.

*   *   *

Les Miserables--and let's get together on the correct pronunciation, lay-meez-air-ahbl, all syllables accentuated equally--is
the world's greatest novel.   And, curiously enough, it is a perfect
scenario, as it stands.   The only problem confronting the producer
of a picture based upon the Hugo masterpiece, is to select the incidents which will best tell the story within the limits of an evening's entertainment.   It has been impossible to make an adequate
speaking play from the book, because the stage drama moves too
slowly.   But it is no coincidence that the Fox production of this
epic follows almost exactly the lines of the Pathé production, made
several years ago.   The incidents used by the Pathé scenarioist are
the logical ones, almost the inevitable ones.   It would, doubtless,
be a grave injustice to say that the Fox scenarioist did his work
after studying the older picture.   The Fox sequence is as follows:

Jean's theft of the loaf of bread; his conviction; his imprison-
ment (both productions using a stone quarry instead of the galleys);
his release; the incident of the bishop's candlesticks; the theft of a
coin from a boy; Jean's rehabilitation as head of a big factory; the
befriending of Fantine; the pursuit by Javert; Jean's voluntary revelation of his past to save another man who has been arrested for his
robbery of the boy; his escape and adoption of Cosette; the treachery
of the Thenardiers; the romance of Marius and Cosette; Jean's
rescue of Javert from the revolutionists; Jean's escape with Marius,

carrying him through the sewers; Javert giving Jean his freedom; the abandonment of Jean by Marius and Cosette, and the final reconciliation.

It is a tremendous story to tell in an evening. The Fox picture is in ten reels, and while it covers all of these points, it leaves the impression of a calm and unhurried creation. Yet there is more "meat" in any one of the incidents mentioned than in most five-reel productions, more humanity, more emotion, and, because it is the undiluted work of a great genius, actually more plot. The growth of a great soul in the heart of a hopeless brute is here epitomized, not in platitudes nor even in mere poetical phrases, but in splendid deeds and magnificent renunciations.

William Farnum as Jean Valjean is powerful and convincing. Not only as the ruthless bear, but, as his soul awakens, as the man whose last thought is of himself, he compels you to say, "He lives. He is." His smooth, unfurrowed cheeks, when Jean reaches the close of his long and troubled life, slightly offend the keen sense of the perfect fitness of things, but this is soon forgotten in his masterly impersonation. Hardee Kirkland has the companion role, the stern, relentless Javert, the embodiment of duty and cruelly consistent justice. He is no less impressive than Farnum himself, though not called upon for such a variety of expressions. He is the portentous diapason, rumbling his menace throughout the story. The scores of minor roles are all well taken. There is no false note. For this thanks is due to the director, Frank Lloyd.

It is a worthy revival. It is a picture that anyone can enjoy at least once a year. It should never go upon the shelf. It is a lost soul indeed that does not feel itself bathed in pure light with the final scene, when Jean, taking leave of life, sees in a vision the form of the gentle Bishop, who bought his soul for God.
> --Randolph Bartlett in Photoplay,
> Vol. 13, No. 4 (March 1918),
> pages 70-71.

□ LET KATY DO IT (Fine Arts/Triangle, 1916)

Eugene Field would have enjoyed this. He might have written it. It is a big heroic of childhood, a nursery story about the Trojan war, in which Ned becomes a little hero for some Homeric lyre, and little Nellie a new Helen.

The plot has possibility. The story is laid--all stories in that respect resemble an egg--in Mexico, present day. A mine owned by Americans is in the center of revolutionary chaos, as are all things south of the Rio Grande and north of the Canal. The Winchester artillery is arranged, against mass attacks, in battery form; i.e., a lever fires a whole row of guns. The attack comes

with Indian stealth and unexpectedness. Most of the men are trapped
outside. In the house at the mine are the children. In previous
days, with much comic anticking, you have seen them snoop to the
gun-deck, get a fill of awed look, and snoop back to their own play
upstairs. Now the makebelieve becomes play on a huge and serious
scale. The comedy takes on the proportions of an American Peter
Pan. The Cholos get the volley-salute, again and again, as the kids
hold the blockhouse until help comes. After a little close-finishing
all is well simply because all are accounted for.

> --Julian Johnson in Photoplay, Vol.
> 9, No. 4 (March 1916), page
> 105.

                              *   *   *

Founded on the novel by Granville Warwick* and scenarioized
with a sure hand by Bernard McConville, the story of Let Katy Do
It, capably directed by C. M. and S. A. Franklin under the supervision of D. W. Griffith, is a simple one. But the development of
the plot with the masterful touches evident in every foot of the five
reels, makes the picture a noted one.

Katy Standish is the family drudge on a farm in Maine. Everybody loafs but Katy. She is kept so busy that no time is left for
her to be alone with Oliver Putnam long enough for the sturdy young
farmer to tell her something he had had on his mind for a considerable period.

In desperation, Oliver accepts an invitation from her Uncle
Dan to help him work a mine in Mexico. Shortly after his departure
Caleb Adams marries Katy's sister Priscilla. In the course of time
seven children make their appearance. When the parents are killed
in a railroad accident, Katy is obliged to act as mother to the flock
of helpless tots. An invitation from Uncle Dan, whose mine has
proved rich, solves the problem of feeding so many mouths.

The seven children are played by a remarkable cast of youngsters, whose parts keep the majority of them on the screen for a
good share of the picture. Violet Radcliffe, George Stone, Carmen
De Rue, Francis Carpenter, Ninon Fovieri, Lloyd Pearl and Beulah
Burns, the precocious little actors, deserve as much credit for the
success of the drama as the grown up principals.

Not once was there the slightest suggestion of the patient
coaching which must have been necessary from the directors. Every child acted naturally.

Even the scene where the Mexican outlaws attacked the house
of Uncle Dan Standish at the mine during the absence of all the
adults, for the purpose of stealing the gold bullion known to be ready

---

*Granville Warwick was, of course, the pseudonym of D. W. Griffith.

for shipment, the child who touched the battery blowing up the trench
prepared for just such an attack, made the scene vivid without any
sacrifice of infantile ingenuousness.

The attack on the mine house by the hundreds of Mexicans
and their repulse by the rifle fire from the building and their subsequent dispersal by the troop of dashing American horsemen in
some respects surpass for swerve and animation many of the best
battle scenes in The Martyrs of the Alamo.

A memorable episode is the stand made by Oliver Putnam in
the deserted hut where he and his sweetheart have taken refuge from
the frenzied crowd of bandits. A mere exchange of glances between
Jane Grey and Tully Marshall when the last cartridge was fired and
the pair was at the mercy of the yelling throngs outside, impressed
the spectator with swift deft touches always at the command of these
players for getting big effects.

Let Katy Do It is a finished production. The story is well
told; the work of the cast shows excellent judgment in the selection
of the players for all the roles, the sets, the locations and the details of costuming all indicate care. Indeed, those responsible for
the picture have left nothing to be done on Let Katy Do It.

--William Ressman Andrews in
Motion Picture News, Vol. 12,
No. 24 (December 18, 1915),
page 93.

☐ LITTLE ORPHANT ANNIE (Pioneer, 1918)

Once in a blue moon a film is produced that shows real genius
in the making. Such a film was The Blue Bird, and such a film is
Little Orphant Annie. The cheaply sophisticated may as well stay
away from this picture; only those who believe in fairies, and who
dare meet face to face the souls of little children, had better attend
its performance. For out of the fragile fragment of verse that is
best-loved of all Riley's child poems by children themselves, a
wonderful picture has been made.

There is only a thread of story: the tale of a little girl in
an orphan asylum, a child of sadness and dreams; a child with a
sight that penetrates the outer shell of the flesh and looks in upon
the things of the spirit. Annie goes to live in a farmhouse, where
there are other children, and she keeps those children in a ferment
of suspense with her ghost tales, her fairy stories, her goblins that
"will get you if you don't watch out."

But Annie is a hero-worshipper. Among her few friends is
Dave, a big-hearted farmer, who is responsible for whatever little
good life has brought to "Orphant Annie." Dave goes to war and is

killed. That is the last stroke of Fate for Annie. She falls ill and
dies, believing that she will join her dear mother of memory in the
Beautiful World.

There is an elusiveness of tenderness and pathos in the picture that reaches the heart. And Colleen Moore endows the character of Annie with a sweet humanness that makes the more plausible
that other ethereal self, which creates around the little girl, Annie,
a world of shadows and mystery. It takes art to make the unreal
seem real, and the delicacy with which the invisible is drawn forth
and made visible gives the picture a strange, almost uncanny, power
and appeal.

> --Chester A. Blythe in The Photo-
> Play Journal, Vol. 2, No. 6
> (February 1919), page 34.

☐ THE LOVE FLOWER (Griffith/United Artists, 1920)

D.W. Griffith's story of a man-hunt in the South Pacific.
Griffith lost his theme in prettying a romance between the pursued
man's daughter and a young adventuress. Does not seem real any-
where but it establishes Carol Dempster as a cinema personality.
Here is a young girl with charm, distinction and vividness. Dick
Barthelmess is not at his best.

> --Frederick James Smith in Mo-
> tion Picture Classic, Vol. 11,
> No. 3 (November 1920), page
> 100.

☐ MACBETH (Reliance, 1916)

Macbeth is great because William Shakespeare invested it with
all the magnificence of his opulent imagery; take away the language
of Macbeth, and as a story it is nothing more than a series of murders with the killer slain at the end. It is not half so good a story,
for example, as was The Price of Power, in which a man's greed
overrides his conscience, makes him a wrecker of lives, and finally
sends his own life crashing down with the others. To film Macbeth,
then, called for something more than two great actors to play the
parts of Macbeth and his lady; it demanded a director who could add
something to the story and produce a new grip, an original suggestion of the subtle psychic forces that drove Macbeth onward in his
crimes.

The Reliance production, with Sir Herbert Tree and Constance
Collier as the stars, is simply a good, straightforward picturization
of the familiar tale of the Thane of Glamis. One hoped much of the

witches, hoped for a stronger suggestion of the supernatural. True,
Director John Emerson's hags are plenty ugly, and fade away in the
accepted manner, as does likewise Banquo's ghost.

But all these things are familiar tricks. Speaking quite seriously, Director Emerson seems tied to a Tree. In a film which
runs nearly three hours one has a right to look for invention, striking effects, tension and mystery.

The one great moment in the film, when everybody forgot the
book, was where Macbeth and his wife wait in their room for Duncan to go to sleep, in order that they may have an opportunity to
murder him. Other scenes alternate--the king's preparations for
retiring, Macduff's premonition of evil--and then back again to these
two tense, staring figures, immobile and portentous. Let the king
pray, let Macduff ride like mad for Inverness, here is tragedy,
poised and ready to strike. In acting and piecing of scenes this is
a master bit.

But there are details that annoy, such as the huge harp with
strings of loose rubber tubing, or some such material, and the projection of a scene wherein the army of Macduff, besieging Dunsinane,
apparently thinks to capture the fortress by gathering in mass formation under the walls, where they will be handy recipients of
molten metal, rocks, and such other missiles, and trying to scare
the defenders out by waving flags on the ends of spears. It is
about time some director with a little curiosity in his makeup, took
a day off to learn how the sieges of castles were actually conducted.
The approved method was to surround them and starve them out,
but that is not dramatic of course.

To return to the main theme, the picture fails of greatness
because it relied upon stellar acting, and after the first few episodes, this acting consisted, on the part of Sir Herbert, of staring
and wobbling, and the staring eye when translated into black and
white, becomes extremely monotonous. Miss Collier was more ver-
satile in her moods, and her sleepwalking scene was decidedly
eerie. Doubtless, to the millions who never have seen Sothern as
the arch murderer, and some actress of the caliber of the late
Helen Modjeska as his temptress, particularly to the millions who
never even have read the classic, this film will be a revelation of
thrills. To us who have been reading and seeing the play for more
years than we care to admit, it brings little of interest. But for
one thing at least, many thanks--the Reliance folks were able to
find material for their captions in the lines of the play itself, for
the most part, even though there does seem to be a difference of
opinion as to the spelling of the word "weird."

--Julian Johnson in Photoplay, Vol.
10, No. 3 (August 1916), page
141.

*   *   *

With few exceptions attempts to place Shakespeare's plays on

the screen have been disappointing.   There has been little Shakespeare and a dull picture.   To say that Macbeth, acted by Sir Herbert Tree and Constance Collier for the Reliance Film Corporation,
is among the exceptions is too much like damning with faint praise,
whereas the production deserves the heartiest and most emphatic
commendation.   It will win on its merits as an interesting, artistic
photoplay, as a faithful representation of Shakespeare's tragedy and
as a masterpiece of expressive acting that truly reflects the genius
of Sir Herbert and the marked ability of Constance Collier.   There
has been much talk about preserving the art of great actors through
motion pictures, but slight accomplishment, either because the players were lost in the new medium, or because the subjects were un-
wisely selected.   Here we have a happy combination of actor and
play, also a director competent to handle a great tragedy--John
Emerson.

Students of Shakespeare who fear a desecration of a masterpiece, or what amounts to much the same thing, a mere skeleton
lacking the mind, the soul and the psychology of the original, will
be given a new insight into the possibilities of the screen.   As Mr.
Emerson adapted the play and directed it, his is the credit for the
production of a picture that not only visualizes the dramatic incidents completely and convincingly, but makes clear the mental processes of Macbeth and Lady Macbeth.   Of course, he could not have
done so much without actors of the first caliber, but it is equally
true that Sir Herbert and Miss Collier received the most valuable
sort of co-operation in making the audience understand.   There is
not the least excuse for missing the vital points of the drama.

In constructing a photoplay of this type the art of a director
is manifested in the scenes he chooses to visualize, scenes that
cannot be shown on the stage, but the meaning of which is commu-
nicated to the audience through subsequent dialogue.   When such ad-
ditions are made it is not altering the original, rather expressing
the same things in the language of the screen, and it is this language
that Mr. Emerson utilizes with fine effect to realize the true spirit
of Macbeth.   The murder of the king is visualized, as are many
other happenings left to the imagination in stage performances, but
never once is anything foreign to Shakespeare's tragedy allowed to
intrude.   When speech is necessary, lines from the play are invariably used, and the arrangement of the scenario necessitates few
explanatory leaders.   It is a treat, indeed, to read so much of
Shakespeare on the screen, even if some familiar quotations are
slightly altered.

Sir Herbert is a virile, compelling Macbeth, possessed of the
rare art that makes possible the communication of emotional states.
Characterization with a psychological background is possible where
such an actor is concerned.   We see the birth of ambition after the
prophesy of the witches and feel the irresistible force of temptation
as Lady Macbeth urges courage that his deeds may fulfill his hopes.
There is infinite variety and subtle shading in the portrayal, as
Macbeth, suffering from the conscience that "makes cowards of us

all, " shrinks before the phantom dagger or the pursuing ghost of
Banquo. Judiciously used close-ups of his wonderfully mobile features enable Sir Herbert to reveal the ever-increasing mental torture that eats into the soul of the usurper.

The Lady Macbeth of Miss Collier is no less impressive, for
she, too, possesses a rich personality perfectly suited to Shakespearean tragedy. She uses natural advantages of face and figure with un-
failing intelligence to indicate emotional feeling and the hard cruelty
of the relentlessly ambitious woman. In the sleep walking scene and
the scenes preceding the tragic death of Lady Macbeth, Miss Collier
reaches the high moments of a superb performance.

But it must not be gathered that the picture depends entirely
upon these two characterizations. Other roles are properly presented
and in the concluding reel, bringing the attack on Macbeth's castle,
there is a stirring spectacular conflict handled on a large scale.
From first to last the production, 7, 500 feet in length, is marked
by artistic lighting, tinting and appropriate settings.

--Lynde Denig in The Moving Picture World, Vol. 28, No. 13
(June 24, 1916), page 2258.

☐ MADAME X (Goldwyn, 1920)

Goldwyn and, more particularly, Frank Lloyd, the director,
have extracted a fine picture from the story of Mme X, which it
would not surprise me in the least to see better all the records
made by Dr. Jekyll and Mr. Hyde. It is a conventional picture in
its approach toward the big scene, as the play itself was conventional, but it is tremendously effective once the big scene is reached.
It is also Pauline Frederick's finest screen performance, a characterization aided mightily by the situation in which the heroine figures,
but one which a less skilled actress could easily have ruined. As
Frederick plays the unhappy mother, arrested on a charge of murder after she has been turned adrift by her husband and sunk to the
gutter as a drug addict, later to be defended in court by her own
son who believes her to be dead, she does not depend upon the pathetic situation in which the woman is placed to carry the scene.
To the contrary, she invests it with a spiritual quality that reaches
through its physical ugliness. Nor is she suffering the pure overlay
of an emotional actress' tricks. She is convincing in the sincerity
of her performance and in the discretion she employs in the most
telling of the episodes. Her court scene is splendidly played, and
as effective melodrama as the screen has offered. The fact that a
second unusually good performance by Casson Ferguson as the son
does not take the scene away from her, as the sons frequently did
in the acted drama, is a further tribute to the actress and her director. Excellent performances in support were those of William
Courtleigh and Maud Lewis, and the photography was especially

good, the detail of the court scene being particularly well staged
and handled.   I think you should see Mme. X.

--Burns Mantle in Photoplay, Vol.
28, No. 4 (September 1920),
page 67.

☐ MALE AND FEMALE (Paramount-Artcraft, 1919)

A truly gorgeous panorama, unwound about the story contained
in J. M. Barrie's play, The Admirable Crichton, with Miss Mac-
Pherson as the composer of the optic version, and Mr. DeMille as
the conductor and expounder.   It is a typical DeMille production--
audacious, glittering, intriguing, superlatively elegant and quite without heart.   It reminds me of one of our great California flowers,
glowing with all the colors of the rainbow and devoid of fragrance.
Sir James' play has twice been timely: when it was written, a great
occasion for sneering at snobbery; and now, when class bickering
and class leveling seem to be going on the world over.   With the
departures and liberties which the photoplay always affords the converted stage medium, the present version, in all its expansion, is
quite faithful to Barrie's incidents, and, as far as I can see, wholly
faithful to Barrie's spirit.   Like all good stories, a summary of
this can be compressed into a few words: In the London household
of Lord Loam, Crichton, a butler, is the real factotum in an establishment of general inability and servility.   When Lord Loam and
his daughter, the patrician Lady Mary, put to sea, it is Crichton
who accompanies the party as major-domo.   And when they are
spewed up by a typhoon on some uncharted coral strand it is Crichton who makes fires with a burning glass, food from the tropic
products, shelter from the forest, and clothes from the skins of
birds and beasts.   Likewise, in the return to nature, it is Crichton
who becomes the natural master--and the affianced lover of Lady
Mary.   But in a return to civilization the old course of life is taken
up perforce; Lady Mary marries her original pursuer, the well-
meaning but inefficient Lord Brocklehurst, while Crichton ties up to
and goes to America with his devoted little slave of all-along,
'Tweeny, the wee maid of the scullery.   So much for the invisible
power of civilization.   One could write a glossary of complimentary
things and use a battery of adjectives without overdoing the description of these various appearances.   With a cast which looks like a
page from the picture Who's Who and with all the strategy of sunshine which his experience and resources could command, Mr. De-
Mille has compounded a fabric upon which adventure is mildly im-
posed upon a main base of luxury, beauty and supreme sensuousness.   What sympathy the piece possesses is carted away wholesale
by the dimpling Lila Lee, as 'Tweeny.   Here Miss Lee realizes,
for the first time, the cinemic dream that Mr. Lasky had when he
espied her shrouded in vaudeville.   Mr. Meighan, fresh in the public mind from his great performance in The Miracle Man, advances
another step by his discreet, forceful, and albeit heartful delineation

of Crichton, the butler who was primarily and always a man.   But
it is upon Miss Swanson that Mr. DeMille lavishes his most insidious
arts.   Does Miss Swanson require a bed--as she does in the introductory passages of the play?   It is such a bed, and such a boudoir,
as have never been seen before.   And in the bed, within the boudoir,
the glorious Gloria is quite literally uncovered to view.   With somewhat more sanity as to coiffure, Miss Swanson then proceeds along
Fashion Way, with a shipful of gowns that are in several ways revelations.   As Lady Mary, she conveys perfectly the hauteur, the
splendor and the almost decadent lure and luxury of a person of her
class--a word which, in these premises, should contain an "h" as
its fourth letter for pronunciation's sake.   In the moments where
the soul of a woman is almost but not quite born in this tigerish and
silken body Miss Swanson does not particularly impress, but at all
times she is assuredly an eyefull, and an eyefull was about all that
Lady Mary could have amounted to in reality.   Theodore Roberts,
as the very earthy Lord Loam, whose noble island occupation is to
get more to eat than anyone else, contributes not only a perfect
portrait, but the most subtle and lingering humor contained in this
mile-long tapestry of sun and sea and gold and flesh.   Mr. Hatton
as a braggart lordling is characteristically effective.   Little Wesley
Barry, as the Buttons of Loam's household, introduces the characters somewhat brazenly by peering through their respective and let
us add respectable keyholes of a morning.   Robert Cain is well disposed as the eventual noble spouse of Lady Mary.   The flashing
beauty of Bebe Daniels illuminates a scene of doubtfully effective
allegory.   The subtitling, perhaps too wordy in places, is mainly a
matter of discriminating intelligence.

--Julian Johnson in Photoplay, Vol.
17, No. 1 (December 1919),
pages 72-73.

*   *   *

That Cecil B. DeMille has proven himself one of the foremost directors on the screen has long been recognized.   It looks as
if he has excelled himself with Male and Female, an adaptation of
Sir James M. Barrie's play, The Admirable Crichton.   There may
be those who will find fault that the original title has been changed
but if they know the British playwright they will appreciate the fact
that he cannot be done successfully on the screen.   So Male and Female is Cecil B. DeMille's achievement any way you look at it.
True he has incorporated Barrie's underlying thought that English
life is divided by sharp contrasts--that equality does not figure in
it except in moments of extremity.   And when stressful events are
over things are as they were in the beginning.

Master and mistress become the servants and the butler and
maid preside when all are cast upon a Crusoe island in the South
Seas.   Remarkably thrilling is this wreck and the suspensive moments contained in the scene are intermingled with flashes of humor,
thanks to Theodore Roberts' keen sense of characterization.   The
butler who had recognized his position with supreme modesty be-

comes a domineering lord. The island scenes are not too long, so
progressive and interesting is the director's action.

It is a remarkable picture, this Male and Female. The story
is well told, the acting is of a superior order despite the fact that
most of the players do not suggest Britishers, and it is produced
with a lavish disregard of expense. It is rich to details and atmosphere and realistic strokes and there is a sob interest that keeps
one fascinated.

--Laurence Reid in Motion Picture
News, Vol. 20, No. 24 (December 6, 1919), page 4142.

☐ THE MARK OF ZORRO (Fairbanks/United Artists, 1920)

In a Douglas Fairbanks film there is always that best promise
of the movie, a good entertainment. The mention of this popular
star's name invariably stirs up visions of an acrobatic youth with an
engaging smile who spends much of his time leaping over and through
everything in sight. But because he is a good actor as well, and
reasonably careful that the stories of his pictures shall be well told
and handsomely mounted, there is also the assurance that they will
be worth while in other ways. The Mark of Zorro is one of the
best of the recent Fairbanks series. It has a romantic hero, who
is the allegedly weakling son of a Mexican don, but who doubles at
odd moments, and especially at night, as a bandit set on freeing the
people of his state from the oppression of their political rulers. As
the happy bandit he eludes the law and engages in wonderfully exciting sword combats with his pursuers, proving himself, incidentally,
the best swordsman in pictures. And in the end he rescues the
trusting heroine as gracefully and with as many thrills as ever accompanied the similar exploits of the knights of old when they as-
saulted the towered prisons of their ladies faire. Marguerite de la
Motte is an attractive heroine. Fred Niblo was the director and he,
too, is to be numbered with the best of the newer and more intelligent picture makers.

--Burns Mantle in Photoplay, Vol.
19, No. 4 (March 1921), page 62.

☐ MEN WHO HAVE MADE LOVE TO ME (Essanay, 1918)

Men Who Have Made Love to Me, presenting the much-
discussed Mary MacLane in supposed love episodes from her own
life, had a bizarre and really compelling interest to me. It was
pleasant to get away from sunset fade-outs and becurled ingenues,
even to the torrid MacLane apartment. Miss MacLane, praise be!,
doesn't try to act, self-consciousness doesn't disturb her and she

surely does hold your attention while she reveals her odd knowledge
of sex psychology thru her piquant affaires d'amour.

--Frederick James Smith in Motion Picture Classic, Vol. 6,
No. 3 (May 1918), page 73.

*   *   *

It is one of those things that never should have been. I,
Mary, came out of the West--from Butte--and when she struck Chicago, the newshounds leaped to the assignment, and Mary got publicity. Her book* was the reason. It was of the frank, soul-
revealing type, and quotes from it made good copy for the papers.
It is apparent that Miss MacLane wasn't gobbled up by the Essanay
because of her film-acting abilities. The ostensible reason was a
desire to cash in on the large publicity. It is not probable that
there will be much of a cash-in. The picture was presented at
Orchestra Hall at a range of prices from 25 cents to $1. Its show-
ing demonstrated it as a highly unsatisfactory, rather anaemic vehicle for a lady who may know how to write but knows nothing of
acting. The Butte brand of vampires is nix. The picture is replete
with radical and ultra subtle subtitles, which smack of Mary's authorship. There is very little story. It appears that several men
fell in love with Miss MacLane, and became imbued with a desire
to possess her. Smoking cigarettes the while, she briefly plays
with each and hands out the fare-thee-well at the finish. However
true to life this may be, it was not brought out strikingly or enter-
tainingly in the picture. Miss MacLane's supporting cast does well
with what has been given it to do. No possible criticism can be
made of the photography. It is excellent. Arthur Berthelet did the
directing. Before production of the picture, there were press ru-
mors Censor Funkhouser** was going to delete certain lurid phases
of the picture. It developed that Funk didn't have to cut much.
Men Who Have Made Love to Me may do well in Butte.

--Swing in Variety, Vol. 49, No.
10 (February 1, 1918), page 45.

*   *   *

Mary MacLane, that very frank lady whose confessions read
more like boasts, tells of six love affairs in Men Who Have Made
Love to Me, appearing in person as the heroine of these battles of
the heart. The lovers are a callow youth, a literary man, an aristocrat, a pugilist, a bank clerk and a married man. Of course,
each of the affairs ends unhappily, some because she was not good
enough, others because she was too good. It is most entertaining.
And all the catchphrases of the easy love-makers are used in the
subtitles. Personally, I think that if these are fair samples of the

---

*Men Who Have Made Love to Me by Mary MacLane was one of the
most sensational, trashy novels of the teens.
**Funkhouser was the head of the Chicago film censorship board.

men who have made love to Mary MacLane, she is entitled to sympathy. There wasn't a "regular guy" in the whole outfit.

--Photoplay, Vol. 13, No. 5 (April
1918), page 111.

☐ MICKEY (Mabel Normand Feature Film Company/Western Import,
1918)

Mickey has been exposed to critical gaze at last and any ac-
cumulated fears with which the reviewer approached the projecting
room, caused by a full year of Mickey advertising, was completely
banished as one after another its seven reels skipped across the
screen. Mabel Normand "struck twelve," so to speak, in Mickey.
For under the direction of Mack Sennett, that master of comedy who
first saw her possibilities in a bathing suit, she attained the heights
as a comedienne. In her role here Miss Normand does some real
acting that makes one sit up and take notice. The title of the picture implies the type of her part. She is a pranky, tomboy girl,
whose adventures both in the mining district and in the ranks of a
certain sort of society, thrilling that many of them are, are filled
with comedy of the kind that only Mack Sennett could create. It is
that quick, spontaneous style of comedy that gives the impression
that it was evolved on the spur of the moment from the players'
ability to sense the situation. It is this style of comedy that always
has been and always will be the most popular. And there is an
abundance of it here. Miss Normand, and her supporting cast as
well, never permit a point to fall short of the spectator.

One is put in the best of moods by Miss Normand's novel
entrance into Mickey, and subsequently there is a regular whirl of
fine comedy introduced. The general store, that locale of so much
of the world's humor, is utilized again in Mickey, put to an original
purpose. Here Mickey enters with her dog and the proprietor objects to the dog. And the dog objects to the proprietor. There is
a grand mixup that contains laugh after laugh. And later when
Mickey is introduced into the home of her rich aunt there is a
further supply of comedy of an unusually high order. First she is
received royally because her hostess believes she owns a gold mine.
And then she is reduced to the rank of servant because her gold
mine proves worthless. But in both stations Miss Normand gets
excellent results.

The story of Mickey has been written with the element of surprise ever in view. One can truthfully say that plain and straightforward as the plot itself is there are many times when the story
takes an unexpected twist. This, of course, serves to ever stimu-
late the interest. After one crisis in the story is completed attention is immediately commanded again because the unexpected happens.

But where Sennett shows his versatility as a producer is in

the fact that the humor of Mickey results from human incidents and
situations.   The comedy is built upon reality.   Beneath every hilari-
ous laugh there is the feeling that it is natural.   And therefore the
laughs are sincere.   And this is the case with each of the picture's
elements.   For of course there are other ingredients besides comedy.   Sennett is too wise a producer to offer such an abundance of
footage offering a single type of entertainment.   There is pathos,
just a little of it, romance in a pleasing quantity, and thrills enough
in a wonderful horse race and a quick and realistic fight, followed
by a sensational rescue of Mickey, to institute a powerful line of
suspense at the finale.   In producing these two episodes, the race
and the fight, the director has shown his appreciation of the technique of building up the suspense.   In both there is thrill upon thrill,
each one just a little bit better than the last, until at their climaxes
the two episodes fairly bring the spectator to his feet out of sheer
excitement and enthusiasm.   The race, with Mickey "up," is con-
stituted of various flashes of the girl urging her horse forward, intermingled with long and fairly close shots of the actual race.   It
is played to its fullest worth.   And it ends with a breathtaking fall.
The horse stumbles and Mickey is hurled headlong over the track.

The fight, which puts an ideal melodramatic climax on the
story, is handled with equal skill.   The scene of action is an old
country place with winding stairs.   The villain has pursued Mickey
to the roof, a slanting peak.   Here she barely manages to hang.
Below the villain and the hero wage one of those exciting, smashing
combats which, in its handling and the manner in which suspense
has been built up, calls to mind some of Fairbanks' best scraps.
But this fight has not the conventional finish.   As the men combat,
Mickey slowly looses her grip on the top edge of the roof and begins to slide down.   There is a sheer drop of a dangerous height
which she seems unable to avoid.   And when the villain apparently
triumphs and sends the hero falling down stairs the cause of virtue
seems about to be dragged about in the dust.   But instead the hero
dashes to the window and grabs Mickey inside to safety just as she
is about to fall from the eaves to the ground so far below.   These
fight scenes alternating with flashes of Mickey in her hazardous predicament on the roof afford some of the finest thrills imaginable.

The story, with its comedy, its romance and its wonderful
thrills, is of the simplest sort.   And simplicity is always greatness.
Particularly when simplicity has so many enjoyable things about it.
The modern-day audience, surfeited with war films and spy melodramas, will welcome Mickey.   It is simplicity itself, it is humorous, human and thrilling and pleasing every minute of the way.   It
was built by a master of his craft.   Interest in it rises as a wave
and culminates in a thrilling crash, like the wave beating the sands.

As for the details of the production, these are appropriate in
every instance.   From the village setting in the early part of the
picture to the contrasting shots in the home of Mickey's aunt there
is ever an atmosphere of reality maintained.   The lighting is effective and the photographic work excellent from every angle.

Miss Normand's supporting cast was well chosen.   Each player is perfectly fitted for his part.   Wheeler Oakman is a fine hero,
Lewis Cody an equally fine villain.   George Nichols was aptly cast
as Joe Meadows, Mickey's guardian.   Minnie, the old Indian who
has appeared in so many pictures, never gave a better performance
than in Mickey.   Minta Durfee, Laura La Varnie and Tom Kennedy
complete the cast.

--Peter Milne in Motion Picture
News, Vol. 18, No. 5 (August
3, 1918), page 790.

☐   THE MIRACLE MAN (Paramount-Artcraft, 1919)

To the reporter whose typewriter daily sifts the news of a
great city the biggest story is not often one of vast concerns or
pompous doings or magnificent expenditures; the biggest story--per-
haps one of small moment compared with the affairs of all the people in his big town--is the story whose unusual happenings or singularly rich humanities can thrill him.   And it is hard to thrill an
old reporter.   The arresting spectacle of death, the red flash of
murder and the dull details of legal and private battle are old grist
in his ribboned mill.   But by so much as he has been hardened to
the round of selfish strife, cynicized by the average bankruptcy of
kindness and schooled in every error that flesh is heir to, by so
much more has he been really humanized.   He discerns motives
that the non-analytical spectator never perceives.   Like a doctor
who deals with the souls as with the bodies of his patients he kin-
dles to the stir of really primitive instincts, and the great underlying struggle of right and wrong in every individual.   The surface
of society is a gloss of insincerity that is seldom broken, even by
the crash of accident or the hammer of tragedy.   But when it is
broken, men and women, in all their splendor and all their frailty,
step forth, and if there is a writing man who does not always thrill
before the procession of genuine humanity he is not a writing man,
but a composing hack.   The thing that made these human beings
swim to the surface of events may be so small that it is unknown
outside a two-by-four flat; it may be so great that its echoes are
heard around the world, but, great or small, it is always essentially the same.   So with the reporter whose business it is to review the mimic editions of human life that we call dramas or novels
or photoplays.   Generally, they are like life as it is lived; conven-
tionalities, glazed in a crust of insincerity.   Never more than a
very few of these compositions burn with the fundamental splendor
of living; seldom one of them uncovers the grand and simple fabric
which is the warp of a human soul.   So the reporter of mimicry
has his equally occasional thrills, along with the reporter of daily
incident.   And when these intoxicating hours do come they atone for
days and weeks of unproductive grind.

Such an evening came to me, at the moist end of a humid

July day, when I saw George Loane Tucker's film production of The Miracle Man unrolled for the first time.

As a study in genuine human beings, as an exhibition of the instinctive triumph of the better nature when that better nature has a chance, as a perfect fabric of life as it is lived--alternately funny as a Chaplin and pathetic as a Warfield scene--and as an adroitly constructed drama, rising from climax to climax and never missing a telling point, I do not recall that the silver-sheet has ever offered anything any better than this, and few pieces as good.

Judged simply as a composition, true both to the canons of and the facts of existence, The Miracle Man stands alongside the previously incomparable Griffith tapestry, Broken Blossoms. In a year and a half the screen has not only failed to furnish their equals, but nothing which in any way compares with them.

Of course Mr. Tucker had George M. Cohan's shrewd, kindly, highly successful play of the same name, and Mr. Cohan, in his turn, had Frank Packard's fine original story as the source of his inspiration. But The Miracle Man on the screen betters its double original even as The Birth of a Nation bettered its original, The Clansman. In both cases there was, originally, a wealth of fact, simple humanity and power, but in both cases the window of the camera has shown these in actual life, moving through vaster fields, and their fact and the power has been multiplied by camera magic as though by a microscope.

Tom Burke finds a particularly easy graft by exploiting a fake Chinatown to visitors in the metropolis. Rose, his girl, suffers the arrowy slings of bruising fortune at the hands of a dope-fiend--for a nice consideration of practical pity. The Frog, who can do a neat dislocation stunt from neck to toes, is a horrible cripple--until the suckers are gone, when he snaps his bones and sinews into their right places and prepares to enjoy the results of his disjointing performance. Even the wily Chinamen play their parts in the nightly hokum. And then, in a chance cupping, Burke happens to read of the Arcadian life as it is led in a small town where, for forty years, a kindly deaf-blind old faith healer, "The Patriarch," has been dispensing calm to aching minds and surcease to bodies in pain. What a chance! He goes to plant his financial machinery and fake goodwill. The Frog, writhing horribly up the long hill, pulls his trick at the physio-pschychological moment--cured! The excursionists are profoundly impressed. A young woman of wealth, exalted out of herself and her mood of ailment, leaves her invalid chair and walks. Rose, artfully planted as "the only living relative," is cashier of the enterprise under Tom Burke's shrewd and dissembling eye. Now comes the great turn in the drama: their fakery a perfect success, their whole arrangement contrived beyond suspicion, the real force of the Patriarch's triumph over illness and sorrow, the mere spiritual power of "a good thought," turns upon them even in their exultance. One by one, it takes them and dissolves, absorbs, obliterates the hell in their hearts. The poor Dope fights away from his needle

--and wins. The Frog finds his trickery becoming increasingly ab-
horrent--he wins. Rose fights a great fight--a double fight, for
she has a greedy soul and a sensual body--and yet she wins. Burke,
the utter materialist, beats back every thrust of his conscience as
though he feared it were a touch of paresis. Yet--at the end--he
wins!

If ever a play made stars, this one will. Whose is the finest
performance? Really, I don't know. I should say that honors are
even, gauged only by the various opportunities. In all the years
that Thomas Meighan has played men good, bad and indifferent, on
the screen he has never done anything which can be even remotely
compared to his virile and engrossing delineation of Tom Burke.
Did you ever think of Tom Meighan, the placid and steady-going, as
a breath-taking emotional actor--an emotional actor as sensitive as
a woman, as true in his depiction of emotion as Tellegen used to be
when he played on the stage with Bernhardt? No, neither did I--
until I saw him play Tom Burke. And, virile and keen as Meighan
is, so Betty Compson, whom you once knew as only as a bathing-
suit comedienne, is keen and true and ultra-feminine in her visualization of Rose. She is a beautiful, sensuous thing indeed. I have
never seen a creature more gloriously physical. Daring as only one
other photoplay-maker can be, Tucker plays the mere man-woman
game to the limit in characterizations which mislead nowhere, and
gloss over nothing. Then, after he has done this with Rose, he
wakes, in an agony of suffering and remorse, the girl's spiritual nature and brings its white flower to perfect blossoming. Lon Chaney
is so good as the Frog that I cannot think of anyone who could have
played that grotesque monster as effectively. Joseph Dowling, as
the Patriarch, is perfect in the great picture, as are W. Lawson
Butt, J. M. Dumont, Elinor Fair and half a dozen other persons of
the allegory.

The sub-titles, for once in titular history, are either perfectly
natural vernacular and dialogue, or else clear, logical statements of
fact. I believe Wid Gunning is partially to be thanked for this blessing. The art-bits which bind titles to picture in a seemly whole are
the graceful contribution of Ferdinand Pinney Earle.

Upon this enterprise, George Loane Tucker steps into that
small but dazzling arena where only the sunshine masters stand.
                                   --Julian Johnson in Photoplay, Vol.
                                   16, No. 5 (October 1919), pages
                                   76-78.

☐ A MODERN MUSKETEER (Paramount-Artcraft, 1918)

Draft the dictionary, order the thesaurus into intensive training, mobilize the superlatives and equip the book of similes for the
first line trenches--A Modern Musketeer has arrived. Here is
Douglas the Fairbanks at his most Douglasish and eke at his Fair-

banksest.   Here is the breaker of all speed records in the speediest
of all forms of entertainment making all his past performances look
like the funeral march of a colony of paralyzed snails.   Here is
Briareus threshing about with every one of his hundred arms at
once.   D'Artagnan, forsooth!   Fairbanks makes the Dumas swash-
buckler seem a popinjay, a milksop, a wearer of wrist watches in
times of peace, a devotee of the sleeve handkerchief, a nursery
playmate, an eater of prune whip, a drinker of pink lemonade, a
person susceptible to hay fever, a wearer of corn plasters, an ha-
bitue of five o'clock teas, a reader of Pollyanna.   Ned Thacker
was born to the tune of a Kansas cyclone, and absorbed the message of the elemental Donnybrook into his small person.   From that
moment his energies consumed him with a desire for adequate expression.   There was not sufficient elbow room in the Kansas town,
so Thacker headed west.   On the rim of the Grand Canyon he found
his proper battlefield.   Even his dynamic soul contemplated with awe
that vast chasm, so that he could barely gasp, "Gosh, what a gully!"
Here, up and down the mile-deep ditch he fought with a nest of outlaws to win The Girl.   He bathes in hairbreadth escapes as a lady
daintily points her immaculate, pink digits at the fingerbowl, and
with no greater disaster.   There is nothing left but for Doug to
scale the bare face of El Capitan in the Yosemite, and he will have
trampled the entire geography of this hemisphere under his never-
slips.   Here and there in the rush of it, one catches glimpses of a
supporting cast, in particular Frank Campeau, Tully Marshall and
Marjorie Daw.   But it is hard to remember just what they did.   Undoubtedly their performances deserve highest praise; the point of the
stiletto is like a needle, but it is not much of a weapon with a few
tons of shells being dumped in your back yard every few minutes.

                              --Randolph Bartlett in Photoplay,
                              Vol. 13, No. 4 (March 1918),
                              page 104.

☐   A MORMON MAID (Friedman, 1917)

        I doubt the propriety of a play attacking an existing sect, even
for performances distinctly beyond the pale.   "The Latter-Day Saints,"
as the followers of Joseph Smith call themselves, have written one
of the strangest pages of American history.   In general practice at
least polygamy seems to have disappeared in Utah, and many of our
staunch Western patriots and good citizens believe firmly in the Angel Moroni, the revelations on the golden plates, and all that.   A
Mormon Maid deals with the militant period of the Mormon church,
and the escape of a gentile from the compulsion of sex-greedy Mormon elders.   There are "Avenging Angels," plotting, broken hearts
and sudden death in this well-told, convincingly written story--which,
as I have said, seems a morbidly unnecessary rehash of a certain
phase of American history.   Mae Murray is the principal artiste.

                              --Julian Johnson in Photoplay, Vol.
                              11, No. 5 (April 1917), pages
                              81-82.

☐ THE MOTHERING HEART (American Biograph, 1913)

        When it was announced some weeks ago that the Biograph
Company would release a photodrama of two-reel length a considerable stir of pleasant anticipation was experienced among those interested in the Licensed pictures. The Biograph Company has long
had the enviable reputation of doing things well, and it has, at
least, lived up to the reputation with The Mothering Heart. After
due reflection we are convinced that it is one of the most notable
productions, from an artistic standpoint, the Biograph Company has
made. Lillian Gish, as the little mother, while showing extreme
youth, interprets her part with pleasing taste and remarkable intelligence. There are moments when the pose which she is caused to
assume seems to bear out too plainly a conscious purpose on her
part. Some of her attitudes of a blank, unseeing nature when the
heart is torn with grief, seem to be held a bit too long for the best
effect. But she has sincerity and, altogether, she is charming.
Walter Miller in the role of the young husband, who is led astray
only to repent, and return because of parenthood properly realized,
exhibits a splendid personality all his own, which is saying much
when we consider the present tendency among some picture players
to copy one another. The basic theme is not wholly new to us; we
have seen it handled before in divers ways, but in such a scene as
we have at the close of this picture where the two estranged parents
lean over the crib where lies the cold form of the baby, we have
another evidence of the Biograph's ability to successfully manage a
most delicate situation. For the girl to have accepted the man back
on his first show of repentance would have been disastrous; but the
need of him and his full regeneration are clearly shown in the final
working out. It is note-worthy that all the principal scenes in the
picture are done close up to the camera, and some of the photographic coloring is beautiful. Particularly is this true of the scene,
"The New Light." One of the most remarkable scenes we have seen
for atmosphere and completeness of detail is the cabaret cafe. It
is a picture that grows upon one with reflection.
                                        --G. in The New York Dramatic
                                          Mirror, Vol. 70, No. 1803 (July
                                          9, 1913), page 28.

☐ THE MUSKETEERS OF PIG ALLEY (American Biograph, 1912)

        As a drama of slum life on the lower East Side of New York
this picture is remarkably impressive. The street scenes and those
laid in the ominous looking Pig Alley carry the touch of reality, and
the characters of the Little Lady, the musicians and the gangsters
are well played. The Little Lady and the musician are lovers, but
he is poor and goes away to earn more money. While he is absent
the girl is insulted by Snapper Kid, the leader of the gang, and being a high-spirited young woman she resents the insult. Later she

goes to a gangsters' ball, and it is Snapper Kid who saves the girl
from the clutches of a designing young man.   This starts a gang
war.   Meanwhile the musician has returned and been robbed of a
pocketful of money by the same Snapper Kid.   How the musician and
the girl finally befriend the young gangster and save him from the
police after Pig Alley has been "shot up" provides a fitting climax
for an interesting tale.

--D. in <u>The New York Dramatic
Mirror</u>, Vol. 68, No. 1769 (No-
vember 13, 1912), page 30.

☐ MY COUSIN (Famous Players-Lasky, 1918)

The consensus of opinion would indicate that the first photoplay in which the famous tenor, Enrico Caruso, is starred, is un-
qualifiedly a success.   Perhaps even the most enthusiastic of the
singer's admirers never fully appreciated the high degree of dramatic art which he is capable of attaining until they saw him in the
double role of Thomaso Longo--the humble maker of images, living
his dream-life in the heart of little Italy--and the cousin of Longo,
the great opera singer, who furnished the matter for the dreams
and gave inspiration to the poverty-stricken, meager existence of
his poor relative.

Briefly, the story is this: Thomaso lives a simple life among
his Italian fellows.   He plys his trade of image-making, and devotes
the passion of his soul to a love for Rosa, the pretty daughter of a
neighboring restaurant keeper.   The great pride of Thomaso's life
is the fact that he is closely related--a first cousin, in fact--to the
world-renowned opera singer, Cesare Caroli, and the very color of
existence is supplied in the boasts that Thomaso makes regarding
this cousin.

Naturally, the cloud of suspicion falls on the humble image-
maker, when a rival suitor for the hand of Rosa begins to imply
that Thomaso is lying; that he is trading on an imaginary connection
in order to draw a reflected glory upon himself.   Rosa listens to
the evil one, and throws Thomaso over.   Here is tragedy of the
deepest variety.   But the cousin was true, after all; and he put forth
a kindly hand to help his humbler relative.   He stoops to visit the
Italian settlement and so prove beyond the shadow of a doubt that
Thomaso's boasts had not been vain.   He brings to Thomaso the joy
of justification and a consummation to a great love.

The picture is well-managed and attractively set.   The contrasts are excellent.   But the real merit of the film lies in the consummate art with which the star himself plays his two parts, and
so gathers to himself the strength of the best that is in his support.
We do not know Caruso, the image-maker; we do know the dashing
Caroli.   As the cousin, Caruso is himself, suave, fashionably dressed,

a familiar figure on Fifth Avenue. As the image-maker he is a lovable, irresponsible builder of Castles in Spain, an impassioned lover, a figure of tragic wretchedness when disappointment and doubt assail him. The man who made Pagliacci famous for intensity of despair, endows this character of the screen with much of the same strength and potency. The choice of vehicle for Caruso's first picture is admirable; the play was made for him, and he has caught the spirit of the new medium as only a genius in histrionic art could catch it.

> --Chester A. Blythe in The Photo-
> Play World, Vol. 2, No. 6 (Feb-
> ruary 1919), page 33.

☐ MY FOUR YEARS IN GERMANY (Warner Bros. , 1918)

        Ambassador James W. Gerard's widely read book, My Four Years in Germany, relating his experiences as representative of the United States Government in the center of Prussianism makes a stirring patriotic propaganda as rendered into film form by Charles A. Logue, who prepared a scenario, and by William Nigh, who directed. Last Sunday night at the Knickerbocker theatre when the film received its premiere presentation, there was hardly a minute when the house did not ring with applause that turned into cheers. All the wily diplomacy with which the heads of the German nation sought to deceive the United States through its representative, all the atrocities witnessed by Mr. Gerard, such as the mistreatment of the English prisoners, the deportation of helpless Belgian women, perpetrated without regard for any sense of international law--these and a large assortment of views of Allied troops on the march make capital seeing for the man who goes into the theatre ready to have his emotions stirred against the common enemy.

        While there is no personal story interwoven with the facts, these in themselves are fully dramatic enough to make the ten reels pass tirelessly. There is no stone left unturned to arouse the audience to a sense that the German manner of conducting war is synonymous with barbarism. One witnesses the heart rending sight of helpless prisoners shot down before German firing squads because "there will be less mouths to feed," of English and Russian soldiers placed in the same pens together so that the former contract diseases common among the latter and feeding of the prisoners as dogs. All of which Mr. Gerard was an eye witness--and more--is utilized to spread the propaganda.

        The sense of humor of the director is ofttimes obvious. It was, indeed, a praiseworthy sense when it came to the production. One long line of actual horrors and of German intrigue would be rather fatiguing without some relief. This is introduced in the way of an element of burlesque on the German Emperor, the Crown Prince and the other war lords of Germany. These touches regis-

tered every time during the initial showing, and they are the kind
that will be appreciated by any audience.

The scenes of real troops with which the film is crowded
are well woven in to the matter picturized from Mr. Gerard's book,
and usually to more rousing effect than if they had merely been
shown by themselves.   When the Kaiser laughs at his enemies it
makes one feel pretty fine when these same enemies are shown preparing for battle with a vengeance.

Halbert Brown, a man who might be mistaken for Mr. Gerard
by his best friend, impersonates him in the picture.   He makes an
impressive and dignified figure of the American diplomat.   Mr. Gerard himself cannot complain, at least he didn't in his speech last
Sunday night.   Louis Dean presented a good makeup as the Kaiser
and had he been imbued with some sense of the autocratic majesty
of the part his characterization might have been perfect.   Fred Hern
and Percy Standing respectively playing Minister Von Jagow and
Secretary Zimmerman succeeded in bringing out the cunning German
diplomacy in realistic style.   Earl Schenck as the Crown Prince,
George Riddell as von Hindenburg, Frank Stone as Prince Henry,
Karl Dane as Bethmann-Hollweg, and Arthur C. Duvel as von Fal-
kenhayn generally have convincing makeups and play to good effect.

Mr. Nigh himself plays the part of a German social democrat
whose excellent convictions are finally overwhelmed by inborn patriotism.   His tragic story terminating with his final stand for helpless
prisoners adds a valuable personal touch to the picture, though it is
not very prominent.   A. B. Conkwright, as his companion in the
Reichstag, in whom blood lust predominates after the outbreak of the
war, also contributes a valuable characterization.

My Four Years in Germany exposes the inner workings of the
German political and military machine and lets its audience know why
America is at war as clearly as did Mr. Gerard's book.

--Peter Milne in Motion Picture
News, Vol. 17, No. 12 (March
23, 1918), page 1768.

*   *   *

My Four Years in Germany is a forceful example of the relations of the films to contemporary history.   It is a faithful and
impressive transcript of Ambassador Gerard's book, screened without the slightest suggestion of melodramatic "punch" or straining
after effect.   The result is a consistent indictment of the German
policy beginning with the Zabern incident and leading to our own
declaration of war.   In the midst of the massing of troops and clashing of armies, there are sudden, poignant flashes of stricken Belgium, which are all the more impressive for their briefness and
simplicity.   The entire production stands apart from the eagle-
screaming variety of war films, which are only too common in these
martial times.   Its value in the interests of sincere, determined

patriotism cannot be exaggerated.   Willian Nigh is the genius of the
production--a combination of fine direction and remarkable assembling and editing.

--Photoplay, Vol. 14, No. 1 (June
1918), page 94.

☐ MY OFFICIAL WIFE (Vitagraph, 1914)*

The wisdom of re-issuing such a box-office attraction as this
combination of stars and play represent can not be questioned.   Miss
Young has not had a greater opportunity to show all her charms than
in this very play which was so largely responsible for her rise to
fame.   In the impersonation of a Russian nihilist, so clever that
she would have accomplished the assassination of the czar himself
had she not overplayed her hand, Miss Young carries her audience
with her in full sympathy even to the glorification of murder itself.
How she thrills at her sinister task!   How she scorns the accom-
modating American gentleman who is like putty in her facile hands!
How instantly she changes her expression from fear, aversion, horror, and contempt to the brilliant smile of the alluring woman who
fascinates all men and makes them do her bidding.

Without Clara Kimball Young, the story might not be so im-
pressive--and without so good a story Miss Young might not show
such fascinating character.   Be that as it may, the happy combination, in its new "de luxe" edition, will be seen in every first class
city, and most of the smaller towns of our country once again, and
will draw more business wherever shown than on its first appearance.
This is bound to be the case.   And the important thing is, the audience will not be disappointed, judging the play by the best present-
day standards.

The story concerns the visit to Russia of the Nihilist Helene
Marie (Miss Young), who succeeds in inveigling an easy dispositioned
American, Arthur Lenox, to pass her by the Russian sentries as his
"official wife."   Lenox (Harry T. Morey) has a real wife, but he
thinks the fascinating woman who pleads that he save her from great
inconvenience is the wife of a college chum, and presumes of course
that once across the border he will receive the thanks of his old
friend for his kindness.   Helene Marie, however, without disclosing
her identity, frightens Lenox with the threat of Siberia if his act be
known; forces him to continue the deception and even finally accompanies him to the Grand Ball where she plans to assassinate the
Czar.   Lenox's American manhood here asserts itself, and he drugs
his "official wife" and carries her back to the hotel.

Sacha Weletsky (Earle Williams), who is fascinated by Helene,

---

*Despite his not being in the United States when the film was made,
Leon Trotsky is often listed as an extra in this film.

follows and the final climax is attained by the elopement of these
two, and the confession of Lenox to the chief of the secret service
that he saved the honor of the secret service by preventing the
Czar's assassination, proves his salvation from Siberia.

L. Rogers Lytton as Baron Friederich, Rose E. Tapley as
Mrs. Lenox and Mary Anderson as Marguerite Lenox are included
in the cast of well known favorites in support of Miss Young. Without these stars this would be an exceptional production. With them,
it has a box-office and artistic value both.
                          --George N. Shorey in Motion Pic-
                            ture News, Vol. 14, No. 24 (De-
                            cember 16, 1916), page 3859.

☐ NEPTUNE'S DAUGHTER (Universal, 1914)

In the film drama, life truly is "one damn thing after another."

"Why don't you go into motion pictures?" some one is reported to have asked an under-sized and under-fed member of the
disengaged.

"Me?" retorted the despairing actor. "Say, if I went into
motion pictures, the first day I'd have to carry 'Jim' Lackaye off
the battle-field."

No one can frequent "the movies" without gasping at the dangerous and difficult feats performed by the players. It is all very
well for Annette Kellermann to swim halfway round the world, as
she does at the Globe in Neptune's Daughter, a picture spectacle
that is New York's nearest second to Cabiria, but one feels sorry
for other ladies who impersonate mermaids in the production, and,
during long stretches of time, soak in the briny deep. One especially sympathizes with little Katherine Lee, a baby mermaid whose
terror of her native element has not escaped the camera, and for
Leah Baird, whose legs having been turned into a tail by a witch,
is compelled to wriggle about on Bermuda's beach and her own tum-
my. Even Miss Kellermann begins to show, by the growing profes-
sionalism of her joy in life, the effects of continual laving.

A contemptuous theatrical manager is said to have characterized Neptune's Daughter, written by Captain Leslie T. Peacocke
and produced by "The Universal," as the story of a king who married a fish. In reality, we have rather an engaging fairy tale, tai-
lored to show the accomplishments and the figure of a star whose
previous public appearances have not called for much tailoring.
King William grants free fishing rights to his subjects, whose first
haul nets Angela and Annette, the two daughters of Neptune. Annette
escapes, swearing an oath to avenge her baby sister, and, turned
into a mortal by the sea witch, walks the earth to destroy the mon-

arch whom she regards as the murderer of Angela.   (Don't ask me
how it is possible to murder an immortal.   Ask Captain Peacocke.)
                                    --Channing Pollock in The Green
                                        Book Magazine, Vol. 12, No. 3
                                        (September 1914), page 496.

☐ OLD WIVES FOR NEW (Paramount-Artcraft, 1918)

        It is extremely difficult to build up a pleasing romance upon
a foundation of divorce.   Add to this difficulty the displeasing fact
that Old Wives for New contains scenes of disgusting debauchery,
and you can appreciate the failure of this elaborate and beautiful and
well-acted picture.   A man of fine instincts, whose wife becomes
lazy, slovenly, and horribly fat, falls in love with a woman of his
own type, and eventually everyone is happy.   There is some power
displayed in the telling of the story, but it leaves a nasty taste.
The cast is remarkable--Elliott Dexter, Wanda Hawley, Florence
Vidor, Theodore Roberts, Marcia Manon, Helen Jerome Eddy, Edna
Mae Cooper, Gustave Seyffertitz, Tully Marshall.   Cecil B. DeMille
directed, and seemed to revel in the most immoral episodes.
                                    --Photoplay, Vol. 14, No. 3 (Au-
                                        gust 1918), page 102.

☐ OLIVER TWIST (Lasky/Paramount, 1916)

        Marie Doro's portrayal of Oliver Twist reminds us of Dick-
ens' other orphans, but of all the sad and luckless little band we
love Oliver the best--perhaps because there have been more heart-
aches over his wrongs.   In the charming little actress, Oliver, as
Dickens conceived him, lives and suffers the bitter trials described
by the beloved author.

        From the first scene where Oliver, egged on by the hungry
boys, has the temerity to ask for more porridge, until his visit to
Fagin in prison, there is not a jarring note.   While some Dickens
lovers may regret that good scenes have been left out of the picture,
they will certainly not be disappointed in what has been put in.   Every member of the company from the "Gentleman in the white waist-
coat" to Bill Sikes, Oliver and Fagin, could have stepped out of a
Cruikshank illustration.   So excellent are the delineations they could
be shown without a line of introduction to anyone familiar with the
Cruikshank and Phiz drawings.   Even the dog is the kind you never
see on the street without thinking of Bill Sikes.

        Miss Doro, white and fragile as a snowdrop, depicts the un-
welcome and unloved child, who with big questioning eyes wonders
that so much misery should fall to the lot of one small orphan.   Miss

Doro's acting is exceptionally good in Oliver's long tramp, after his escape from the coal cellar, when footsore, his tired little legs give way under him and he sinks down by a milestone.

Oliver's innocent belief that he has found an honest friend in the Artful Dodger, his ingenuous pleasure and willingness to learn the deft game taught in Fagin's school of pickpockets, are faithfully represented. The child's horror when he discovers that his new friends are thieves shows that although the "Board" had kept Oliver's stomach empty they had filled his mind full of the eighth commandment.

James Neil catches the spirit of Grimwig, who conceals a tender heart under a testy manner. He predicts that Oliver will go back to the thieves and not come home with Mr. Brownlow's books and change. Grimwig is shown to be as disappointed as Dickens intended the character to be, when the boy fails to return. The murder of Nancy is accomplished better than film murders are generally. Sikes, splendidly played by Hobart Bosworth, is shown with his big stick; blow after blow descends, but by a clever Lasky lighting device we do not see the blows fall on the crouching woman. Tully Marshall was Fagin, the merry old gentleman who brought sadness to Oliver.

The spirit of the author pervades every scene. The moral that Dickens hoped his story would teach is apparent. Sin and crime are not made attractive and much good comes out of great evil. Parents should take their children to see Oliver Twist; it carries a lesson to all besides being a genuinely entertaining picture.

--Agnes D. Camp in Motion Picture
News, Vol. 14, No. 25 (December 23, 1916), page 4037.

☐ OVER THE HILL TO THE POORHOUSE (Fox, 1920)

Here is a production that is going to take its place among the season's best by universal acclamation. It is a simple tale of simple American folk based on a poem by Will Carleton which for eight reels ties knots in the heart strings, and, in the prologue, by its remarkable picturization of family life in a small town twenty years ago, rises to the heights of the most artistic comedy and subtle pathos.

Over the Hill is going to win Director Harry Millarde a seat in Moviedom's Hall of Fame. Next it is going to earn for Mary Carr, who plays "mother," the applause and gratitude of the picture-lovers of the country. Her role is a crystalization of the ideals of mother-love, mother-devotion, and mother-understanding, and her acting, especially in the second act, is the most beautiful, the most exquisite, and the most touching feature of the production. William

Welsh is "father," and he is almost as effective as "mother," although his role is of less importance.

The prologue opens with the six children still young. Here too, the youngsters are splendid little stage folk. Harry Millarde's master hand makes this simple tale of carefree boys and girls and their worried mother, so thoroughly human that an audience will be laughing with tears in their eyes. The action jumps to twenty years later, and the casting cannot escape notice. It is as if each child had grown up over night. The story revolves around "mother," neglected by her married children, and Johnny, her scrapegrace son, who alone remains in the old home, and who suffers a jail sentence to save his guilty father. The old lady wanders from the home of one child to another, unwelcome, until finally Johnny returns to save her from the drudgery of the poorhouse, punishes his hypocritical brother, and reestablishes his mother in her old home.

The only possible objection to the picture, from an exhibitor's standpoint, is the title. It smacks somewhat of the cheap melodrama of by-gone days. Music will help it immeasurably, and it should not be run without a rehearsed orchestra.

We will take off our hats to Harry Millarde, Mary Carr and all the rest who helped to make Over the Hill what it is. To Will Carleton's poem, a slighter doff--for in other hands it might have been made into a hash of exaggerated characterizations and strained drama. As it is, it is eight reels of a "mother" picture without mawkish sentiment or strained, artificial pathos--a feast of tears and laughter that will satiate the appetite of the box office.

--Matthew A. Taylor in Motion Picture News, Vol. 22, No. 15 (October 2, 1920), page 2703.

*   *   *

Over the Hill is based upon two poems by Will Carleton, "Over the Hill to the Poorhouse" and "Over the Hill from the Poorhouse," which were so widely known in the days of our grandmothers. It is only natural, therefore, that the super-sentimentality which characterizes the literature and music of that past generation should have left its mark upon the photoplay version of the poems. Over the Hill is frankly thematic. The note of mother-love is iterated and reiterated. The iteration and reiteration of this note tends to create a decided dissonance before many hundred feet of film have passed by.

Nevertheless, the photoplay has indubitably attained to a height well above its immediate contemporaries. Ever since the days when the Greek unities were discarded in favor of greater leniency as to time, place, and subject, the relation of the time lapse to the main dramatic fabric has been a point of constant controversy. Upon the screen it has become almost an immutable law to eliminate the long time lapse whenever possible, since the tense of the screen is me-

chanically the present tense, and because the few seconds which
must necessarily bridge over the lapse of years cannot fail to be
unconvincing. Over the Hill throws to the winds this meticulous
care concerning time lapses, and allows a break of twenty years to
disturb the sequence of its story. But it is the skillful handling of
this break in the narrative which gives the picture a claim to ingenuity and achievement. The lapse of twenty years is bridged in
two ways, first by the matching of types in the cast, and secondly
by the character delineation. The children are merely children in
the first half of the photoplay; yet the audience finds no difficulty in
recognizing these children grown up, in spite of the fact that the
parts are played by other actors. So well dove-tailed are the physical attributes and the general bearing of the children and the young
men and women who are their counterparts, that the little Isabella,
the little Isaac and the little Johnnie are readily discernible in the
Isabella, the Isaac and the Johnnie of the second half of the play.
The prologue of the picture, therefore, serves a greater purpose
in the plot construction than that of being merely amusing. It fulfills the definite dramatic function of foreshadowing the mother's
sacrifices, the father's lack of moral stamina, the parsimony and
hypocrisy of Isaac, the devotion and self-abnegation of the boy John.

Some of the most poignantly dramatic scenes are those between father and son. And there is an excellent bit of acting when
Johnnie shakes Isaac's hand in order to guard his mother's newly
found happiness against the faintest shadow. We may have no faith
that the bent twig of Isaac's nature will not revert to type when the
immediate stress of emotion is lessened. It is enough for us, however, that Johnnie should make this last sacrifice of his bitterness
of soul with such a gallant spirit.

Pictorial appeal is strangely lacking in Over the Hill. There
are remarkably few exteriors, and even these few do not call in the
aid of natural beauty to refresh the eye, or to intensify the dramatic
elements in the plot. Yet there is a certain harmony of setting
running through the picture, an impression of unity that is gained by
preserving the background representative of a certain type of rural
American home. This atmosphere is not destroyed by any sudden
shiftings into superlative luxury which so many producers consider
essential to Broadway "super-features." The simplicity, the home-
liness of the settings, is in keeping with the characters and the
story, and this sense of the fitness of things is in a measure a
manifestation of artistic principles.

There is one other point about the picture to be commended.
There is no triangle, no tertium quid, all too familiar in a certain
type of cinematic production. The love interest confines itself almost entirely to filial devotion. Yet the play manages to hold the
attention of the audience throughout. It is refreshing to know that
the overexaggerated idea of romance can be eliminated upon occasion.

--Exceptional Photoplays, No. 3
(January-February 1921), page
5.

☐ THE PAINTED LADY (American Biograph, 1912)

     The acting of the principal character in this picture is mar-
vellously effective.* It deserves a place among the most artistic
accomplishments of any player before the camera, and is an answer
to those who claim that subtle mental conditions cannot be expressed
by means of pictures. This actress shows the value of restraint
and the remarkable results to be attained by well judged facial expressions. She expresses tragedy as it has seldom been expressed
in a photoplay, and her method might be studied with profit by other
actors in the same field. The story to which she contributes so
largely is a simple, direct and sincere tragedy. The eldest daughter
of the family has obeyed the precepts of a stern father and resisted
the temptation to use paint and powder for her personal adornment.
She goes to an ice cream festival and is neglected by the young men
of the village, who flock around the rouged and overdressed younger
sister. Then there appears a dapper young man from the city, who
for purposes of his own seeks an introduction to the neglected girl.
He is her first sweetheart and she confides in him the extent of her
father's wealth. That night, thoroughly disguised, he enters the
house intent on robbery. The girl hears the noise in the room below, goes downstairs and shoots the man, not realizing who he is.
The emotion following the discovery of his identity causes the loss
of the girl's mind, which is never recovered. She has imaginary
meetings with her lover, and finally dies standing on the rustic bridge
where they first met. It is a picture of genuine tragic power.
                              --D. in The New York Dramatic
                                Mirror, Vol. 68, No. 1767 (Oc-
                                tober 30, 1912), page 31.

☐ PANTHEA (Selznick, 1917)

     Panthea. Here is another screen novel: directly told, staged
with an eye both to artistic lighting and dramatic effect, true to life
even in its most melodramatic moments, tingling with suspense, sat-
urate with sympathy. All of which sounds as though we considered
it the best picture of the month. We do. It is one of the best photoplays in screen history, and if there were more like it every interpretative art would have to cinch its figurative belt and prepare to
fight for existence.

     All of this notwithstanding a watery and ineffective ending;
where both author and director seem to fatally hesitate between
marshmallows and catastrophe, and, having a mind to neither, un-
comfortably straddle a problem picket fence.

     Panthea first served the serpentine Petrova, when the Shuberts

_____
*The actress in question was Blanche Sweet.

introduced her as their tragedy white hope. At this time it was an
alleged transcript of turgid life, and considerable sapolio might have
been used in its sordid corners.   Here, with the exception of the
wavering finale, it is all quite antiseptic--there are deep thrusts
and wide wounds, but they are made with clean swords.

Panthea herself is a piano graduate of the Moscow conserva-
tory.   At her keyboard valedictory a number of impresarii attend,
among them a Baron.   The Baron sizes up Panthea's person rather
than her performance, and connives with his friend, the Moscow
Chief of Police, to have Panthea raided on a charge of Nihilism.
Then he--the Baron--may demand and secure her release, thus establishing himself forever in her good graces.   But it happens that
Panthea's brother--presented by his parents with the not uncommon
name, Ivan--is really a Nihilist, and is holding vigorous revival
services of his own kind when the fixed police arrive to arrest Panthea.   The sham turns into reality, Ivan flees, and a soldier is
killed.   Now the Baron will have to extend himself indeed--but Panthea, helped out of a vaulty prison by a common soldier who had
once been her schoolmate, escapes to England.   She is pursued by
a secret police agent, on the same boat.   There is a wreck off the
English coast, and Panthea, unconscious, is carried to the Mordaunt
estate.   Gerald, the piano-playing younger son, immediately discovers a soul-and-music affinity, and they trip off to Paris, where
they live in happy married life for a year.   Gerald would be an
Anglo-Saxon Verdi, and wilts daily because he cannot get his opera
produced.   Panthea goes to a French manager who is about to turn
her down when a distinguished visitor from Russia sees her card.
It is no great surprise to learn that it is our old friend the Baron.
Panthea is in the toils again.   She makes the compact to save her
husband's life, while the Baron, Scarpialike, arranges to have her
pinched as soon as his personal purpose is accomplished.   But a
weak heart gets him in her parlor, and he does not long outlive his
culminary villainy.   The police agent is on hand, and starts back
to Russia with her.   The final fadeout is upon her and Gerald, camp-
ing in the Siberian snow, while he assures her that the English dip-
lomatic machinery must even now be grinding the grist of their formal release.

The direction is Allan Dwan's, and he manifests that same
leisurely, perfect passion for detail that he showed in Betty of Greystone.   The lieutenant who comes to arrest Panthea in the early episodes is the perfect picture of the "well, it's all in the day's work"
type of blase young militarist.   Wonderful is the relevatory close-
up when the Baron attends Panthea's recital: all the other old men,
we infer, are watching her hands, for there is a great keyboard
close-up; but when it is the Baron's turn we get a close-up of Panthea's shapely foot and promising ankle, upon the pedal!   Equally
subtle is the first view of the Baron in the Parisian office; he is
in a deep chair, back to us, and only his eager hand, reaching for
Panthea's card, is visible--but we know that it is he.

The lighting of this play sets a new mark in photodramatic

illumination. The tone in the main is deep, as it is with most of
Dwan's plays, but it is never gloomy.

Norma Talmadge plays Panthea with a verve, abandon and
surety which denominates her queen of our younger silver-sheet
emotionalists. There is no woman on the depthless stage who can
flash from woe to laughter and back again with the certainty of this
particular Talmadge. She is 100 percent surefire. Rogers Lytton,
as the Baron, surpasses all his other efforts. Earle Foxe plays
Gerald in psychopathic correctness. George Fawcett is totally disguised as the sinister Chief of Police; Murdock MacQuarrie comes
to the fore with all his fine old melodramatic resource as the Secret
Agent, and the rest of the faultless cast includes such players as
William Abingdon and Winifred Harris.

There are several points where the plot wears perilously thin,
but the craft of the director and the artifices of the players send
the beholder skating safely across.

--Julian Johnson in Photoplay, Vol.
11, No. 5 (April 1917), pages
77-79.

☐ PASSING OF THE THIRD FLOOR BACK (Ideal/First National,
    1918)

Made famous in this country and in England by the acting of
Sir Johnston Forbes-Robertson, Passing of the Third Floor Back,
Jerome K. Jerome's stage play, has been put into screen form by
Herbert Brenon, and is now being released by the First National
Exhibitors' Circuit. Sir Johnston plays his original part of the
Stranger. Those who saw the play on the stage will miss the star's
chief asset--his melodious voice--but the same gentle dignity which
was so winning in the spoken play is brought out equally well on the
screen, and the beautiful sentiment of the story cannot fail to reach
the heart of every spectator. Several changes have been thought
necessary in the plot, the greater freedom of the screen allowing
them to be introduced. As originally written every scene took place
in the parlor of a London boarding house.

Passing of the Third Floor Back is a modern allegory. Its
action is all fashioned to drive home the lesson that selfishness is
at the bottom of the misery of the world. The inmates of the boarding house shown in the picture are trying their best to show their
worst side to one another when a new lodger arrives. He is a man
in whom the spirit of Christ is reflected. Every word and every
action of his reveal his thought and care for those about him. To
each one of his fellow lodgers he shows a way out of the difficulty
into which his own folly has led him. The dishonest landlady, the
immoral little slavey, the father and mother who are willing to
sacrifice their daughter for the sake of a wealthy marriage, all are

taught the true meaning of life. It is to be hoped that the screen
version of the play will repeat its stage success.

--Edward Weitzel in The Moving
Picture World, Vol. 36, No. 6
(May 11, 1918), page 895.

☐ PASSION (Union-Ufa/First National, 1920)

    The greatest fault of this extraordinary picture lies in its
title. Passion is an entirely misleading name for an historical picture dealing with the life of Du Barry and the French court of her
time. Such a title is not only misleading but in very bad taste.
The National Board of Review is strongly of the opinion that the
choice of such lurid titles as Passion, Sex, Jealousy, and so forth
is a short-sighted policy even where titles of this nature are more
appropriate to the theme of the picture than is the case here. While
they may attract first audiences in the cosmopolitan centers they
are more likely in the long run to repel than to attract the better
part of the general public throughout the country.

    With this one reservation the picture deserves almost un-
qualified praise. The life and adventures of Du Barry are perhaps
not the most inspiring theme for a picture of the first magnitude,
but the story of her rise and fall is full of dramatic material even
without the embellishments added by her biographers and the glamor
which the period in which she lived has thrown over her. She was
the last of the great mistresses at the French Court of the eighteenth
century and perished miserably in the revolutionary upheaval which
for a time put an end to kings and mistresses.

    Du Barry's story unfolds appropriately against the background
of fading glory which marked the decline of royalty in France. To
the producer it presents the opportunity to work with bold strokes
upon an historical canvas on which the whole culture of a period can
be reflected. It calls for fidelity to detail in costume and manners
and for authentic historical setting. Anything less would fail to lift
the story above the level of a tawdry presentation.

    It is very gratifying to find that this first foreign picture of
importance to be shown in this country since the war sets a standard of which our best producers may well be envious. Mr. Ernst
Lubitsch, working with an international cast and with the palaces of
Europe to choose from for his settings, has achieved an excellence
in this type of screen spectacle which will not be easily surpassed.
The appointments of the interiors are made with a care that will
bring delight to the student of the Louis XV period of decoration,
while the formal garden exteriors that represent Versailles recall
the works of Watteau.

    When the story plunges into the events of the French Revolu-

tion, Mr. Lubitsch shows a skill in crowd composition and the dramatic clash of massed groups which proves that he knows how to
get his effects without overloading his scene.   He achieves a maximum effect with an economy of means which never leads him into
exaggeration.   In this part of the picture he has hastened history
along a little too fast by putting the Revolution immediately after the
exile of Madame Du Barry and entirely omitting the reign of Louis
XVI.   But he is artistically justified in this because he purposes to
show to how great an extent the dissoluteness of the Court mistresses
helped to bring about the French Revolution.   And he may have also
had in mind that the story of Marie Antoinette is too good a film
to lose by treating it as a mere incident.

But all of Mr. Lubitsch's skill would not suffice to make this
an exceptional picture if he had not been able to depend upon his
actors.   The cast is headed by Pola Negri, an actress of great
reputation abroad, who looks rather like Geraldine Farrar must
have looked at the beginning of her career.   The role of Du Barry
is presented with fire and imagination.   But Pola Negri is only one
of many.   The part of Louis XV is superbly played as is also that
of the Duke de Choiseul, not to mention Armand, the lover, and the
Count Du Barry.   We do not remember ever having seen a cast of
such a high average of talent.   Even the smaller roles are portrait
studies and our attention is often arrested by a group of half a
dozen figures which stand out with the clarity of a Rembrandt painting.   This will be particularly noticeable to American audiences
who are used to seeing one or two artists of distinction surrounded
by third and fourth rate talent.

--Exceptional Photoplays, No. 1
(November 1920), page 3.

*   *   *

The first picture to come from Europe since the war is the
German made Du Barry, which has been renamed Passion for the
American public.   If this magnificent production is a criterion of
what we may expect from foreign countries, by all means let us
have more like it.   The natural thing in passing judgment on a European product is to compare it in every department with the productions made on this side of the water.   Passion compares favorably with any spectacle ever produced in this country and surpasses
them all in the interpretation.   Really it is the biggest thing to
come from Europe since Cabiria, and the fact that it bears a German origin should not stand in the way of having it accepted as a
work of art.

Super or pseudo patriots may raise a feeble cry against it,
but they have no ground to stand upon since it is in no way an effort at propaganda.   A bone of contention with most producers is
the harboring of the false idea that the public cannot become recon-
ciled to costume pictures.   But isn't this conclusion born from the
inability of American directors to stage a costume feature properly?
Go back fifty years and any picture would become a costume play.

Passion goes back two centuries and smashes the costume bugaboo
to pieces.   Why?   Because there is intelligent effort behind it.

The point which impressed us the most is the painstaking
direction and acting.   Each player is seemingly familiar with his or
her part.   There is evidence in the picture of the very closest co-
operation.   Seemingly years of rehearsals have been spent in making
this picture perfect.   And that is the lesson to be learned from the
Germans.   If it took fifty years to prepare a perfect war machine,
they would take the same length of time in peace to prepare something equally perfect.   In passing on the merits and demerits of
Passion, one may say that its faults are minor ones, while its virtues will be talked about for months.   The titles could be better
which may be due to a poor translation.   And intimate details are
missing which may be due to the cutting.   But it carries a magnificent sweep and tells a tale of Old World romance and intrigue that
is completely fascinating.

The life of Countess Du Barry, the famous courtesan of Louis
XV, is presented accurately, vividly and artistically.   There is not
a false touch--not even in the minutest detail.   And the acting is in
a class by itself.   Pola Negri, the Polish star, gives a performance
that has never been equalled in its color, vitality, passion, shading
and emotional depth.   A woman of the world one minute, she becomes a simple child the next.   No mood of feminine nature is
missing.   She is the eternal enigma-woman, to the life.   Her support is magnificent.   Each player down to the most humble extra is
blessed with genuine talent.   And when the climax comes showing
Du Barry carried to the guillotine, it brings a fitting conclusion to
a truly big picture.   The mob scenes are handled with machine-
like precision.   The sets and details are faithful and impressive.
Passion carries great dramatic, historical and educational values.

--Laurence Reid in Motion Picture
News, Vol. 22, No. 18 (October
23, 1920), page 3265.

☐ PATRIA (International Film Service, 1917)

Following the unwritten serial law this chaptered violence is
packed with mechanical desperation and explosive incident.   Things
happen as fast as they do in a rarebit dream, and with almost as
much reason.   It seems strange that no one puts out a sensible
serial of real life.   Had not the Mexican interlude sent Rupert Hughes
away from Gloria's Romance just as that unlamented repeater was
beginning, I believe we would have had a real-life story there.   I
think the continued and ferocious Jap-baiting in Patria is more than
questionable.

--Julian Johnson in Photoplay, Vol.
11, No. 5 (April 1917), page
172.

☐ PEGGY (Kay-Bee/Triangle, 1916)

Peggy, it seems to me, was a case of dramatic buck fever.
Producer Ince has never issued a drama showing more care or endeavor, but the labor murdered the inspiration. No pretty wanderer
into the camera's field ever photographed more exquisitely than Billie
Burke. The whimsical little twitches of her lips, the elfin glimpses
of her eyes, the cascades of her laughter have been faithfully written down sixteen times a second. No star this season--she is truly
entitled to the stellar name, no matter how carelessly the planets
are batted about by the press-agents--has twinkled out of such a
surrounding constellation. No more lavish inanimate investiture has
ever fortified an animate representation. But--

The story does not convince. Movement has been artificially
retarded until even casual gestures have lost their natural significance. The romance is not real.

We can understand Peggy Cameron's despair at leaving upper
Broadway for a Scotch village, and we can pardon the despair of the
Scotch village when she comes tearing through it in a white racer on
the Sabbath. But the follow-up does not fulfill the promise of the
beginning. Her night ride in the storm is as unconvincing as her
sudden love for a young preacher of Calvinism whom she teaches to
smile. When she entered the meeting to tell on poor Colin I confess
I thought her a tattle-tale. He wanted to marry the wronged girl,
anyway. Couldn't this situation have been worked out more to Peggy's glory? The episode in the "pub" also begins well--and ends
drearily.

I wonder if the reverend Bruce and his irreverent bride remained in Woodkirk? And what do the Woodkirk good wives think
of her--her sleeping things, and her habitual overalls?

Here's a cast that glistened like spatterings from a Bessemer
converter: William H. Thompson as the elder Cameron; Charlie Ray
as his son; Gertrude Claire as Mrs. Cameron; William Desmond as
the husky young Dominie.

The best thing this picture did was its introduction of a superlative screen comedienne. In one picture Billie Burke takes her
place beside anyone you might name for sheer silversheet ability.
                              --Julian Johnson in Photoplay, Vol.
                              9, No. 5 (April 1916), page 102.

                    *   *   *

Given a clever and attractive artiste, Billy Burke's fine comedy opportunity, such as Gardiner Sullivan can provide, and the capable directing of Thos. H. Ince, what else than delight could be expected at this stage, when good scientific work is taken for granted?
Billie Burke is a born screen actress--she was probably a tomboy

earlier in life. Back of her fascinating vivacity are the high spirits
of sound health--she is a fountain of natural energy and seemingly
exhaustless vigor. Every movement, however nicely balanced by
training, springs from the natural impulses of a woman to whom
mere existence is a pleasure. Such, at least, is the impression
she conveys to those who rejoice with her, whether she is merely
amusing herself, or whether she is shattering some old-world pessi-
mism.

Peggy is called upon to leave America and visit her uncle in
Scotland, and the most amusing part of the whole story is that of
her arrival on Sunday. The good people are all at church, a group
of hard, undemonstrative, sanctimonious, just-but-not-merciful Puri-
tans, like those who settled New England and left their sturdy impress on our race. In the distance is seen a whirl of dust and
white streak, Peggy speeding the limit in her raceabout. Chickens,
geese and humans are scattered like autumn leaves along the village
street, and Peggy hits the center of religious activity like a meteor
just as the kirk is letting out.

Such is warm-hearted and impulsive Peggy. She becomes
modified--the characterization is very subtle--but she dares in the
end to smash provincial egotism when an erring girl, one who loved
not wisely but too well, is brought to harsh social judgment. Peggy's character is the sweet and lovable one of our Southern girl,
one whose purity springs straight from the heart, along with that
tender commiseration which sometimes makes this hard old world
of ours a little heaven in itself.

--Louis Reeves Harrison in The
Moving Picture World, Vol. 27,
No. 4 (January 22, 1916), page
620.

☐ THE PENALTY (Goldwyn, 1920)

Here is a picture that is about as cheerful as a hanging--and
as interesting. You can't, being an average human and normal as
to your emotional reactions, really like The Penalty, any more than
you could enjoy a hanging. But for all its gruesome detail you are
quite certain to be interested in it. It at least offers an original
story, and heaven and all the angel fans know how scarce they are.
Also it has been screened by that crafty Goldwyn crew with a good
sense of the dramatic episode and a free employment of theatrical
tricks. Chief of these is the trick of making Lon Chaney "what he
ain't"--a perfectly good legless wonder--by bending his legs back at
the knees and strapping them against his thighs. You can see the
strap arrangement, and you know the long coat conceals the feet, but
you are extremely interested in watching him try to fool you. Then
there are several sets of trick scenery--a practical fireplace that
slides up into the chimney and reveals a secret cavern below,

flaring, as it were, with the white hot flames of hell; rope ladders
hung below peek-hole windows that the legless one may climb up like
a misbegotten spider to take a look around; trap doors through which
the investigating youth in search of the heroine is shot down to the
villain-infested depths below.   Chaney's role is that of a man who
has sworn to be revenged upon society in general, and one man in
particular, because, as a boy, he was crushed in a traffic jam and
had both legs amputated above the knee by a careless surgeon who
might have saved them.   Legless, but bitter, he becomes one of
those "rulers of the underworld" who have only to push a white but-
ton to summon an army of cutthroats, dope fiends and fancy lady-
fiends.   But after getting all his enemies in his power the wicked
one is restored to the world of decent men by an operation which
removes a blood clot from his brain, and while he is later killed
by one of his old pals the happy ending is provided by the appearance of Mr. Chaney with legs attached.   It is a remarkably good
performance this actor gives, and he is capably assisted by Ethel
Grey Terry, Kenneth Harlan, Claire Adams and Charles Clary.
Wallace Worsley's direction helps the picture a lot.   Charles Kenyon and Philip Lonergon wrote the scenario, from a Gouverneur
Morris story.

> --Burns Mantle in Photoplay, Vol.
> 19, No. 3 (February 1921), page
> 66.

*   *   *

In spite of a most unique and powerful characterization by
Lon Chaney, one which will compare favorably with his never to be
forgotten "The Frog" of The Miracle Man, and a decidedly different
basic plot, The Penalty fails to deliver much in the way of screen
drama.   The picture is episodic, jumping to various essential scenes
with such rapidity and cutting back and forth to different sequences
that have to be carried along in such a way that most of the suspense of the offering is killed.

It would look when reduced to bare basic plot as if this would
have made much better serial material.   The whole idea is wildly
improbable, the romance connected with it inconsequential, and its
multitude of characters get lost in condensing the book into feature
picture length.

Only one thing stands out as worthy of any great amount of
praise.   Mr. Chaney has a role that even outside of its uniqueness
in that he plays the part of a man without legs, the illusion being
perfect, which gives him ample opportunity to demonstrate that he
is a great actor.

From a technical standpoint the picture is up to standard.
All the sets, a rather unusual number of exacting interiors being
required, are excellent, while lightings and photography are note-
worthy.   The supporting cast is good, but no single player succeeds
in making his role amount to anything from an audience standpoint,
except Mr. Chaney.

The Perils of Pauline   197

The twist in the plot at the end of the picture saves the offering somewhat and perhaps this fact and Mr. Chaney's characterization will get it over. An occasional title is good, but most of them are commonplace necessaries to tell what is happening.

The fame of the novel from which the picture is adapted and the considerable following which Lon Chaney has acquired ought to make the feature a very good box office attraction.
                              --J. S. Dickerson in Motion Picture
                              News, Vol. 22, No. 23 (November 27, 1920), page 4155.

☐ THE PERILS OF PAULINE (Eclectic/Pathé, 1914)

The motion picture serial has come to stay. Serial novels have long held a commanding position in the magazines; but one of the most popular of these has concluded that they are no longer popular and is offering a complete novel with short stories. No one will deny that this, from the reader's standpoint, is a wise move; for the serial in the magazine, especially the monthly, was, except in cases of "three decker" novels, only a business expedient to induce an even, dependable distribution. But, quite on the other hand, the requirements of an evening's entertainment in a motion picture theater that accents the mechanical difficulties of presenting long stories would have made the serial picture imperative. The modern spectator wants variety and won't stand being wearied. The serial picture is so vivid and the impression it leaves on one is so clearcut that the period of waiting between installments is rather a pleasant experience than otherwise. This is going to work out distinctly for the good of the business; for the serial that isn't vivid and doesn't leave an impression deep enough to last over the gap, is going to be the sharpest kind of frost. The serial that doesn't "get over" had better not have been made. By the same token, the serial picture that does get over with a real punch is going to be a great moneymaker. The Perils of Pauline seems, on this account, to this reviewer, an ideal offering for the exhibitor.

There are several things that contribute to its excellence as a show. There are big prizes offered to spectators clever enough to solve certain mysteries that come up in the progress of its story, and we may add at once that these mysterious things are not, so far, in connection with the plot and we feel sure that they will not hamper the interest in the story at all. But even better than the $25,000 in prizes that are offered is the good quality of the entertainment. Only the first installment, the first three reels, has as yet been shown to us. We know nothing of the rest of the picture; but are sure that this part is good and when it closes we are, in our hearts, certain that Pauline, charmingly portrayed by Pearl White, is in real danger from the much trusted but very villainous secretary (Paul Panzer) of her foster father, now dead. By the old

man's will, the precious secretary will inherit, "if anything happens"
to the heiress.

Miss White hasn't had so good a chance in a long while to
show her art, and she plays this picture's ingenuous heroine with
the truly wonderful naturalness that she has so surely at her command. Perhaps she doesn't always hit square in the center of the
effect she desires; but she does it so often that she continually commands the heart-interest of the audience. Mr. Panzer, in the villain's part, finds it his duty to intensify this. His work on the audience is, of course, through the heroine, and in the playing that
he is doing and will do, he stirs an antisympathy that is every bit
as worthy of praise; for the audience takes it with the left hand, so
to speak, and affectionately hands it back to the heroine with its
right. Crane Wilbur, as the hero, has little chance in this beginning portion. The character is still colorless and we can hardly as
yet criticize the player. The picture's weakest point is in its relief. The "comedy" gaucherie of the outdoors man, a sort of gardener, but too much of a fool to tend a garden, is weak and not
less so is the "fall" of the butler who is running out to the gate to
help the gardener bring in the mummy box that comes to the house
shortly before the heroine's foster father dies. The old man is
drawn very well. He has now passed away and will not appear
again--at least we presume so. The mummy, who comes to life
while the old man dreams, is graceful and pleasing. There is also
a very fair "tough" character in the story. All the characters, except Miss White, are guilty, now and then, of over-registering their
points.

The mechanical work is meritorious, and we wish we could
say that the photography, the prints, are perfectly clear and serv-
iceable. That the thickness of the photographs in some of the scenes
fails to hinder our comprehension of the story, speaks well for the
simplicity and clearness of the script. At the opening of the double
exposure scene in which the mummy comes to life, an awkward jump
is noticeable; but the unsubstantial figure flits about the room in the
best possible way and goes back to her mummy case again in so
perfect a closing of the double exposure that the eye can detect no
manipulation at all; it is done as naturally as dream.

The story has a story within a story; for Pauline is a bud-
ding writer and has got one of her novelettes accepted and printed
by the Cosmopolitan Magazine and the old man, her foster father,
reads it to us (in pictures) without wearying us at all. She doesn't
want to get married to the hero for a year; she wants to see life
first so that she can write things worthwhile. In the old man's will,
her part of the fortune is left in charge of the secretary until she
gets married. As the picture's first installment ends, it is clearly
to her interest to elope with almost anyone; but what she really does
do is left undecided as yet till the next of the series.

--Hanford C. Judson in The Moving
Picture World, Vol. 20, No. 1
(April 4, 1914), page 38.

☐ POLLY OF THE CIRCUS (Goldwyn, 1917)

There are many things to distinguish this first Goldwyn release from contemporaneous screen productions. Naturally Mae
Marsh is the outstanding one. Its completeness of detail, its superb light effects, and its realistic settings are others. Lastly the
manner in which the story holds up under eight reels is a point not
to be overlooked. That it never for a moment becomes tiresome
despite its precarious footage is a lasting attribute to the appeal
and strength of Miss Margaret Mayo's play as adapted and arranged
for the screen.

Miss Marsh again demonstrates her right to be termed the
best actress of the shadow stage. A simple scene in Polly of the
Circus is sufficient to drive that assertion home with great force.
When she believes that the minister wants her to leave his home,
Miss Marsh as the dismayed Polly is so expressively doleful about
it that it makes the spectator almost want to cry for her. There
are other episodes too, which an actress of less ability could hardly
have handled with such significance as does Miss Marsh. In the
lighter scenes which outnumber those of a serious nature she is
equally as good. One can feel the outlet of all the pent up play of
years of playless life when Polly first begins to cavort around with
the village children and drag the minister into a game of blindman's-
bluff.

The humorous note in Miss Mayo's play is the dominant one.
Polly's initiation into home life, the way in which the minister's
first sermon impresses her, her pranks with the village children
are episodes which can defy the gloomiest spectator to remain sour.
The comedy supplied by the two old negroes is not to be forgotten
either. But the thrills come in equal numbers. The accidents in
the circus ring, the horse race and the final burning of the large
tent and the scurrying away of the people are as dominant in their
side of the dramatic scales as the humorous moments are in theirs.

The settings of the picture, designed by Everett Shinn are
appropriate to the last letter. There is nothing elaborate about them
yet their very plainness only serves to accentuate their realism.
The technical end of the production has also been attended to by a
real artist. Such realistic light effects as the various scenes bring
forth, it may safely be said, have never been paralleled on the
screen before.

Worthy of considerable attention is the appearance of an entire circus in a great many of the scenes. It is a small town circus and so nothing might be lost in the way of sincerity and faith-
fulness of detail. The Goldwyn Company hired a real one, from
wagons and tents to performers. Much of the story transpires under
and around the big top and the various details incident to the life of
Polly and her circus companions lend unusual color to the production.
It affords opportunities for both comedy and drama and neither class
has been neglected.

Charles Horan was in charge of the direction and he has set a high mark for both the Goldwyn Company and himself. The supporting cast including Vernon Steele as the minister and Charles Eldridge as the faithful old clown is one of the best ever assembled.

--Peter Milne in Motion Picture News, Vol. 16, No. 12 (September 22, 1917), page 2035.

☐ POLLYANNA (Pickford/United Artists, 1920)

The popular pose, I know, is to make light of tears in the theater--to declare that anything that inspires weeping must necessarily be cheaply sentimental; that all the tears of all the actresses are crocodile tears, and all their suffering the most artificial sort of make believe.

Probably the heroine with the moist cheek is smeared with vaseline, and rises from her bed of pain to curse her cameraman for not having given her more footage in the close-up. (Incidentally, I loathe that death stab to illusion, the tearful close-up.) And if some one were to tell me that the crippled lad who is made straight and sound by a trusting faith, once he hears the shutter of the camera click, skips off the lot with a raucous cheer of joy to beg the loan of a cigarette from the venerable healer who has performed the miracle, I should believe it.

Still, under the spell of the illusion, I weep for him, and am unashamed. To me, for the moment, he stands for all other miserable souls who suddenly have been plunged into a great happiness. Twenty years of playgoing did not save me from an embarrassed exit when they turned up the lights on the acted performance of A Poor Little Rich Girl and I was caught sheepishly dabbing a pair of red eyes with a moist handkerchief as I stumbled up the aisle.

Naturally, therefore, the acted play, or the incidental scene, or the individual performance of the trained emotionalist that wins what I am pleased to consider the tribute of tears from me appeals to me as representing a measure of perfection achieved in that particular phase of playmaking. So it was with Pollyanna and Mary Pickford's performance therein.

Analyze Pollyanna and you find it conventionally sure fire. The plight of the "glad" girl is the hokum of the theater at its hokumist. The "glad" game itself, robbed of the thing it stands for, which is the beautiful optimism of youth and the earned rewards of "playing the game" and "being a thoroughbred," is a deliberate bid for your kind applause. It reeks with the sentimentalism of the theater at its baldest. But during its performance in the theater it is a good game, and a cheering one. A week of it and you might strangle Pollyanna. For one afternoon or an evening she is an inspiration.

Miss Pickford, too, has the supreme gift of the artist--which is the gift of compelling your belief in her. You hear much of the great actors who submerge completely their personalities in the characters they assume. But you may have noticed you never see them. You always hear about them. They are like the hoop snake of youthful memory. It was your uncle or your grandfather who saw one. The personality that is strong enough to focus and hold your attention upon it is too vital, too vivid, too real a thing to be submerged. And the great actors, of either screen or stage, are those possessed of such commanding personalities that in place of being able to submerge themselves in a character do exactly the opposite. They so envelop and emphasize the character that they substitute their own personalities and literally force your acceptance of them as the person they pretend to be. Their art, and the quality of their art, is in the completeness and the fineness of the substitution. If this were not true the Booth Hamlet would have been little, if any, different from other Hamlets, and the Mary Pickford heroines no more than a professional model for her imitators. Not, that I am comparing Mary with Booth. That would be unfair to Booth.

Miss Pickford is, for example, probably old enough to be the mother of the lad who plays Jimmy Bean to her Pollyanna. This suggestion may vaguely obtrude itself when they are placed next to each other in the close-ups. But the spirit of her performance is as convincingly youthful as his, and though her waistline is more mature, her heart is as light, and the sparkle of her eyes as bright. So far as your impression of Pollyanna is concerned, she is the best little playmate he ever had.

Miss Pickford's division of the United Artists' Corporation has done well with Pollyanna. It is sweet, but not drippy. It tells an interesting story without recourse to conventional drama. The cross aunt (Katherine Griffith) to whom Pollyanna, the orphan, is assigned, is neither a brutal shrew nor an animated New England conscience. The "glad" game with which the heroine sandwiches her adventures is emphasized, but not unduly stressed. And Howard Ralston's Jimmy Bean is a delight.

It requires a director with taste, a star with intelligence, to obtain these results. Working together harmoniously, such combinations will prove the saviors of the screen. More, and more, and still more power to them, say I. The trick is to find directors of taste and stars of intelligence. In this instance Paul Powell is the gentleman concerned.
--Burns Mantle in Photoplay, Vol. 17,
No. 5 (April 1920), pages 64-65.

☐ THE POOL SHARKS (Gaumont/Mutual, 1915)*

W.C. Fields, famous juggler and comedian of the Follies, is

---

*Pool Sharks marked Fields' screen debut.

featured in this slapstick. Admirers of Fields will find his screen
work neither as subtle nor as laughable as his stage performance.
There is plenty of good fun in the picture, however, and much of
the "business" is new. The action centers around a pool contest
between two rivals, the winner of which is to marry the disputed
girl. Some pool playing develops such as De Oro never saw. Mr.
Fields has very good support.

--"Tabloid Reviews for the Busy
Exhibitor" in Motion Picture
News, Vol. 12, No. 13 (October
2, 1915), page 85.

☐ A POOR LITTLE RICH GIRL (Paramount-Artcraft, 1917)

The film version of Eleanor Gates' play. A chain of incidents presenting Mary Pickford as a very saucy, tomboyish little
girl. The element of pity which, if we recollect correctly, was the
prevailing emotion of the stage version, is lacking here. Nevertheless, a thoroughly enjoyable entertainment, lavishly produced.

--Hazel Simpson Naylor in Motion
Picture Magazine, Vol. 13, No.
5 (June 1917), page 14.

*   *   *

It may be as well to start off with the statement that those
who remember the heroine of the stage play when they see the screen
version of Eleanor Gates' A Poor Little Rich Girl will be introduced
to an entirely different Gwendolyn in the person of Mary Pickford.
The writer of the scenario has used the utmost freedom in departing from the original work, and Miss Pickford has followed the scenarioist's example. The Gwendolyn of the play was a somewhat top-
lofty little miss who seemed born to the purple and never forgot her
station in life. Her airs and graces appeared to harmonize with the
rather artificial story and its many touches of symbolism; the moving picture star's Gwendolyn is a very human, lovable child who is
just aching to break away from all restraint and play in the dirt
with the street children.

The wisdom of these deviations admits of no dispute. As a
stage play A Poor Little Rich Girl harped too long on one key, and
there was altogether too much made of the delirium scenes. These
points have been judiciously shortened and the additional matter is
along the comedy lines that Mary Pickford does so well. The biggest laughs in the picture occur in the new material and are the results of such dependable bits of comic business as leaky plumbing,
a mud-throwing contest--in which the gardener is obliged to turn the
hose on his young mistress before he can recognize her--and the
seating of a priggish young lady on a plate of chocolate cake. Other
and more original bits are sprinkled all through the screen play, and

little Miss Pickford extracts the last ounce of fun from them with
that deft touch of hers which knows just how far to go, and never
lacks the saving grace of a sure sense of humor.

A separate paragraph is due the star for her portrayal of this
eleven-year-old girl. Entirely free from the stock tricks of the ordinary child impersonator, she looks the part amazingly well, especially in the close-ups, and acts it with a skillful blending of her
own personality and that of a bright and winsome "kiddie" that makes
the illusion perfect. Her Gwendolyn will rank as one of her best
screen creations.

As aids to such a pleasing achievement Miss Pickford has
been surrounded by a company excellent in every respect, of which
Charles Wellesley, Frank McGlynn, Emile LaCroix, Charles Craig,
Frank Andrews, Madeline Traverse, Marcia Harris and Maxine Hicks
are members. Artistic direction has been given the entire production by Maurice Tourneur, and every adjunct in the way of appropriate settings has been provided by the Artcraft Pictures Corporation.

--Edward Weitzel in The Moving
Picture World, Vol. 31, No. 11
(March 17, 1917), pages 1760-
1761.

☐ POPPY (Selznick, 1917)

Poppy is the best vehicle Norma Talmadge's talents have ridden in since Panthea; and in many ways it is a marker screen play,
for, like the Cynthia Stokely novel from which it was adapted, it has
an unwonted freedom from the conventional manner of narration, and
a remarkably effortless play upon and development of human character, both in its men and its women, rather than the fruitless stalk-
ing of the usual bad puppets and good puppets and mediocre puppets
who are at once the furniture and cogs of contemporary screen drama. This author starts with the assumption that all her mimic people are more or less wicked, and that it's up to the years, experience, chastening sorrows and perhaps some love to make them a bit
better, if not really good. Which is about like real life--isn't it?
The action passes mainly in South Africa. Poppy Destin, bound out
to a Scotchwoman who is a sort of super-Boer, vamps away to the
swamps and freedom. Luce Abinger, a gentleman of slightly preda-
tory instinct, finds her at the gate of his compound; takes her in,
educates her, and, upon the verge of a departure for England, marries her with a French ceremony which she believes is legal adoption. The author now steps heavily upon the accelerator of probability when she asks us to believe that a young man wandering in the
delirium of fever can be a genuine Don Juan; but after this shoal the
tale flows in smooth lifelikeness to its conclusion. Poppy sails to
London, struggles for literary success, and beholds her beloved
little nameless boy die in a fall from a window on the very day that

triumph came. Eventually, back to Africa, where she divorces
Abinger, and, after enduring a barrage of moral stone-throwing by
a lady who lives in a large glass house, she weds Sir Evelyn Carson, her rare knight who could unite a temperature with temperament.

The easy, human performances of most of the people in this
play assure us that screen naturalness not only endures, but flour-
ishes.   Miss Talmadge passes perfectly from short-frocked, bar-
barous childhood to slightly satiric, elegant maturity.   There is not
another camera woman who could so contrive this character's long
range and unexpurgated catalogue of every female emotion.   Eugene
O'Brien is so fine as Carson that we wonder why we don't see more
of his work before the camera.   Frederick Perry brings all the assets of his acting maturity to Abinger, and there is a wonderful
colored woman the cast doesn't name.   Edward Jose is stamped by
this picture a genuinely big-time director.

--Julian Johnson in Photoplay, Vol.
12, No. 3 (August 1917), page
84.

☐ THE PRIDE OF THE CLAN (Paramount-Artcraft, 1917)

The tenderness that is attached to almost everything Scotch
makes The Pride of the Clan a very effective setting for the second
of the new Artcraft pictures featuring Mary Pickford.   The little
actress is consistently "bonnie" through five reels of sentimental
Scotch drama with the scenes laid on a bleak coast which might indeed be the wave-hammered shores of Scotland.   The story is not
as strong as might be in itself, and, without the winning personality
of Mary Pickford, would not be so pleasing, but her characteristic
stage business builds up the weaker situations, and, with the assistance of the excellent details in the direction of the piece, serves
to hold the interest of the audience.   It is the story of a little Scotch
girl Marget, who lives alone in the hulk of an old fishing boat which
belonged to her father, who was drowned at sea.   She is formally
betrothed to Jamie, a young fisherman, and the two are about to
settle down to the simple life of the villagers when a titled mother
appears and claims Jamie as her long lost son.   Marget confidently
expects to be taken away with Jamie when he goes to the city to be
a fine gentleman, but the two aristocrats appeal to her unselfish
love and persuade her to give Jamie up for his own good.   The
broken-hearted lassie cuts her boat loose from the shore and drifts
into a sea which nearly sinks the frail old hulk, but she is rescued
at the last moment by Jamie, who carries her to his mother's yacht,
where she is restored by hot lemonade and the kindly attentions of the
two repentant parents.

Mary Pickford gives to the character of the Scotch lassie all
the quaint tricks of manner that have endeared her to thousands.

Matt Moore plays the part of the young fisherman with touching simplicity, and the minor characters, especially the types about the
fishing hamlet are excellently chosen.   The scenario is well developed but is slightly marred by a number of superfluous titles, which
are put in feeble and quite unnecessary rhyme.

An Artcraft suggestion for the benefit of exhibitors is worth
repeating.   They publish a list of Scottish Societies throughout the
United States and Canada, and advise the owners of moving picture
houses to get in touch with them and give special nights in their
honor.   In most cases, however, the name of Mary Pickford alone
will pack the houses without any further efforts toward advertising.

--A.G.S. in <u>The New York Drama-
tic Mirror,</u> Vol. 77, No. 1986
(January 13, 1917), page 26.

*   *   *

Mary Pickford's second Artcraft release is a picture that is
good to look upon.   <u>The Pride of the Clan</u> is sweet, wholesome,
moving.   Practically all of it is in the wide outdoors; and the exteriors are of the upper half of the New England shore, where the
ocean smashes into real rocks.   We see a genuine New England
gale, and it makes for atmosphere.   Elaine Sterne has adapted, and
adapted well, a story of the western Scotch coast.   Director Maurice
Tourneur has peopled his scenes with types of fisherfolk who seem,
as many of them undoubtedly are, the real thing.   Surely there is
about them the salt of the sea, as to those who know them they are
in a bad pinch the salt of the earth.

Mary Pickford has as Marget MacTavish in <u>The Pride of the
Clan</u> a story made of her own cloth and to her own measure.   It
gives her full opportunity to bring into play the varying moods of
which she is mistress--of sunshine and shadow, of playfulness and
of struggle against impending death.   There is romance, too, of the
happy sort, in which Marget is indirectly a beneficiary.

The story opens with one of the tragedies of the sea with
which fishing communities are only too familiar.   We see the small
craft beaten about by the waves off shore; we see a mast fall.   The
loss of the crew means that MacTavish, the head of the clan, is
gone, leaving Marget as the head.   It is not until she takes the
MacTavish lash and forces attendance at church that she assumes
the real leadership.   She plays no favorites.   There are tender
scenes, too, in abundance--of the love-making between Marget and
Jamie, of the betrothal, of the renunciation, and of the reunion.

Matt Moore is Jamie, and finely he plays the part of the
Scotch boy who after his betrothal to Marget learns his mother is
the Countess of Dunstable.   It is an excellent performance.   Ed
Roseman is Pitcairn, the humble misanthrope whose failure to real-
ize on his prayers has turned his heart against religion.   Kathryn
Brown Decker is the Countess and Joel Day the dominie.

Among the incidents that stir are the meeting of the mother
of Jamie and the woman who all his life had mothered him, who had
concealed from the boy the fact that he had any mother other than
herself; the meeting of mother and son; the refusal of Marget to re-
tract her renunciation, and the falling to his knees of Pitcairn when
he sees the little craft bearing the head of his clan slowly sinking
in the water.

The struggle of Marget in the cabin of the boat and her rescue by Jamie will thrill. A door has swung across the trap leading
into the cabin, and with her kitten in her arms Marget is imprisoned
with the water rising about her. One of the more striking scenes
is the betrothal ceremony, with the lovers facing each other across
the big stone, with the townspeople and the surf in the background,
the whole dimly lighted by the flares carried by the many spectators.

The Pride of the Clan is a strong picture, well staged; and
it is worth noting that in its entire length there is no trace of a
villain.

--George Blaisdell in The Moving
Picture World, Vol. 31, No. 3
(January 20, 1917), page 354.

☐ PRINCESS VIRTUE (Bluebird/Universal, 1917)

The screen career of Mae Murray, whose latest appearance
in moving pictures shows her as the heroine in a five-part Bluebird
screen version of Louise Winter's novel, Princess Virtue, has been
in the nature of a surprise. Starting as a dancer, her first parts
in photoplays were of the light, ingenue order, and she contented
herself with giving a somewhat indifferent imitation of a well-known
star. Then came the leading role in a feature picture that started
with the usual comedy scenes, but developed into a drama of serious
import. And here the actress found herself, and acted with a
strength and sureness of method entirely unexpected. In Princess
Virtue she is called upon to portray a most artificial young minx
and succeeds in making her considerably more unconvincing than the
author has drawn her. She wriggles and twists through the part and
relies upon an overworked "baby stare" to express whatever emotion
has her in its grasp. The atmosphere of the story is supposed to
be that of the smart society set of Paris, and the actress has indulged in a make-up that gives her the appearance of a wax doll.
All in all, the picture is about as true to life--at least, and life
worth living--as some of the Family Story Paper romances of thirty
years ago.

The heroine of the Louise Winter novel is the daughter of a
young Bostonian of wealth and position, who married a chorus lady
and died about seven years later. His widow goes to Paris with the
child and eventually becomes the wife of a Russian count. The girl

grows up after the manner of a hothouse plant and exhibits about the
same amount of animation. She cannot make up her mind which of
two suitors she prefers until a cousin from America arrives and
convinces her that he is a better man than either of them. He does
this by punching one of the suitors in the jaw and then fighting a
duel with him for engaging himself to the "Princess" and continuing
his attentions to a lady of much notoriety but little reputation. The
cousin from America is desperately in love with his Paris-raised
relative, but, thinking his case a hopeless one, sets sail for home.
One night, as he leans over the rail, a small foot touches him
lightly on the knee. The foot belongs to a lady in a steamer chair,
and the chair belongs to the "Princess." There is also a plentiful
supply of moonlight at hand, so the story is finished in the proper
romantic surroundings.

Wheeler Oakman, as Basil Demarest, is manly and likable,
and the two suitors are well played by Paul Nicholson and Jean Her-
sholt. Lule Warrenton, Clarissa Selwynne, Gretchen Lederer and
Harry von Meter are also efficient. The scenario was made by
Fred Myton and produced by Robert Z. Leonard.

--Edward Weitzel in The Moving
Picture World, Vol. 34, No. 7
(November 17, 1917), page 1033.

☐ THE PRISONER OF ZENDA (Famous Players, 1913)

With this four-act film drama the producers have leaped to
the pinnacle of moving picture fame at one gigantic bound. The
Prisoner of Zenda, as shown at the private exhibition in the Lyceum
Theater, bears a message of hope and cheer to every friend of the
motion picture and vindicates, beyond all cavil, American supremacy
in the world of films. We have seen a new standard in dramatic
architecture for screen purposes and we have witnessed an ensemble of American artists, in whom their debut in the new art called
forth the very best that was in them. Indeed, before I go any further, let me state right here, that the function of the critic now resolves itself into the difficult if pleasing task of a proper and orderly
distribution of credits and tributes.

The direction of The Prisoner of Zenda, I believe, was largely a work of intelligent and enthusiastic co-operation. The skill of
a talented, experienced and ardent master of the silent drama is apparent at every turn. Mr. Porter knew the possibilities of his instrument and made the camera's conquest quite complete. He has
disarmed and delighted the most captious of critics by the daring
but entirely successful use of all those advantages which are peculiar
to the motion picture and which the conventional stage can never
hope to share. Take but one example. The judicious employment
of outdoor scenes knitted the splendid story into a rapid and continuous whole, of which neither novel nor stage can give us even the

shadow of a conception. The audience, mostly composed of theatrical people and perhaps somewhat inexpert in moving picture work, was quick to appreciate these advantages of the new invention and broke into applause whenever the action of the drama was carried on in the theater of Nature. To be sure all the outdoor settings were happily chosen, but the ordinary motion picture audience is well used to such settings and takes even the best of them as a matter of course.

Let it be made plain that "the new standard" applies to this production from every angle. In the matter of interior settings I can recall nothing finer and more painstakingly finished. To Mr. Richard Murphy is due much of the credit for this novel and charming feature of the production. A hundred pairs of critical eyes swept up and down the screen and gathered nothing but delight. Everything was perfect, the scenes of The Coronation, the appeals to the populace in the streets of Strelsau by Black Michael and the pseudo-King, the procession to the Hall of State; no detail had escaped the watchful eye of the directors.

The marvel of the performance was the acting.

No such cast ever showed its varied skill and power on the screen before. Of Mr. Hackett in the leading role it seems scarcely possible to speak with becoming praise. He knew he was acting for posterity and he acted with an enthusiasm born of a very great and sincere love for his novel task. Superbly fitted for the task by generous nature he gave us an ideal portrayal of the difficult dual role of King Rudolf and plain Mr. Rassendyl. Though it was his first attempt on the silent stage he was in thorough accord with the camera and the mind that directed the camera from the first turn to the last. The love of honor and of justice, the English readiness for sport and perilous adventure, the absorbing devotion of a true man to a true woman, the turmoil and intrigue in the mythical kingdom, the loyalty of faithful retainers--all the qualities that account for the response of the popular heart to the appeal in Hope's novel are found in convincing realism on the screen. The fatal American defect of neglecting the cast to make the star shine all the brighter is here conspicuous by its total absence. The ensemble was in every way worthy of the star. It seemed to me that Miss Beatrice Beckley had solved better than most artists who are new on the silent stage the problem of maintaining poise in pantomime. Without that poise, directed by superior art and intelligence, the pantomime is either too mechanical or overacted. Mr. Torrence as Black Michael acquitted himself in a clever manner. Seeing himself he will realize that acting before the camera gains little from overemphasis in speaking and shouting. Miss Haines was fully equal to the somewhat thankless part of Antoinette. Mr. Hale gave the camera a fine impersonation of Rupert of Hentzau, while the Messrs. Coulter and Randall got all the rich humor and the touches of pathos out of Sapt and Fritz.

We owe much of the excellence of this production to the har-

monious working of masters on the speaking and on the silent stage.
There never was any just enmity between them and what enmity
there was must be characterized as strictly one-sided and confined
to the prejudices of some lights on the speaking stage.   Perhaps I
should say managers instead of lights.   The motion picture will help
the dramatic stage and vice versa.   Drama is of the motion picture
but a part, but it is the stage's whole existence.

The Prisoner of Zenda has, I think, another mission than the
mere making of money.   It merits particular praise because it is
an appeal to the finer feelings and the better taste.   No one can deny
that the large quantities of trash that have with painful consistency
been poured forth from certain studios too numerous to mention had
begun to vitiate public taste and even to debauch it.   Here is the
counter-current which, let us hope, will crowd the cheap and the
incompetent far into the rear of the procession.

Frightful monstrosities have been committed in the sacred
name of kinematography and such atonements as this wonderful production are needed to blot out the transgressions.   I believe the public will flock to the newer, better, higher, cleaner and more artistic standards.

The higher ideals of these producers shine out even in some
of the minor things and of the latter the program given out deserves
most honorable mention.   Typographically and from a literary viewpoint it harmonizes with the supreme merits of the production itself.
The faults of projection in a house hitherto a stranger to motion pictures may readily be forgiven, but what was the matter with the music?
                                          --Edward Weitzel in The Moving
                                            Picture World, Vol. 15, No. 9
                                            (March 1, 1913), pages 871-872.

☐   PRUNELLA (Famous Players-Lasky/Paramount, 1918)

The screen has, we believe, achieved nothing happier than
Prunella, adapted by Paramount from Granville Barker and Laurence
Housman's fanciful romance.   Here Marguerite Clark plays the fascinating little character she portrayed in Winthrop Ames' production
of Prunella several seasons ago.

Prunella is an innocent little orphan, reared by three strait-
laced maiden aunts, Prim, Prude and Privacy.   She lives in a quaint
garden, alone from the world, until a troupe of strolling players
passes--and Pierrot slips thru the hedge.   Then, caught in love's
net, Prunella runs away with Pierrot and becomes Pierrette.   Two
happy, carefree years pass, as the players wander from country to
country.   Finally Pierrot, chafing at the seeming bondage of his
marriage, deserts Pierrette.   But loneliness soon enters his heart
and he longs for the old love of Prunella.   So he returns to the
garden, now desolate and unkept, seeking to stir old memories.

There, too, comes Prunella, likewise drawn by dreams of the past, and the two are united, for Prunella forgives Pierrot, knowing that at last he understands the real meaning of love.

The whimsy of Prunella has been admirably caught.   Maurice Tourneur, who produced it, has utilized the new impressionistic stage art thruout.   He has achieved a splendidly sustained atmosphere of fantasy and some screen pictures of rare imagination and suggestion.   The strolling players' caravan, the wanderings of the troupe thru strange lands and the scenes in Prunella's garden are handled with the feeling of a painter.   One scene, a striking study in blacks and whites, stands vividly in our memory.   It shows the lonely Pierrot at a table, while an endless chain of shadows pass the curtained windows in the background.

The weakness of the screen Prunella lies in a failure to characterize Pierrot, Scaramel and the subordinate allegorical characters.   Miss Clark's Prunella is a fascinating thing of thistledown, sympathetic and completely charming, and, we believe, the best film contribution of her career.   But the other folk are mere characters moving thru scenes of singular imaginative beauty.

--Frederick James Smith in Motion
Picture Classic, Vol. 6, No. 6
(August 1918), pages 60 and 62.

*   *   *

Prunella comes to the devotees of moving pictures with these questions: "Do you want pictures to stand still or go ahead?   Do you want to continue forever watching the unwinding of tales of commonplace things of life, or do you want to broaden your mental vision?   Do you want poetry now and then, or do you insist upon always having prose?   Do you want the screen to reflect the highest art of which it is possible, or are you satisfied to hold it down to everyday life?"   According as Prunella wins the enthusiastic approval of the public, or slips by with just average attention, will these questions be answered.   It is a fantasy--a tender little story of an adventure in love by a little girl who has been secluded from life and kept in ignorance of love.   It is told with the most delicate art, the characters being picturesque marionettes.   Pierrot, Scaramel, Coquette, and many other mummers.   Even the scenery is of the spirit of masquerade, consisting of quaint miniatures of house, trees and gardens.   Marguerite Clark, whose entrance into pictures was brought about through Mr. Adolph Zukor's admiration for her work on the stage in this play, has never been half so charming, except perhaps in one or two of her fairy tales.   The entire moving picture business and profession owes Mr. Zukor a vote of thanks for having the vision and the courage to put squarely to the public the question of whether or not movies shall remain movies forever, or advance to a point where they can stand on the same high plane as the other fine arts.

--Randolph Bartlett in Photoplay,
Vol. 14, No. 3 (August 1918),
page 80.

☐ QUEEN ELIZABETH (Famous Players, 1912)

Historical accuracy, swift and clear action, a sustained splendor of settings and the supreme art of Sarah Bernhardt combine to make this play stand out as a rare and most creditable achievement. It has always seemed strange to me that one of the most commanding and fascinating characters in English history, Queen Elizabeth, has received so little attention at the hands of the dramatists of her own country. Historians have explored every nook and corner of the Elizabethan period and have delineated the character of the queen with indefatigable zeal; painters and sculptors have only been a little less enthusiastic, but the English stage has not kept pace with the historian, the painter or the sculptor.

It would be too much to say that this play fills the gap.   It deals with but a minor episode in the life of the famous queen, but it does so in an impressive, masterful manner; the whole performance is marked by dignity and an unmistakable care in the preparation of every detail.

The story of the plot, upon which this fine reproduction of the days of Elizabeth is based, is both simple and pathetic and may be told in very few words.   It is the tale of the tragic romance between the queen and the Earl of Essex, which began with a promise of an ardent and not ignoble love and ended in a tortured royal heart and a knightly head trembling beneath the sharp edge of the headsman's axe.   It is a tragedy surely not unworthy of the genius of Sarah Bernhardt.   This great artist had her own conception of the character of Elizabeth.   It was not the traditional Elizabeth, crafty, calculating and not at all emotional.

So superb is the art of Sarah Bernhardt that she made her conception, which is that of a passionate woman, dominated wholly by her affections, seem not impossible.   No student of history could pay a greater tribute to her art than to say, that she successfully defied a well-known historical fact.   Throughout the play, which consists of three reels, she exhibited her best powers and won from her audience such keen sympathy and compassion as the real Elizabeth could never have expected, the difficult part of the Earl of Essex was rendered with fine skill and that portrayal acting largely accounts for the tense interest which the play creates in scene after scene.   The parts of the Earl of Nottingham, the Countess of Nottingham and Lord Bacon leave nothing to be desired.

The most remarkable part of this play is its accuracy in historical detail.   What has been so often urged in these columns, the co-operation of the scholar and historian in the preparation of historic feature films, has been most literally carried out here.   The procession to and from the court was a masterpiece of historical cinematography in spite of the fact that the scenery was painted when it might just as well have been natural.   The mournful pageant itself was true to recorded history in even the minutest detail.   Going to the place of trial the headsman, who brought up the rear of

the grim procession, had the edge of the axe turned away from the
earl, while after the latter's conviction and sentence it was turned
toward him.   This may appear to be a trifle, but it shows and characterizes the extreme care that was taken to produce something creditable, in which even the most fastidious of critics can find no just
cause for censure.   This gratifying study and elaboration of detail
is present in every inch of the three reels; it marks the costumes,
the decorations, the furniture, the tapestry, the military uniforms,
even the painted architecture of the Tudor period.   When motion
pictures present such a faithful study in history no praise can be
too great for them.

Like other great features Queen Elizabeth will win hosts of
friends for the motion picture.   Of its value as a teacher of history
there has never been a more conclusive proof than this play of the
Famous Players' Film Company.   There are some minor points
which it might be well to have commented upon and explained by a
competent lecturer, as for instance the relation of Lord Bacon to
Essex, the queen's handling of the sword in the last scene, the
cause of Elizabeth's leaving Essex just before the coming of the
Countess of Nottingham, while the anonymous accusing letter was
lying on her desk.

Two scenes in this feature are especially pathetic and im-
pressive--the last scene in the first reel, which shows the leave-
taking of the Earl of Essex and the Countess of Nottingham, and
the last scene of the third act, portraying the death of the queen.
I cannot imagine a finer cinematographic description of the tragic
solitude of Elizabeth's last years on earth and of her pitiful, almost
inglorious end.   The great Tudor Queen, whose heart leaps with
patriotic joy, when, in her prime, she hears of the defeat of the
Armada, has changed to a vain, old woman, at once wishing flattery
and despising it, forbidding the presence of mirrors at the court,
for fear of learning from the truthful leaded glass the sad revelation of her faded charms and her approaching end.   Sarah Bernhardt
rose to the situation in this scene with consummate art and gave an
example of her acting, which will linger in the beholder's memory
for many a day.   She prepared the hearts of her audience for the
fitting final words on the screen. "Sic transit gloria mundi." "Thus
passes away the glory of the world."
                                    --W. Stephen Bush in The Moving
                                      Picture World, Vol. 13, No. 5
                                      (August 3, 1912), pages 428-429.

☐ QUO VADIS? (Cines, 1913)

Some time ago, when reviewing Pharaoh, King of Egypt, by
Cines, I made the assertion that when the Societa Italiana Cines at-
tempted to do a big thing it was always done well.   In the case of
Quo Vadis? the assertion is altogether too tame, and even to say

that the production is "superbly well done" falls short of the mark. But the mere use of superlatives is inadequate to do justice to any great work; there must be careful analysis and a keen study of the component elements, as well as a nice appreciation of what constitutes their harmonious arrangement and treatment in the synthetic whole.

Surely one of the most vital and indispensable requisites in the production of such a subject as Quo Vadis? is that of atmosphere, by which, in this case, for the lack of a better term, is meant the subtle power of translating the beholder into the midst of old Rome when the early Christians were looked upon as members of a pernicious secret society, when the last of the Caesars and his favorites drained to the dregs the cups of the revelling and cruelty, and when arenic spectacles included fights to the death of gladiators and the devouring of men, women, and children by ravenous beasts.

The Quo Vadis? of Cines does more; it gives us a view of Rome, burning, one of the most impressive spectacles ever pictured. Nowhere else could this have been done with equal fidelity; for the style of architecture has changed but slightly, though the narrow, tortuous streets of the old city have been replaced by broader, straighter avenues and the buildings made more substantial, while those in charge of the selection of the sections in front of the camera were perfectly familiar with the appearance of the old. Where else could the hiding places of the early Christians have been pictured so realistically? The catacombs and the other underground retreats of the new sect in Rome would have been imperfectly reproduced had the pictures been made in any other country. And where else could the vast amphitheater, with its perfect outlines and faithful observance of the minutest details, have been secured? One is actually impressed, as he looks at the flying chariots in the arena, the clash of the gladiators, the shimmer of the white garments of the vestal virgins, on a section of the amphitheater immediately to the right of that occupied by Nero and his court and patrician followers, the huddled-up crowd of devoted Christians calmly, or affrightedly, awaiting death in the arena, and the rush of the hungry lions on their prey, one, I say, is actually impressed, for the moment, that he has forced his way back through the past, for a period of some nineteen hundred years, and is gazing into the face of Nero with its imperious and cruel lines.

Are there yet other examples needed to accentuate the omnipresence of atmosphere throughout this photodrama? If there be, come with me to the last banquet of Petronius, the Arbiter, the Canon, of Court taste at the time, who, after drinking his last drink, crashes the costly and exquisitely fashioned myrrhine bowl on the floor so that Nero may not possess it, and then smilingly bleeds to death. View also the banquets at the Imperial Palace and on the Pond of Agrippa. There you have extravagant expenditures on costly wines and rare delicacies; lavish display of dress and ornament and furnishings, with flash of wit and show of fair beauty, intermixed with beguiling coquetry and shameless debauchery.

And atmosphere is accompanied by fine dramatic construction and treatment. Interest becomes more tense as the photodrama proceeds, with climax succeeding climax--each outrivalling its immediate predecessor--until the scene showing the great amphitheater is reached and eclipses all of them. The photodrama follows closely the story by Henryk Sienkiewicz, but I am of the opinion that the scenes in the Imperial Gardens, showing the Christians being burned alive as human torches, might better have been omitted for the sake of dramatic effect. The only scenes which can follow that in the arena acceptably and effectively are the flight and death of Nero.

It is, perhaps, necessary to note here, in view of the tremendous impression which a presentation of Quo Vadis? creates, that the story by Sienkiewicz does not conform strictly to historical facts in certain places. The photodrama conveys the impression that Nero gave orders to fire Rome. Most of the writers since Tacitus have conveyed the same impression, but the best scholars are agreed that the fire occurred by chance. The fire broke out at night near the Great Circus at the base of the Palatine and Caelian hills, raging for six days, when it seemed to have spent its fury, then suddenly broke out again on the north side of the city and continued for three days more. Nero was at Antium, thirty-five miles away. "His own palace and all its treasures were lapped up by the flames. He opened the Campius Martius by the river side and all the public buildings on it to harbor the homeless. He built shelters in his own garden to house them. He hurried up stores from Ostia and the neighboring towns to feed them, and fixed the cost of corn at one-half the prevailing market price. Though conspirators sought his life, he roamed the city all night alone as his noble palace flared away to ruin. His efforts at succor and his careless exposure of his person were, however, quite useless to restore his reputation, and the ruined denounced him as the author of the conflagration. Men whispered that he had been seen on the tower of Maecenas, on the Esquiline height, clad in habit of the stage gazing down on the lurid inferno beneath, revelling at sight of the beauty of the flames while chanting in wild glee the song of Illium's (Troy's) capture. To ascribe the fire to its real cause, chance, would never appease the mob of Rome." But Nero supported gladly the charge against the Christians and indulged with fiendish cruelty in their massacre.

A striking feature of the production, and one that cannot fail to please the eye of the most critical, is the care bestowed on detail. One fails to find, even in a great mob scene, a single instance where something better than that which happens could be suggested. Watch the crowds dashing frantically through the burning streets, the streams of humanity sometimes rushing in opposite directions. Is it not panic conceived fully to the letter? Or take the patrician throng in the great banquet scene, in the Imperial Palace, after the Empress Poppaea has retired, her exit being the signal for still greater license and more delirious revelling. Or again refer to the death scene of Petronius at his last banquet. What amazing painstaking has been taken in their rehearsal as in all the other big scenes of the photodrama! And the almost inter-

minable array of costumes, interior furnishings and properties!
What a labor these must have cost the archeologist! Indeed the perfection of detail makes one wonder while he sings its praises.

The photography and technique of this eight-reel photodrama
are in full keeping with its other excellent features. In several
cases one is treated to scenes with extraordinarily beautiful light
effects. Take, for example, the scene in the underground room
where Lygia is nursing Vinitius back to health, after she has saved
his life from the wrath of Ursus. Could there be finer depth and
definition in moving pictures than are shown there, or greater soft-
ness? Another example is the scene showing the baptism of Vinitius
by the Apostle Peter, where we have shadows photographed, yet every person and object in the room are clearly and softly defined.

And now the acting. What a splendid assemblage of histrionic
talent! Or should I more happily say photodramatic talent? G.
Serena as Petronius is undoubtedly our favorite among the leading
parts. A. Mastripietri as Chilo commands attention next for forceful, artistic character acting. But it is really like splitting hairs
to praise any one of the principals at the expense of the others in
the cast. A. Novelli as Vinitius, C. Moltini as Tigellinus, Miss
L. Giunchi as Lygia, C. Cattaneo as Nero, Mrs. O. Brandini as
Poppaea, J. Gizzi as the Apostle Peter, L. Lupi as Aulus Platius,
Mrs. A. Cattaneo as Eunice, and B. Castellani as Ursus are other
bright stars in the firmament of this extraordinary production.
                                   --James S. McQuade in The Mov-
                                   ing Picture World, Vol. 16, No.
                                   7 (May 17, 1913), pages 681-682.

☐ REBECCA OF SUNNYBROOK FARM (Paramount-Artcraft, 1917)

Mary Pickford goes back to short dresses and juvenile ways
in Rebecca of Sunnybrook Farm, an adaptation of the book by Kate
Douglas Wiggin and Charlotte Thompson. It offers her as many
chances as a specially prepared vehicle might and she proceeds to
display her talents in them to such winning effect that one is tempted
to describe the results as her best picture. However, such an expression is bound to yearn for a hearing after each Pickford picture.
It is better to say that Rebecca of Sunnybrook Farm meets all expectation and belies all description, which is in the way of an apology
for the remainder of the review.

A crowded Strand audience of the matinee species sat and
laughed at every comedy touch and wept with equal sincerity at every
pathetic moment. Miss Pickford gloriously succeeds in giving a
faithful representation of an honest-to-goodness, true-to-life girl,
not yet a lady but "the makings of one," as Rebecca remarks in a
subtitle. The subtitles, by the way, are excellently chosen and
placed. Frances Marion who made the adaptation has seen to this

and her judgment has stood her in good stead in every instance.
The more difficult work of forming an even and continuous scenario
was done in that precise and technically faultless style that has
stamped her many efforts of the past.

The various episodes comprising the greater part of the picture depicting the life of Rebecca while in the care of her straight-
laced maiden aunts are filled with a humor that is irresistible. Her
efforts to keep off the polished floors by leaping from rug to rug,
the play circus promoted by Rebecca and her companions and the
selling of the soap in order to obtain a present for a poor family
with the wrappers, are phases which call for rounds and rounds of
laughter. And toward the end the action changes, quick as a flash,
from humor to pathos when Rebecca witnesses the end of the once
cranky old aunt with tears streaming down her cheeks. But to enumerate these episodes only calls to mind other less prominent but
just as effective. Rebecca has no weary spots. It is entertaining
from first to last and, like the majority of the Pickford pictures,
is universal in its appeal.

Marshall Neilan, directed. Those who are acquainted with
his work need not be told that every scene is artistically presented.
The storm effects he has introduced are marvelous in their realism.
Josephine Crowell and Mayme Kelso interpret the maiden aunts to
a striking degree of perfection. Eugene O'Brien is a fitting Adam
Ladd, while Marjorie Daw as Rebecca's playmate does capable work.

--Peter Milne in Motion Picture
News, Vol. 16, No. 12 (September 22, 1917), page 2035.

*   *   *

It was inevitable that one of the most popular child heroines
in recent fiction should be portrayed on the screen by the most popular film ingenue. Mary Pickford's "Rebecca," while retaining the
charm of the quaint little character in the book, is so closely identified with her own personality that it is difficult to tell where Mary
Pickford begins and where Rebecca stops. Thus the wholehearted
applause that greeted the film on its presentation at the Strand Theater was divided between the two personalities though on the whole it
was the screen heroine that predominated and we have a coquettish
Rebecca with ruffles and Mary Pickford curls instead of the plain
gingham and sleek black braids of the Kate Douglas Wiggin heroine.
There can be no question about the instant response that this character will gain from motion picture audiences for the crowds that
packed the Strand laughed at Rebecca's escapades and wept over her
tribulations with very evident and spontaneous sincerity.

The story follows the incidents of Rebecca's childhood with
only a hint at the romance in her later college days. Most of the
audience were familiar with the career of the little New England
girl who leaves a large family of brothers and sisters and a mort-
gaged farm to live with two severe and exacting maiden aunts. In

the course of her placid life in the village she contrives to bring
joy into a destitute household, pay off the mortgage on her mother's
farm and win the admiration and later the love of a handsome and
wealthy stranger.

Mary Pickford was admirably supported by Eugene O'Brien
as the hero from the city, and by Josephine Crowell as the crabbed
maiden aunt.   The New England types were well selected and the
setting in a Maine village was delightfully quaint.

For those who prefer Mary Pickford in her most juvenile and
ingenuous mood, this character study will prove one of the most
charming of her recent output.

> --A.G.S. in The New York Dra-
> matic Mirror, Vol. 77, No.
> 2021 (September 15, 1917), page
> 18.

☐ THE RED LANTERN (Metro, 1919)

A year of Chinese plays reaches its climax in this huge ca-
cophonous symphony of colorless lacquers and soundless gongs and
gray shadows of yellow men.   The material upon which Nazimova
of all races builds her saffron tragedy is a novel by Edith Wherry,
descriptive of life in the Peking foreign legation about the time of the
Boxer horror, nearly twenty years ago.   Mme. Nazimova plays two
parts: Mahlee, an Eurasian, and Blanche Sackville, in reality the
unsuspecting half-sister of Mahlee.   Notwithstanding an intensely dramatic role by the star, it is as a spectacle more than as a play that
this story concerns us.   The Eurasian is a solitary; he is distant
kin to two races and is not admitted to close relationship by either.
So with Mahlee, raised in a mission, and not realizing until she as-
pires to the hand of the household's son that she is as much a thing
apart from fair-skinned folk as a mulatto in Alabama.   It is then
that she turns to her Eurasian pursuer, the villainous Sam Wang,
who has studied medicine in America and has returned to be an insidious force for both good and evil among the people to whom he,
too, is just a cousin.   The drama of destiny works as swiftly after
her surrender to Sam Wang--spiritually, at least--as it did slowly
before.   Wang, the inside agent of the Boxers in Peking, needs a
personality about whom he can weave false magic; a superwoman to
sway the credulous yellow rabble in an incense of fakery.   Mahlee,
grasping her one hour of infernal glory, becomes that woman.   The
end, of course, is defeat and death, but by the hokus-pokus invented
long ago to appease the populace when they clamored against the
death of a heroine, the star survives pleasantly and innocuously in
her other personality, Blanche Sackville.   I doubt if any such gorgeous Celestial pageant as this Feast of Lanterns has ever been seen
outside China itself.   And I have seen some Mongolian spectacles--
believe me!--in California.   It is this barbaric splendor of both in-

terior and exterior, this atmosphere of little lilies and heavy incense, this silent din of bronze gongs and falsetto voices, which
most engages the beholder; after, possibly, the performance of Nazimova herself. I feel sure that the star's bizarre costumes will
enchant every woman in the land. They may or may not be Chinese
--for all I know--but they are wonderful; so wonderful that they
might in themselves influence the fashions as occasionally the tog-
gery of great stage plays has done. Nazimova's performance is on
a high level of excellence without any startling distinctions, unless
her sharp and remarkable differentiation between Mahlee and Blanche
Sackville is such a distinction. That shrewd actor, Edward J. Connelly, plays perfectly the very small part of General Jung-Lu, and
Noah Beery is a wicked Sam Wang who suggests only the European
part of his Eurasian ancestry. The book is a flexible, workable
one, rather than an essay which rises at any place to great power
or suspense. The same may be said of Mr. Capellani's direction.
The only actual detriment the piece has is a set of commonplace,
utterly undramatic subtitles. How Maxwell Karger permitted such
a dull set of words to go out with his veritable optic music is hard
to understand, for these sayings are formula stuff to the last degree,
no more reminiscent of Celestial surrounding than a tea-cup made
in Dresden.

                                    --Julian Johnson in Photoplay, Vol.
                                    16, No. 2 (July 1919), page 77.

                          *   *   *

     We went to see The Red Lantern Alla Nazimova's latest photo-
play, with high anticipation, but the thing left us cold. Not thru any
fault of Nazimova, however. The story, based on Edith Wherry's
novel, has simply been swamped in gorgeousness. Before such massive and glittering backgrounds, all personal interest dwindles. We
lost all desire to know the fate of the little half English-half Chinese
girl who, raised and educated to Western ideals by missionaries,
suddenly falls in love and comes smash up against the blood barrier.
Embittered, she falls in with a plot against the white race, poses
as the goddess of the red lantern to lead the Boxers, and, in the
end, loses her life. Nazimova plays this girl of contrasting racial
moods finely, in fact it is her best performance since Revelation,
but the humanness of it all is crushed beneath tons of scenic trappings. Where an imaginative director would have suggested, thus
keeping interest centered upon the main figure of his theme, Director Albert Cappelani has crowded thousands of supers and a fortune
in Oriental architecture upon the screen. Result--cold gorgeousness.
The Red Lantern will dazzle your eye, but it will never touch your
heart. Nazimova plays both the pseudo-goddess and her English
half-sister. Noah Beery gives a vivid performance of Warner Oland
as the scoundrelly leader of the Boxers.

                                    --Frederick James Smith in Mo-
                                    tion Picture Classic, Vol. 8,
                                    No. 5 (July 1919), pages 81
                                    and 83.

☐ REGENERATION (Fox, 1915)

A more sympathetic and stirring picture of slum life than
that found in Raoul A. Walsh's production of Owen Kildare's Regeneration need not be desired. As a human interest story, strong and
true in its characterizations, and as a spectacle introducing a wonderfully realistic depiction of a fire aboard a crowded excursion
boat, the photoplay scores an emphatic success. The production is
most artistic in detail and accurate in presenting the depressing
squalor of tenement life on the East Side of New York. Moreover,
the two principal characters, those of Owen and the pretty settlement worker who brings about his regeneration, are notably well
handled by Rockcliffe Fellows and Anna Q. Nilsson.

In its original form, the story used in this picture was an
actual human document rather than a work of fiction. A product of
the East Side slums, Kildare did not learn to read or write until
after his thirtieth year, and his first book, My Mamie Rose, was
based on the facts of his own youthful life. Parts of it were a beautiful tribute to the young school teacher who inspired a desire for
knowledge and saved him from the career of a gangster. Dramatized for the stage, the story was called The Regeneration.

The photoplay is thorough in presenting the life of Owen from
childhood and showing how he is the natural product of an unfavorable
environment. Director Walsh was fortunate in his selection of types
that are in no way an exaggeration of those to be found on the streets
of the East Side and in the dives frequented by Owen. There is a
grim sort of humor in many of the scenes; there is an abundance of
excitement in others, and throughout, the picture carries a genuine
heart interest that cannot fail to move an audience.

                              --Lynde Denig in The Moving Pic-
                                ture World, Vol. 26, No. 1 (Oc-
                                tober 2, 1915), page 94.

☐ REMODELING HER HUSBAND (Paramount-Artcraft, 1920)

This is a woman's picture. A woman wrote it, a woman
stars in it, a woman was its director. And women will enjoy it
most. It does an unusual and daring thing; it presents the feminine
point of view in plot, in captions, in sets and acting. Our worthy
contemporaries of the various film trade journals took a good crack
at it. They have to take a good crack at something. But at the
Rialto in New York, where this review was accomplished, the audience just sat back and howled--and there were men there, too.
Lillian Gish has gone back to acting, but we'd like to tell her that
she is almost as good a directress as she is an actress--and that's
going some. Little things count in this picture; details are not

overlooked. Dorothy Gish is just--Dorothy Gish, which is enough
for most people. There is no-one like her, and when she gets good
stories she should lead her class. James Rennie, recruited from
the legitimate, is a gratifying leading man.

--Burns Mantle in Photoplay, Vol.
18, No. 4 (September 1920),
page 106.

*   *   *

Only the presence of Dorothy Gish, with her undeniable charm
and inimitable comedy, saves this piece from becoming a tiresome
entertainment. We can think of no other actress who can endow the
tried and true role of the young bride, whose object is to tame her
husband, with so much color and personality. Whatever appeal this
picture has is found in her performance, although it must be said
that her leading man, James Rennie, a newcomer to the screen,
gives a distinctive bit of acting. He catches the spirit of the part
with true comedy insight--never for a moment losing his balance
and overstepping the mark.

The idea is indexed in the pigeon-holes of producers' desks,
who cater to farce-comedies, as Number 1. It is lugged out repeatedly, although there is never any attempt to refurbish it--or dress
it up with novel headlights. In this case Remodeling Her Husband
runs true to form. The pattern is complete in every particular.
You have the young bride who simply adores her husband and is
happy to settle down in marital bliss; you have the equally young
groom who is determined to indulge in just one more fling. His
flirtatious disposition carries out the conflict--which is mostly a
series of scenes capitalizing his ability to alibi himself and his
spouse's efforts to bring him to account.

There is a goodly amount of comedy business established in
this mild but pleasant action due to the star's sure-fire touches,
coupled with appropriate dialogue. Finally she is provoked into
leaving him when he simply can't make his eyes behave. He is a
trifle ashamed of her because she hasn't the dash and style of the
w. k. flapper. Well, the upshot of it is she goes into business
and after being separated hubby realizes what a wonderful girl she
is and becomes repentant. And thus to the final clinch. There
are moments when the action drags, but for the most part Dorothy
Gish is there sending out shafts of her quaint humor. The idea is
hardly big enough for feature expression, but the continuity is so
even, the direction so spontaneous, the acting so spirited, that the
lapses aren't unduly noticeable. Lillian Gish shows her versatility
as the director and her ability to make the most of the story is a
creditable achievement.

--Laurence Reid in Motion Picture
News, Vol. 21, No. 26 (June 19,
1920), page 5011.

☐ REVELATION (Metro, 1918)

The most vivid screen playing of months was contributed by Alla Nazimova in Revelation, Metro's adaptation of Mabel Wagnall's A Rosebush of a Thousand Years Ago. It is the story of the spiritual regeneration of a fascinating little pagan, a grisette who poses as the Madonna. Mme. Nazimova plays Joline, a cabaret dancer, who becomes the mistress and model of a young American painter. How Joline poses as the Holy Mother when the artist goes to paint an old legend of the virgin among the branches of a monastery rosebush, which caused the bush to burst into bloom; how the dead branches again blossom under her hand in a second miracle; and how the woman, spiritually stirred, renounces her old life and leaves her lover, form a picturesque story. The plot slumps to a conventional ending when the American, now a soldier for democracy, is brought wounded to the monastery where Joline is a war-nurse. There they are married by the prior.

Nazimova shades the spiritual growth of the grisette brilliantly, but she really does her best work in depicting the fiery, untamed girl of the Latin Quarter, a creature of passions and whims, who lives but for the moment in her love for her artist and who jealously fights the approach of any one else with the fury of a tiger. Personally, Nazimova fascinated me as the little devil of the boulevards, but lost my interest when she saw the light.

Any cabaret with a Bacchanite dancing with the splendid abandon of Joline would be successful beyond calculation. Nazimova proves the value of a fine dramatic skill. In a single scene she can depict graphically the fleeting flashes of a hundred moods. I respectfully nominate her pagan Joline as the most fascinating screen characterization of the screen year.

Charles Bryant is excellent as the painter, Bigelow Cooper gives poise and distinction to the role of the worldly Parisian, and Syn de Conde makes his bit as an apache stand out. I congratulate George D. Baker on his direction. But all these things can't hold up the last two reels of Revelation.

--Frederick James Smith in Motion
Picture Classic, Vol. 6, No. 3
(May 1918), pages 52-53.

*   *   *

Although we speak of moving picture "plays," it has become evident that they are not to be considered from the theatrical or dramatic point of view. Although they employ actors and have plots, they are made for a different medium and for a different public. Besides, they are so transitory, except in the case of unusually pretentious efforts, that they are not subject to review except in their own trade organs and in the daily prints. They are like the Irish-

man's lively insect--you put your finger on him, and he isn't
there.

For instance, at this writing there is on view in New York
a "movie" which comes very near to being a play, in the dramatic
sense. If it was likely to remain long enough at any one place for
the public to rely on finding it, it would be entitled to a review as
a dramatic production. As the moving picture business is conducted,
it would take a detective, a divining rod and the mystic gifts of a
seventh-son to find out where it could be seen.

The play in question is Revelation, and it is remarkable in
the fact that it comes nearer to being a play performed consecutively
without the usual exasperating "movie" tricks than anything shown on
the screen for a long time. There is a miraculous episode--the
Virgin appearing in a rose-bush--where photographic trickery is used
legitimately. Nazimova impersonates the story's heroine, and although her voice is not heard, she has never appeared to greater
artistic advantage. The character of the artiste's gamine model,
changed by a credible experience in religion to a woman of character, gives full range to her versatility and to her command of physical expression. It may not be possible to see Revelation now, but
it is worth noting that there has been one "movie" which approached
being a real drama.

                              --"Metcalfe" in Life, Vol. 71, No.
                              1486 (March 14, 1918), page 422.

☐ THE REWARD OF THE FAITHLESS (Bluebird/Universal, 1917)

This latest five-reel Bluebird, The Reward of the Faithless,
is not, like the fabled bluebird, for happiness. It is a heavy dramatic offering whose sombre plot depresses while its very doleful-
ness fascinates and holds the interest captive. Most of the scenes
are laid in Russia. Although the photoplay ends as happily as could
be expected under the circumstances, there is a tragic strain that
can be heard above the final song of great happiness. The picture
convincingly proves the tradition of the family of one of the characters to the effect that great happiness can come to a member of that
family only through great sorrow, and we see most of the sorrow,
but little of the happiness. The story has the saving grace of a
degree of originality, and was written by Magnus Ingleton.

Wedgewood Nowell and Betty Schade head an excellent cast.
Upon these two and Claire Du Brey falls work that brings into being
their every iota of dramatic ability, and they never once fail a situation, some of which are quite difficult of interpretation. A good
characterization is done by William J. Dyer. Nicholas Dunaew
proves himself adequate, as does also Richard Le Reno.

The picture has received careful and artistic production by

Rex Ingram, some of the lightings being especially effective. Photography throughout is excellent.

There are several points in the story at which plausibility is considerably stretched. For instance, the adventurer's wife apparently dies when the man and the one-time woman of the streets, who has been taken into the home, fail to give her prescribed pills. We see the wife in her shroud, and believe her to be dead. But she isn't. She comes out of her comatose trance when her first lover mourns at her side.

--Ben H. Grimm in The Moving
Picture World, Vol. 31, No. 6
(February 10, 1917), page 868.

☐ ROMANCE (United Artists, 1920)

The long-heralded screen version of Edward Sheldon's famous play, Romance, with Doris Keane playing her identical role, has reached the exhibitors and the public and the verdict is sure to be "an artistic production." The name of the star may not be familiar to the majority of picturegoers and there may not be much box-office value attached to it. Still the average patron is ever in search of a new type. From that standpoint the star is certain to please any one tired of the personalities who are presented every other week. She brings to the screen a fragrant personality, even though her histrionic capabilities are smothered through its limitations. Yet she screens well and conveys a spiritual quality in her work.

The picture itself is lacking in physical action, there being scarcely a scene of situation or climax. So it is dependent upon its theme of broken romance for sustaining value. And it must be said in all fairness that action which presents nothing else but impassioned and often sentimental love-making has a tendency to become wearisome at times. The picture follows the play very closely, the subtitles being genuine excerpts, and carrying on its thought exceedingly well. And the treatment is identical with the original, even to the prologue and its subsequent development. A young man contemplating matrimony approaches his grandfather on matters of love and the old gentleman's imagination travels back to the heyday of his youth--to the big romance of his heart.

His account of it makes up the moving moments of the play. He is a clergyman in love with an Italian opera singer and the conflict is generated in his effort to rise above worldly things and take her with him. But she is of the flesh and the romance ends with a deep note of pathos. It is hard to reconcile the conduct of the young dominie with his religious doctrine. And his action, to some, will be a big pill to swallow. Chet Withey, the director, has brought out all the atmosphere. The scenes are well arranged and he has guided the players to get the most from them. Basil Sydney

as the romancer plays with a good deal of fire and persuasion, while
Norman Trevor brings a balancing note with his admirable restraint.
The picture will certainly appeal to those in search of romance or
who have lost it in the days when love was young.

--Laurence Reid in Motion Picture
News, Vol. 21, No. 22 (May 29,
1920), page 4545.

☐ A ROMANCE OF HAPPY VALLEY (Paramount-Artcraft, 1919)

One of the famous indoor motion picture sports is to joke
about THE "great American motion picture." With A Romance of
Happy Valley, D. W. Griffith has at least created A "great American motion picture." It is a beautiful, heart-gripping and genuine
story of a little Kentucky town in the days before any one thought
of a great world war.

In many of his productions Griffith has pictured various phases
of American character, but he knows Kentucky a little better than
any other place, for that is the place of his birth, and others that
know the same country will appreciate how perfectly he has pictured
its people. It is to that section what the stage production, Way Down
East, was to New England--and it is just as sure to have as wide an
appeal to every section. We saw it in the crowded Strand theatre,
crowded with New Yorkers, and we believe that many of these did
not quite "get" the full spirit when the master craftsman really "kids"
New York. It is going over with great enthusiasm at the Strand; it
will go even better in other sections.

It is a simple little story--a story of a boy and a girl of the
Kentucky village and their love; of the boy's desire to go to New
York and win a fortune, but of the church-going people being afraid
of his fate in the wickedness of the great city. He "backslides" and
goes, promising the girl that he will be back within a year; but other
years, till seven, pass without his coming. The father now faces
losing his home and is desperate, and when the son returns, so
changed that he is not recognized, the father is tempted to try to
rob him. Then Griffith has laid a plot that grips and amazes. We
wouldn't try to tell patrons the full story of the picture. They need
to see it portrayed in the Griffith way.

Robert Harron and Lillian Gish do the very best work of their
careers, and there is a notable supporting cast. Griffith has pictured
the negro characters better than in any production that we have seen.
The settings are the simple ones of the country town, with most of
them exteriors. The photography is of the highest order, the close-
ups being unusually convincing.

We believe that most of your patrons will laugh a lot and cry
a little and that they will leave your theatre the best advertisers for

this picture that you ever had. Its appeal is universal, and you
needn't be afraid to put your personal guarantee behind it.

--R. E. Pritchard in <u>Motion Picture</u>
<u>News</u>, Vol. 19, No. 6 (February
<u>8, 1919</u>), page 918.

☐ ROMEO AND JULIET (Metro, 1916)

Metro Pictures Corporation has produced for the screen
Shakespeare's <u>Romeo and Juliet</u>. It is a great production, one that
easily will rank with the best kinematographic efforts that have gone
before. It is a subject that should appeal alike to the Shakespearean
student and the man to whom the linked names of Romeo and Juliet
have only the remotest significance. Plainly, it has been the aim
of the producers to visualize the story of the world's greatest love
tragedy just as it was penned by the hand of the master. They have
neither subtracted from it in any essential detail nor have they added
to it.

Best of all, the textual accompaniment to the photographed
action is the language of Shakespeare. Right here is a good place
to say that the leaders constitute of this picture a thing apart. We
have all heard it said that the works of the Bard of Avon are not
for the screen--that the "upright stage" robs them of their matchless dialogue. The Metro production measurably disproves the assertion. Elaborate use has been made of the text. Artistically and
clearly presented are these gems of the world's best literature;
there is no possibility that their majesty will be marred by those
who are "capable of nothing but inexplicable dumb-shows and noise."

To the making of the picture Director John W. Noble has
contributed his best work for the screen. The scenario was prepared by John Arthur, Rudolph De Cordova and Mr. Noble. The
director was assisted in the staging by Edward Elsner and Mr. De
Cordova. There is no need to tell us these men were given carte
blanche. The result speaks for itself.

Francis X. Bushman and Beverly Bayne head the cast. It is
an ideal combination. Mr. Bushman, above all else, possesses the
physique of a "well-governed youth," of "a man to encounter Tybalt";
he appears to unusual advantage in the scanted garb of the period--
in the language of Juliet's Nurse, "his leg excels all men's." He
fits the part, and he plays it. Miss Bayne is a rare Juliet. Kindly
endowed by nature in figure and feature, she has entered into the
interpretation of the role of the heroine with marked sympathy and
feeling.

Supporting these two is a splendid cast--and also perhaps the
longest in the history of motion pictures. There are exactly one
hundred names in the list furnished by the company. Space forbids

mention of more than a few. Robert Cummings is Friar Laurence,
a fine performance. Adella Barker is the portly Nurse to Juliet.
Joseph Dailey is Peter, the Nurse's servant. These two contribute
to the somber story the sole touches of lighter color. W. Lawson
Butt is Tybalt, a heroic figure; Edmund Elton and Helen Dunbar are
the Capulets, Eric Hudson and Genevieve Reynolds the Montagues;
Horace Vinton is the Prince.

Romeo and Juliet will appeal to picture lovers as an all-
around production. It will possess a distinct double appeal--to the
eye and to the mind--that of the action and that of the text. At the
Broadway theater on the initial presentation, October 19, nearly two
hours and a quarter were devoted to the running of the eight thousand
feet of film; yet the movement at this normal speed is sharp, the
best of evidence the scenes have been trimmed to a hair. Approxi-
mately a full reel is devoted to the single scene of the balcony--that
where Romeo climbs the Capulet wall following the "accustomed
feast" of the Capulets and from the ground underneath Juliet's window converses with his new-found love. Of the twelve thousand inch-
es of film devoted to the portrayal of this great epic of the stage
not a single one is superfluous. It is the dramatic height of the
play as we see it on the screen. The remainder of the story holds,
but this particular scene markedly moves.

As has been said, the story runs with fidelity to the text. It
is told so clearly that lack of knowledge of the book is no bar to
full enjoyment of the production. Pictorially the subject is notable.
The studio interiors and exteriors--especially those of the streets of
Verona--are unusually elaborate. For the home of the Capulets Director Noble has employed a great castle which he discovered in the
neighborhood of the metropolis, a setting which most happily fits the
requirements of the story.

Metro has done the screen a distinct service. Not only has
it lavished its best on the adaptation of a great tragedy; not only has
it brought it out in all its strength and beauty, its glamor and romance, for the education as well as entertainment of countless thousands who heretofore may have had slight acquaintance with it or
concern about it. It has demonstrated that Shakespeare dead three
hundred years penned in his youth lines that stamp him the greatest
title builder in the world of to-day.

> --George Blaisdell in The Moving
> Picture World, Vol. 30, No.
> 5 (November 4, 1916), page
> 685.

*   *   *

There has been a tradition that eternal Shakespeare is the
foundation of everything dramatic, and that his name must appear
sooner or later before any theater in the world. The two-
dimension stage has now done much to confirm that tradition.

Romeo and Juliet was last month's biggest endeavor.* Bill of Avon
became not only a scenarioist but a caption-writer, and his titles,
notwithstanding their preparation some centuries in advance, were
at moments snappy and humorous as Keystone; at others immeasurably poetic, profound or dramatic; and--here's the proof of this un-
aging pudding--there was not an instance in which the Elizabethan
Turnbull-Sullivan's stuff failed to get over, and get over big.

We have the Metro organization to thank for a sunpainting of
the great Veronese love-tragedy, for if Metro hadn't thought of it
it's empty spools to a reel of The Birth of a Nation that Fox wouldn't.
Not a nice thing, this foxy faculty of pinning himself to everybody's
coattails, yet he at least gives all his imitations with profound energy
and prodigal extravagance.

While Metro's is the one entertainment worth perpetuity, Mr.
Fox will carry the gospel of real drama far, and in his great chain
of theaters, will present a highly satisfactory and reverently handled
Shakespeare film before thousands who would not otherwise see it.
Therefore Mr. Fox, despite his copy-cat propensities, is in this instance a benefactor, for in our optic play-shops we have too many
pieces and too few plays, too many dully diluted dime-novels and too
little of the grandeur of life.

Here's something to think over: one successful Shakespearean
film production such as these twins does more to spread dramatic
education among the people in general than all the "classic" revivals
of Sothern, or Mantell, or Warde, in a decade. Reckless statement?
Not at all. Figure not only your audience-per cent; remember that
people who go to see Shakespeare in a talk-shop go with a stiff sense
of duty, and usually take the magic lines and majestic situations like
a dose of spring medicine. Ever hear anybody talk about Shakespeare coming away from a Sothern blank-verse orgy? They go to
see Sothern, and they endure Shakespeare.

But the folk who attend these two Romeos are really entertained. They trek thither for a real show. Of course, they may
wish to see F. Xavier in tights, or Theda as a good baby for once
in her life, but it is the spell of the play which holds them. It is
Shakespeare--not Mr. Rowland or Mr. Fox, Mr. Bushman or Mr.
Hilliard, Miss Bayne or Miss Bara, who is the real star of the
screen.

From time to time the little fluttering hearts whose musky
notes grace the whittled pine desk of our blind, deaf, ninety-year-
old answer man make much wailing to-do and what-not over this department's "abuse" of Mr. Bushman. Abate, gentle cardiac earth-

*Julian Johnson here provides an overview of both the Metro and
Fox productions of Romeo and Juliet; for obvious reasons the two
films were released simultaneously.

quakes, for as Romeo this department found Mr. Bushman not only
in the best role of his career, but doing the best acting he has ever
shot into the transparencies. Medically, we might term Mr. Bushman the acting hypochondriac. He has always been thinking of himself and his pretty clothes and his sweet biceps and grand smile--
and forgetting his character. He may have been "scairt" into doing
a superb Romeo by the overwhelming splendor and tradition of the
woeful Italian lad; nevertheless, the fact remains that he is a superb
Romeo, performing with discretion, dignity, an unusual amount of
reserve and astounding sincerity. As Romeo Mr. Bushman fills the
eye. The trappings of our ancestors, who wore the clothes of the
chorus and buttoned themselves up with shoe-strings instead of discs
of horn, admirably caress his well-plaited muscles. Mr. Bushman
is one of few screen lovers who can be unutterably earnest, clean
and wholesome at the same time.

Miss Bayne is the sweetest of Juliets, but one could ask a
little more fervor, at moments. This Juliet would scarcely have
risked immurement in the grisly tomb of the Capulets. I think she
would have married her cousin, heckled him into an affinity's arms--
then the divorce of outraged chastity, and Romeo; provided Romeo
had waited. In the tender, childish moments of Juliet's love she
may be characterized only by the word "exquisite."

An easy third in the race for Metro honors is Robert Cummings' Friar Laurence. I must confess an ignorance of the period
which makes me unable to say whether Friar Laurence was a bearded
or a shaven monk; but I believe he was bearded, and in this--if my
supposition is correct--Metro is right, and Fox wrong. At any rate,
Cummings moves behind a hirsute curtain that would honor an Is-
raelitish patriarch, and is a wholly lovable celibate and friend to
humanity.

As to associate pantomimists, Romeo and Juliet are adeptly
surrounded, and the cast in general is satisfying without having individuals of particular note, unless one speaks of the fine Mercutio
of Fritz Leiber, W. Lawson Butt's energetic Tybalt, and Peter,
quaintly played by Joseph Dailey.

In direction, location, costuming, scene-making and general
equipment, Metro has never approached this picture. Seldom has
any stage enterprise shown such a real period as these scenes glimpse.
The ghostly procession past the bier of Juliet when she, in imagination, wakes untimely, is as thrilling a piece of fine art as has been
conceived for such a situation. The marriage scene is beautifully
rendered. The Metro organization proved its Shakespearean devotion
by the use of so many literal transcripts as titles that the sheet
could endure some eliminations very nicely.

When Fox changed the guard for Corporal Don Jose, in his
production of Carmen, he brought in a regiment, and the gun-hands
knocked off like the charge of the Light Brigade. This incident is
dragged from the well of history not to deride Carmen, which was

a lively show, but to illustrate Mr. Fox's disbelief in doing anything
by halves. Romeo and Juliet, here, is a pageant, a glittering spectacle, a tumult of passion and punch.   The Capulet manse lives up
to the I. W. W. idea of John D. Rockefeller's home.   A street-
fight is nothing less than Civil war.   No keeper of an inn of that
period had as many beds in his establishment as this Juliet seems
to possess.   There are couches and reclining places everywhere.

Histrionically, Miss Bara is a better Juliet than Miss Bayne,
for she brings to the play's tropic moments all the steam-heat that
the cool Beverly lacks.   Here is a consistent and more convincing
acting performance--but it is always acting.   There are breath-
catching moments in little Beverly's assumption when she seems a
very real and helpless child, caught in the tentacles of an octopian
fate.   At other moments, such as the balcony farewell and her defiance of her father, Miss Bara has Miss Bayne standing still while
she sweeps by like a whirlwind.   So there you are.

Harry Hilliard is altogether satisfactory as Romeo.   He is
a youthful lover, he has many, many sets of wonderful scenery, all
of which he wears well; and he has a sort of fine, clean sincerity
necessary to such a being.   Nothing worse as Romeo could have
been imagined than our modern, over-vamped type of stage lover.
Both organizations steered clear of this.

Glen White's Mercutio is splendid, and John Webb Dillion is
a fine Tybalt.   Alice Gale as the nurse deserves especial commendation.   Walter Law, an unusually careful and intelligent actor, gives
the conventional portrait of Friar Laurence.   Picking on form, one
would say that Law would sweep the field as Friar Laurence; the
fact that he doesn't may be accounted for by direction and the scenario.

Though the front families of Verona seem to live in the town
hall, there are many locations of enchanting beauty and reality scattered through the thousands of feet of this picture.   The director--
or Mr. Fox--had a novel notion of improving Shakespeare by adding
some comedy for the best little funny bet at her weight in America,
Jane Lee.   Shakespearean text are used discreetly in the subtitles.

Metro's Romeo and Juliet seeks as its goal the artistic per-
petuation of a great story.   It is just that.

Fox's Romeo and Juliet aims to be a thrilling entertainment.
It is.

> --Julian Johnson in Photoplay, Vol.
> 11, No. 2 (January 1917), pages
> 96-100.

☐   THE ROSARY (Selig/V-L-S-E, 1915)

The Rosary is a big picture, and its bigness does not rely on

its length, but mainly on artistic production, which includes, of
course, direction, acting and the other elements which contribute to
a well visualized story.

After viewing the seven reels twice, once on each of two con-
secutive days, I was forced to the conclusion--so far as my individual opinion is concerned--that there was only one important discordant
note in the harmony of this feature's run. That is the lack of sufficient motive in the story to convince a thinking mind that Kenward
Wright could have been the arch villain he shows himself to be in
this photoplay. I was rather astonished, indeed, to discover that
such vindictive animus existed in the heart of Wright against Bruce
Wilton; for we see them in the picnic scene with the sisters Vera
and Alice Wallace, and Wright is seemingly well satisfied in the
company of Alice, the least attractive of the two, while we discover
that Bruce and Vera are in love. Only once did I catch Wright cast
a longing look in the direction of Vera and that when she and Bruce
walk off to moon by themselves, leaving Wright and Alice to follow
their example. Surely this look is not sufficient to prepare one for
the fiendish hate soon afterwards expressed by Wright, in the ruin
of the man who has always been his friend, and who still believes
him a friend.

Aside from this single exception, The Rosary made a strong
appeal to me. Director Campbell deserves great praise for the settings he has given this photoplay. Whether it be in old Ireland or
New York, the scenes are nicely appropriate. Particularly are we
interested in the scenes surrounding the village home of young Brian
Kelly, afterwards Father Kelly. The interior of the home itself has
the atmosphere of what such a home meant about 40 or 50 years
ago, in the south or west of Ireland. What a realistic picture is
the scene showing Brian's defense of his little playmate and sweetheart, Madge Callahan. Or that fishing scene after the fray is over,
or the welcome given Brian on his homecoming several years afterwards! How the old jaunting car, weak in its springs, sags as it
jolts over the rough cobble stones, and how the villagers, in their
haste to catch sight of Brian, jostle against goats or trip over the
waddling geese! The interior and exterior of the village church, of
which the good Father Ryan--who is young Brian's heaven-sent friend
--form a study in the art of lending atmosphere and color.

When young Father Kelly finds his life work in the United
States, we note that the settings are just as carefully and appropri-
ately selected. The interiors of the Wilton mansion, of Father Kelly's apartments in the tenement district of New York, and the exterior showing the unfinished doorway of the new Church of the Rosary (contributed by Bruce Wilton to his good friend and old tutor,
Father Kelly, before the crash to his fortune came) are all worthy
of intelligent appreciation. When it is remembered that many of
these five scenes are tinted, the fullness of the effect will be better
apprehended.

The acting in The Rosary is excellent. Not since I saw my
deceased friend, Harry Cashman, in the role of a venerable priest,

in Essanay's Sunshine, have I been so moved by anyone else in a
similar role as by Charles Clary, in the part of Father Kelly. In
this case the role is far more exacting, as the priest is seen while
he is a student and then afterwards throughout long service in the
church. The gradual aging, which requires most artistic simulation,
is most skillfully accomplished, both in action and make-up. Indeed
the characterization has the force of a mighty appeal for good, so
deeply impressed does one become by the saintly and noble character of this good man. Many fine heart touches are made by Mr.
Clary here and there, by little bits of "business," which convey the
delicate effects of light and shade in a masterful portraiture.

Miss Kathlyn Williams, it seems to me, can renew her girl-
hood at will, judging from her winsome impersonation of Vera Wallace. In the strong, emotional scenes between Bruce Wilton and his
wife, Vera, Miss Williams meets the requirements fully. Wheeler
Oakman has added quite materially to his laurels by his impersonation of Bruce Wilton. I must compliment the young lady who played
the part of Madge Callahan--grown up. Her acting is quite spirited,
and she succeeds in convincing one that in affairs of the heart a
girl will oppose even the church to win the object of her choice. I
would like to mention others, equally deserving, but space forbids.
--James S. McQuade in The Mov-
ing Picture World, Vol. 24, No.
13 (June 26, 1915), page 2105.

☐ SCARLET DAYS (Paramount-Artcraft, 1919)

Since David Griffith gave us his epic, Broken Blossoms, we
again look forward to new productions emanating from his studios
with something of the expectation we once awaited his old-time Bio-
graphs. Mr. Griffith's latest, Scarlet Days, is a tale of the mining
camps of '49, built around a young outlaw, Alvarez, said to have
been a real character of California history. There is nothing particular about Mr. Griffith's melodramatic opus, altho Mr. Griffith,
by a multitude of tiny touches, gets a little closer to what the real
pioneers and dance-hall favorites must have been. But Scarlet Days
is distinctive in at least one item: Richard Barthelmess' portrayal
of Alvarez, a sensitive, finely attuned romantic performance. Little
Clarine Seymour makes a Mexican spitfire stand out and Eugenie
Besserer gives a very commendable presentation of a grey-haired
mining camp belle.
--Frederick James Smith in Motion
Picture Classic, Vol. 9, No. 5
(January 1920), pages 56-57.

☐ THE SEA-WOLF (Bosworth, 1913)

I would characterize all of Jack London's stories as preemi-

nently filmable.   As Mr. Bosworth is even to the most superficial
eye peculiarly fitted for impersonating types of the Jack London pen,
the combination which makes its bow to us with a seven-reel filming
of The Sea-Wolf is most propitious.   It is a first effort and it is
creditable and gives promise of splendid things in the future, but it
is not an unqualified success.   Even such filmable stories as those
of London cannot be allowed to go upon the screen undramatized.
The process of adaptation must be a process of elimination, too,
and the tendency even in such a picturesque tale, so rich in episode,
must be toward simplifying and strengthening the action.   In these
requirements the present production has not reached perfection, but
I am glad to add that everywhere the spectator meets glorious pictures and the subtle touch of the London variety of genius.

No praise can be too high for the settings and for the photography.   The spirit of the ocean, which London conjures with such
enviable ease, is on the screen and travels from the screen to the
delighted audience.   The attention to detail in all nautical matters,
the characterization of the types of sailors, who sail in the London
stories--and we all know they are true enough sailors and always
mighty interesting--leave not the least thing to be desired.   I think
a word of acknowledgment is likewise due to the cameraman, whose
task was a heavy burden.   He has done well.   The realism for which
a London story affords such fine chances is not lacking.   It is convincing no less than exciting.   Take the accident.   It has every appearance of being real, and the cheers the scenes brought forth from
a rather critical audience were well deserved.

Far the most difficult part of the whole production was the
rendering of the "Sea-Wolf."   Mr. Bosworth had the physique and
the artistic size required by the part, though in the characterization
he was not quite as strong as in the "straight" acting.   He seemed
in the early part of the story not quite certain of his ground, but as
the action advanced to the great dramatic moments he electrified the
audience by his masterly portrayals.   He does not always succeed
in expressing a mood, but a passion he can express according to
Shakespeare.   He found his footing at the first great dramatic moment and never lost it afterward.   It was his acting which was chiefly
responsible for the sharp revival of interest toward the end of the
story just as the action was beginning to drag.

His support was fair.   Viola Barry, the only woman in the
story, is conscientious in her work.   It would have been better if
she had not emerged from the shipwreck with her makeup in a flour-
ishing condition.

I think five reels would have been much better than seven.   In
saying this I realize very well that the adaptation for the screen may
be allowed on a much more generous latitude than an adaptation for
the conventional stage.   Indeed many of the incidents of the story,
though they do not carry the action forward by the fraction of an
inch, are entirely welcome to the motion picture audience.   What
could be more interesting than the rough but good-natured comedy of

the sailor folk? The throwing overboard of the cook and "washing" him because of his contempt of sailors' stomachs, the appearance of a man eating shark going in the direction of the unlucky cook and finally the capture of the monster are incidents that add not a little to the charm and the general effect of the story. Other scenes, however, were painfully superfluous. The lingering of the poet and the critic on Endeavor Island was altogether too long and the action in the last thousand feet could have been fully brought out in less than five hundred feet without the least danger of crowding. The trips to the boat and the final incidents on it might profitably have been cut even at the risk of cutting the story itself. These and other scenes that might be mentioned in different parts of the production have not enough humorous or spectacular value to allow them to detract from the central theme of the story.

The motion picture art is in a fair way to profit by further screen adaptations of the London stories. I predict that in his second venture Mr. Bosworth will touch perfection. He has the ability and he has the ambition which is justified and useful only as it is supported by ability. There was a lavish expenditure of money in the production, an item that counts for much when the money is expended judiciously, as it was in the present case. Every friend of the good motion picture will hail the present and the future work of Mr. Bosworth with sincere joy. We cannot have enough good, clean, thrilling pictures of adventures at sea and in strange lands.

--W. Stephen Bush in The Moving
Picture World, Vol. 18, No. 5
(November 1, 1913), page 480.

☐ SEVEN KEYS TO BALDPATE (Paramount-Artcraft, 1917)

George M. Cohan's second appearance on the Artcraft program is by way of an adaptation of the comic-mystery play, Seven Keys to Baldpate, which enjoyed a remunerative run on Broadway not so many years ago. It is, indeed a laughable and, at the same time, intensifying piece of work. The various mysterious characters and mysterious events that respectively visit and involve the abstracted author while in the seclusion of Baldpate Inn come thick and fast, while the general tone of the production swings alternately between the surprisingly melodramatic and the ridiculously farcical. The ending which displays a fade-in to the author finishing his book and which reveals the fact that the wild happenings of the previous scenes were manufactured by the man himself, is big in its quality of surprise, but not so startling in its effect as it was on the stage. Such a trick has been employed too often in pictures to draw more than a passing "Oh" from an audience.

The only George M. has improved his picture work over his first production by holding himself in check. He still, however, utilizes his hands as much if not more than his face and is constantly

on the go. But such traits are identical with the actor, and while
he would certainly appear to better advantage if he held himself still
more in restraint, his personality then would not be the thing peculiarly Cohan that it is now. On the whole, he puts over every humorous point with a significance that the spectator can never doubt.

The staging of the picture under the direction of Hugh Ford
is modeled after the original play as much as possible. The hotel
set is excellent, and the many rapid entrances and exits of the characters have been handled deftly. The photography and lighting merits
the warmest praise.

Anna Q. Nilsson makes a most suitable opposite for the star
and of the remainder of the supporting cast Armand Cortes is the
outstanding figure because of the extreme manner in which he bur-
lesques a heavy's role. Seven Keys to Baldpate, with George M.
Cohan, should, all in all, prove an attraction over any theatre--and
likewise in any theatre.

The Story and Players

George Washington Magee (George Cohan) makes a bet that he
can write a novel in twenty-four hours. His adversary sends him to
his summer hotel, Baldpate Inn, where he may have absolute quiet.
There is only one key to it, he is told, and that is in his possession. But as soon as G. W. Magee starts writing, a succession of
startling events occur. There proved to be seven keys to Baldpate,
and when the seven persons gain admittance to the lonely inn, a wild
and furious melodrama is unfolded before the eyes of the bewildered
author. All he succeeds in doing is to fall in love with the heroine
of it. Then the characters disappear, and it is discovered that Magee has been writing all the while. The heroine of the story turns
out to be a newspaper woman, who comes to interview him later on.

The various characters of the melodrama are enacted by Elda
Furry, Corrine Uzzell, Joseph Smiley, C. Warren Cook, Purnell
Pratt, Frank Losee, Eric Hudson and Carlton Macy, besides those
already mentioned.

--Peter Milne in Motion Picture
News, Vol. 16, No. 11 (Septem-
ber 15, 1917), page 1856.

☐ SHERLOCK HOLMES (Essanay/V-L-S-E, 1916)

Speaking in sporting parlance, which by the way seems particularly appropriate in the present instance, the Essanay Company
has scored a clean and decisive knockout with the film version of
William Gillette's stage success--Sherlock Holmes. It is not merely
a photodrama with a punch--it is a screen triumph with a varied

assortment of punches, and veritable triphammer punches, all of them. Sensational to the 'steenth degree, vibrant with rapid action, it grips and holds the attention of the spectators from the first to the seventh and final reel.

Granted that some of the thrilling situations may seem a trifle exaggerated on calm reflection, be it understood that there is no time for reflection of that type when one is engaged in watching with breathless interest the battle of wits, liberally intermixed with physical struggles, between the omnipotent detective of Conan Doyle's creation and the forces of crime, guided by the master mind of Professor Moriarty. Mr. Gillette made the role of Holmes an unforgettable characterization before the footlights. With the assistance of the motion picture camera he has more than duplicated his success in the "legitimate," for the silent drama production here lends itself to an infinite variety of detail impossible of attainment on the boards.

In the hands of a less capable director than Arthur Berthelet, who is responsible for the handling of the play, or left to the mercy of a mediocre cast, the feature would have fallen far short of its present excellence. But the directing is admirable and the talent supporting the star leaves nothing to be desired, with the result that Sherlock Holmes goes forth to the public bearing the stamp of critical approval by all who witnessed its private showing.

Where such a uniform standard of excellence is preserved throughout, it is a difficult matter to select any particular stage of the tale in preference to others. But if a selection must be made, possibly the most thrilling scene is that in which Professor Moriarty and Holmes face each other in the latter's room, when the detective thwarts the arch criminal's designs upon his life. In this connection it may be said that Ernest Maupain, as Moriarty, divides honors equally with Mr. Gillette. Moriarty's slow, venomous approach toward the man he hates, the snake-like glitter of his vicious eyes, the storm of passion which shakes his robust frame, the frenzied outbreak of baffled rage made manifest when he dashes the empty and useless revolver with which he has tried to shoot his enemy to the floor is the climax of melodramatic realism. As a foil to the savage fury of Moriarty nothing more striking could be imagined than the cold aplomb of Holmes, his cynical sneer, his calm disdain as he indifferently turns his back on his frantic foeman and applies a light to his pipe. It is a whirlwind of passion beating vainly upon an iceberg, a remarkable bit of acting warranted to linger in the memories of the spectators.

Another exciting episode is the attempt of Moriarty's band of crooks to trap Holmes in their den in the suburbs, when the latter not only defeats their aim, but rescues Alice Faulkner from the house of death. A vein of humor is injected into this scene by Holmes' sardonic comments on the futile efforts of his enemies to ensnare him, and the parading of the prisoners past him by the police, as he lounges carelessly in the street, complete master of the situation.

According to the plot, Holmes is retained by the members of a noble foreign family to recover certain documents which, if made public, will bring scandal upon them. The papers are held by Alice Faulkner, whose sister has been ruined by a relative of Holmes' clients. She intends with their assistance to obtain revenge upon the family of her sister's seducer. Alice falls into the hands of a band of crooks, of whom Moriarty is the head. They are anxious to obtain the papers for blackmailing purposes. Holmes visits the house where Alice is detained, finds the papers, but restores them to her, saying that he will not retain the documents until she gives them to him of her own will.

Then commences a war between Professor Moriarty and Holmes. How the detective meets plot with counter-plot, outwits the crooks, jails Moriarty and the members of his band, wins Alice's affections and restores the papers to his clients, it is not necessary to relate in detail. In the finish the tender passion triumphs, when Dr. Watson, Holmes' faithful colleague, steps outside his apartment, closing the door behind him and leaving the detective alone with the girl, a final closeup revealing the lovers in an attitude that indicates the clearing away of all misunderstandings between them.

Marjorie Kay endows the role of Alice Faulkner with distinctive grace and charm; Edward Fielding is effective as the amiable Dr. Watson, and the work of the remainder of the cast cannot be too warmly commended. The narrative is so sharply outlined by the expressive pantomime employed that few subtitles are necessary to the continuity of the drama, and those shown are decisive and to the point.

It is seldom that such good use is made of "fade-outs" and "close ups" as in this production, and the photography as a whole, in its tinting, its handsome interiors and exterior views, is on a par in artistic merit with the clever acting which establishes Sherlock Holmes as an undoubted super-feature of filmland.

--P. in The New York Dramatic
Mirror, Vol. 75, No. 1952 (May
20, 1916), page 25.

*   *   *

Essanay has made a seven part feature of Sherlock Holmes that should have a very strong call from exhibitors and "make good" with picture patrons. Added to this, the name of William Gillette as the star makes for an ideal combination "on form." The "form" is lived up to by the scenario, made by H. S. Sheldon, the cast selected, the direction, and the detail--all of which appears to have been given intelligent and careful consideration. For instance, the double doors on hotel rooms in a continental hotel, portieres on the inside of doors in an English house, the baggage rack on top of a London cab, etc. It seems a pity to have to find a flaw in any of the detail, but as so many things are to be commended, one criticism

shouldn't be objected to. In order to create a fire in the home
where Mary Faulkner is kept prisoner so she may become alarmed
and reveal the hiding place of the letters upon which the plot hinges,
the butler throws over an oil lamp. No London town house used
lamps in the Holmes days, and if this one did, there should have
been evidence of other lamps about the remainder of the residence.
But the going to all the trouble of securing a good imitation of the
exterior of Holmes' house in Baker Street, London, is alone sufficient to "stand off" the lamp faux pas. Then again the assembling
has been done with much more care than is usually devoted to this
important part of a feature. The scenario creates suspense within
the first very few minutes, and never lets up, not even for comedy,
throughout the seven reels. It is intensely gripping and interesting,
carrying with it the bare outline of the love of Holmes for Miss
Faulkner, and studiously avoiding any reference to Mr. Holmes' ad-
diction to the needle. While all of the parts are well played, the
one standing out strongest, next to the star, is that of Moriarty as
portrayed by Ernest Maupin. The picture is so good it would hold
interest if called by any other name and without starring Mr. Gillette.

> --Jolo (Josh Lowe) in Variety, Vol.
> 42, No. 11 (May 12, 1916), page
> 18.

☐ SHORE ACRES (Metro, 1920)

The real star of this picturization of James Herne's stage
classic is Edward J. Connelly. His Uncle Nat is a finely drawn
study that no other actor in our collection could have accomplished
as well. The melodrama which your mother or grandmother could
tell you about has been carefully, almost too painstakingly done by
Rex Ingram. Alice Lake does not equal her fine appearance in
Should a Woman Tell? All in all, it's a praiseworthy production.

> --Burns Mantle in Photoplay, Vol.
> 18, No. 1 (June 1920), page 99.

☐ SHOULDER ARMS (Chaplin/First National, 1918)

Charlie Chaplin came to town in Shoulder Arms, which, to
us, is the one screen classic of the war. In fact, after watching
Chaplin as a khaki hero, we can never take another war drama
seriously. Memories of Charlie drilling with the awkward squad,
his well known feet the despair of a nerve-racked drill sergeant;
of his combat with cooties; of Chaplin slumbering to sleep in a hut
filled with mud and water; of----But why spoil the joy of fans by
telling the humorous twists of Shoulder Arms? Let it suffice to
say that Charlie captures William Hohenzollern, the crown prince

and Von Hindenburg with neatness and despatch.   And if there's any
funnier scene than the episode where Chaplin camouflages himself
as a tree and is pursued by a fat and worried Hun thru a forest,
we would like to see it.

There isn't a single dull second in Shoulder Arms, which
shows in many ways just why Chaplin maintains his amazing grip
upon the affections of fans.   First, the comedian takes months to
make three reels of comedy, developing his fun carefully, discard-
ing here and building up there.   He doesn't rush his productions
out.   He whets interest and has the public waiting for him.   Secondly, he never duplicates.   Every comedy is different, not only as to
action, but characterization.   All this in comment upon his business
acumen.   Above all else, Chaplin is a truly great actor.   He is
human--touching when he wishes to be.   His little soldier in Shoulder Arms isn't a mere merry manikin going thru a maze of comedy
situations.   He is a human figure, sometimes even a pathetic one.
Audiences do not merely laugh at him.   They love him.

Some one has said that Bruce Bairnsfather's cartoon character, Ole Bill, personifies the British Tommy's spirit in the war.
Charlie Chaplin's little soldier certainly personifies the American
view of the struggle.

Shoulder Arms marks the last appearance of Edna Purviance
opposite Chaplin.   And his brother, Syd, returns to the films as a
bunkie.
                                        --Frederick James Smith in Motion
                                           Picture Classic, Vol. 7, No. 5
                                           (January 1919), page 48.

☐ SICK ABED (Paramount-Artcraft, 1920)

This farce was funny in the legitimate.   It is anything but
funny here.   One goes drearily back to one's desk after seeing it,
asking the old corona "Can such things really be?"   Sam Wood is
usually a good director; but here he was working on the principle
that there has got to be a guffaw in every scene, boys.   He didn't
do a thing to Wallace Reid, who, over-made-up, at times looks
positively pretty.   There's a nurse in it--a beautiful nurse who
never got any diplomas in nursing, but a lot of them in looks.   Bebe
Daniels.   No wonder Wally didn't want to get well.
                                        --Photoplay, Vol. 18, No. 4 (Sep-
                                           tember 1920), page 106.

☐ THE SINKING OF THE LUSITANIA (Winsor McKay/Jewel, 1918)

In this latest animated cartoon which was exhibited at the

Strand theater, New York City, during the week of April 28, Windsor McCay has surpassed in tragic realism anything of the kind that has yet been attempted. In fact we believe that The Sinking of the Lusitania is the first tragic subject that has been presented by means of animated drawing. Its sole purpose, apart from artistic effort, is evidently to instill patriotism in the hearts of spectators and further hatred, if possible, for the German perpetrators of frightfulness. It is tremendously realistic, even the fantastic coils of smoke writhing about the doomed vessel reflecting the terror and agitation of the moment. It tells its story clearly, recalling effectively those first bitter moments of America's sorrow and resentment toward the common enemy.

The cartoon represents 25,000 drawings on separate sheets of celluloid, which it is said to have taken McCay two years to complete. It took eight days to photograph the drawings one at a time. Each detail from the sighting of the Lusitania by the German submarine to the actual sinking of the ship is shown. The lowering of the life boats, the tilting of the vessel bow first, the leaping into the sea of the terrified victims, and all the other pitiable sights that the situation presented are vividly shown in the picture.

> --Margaret I. MacDonald in The Moving Picture World, Vol. 36, No. 7 (May 18, 1918), page 1034.

☐ SNOW WHITE (Famous Players/Paramount, 1917)

In Snow White, Marguerite Clark repeats her former successes and adds another link to the chain of attractive plays which the Famous Players have furnished her. That they have not before delved into the unlocked treasures of her past stage successes is remarkable. This is the first appearance of this favorite of favorites in a play which she made a success before her transfer to the silent drama for expression of her charms.

As all know, this is a Grimm fairy tale, translated with all the charm and wealth of material for story-telling entertainment into a six-part photodrama of which the Famous Players Company may well be proud.

From the opening prologue, in which Snow White's arrival into this world through the beneficent auspices of a kindly stork is shown, we pass through several fantastic scenes, including a very clever transformation of a tableful of dolls left by Santa Claus into real little beings, to the point in the story where the wicked Brangomar is transformed into a beautiful Queen by the Witch Hex, and promises to give her heart to Hex in return, upon the betrothal of the Princess Snow White. So Snow White is kept always in the kitchen, like Cinderella, while not in rags, yet in calico, and supposedly unattractive dresses, which appear attractive on this petite little lady.

One day she goes to seek three ducks for dinner, and meets in the forest the Prince Florimund, who takes an instant fancy to her. Little does either realize that this prince is to demand her hand as "Princess Snow White," shortly afterward.

The wicked Brangomar, discovering the love of the Prince for Snow White, orders Snow White killed, but the man she chooses to command to do this terrible deed cannot bring himself to perform it, even under the fear that his own children will be sacrificed if he doesn't.

He tells Snow White his mission, and a way is found to seem to comply with the command, by substituting a pig's heart for Snow White's, which Berthold the huntsman duly delivers to the wicked Brangomar.

Left alone in the forest, Snow White finds the seven dwarfs, in their quaint retreat, and endears herself to them. Meantime the mirror tells Brangomar where Snow White has gone, and she makes two attempts to poison her. The last seems about to have succeeded, when Snow White suddenly awakes to find the poisoned apple lodged in her throat, so it only caused a temporary stupor, and the witch, relenting, appears just in time to see the transformation of the cruel Brangomar back into her original ugliness by the breaking of the magic mirror which has protected her and been her talisman.

In this play Miss Clark is charming beyond words to describe. She fits exactly into the role of the Princess Snow White, and Creighton Hale as Prince Florimund is a likely match for her charm and beauty.

The many clever tricks of photography and novelty which helped perfect the illusion speak of infinite pains in giving this worth while fairy story an adaptation worthy its former stage success and the vast number of persons who have been fascinated by it as a fairy story. The pet bird which entered into the plot wonderfully in several places, will be the talk of the children for months. This feathered member of the cast seemed to have a real personal affection for Miss Clark, and saved her life time and again as a reward for her kindness in liberating it from its cage early in the story. It led her to the dwarfs' house. It brought the rope to Berthold which enabled him to escape from the prison, it told the bunny that told the dwarfs of the impending peril of the deadly comb, and was really the hero of the play. The children will surely love that bird.

Grown people will enjoy this play fully as much as the children, and we know the children will just rave about it. There is a combination of fancy and fascination, of fine interpretation of a classic role by Miss Clark, not to mention individual scenes of surpassing beauty, which will entitle this subject to first recognition in the motion picture hall of fame. H. Lyman Broening is responsible for the excellent camera work.

--George N. Shorey in Motion Picture News, Vol. 15, No. 1 (January 6, 1917), page 113.

☐ THE SPIRIT OF '76 (Continental, 1917)

The author of The Spirit of '76 served a year in prison for
directing in the picture a hot political fire against one of our allies,
and producing his work during the Great War.   Up to the present
this country has not attached a prison sentence to artistic crimes.
Offences against good taste and common sense bring no greater penalty than loss of patronage.   This is fortunate for Mr. Robert Gold-
stein.   He has ground out a crude concoction of fact and fiction,
purporting to deal with some of the most momentous episodes in
American history, and filled it with astonishing and mirthful anach-
ronisms thrown in for good measure.

Produced in 1917, our good neighbor, George V, and his
subjects need not be in the least disturbed because The Spirit of '76
comes right out and says that his Majesty George III, of unsavory
memory, was a bit of a blackguard and very much of a rogue.   Over
half a century ago a truthful subject of the English Crown, one
George William MacArthur Reynolds, wrote a book which gave Mr.
Guelph of the third reign a character that smelt to heaven and out-
ranked by many degrees the rankest allegations of the American
scenarist.   This book, The Mysteries of the Court of London, has
been sold openly in this country for the last fifty years and can still
be obtained at the public libraries in the large cities, without the
slightest danger of giving birth to an international imbroglio with the
British Government--although there are very good grounds for sur-
mising that this same unblushing human document was the inspiration
and fountain head from which the author of the photoplay under discussion drew the form and color of his own historical romancing.
That sweet smelling complication, the ardent lovers who discover
that they are brother and sister, is one of the love motives of the
story.

A list of the big historical moments in the picture includes
Patrick Henry's speech before the Virginia House of Burgesses,
Lord Chatham's death, Paul Revere's ride, the Signing of the Declaration of Independence and Washington at Valley Forge.   However
crudely presented, these immortal "footprints on the sands of time"
command respect and deep emotional reaction.   But they are power-
less to save the picture from mental derision when it is shown, if
the director be correct, that George III bought the royal coffee cups
for His Majesty's breakfast table at a local ten cent store; that his
morganatic Queen wore a pair of stays of the 1921 model; that at
the battle of Cherry Valley, 1777, the British commander, mindful
of his soldier's comfort, marched his troops along a concrete side-
walk, and that the rafters of the houses destroyed by the British, at
that period, were planing mill stock and so scant as to come under
the building laws of today.   But the crowning absurdity is reached
when the gentleman intrusted with the visualization of an Indian witch
cinches his claim to having the right dope on the brother-and-sister-
ardent-lovers business by beating his breast and exclaiming, "I am
your mother!"   The mystery is never explained.

The acting belongs to its day, and serves to illustrate the
vast improvement four years have brought.   There is much sawing
of the air with both hands, and rolling of the eyes.   The performance of one member of the cast stands out from the otherwise unbroken level like a lofty mountain peak.   George Cheeseborough as
Walter N. Butler, embraces in his work the best results of the
latest methods of screen acting.   The part is not a long one, but
history credits Butler with being "One of the most cruel scourges,
as he was one of the most fearless men of his native country."   Mr.
Cheeseborough carries out this description of the man by doing a
cold blooded murder with a calm indifference that seems as natural
to him as the air he breathes.   His knife fight to the death with an
Indian is also in keeping with Butler's reputation; not a move or an
expression is a hair's breadth out of the way.   There is something
predictive in everything he does.   The Spirit of '76 is a great theme.
Let us hope that some day it will be given an adequate interpretation
upon the screen.

Exploitation Angles: Sell this to the Sinn Feiners and the
pro-Germans, who are most apt to be interested in this production.
Some adaptation of the famous painting of the same title as this picture will work out well for street use.

>   --Edward Weitzel in The Moving
>   Picture World, Vol. 51, No. 6
>   (August 6, 1921), page 634.

*   *   *

Oh, propaganda!   What crimes are committed in thy name.
The Spirit of '76 was first designed as German propaganda.   But
the Germans, after seeing the film, evidently disowned it.   So now
it is called Irish propaganda.   Whatever its political significance,
it resembles nothing so much as a fourteen-reel Ben Turpin comedy
without the talented Ben.   If this is a specimen of the real spirit of
'76, how did we ever manage to win the revolution?

>   --Photoplay, Vol. 20, No. 5 (Oc-
>   tober 1921), page 94.

☐   THE SPOILERS (Selig, 1914)

In choosing the picture version of Rex Beach's stirring novel,
The Spoilers, as the opening film feature of the new Strand Theatre,
manager S. L. Rothapfel exercised excellent judgment.   To the rabid
movie fan--the one who revels in action, excitement and a panoramic
succession of real life adventures--this picture hands him a wallop.
The picture made the biggest kind of a hit with the Strand's opening
night audience and although it ran along more than an hour the film
held the closest attention until the very end.   As a rule movies of
the melodramatic sort are expected to have several thrills but this
story has been so realistically told by the camera one is handed
thrill upon thrill.   As a movie production it beats the book.   Colin

Campbell is given the credit of having staged the production yet
one familiar with the book and Beach's style of description and love
of adventure, can readily see that Beach had an important hand in
the staging of his novel before the camera. While credit is due
Campbell for his studio and exterior work, Beach should not be forgotten in the handing out of praise for the success this picture is
going to attain before the summer season is very far advanced.
The Spoilers is a red-blooded, peppery story that will catch wide-
awake, live Americans. The photoplay follows the book so closely
one can forgive the author and director for having digressed the
rules a little and played several incidents up a little differently.
But these changes, while making the story stand out stronger in
photoplay, are such that no one will register any kick about the film
not sticking pretty close to the text.

On the Strand program only eight of the characters were programmed. As there were others in the cast as essential and who
did some great work in putting the movie over, it's too bad they
were not carded. William Farnum is the Glenister of the picture
and a manly, strong, rugged, healthy character he made of it. He
handled the strenuous role of the big miner so capably there was
no fault to be found with his acting. Farnum has broad shoulders
and a deep chest and they stand him in good stead in the rougher
climaxes of the picture. Thomas Santschi was McNamara and he
made the villainous role loom up in the wicked manner in which
Beach described him in the book. He appeared to be much slenderer
than Farnum yet in the big fight scene he held his own well. Kathlyn
Williams looked after the Cherry Malotte character so effectively it
is doubtful if any other actress could have improved upon the part.
As for Bessie Eyton's interpretation of Helen Chester she is due for
all the bouquets that will come her way. Her hardest scenes were
the escape from the boat and the fight in the mountain resort. She
met them both and many other with consummate skill that few movie
leads possess. Frank Clark was superb as the "silverhaired old
Texan pirate, Dextry." Wheeler Oakman was Broncho Kid and he
did the role without exaggerating it from the book's standpoint.
Marshall Farnum played Lawyer Wheatin, but didn't have much to
do, while E. MacGregor was a capable Judge Stillman. The men
who played Slapjack Simms, Wilton Struve, Jos Galloway, the Marshal Vorhees, and Mexico Mullins were excellent supporting players.
In staging The Spoilers, Rex Beach had the Selig Co. re-enact the
story of the Alaskan dance halls and gold fields at the California
plant (Selig's) where a second Nome and surrounding country were
built under the author's direction. In subtitles many phrases, word
for word from the book, are employed to good advantage. Some of
the captions were in green letters, others in a lighter shade.
                                        --Mark in Variety, Vol. 34, No.
                              7 (April 17, 1914), page 22.

☐ THE SQUAW MAN (Lasky, 1914)

One of the best visualizations of a stage play ever shown on

the screen, The Squaw Man, was a source of surprise and delight
to me, and to the able critic at my side during the private exhibition, from beginning to end. Credit must, however, be given almost entirely to the direction and interpretation, the direction in
this case embracing both form and treatment of an almost flawless
production. To the lucid arrangement and delicate appreciation of
dramatic values, to unwavering logic and consistency, to the pains
taken in those tiny details which make action realistic, to the per-
vading sense of beauty, and to highly intelligent interpretation,
quickening interest in the outcome, must be ascribed the charm this
feature is bound to exert.

I have not seen Oscar Apfel's name* made prominent in connection with this winner, but I recognize his handiwork without difficulty. Cecil DeMille, I am told, put his heart and soul into making The Squaw Man an unqualified success, but his unbounded enthusiasm could only act as a support to the unhampered skill and decided native ability of the active director. First honors must go to
the gentleman whose discriminating judgment cleared the path of this
notable production of a thousand thorny errors. Dustin Farnum's
unobtrusive and masterly characterization ranks next in value--he
was largely responsible for the "surprise and delight" already men-
tioned--for he has certainly grasped the essential principles of
screen interpretation. His performance is so manly, so apparently
devoid of stale artifice, that I could only regret that he was not representing a typical American.

The general theme, that of frenzied self-sacrifice on the part
of a blameless man for the sake of a villain who happens to be a
member of the same family, "for the family honor," whereby he
blasts his own career, has been very popular with lady novelists
since Ouida used it, and variations of it have been seen on both
stage and screen until it has become almost as familiar as "Mary
had a little----" but it is time that it should be shelved, along with
a lot of overdone expedients. Nothing in the photodrama is less
conducive to progress in the new art than this old billposter theme.
But it is all the more creditable to the producers that they have presented with exquisite charm what is no longer considered to be within
the bounds of common sense. The truth is that they have depended
upon a rattling good story of adventure, running with unbroken unity,
sustained by a character of magnetic personality, through perils at
sea and on shore.

To begin at the beginning, Jim Wyngate, with whom we are
better acquainted as Dustin Farnum, agrees to be the scapegoat for
his relative, the Earl of Kerhill, who has embezzled the funds of
Wyngate's regiment, and, as soon as Jim is disentangled from a lot
of other officers that our affections may be fastened upon him, he

---

*From the evidence available, Apfel appears to have been largely
responsible for the direction of the film, although, of course, the
film today is always credited to DeMille.

leaves England in a trading schooner, and the real fun begins.   He
has been followed by a detective.   Every small boy in the audience
and a large portion of the big ones will begin to sit up and take notice when Jim gets busy with that detective.   Jim is every inch an
athlete, and he does not mince matters as they do in stage struggles.   He succeeds in making a fool of the spy at the end of a game
fight and soon after performs greater feats, when the ship catches
fire.   The fire scenes aboard ship are made plausible by using an
actual vessel, sailing in the open, and there is a delightful fidelity
to legitimate requirements not ordinarily seen in the escape of crew
and passengers in the boats.

Jim is picked up by an American vessel, landed in New York,
and gradually drifts from the lurid White Way to ranch life in the
far west, accompanied by "Big Bill," whom he has saved from the
deft "touch" of a tango artiste.   They arrive at a railroad station
that is a veritable gem of its kind--we look through the combination
bar and station, where cowboys assemble at train time, to the track
on which actual trains are passing.   Some of the high scenes occur
in this room, and the view of cars running without gives them an
unusual atmosphere of realism.   Jim gets into difficulties there with
Cash Hawkins, and the latter is shot dead in the station by an Indian
girl, a veritable one, and a remarkably fine actress, when he attempts to murder Jim in cold blood.

It is not altogether a pleasing spectacle to see white women
impersonating Indian squaws, and they are seldom, if ever, successful at it; on the other hand, Indian girls who can awaken and hold
sympathy for their roles are few and far between, but Princess Red-
wing performs her part with exquisite fidelity and great depth of
feeling.   The play's highest merit is the opportunity it affords this
accomplished actress.   The love of this child of the forest for the
splendid specimen of manhood injected into her dull career forms the
most touching and beautiful part of the story, and it was probably
the essence of interest in Royle's stage version.   So artless, so appealing to the protective instincts of true manhood, so self-abnegating
is that love, that it is bound to make heartstrings throb in the audience.

It is quite probable that both Royle and DeMille, when they
come to study this characterization from the viewpoint of spectators,
will realize that the art of producing moving pictures is to be measured by its own canons alone.   Both may perceive that this new
method of thought transmission has a grander scope than the boxed-
in stage presentation once they are enfolded in the charm of its
method of telling a story.   Its directness, the lack of intervening
utterance, its very silence, all contribute to a fascination long proven
to exist, not only for the mixed audience, but for those familiar with
superior examples of the older arts.   When these gentlemen come to
us, as they surely will, with the finest products of their creative
talent, unhampered by what they have learned in a totally different
medium of expression, with a cause that is compelling, it will be
with quickened fondness, for what can give such free release to their
forces.

Note the characterization in action of the Indian maid when the man she loves goes snow blind, when she follows the trail of his horse until she finds it where he was thrown, and thereafter trails his steps to the sulphurous crevice into which he has fallen. Note the impression made by witnessing her patient courage and native resource in the almost insurmountable task of rescue, the comparison suggested of her sturdy and simple devotion to the dependent and resourceless man hunter of civilized society, the lady who affects to steer the boat while man does the rowing, who relies on sex attraction rather than sex qualification. The physical superiority and mental alertness of the woman enjoying fewer advantages could never be so forcibly presented in the related narrative as in the pictured story.

Note the compelling beauty and nobility of actual scenery as compared to stage affectations. The complex impression produced is powerful enough to make one subscribe to the view expressed by a great creative critic, "Art's first appeal is neither to the intellect nor to the emotions, but purely to the artistic temperament that guides civilized man back to nature for relief." The same critic said, "I hold that no work of art can be tried otherwise than by laws deduced from itself; whether or not it be consistent with itself is the question." Note the Indian maid "fighting it out alone in the foothills, only nature looking on," the distance tragically mellowed by a setting sun--how fascinated we become by this visible world of form and color, not only because its delicate beauty is so appropriate to a communion of a human soul with the spirit of the Great Invisible, but because of its imaginative insight and poetic aim!

This one scene might well have been the last, discovering, as it does, the finest sentiment of the story, the tortured appeal of a human heart--"will we ever come to our own?" Sickened with pursuit of the unattainable, how often have each of us secretly communed with something we only vaguely recognize as a power that makes all our boasted ones pitiful. Such occasional glimpses may be less intelligible than those more commonplace, but they belong to life in its artistic entirety, enter a sphere of deep feeling, stir the nobility too often dormant within us, rouse our better selves. The touches of great beauty contain a secret of success known only to screen presentation--they cause us to surrender ourselves more completely to the story that is being told and to love this new art for its own sake.

--Louis Reeves Harrison in The
Moving Picture World, Vol. 19,
No. 9 (February 28, 1914), pages
1068-1069.

☐   STELLA MARIS (Paramount-Artcraft, 1918)

Two things impressed me most in the past four weeks: the

playing of Mary Pickford in Stella Maris, and of Elsie Ferguson in
Rose of the World. These two vehicles are adapted novels, by the
way.

Stella Maris, Artcraft's visualization of William J. Locke's
story, has been pronounced the greatest effort of the Pickford career. Why? Because she is permitted to get away from curls and
cupid-bow lips to a character rôle with pathos and humor. Miss
Pickford used to do these parts back in the old Biograph days, but
people seem to have forgotten. The truth is, Mary Pickford is an
actress of infinite humanness, sincerity and personality. And Stella
Maris gives her opportunities to prove it.

The charm of the Locke novel has been torn away until little
more than a conventional movie scenario remains. John Risca, his
married life a wreck, centers his love upon a wealthy little cripple
girl, Stella Maris, who knows nothing of life outside her room.
Risca employs a little orphan waif, Unity Blake, in his home. Little Unity loves Risca in her own pathetic way, and, when she realizes that the man's drunkard wife stands in the way of his happiness,
she kills the woman and herself. Thus the way is opened for Risca
to marry Stella, now able to walk thru an operation and coming face
to face with the sordid things of life for the first time.

Miss Pickford plays both Stella and Unity. She suggests the
growing disillusionment of Stella admirably and does Unity relentlessly. The Pickford is hardly recognizable in the slatternly little
slavey.

Stella Maris is away above the screen average, but it isn't
Locke. That is, you will admire the dexterity of double photography,
but you will regret the loss of Locke charm.
                              --Frederick James Smith in Motion
                                Picture Classic, Vol. 6, No. 2
                                (April 1918), pages 36-37.

                    *   *   *

The original of Stella Maris will never reach any such audience as this beautiful screen version, nor with anything like the
power given by Miss Pickford's exquisite interpretations. Words
are too feeble and inadequate. The printed story is a poor thing in
comparison. It contains a lot of old and insincere adjuncts of plot,
a merely clever readjustment of well-known artifice, in type. Suddenly these are transformed, as by the wand of a magician, into a
strong and unified story clothed with great imaginative charm, emotionally appealing through what seems to be the finest work Miss
Pickford has ever done, the whole rising in dignity to a play of social significance.

The story is an old one, that of a girl kept pure and good in
a life so sheltered that she is unaware of the world and its hard
struggle, then the bitter disillusion. Such is the theme and the plot

248   Selected Film Criticism

so far as the main issue is concerned, with a side one, the contrast of another, similar girl's life of hardship. The idea is vital
in so far as it is humanitarian, but the screen version rises far
above the novel through pure artistry of development and most of
all through a contrast little short of marvelous made by Mary in
her dual roles. She is amazingly sincere this time, daring to look
positively commonplace and unattractive as a mentally and physically stunted child from an orphan asylum, but she might never
have consented to it without the ever-present contrast of her lovely self as
Stella Maris. Those who have thought her merely pretty have a
new think coming to them in this play. Those who like her straight
through will sit amazed to note the transformation she succeeds in
making of her personality. One might reasonably conclude from
this exceptionally fine performance that personality consists of conduct, clothes and the way both are worn.

I have watched the career of Mary Pickford since I reviewed
the one-reel stories in which she made her first appearance--that
was under Griffith in the old Biograph days, and I have never seen
her in a more satisfying performance, true to life and to art, dramatic rather than theatric. Even as quiet little Stella Maris, whose
happenings are not those of intense action, she succeeds in affecting
the heart and the mind of the spectator by some exquisite portrayals
of character. She seems to have become transformed by her own
experience and study to a creature of finer spiritual force, though
she loses none of her dainty charm as a comedienne. The play
should be "the thing" to achieve lasting success, but Mary is one
of the very, very few who can make most dramas appear secondary
to their interpreter.

The Strand presentation was admirable, the house packed with
a long waiting line outside, and the audience profoundly interested
from beginning to end.

--Louis Reeves Harrison in The
                                    Moving Picture World, Vol. 35,
                                    No. 7 (February 9, 1918), page
                                    864.

                    *   *   *

Stella Maris is a photodrama based upon the novel by William
J. Locke. One little girl is an invalid from childhood, but all the
resources of wealth and kindness are centered upon her life and she
is happy. She knows nothing of the cruelties of existence. Another
little girl is a drudge in an orphanage, and has never known what it
is to be loved. A journalist is one of the friends of the little invalid. His dissipated wife takes the drudge from the asylum to be
her private slave. In a moment of rage the woman nearly kills the
drudge, and is sent to prison. The journalist, pitying the little victim, adopts her, and for the first time in her life she learns the
taste of kindness. As the years go by, the little invalid is cured,
and she and the journalist love each other. The dissipated wife,
her sentence expired, discovers this and gloats over the fact that

she can keep them apart.   The drudge, understanding that the happiness of the one being in the world who has been kind to her, is at
stake, cuts the knot with a tremendous deed of self sacrifice.

Mary Pickford plays both roles--the happy invalid and the
drudge.   Prettiness was required for the one, cleverness for the
other.   You may find it difficult to believe that the hungry looking
creature, with stooped shoulders, plastered hair, crooked mouth,
and awkward manner, is Your Own Mary.   Only in rare moments
does she relax into a certain curious semblance of her own lovely
self.   The fact remains.   There are cleverly photographed scenes
in which the drudge and the invalid both appear, and talk to each
other.   Then the contrast is brought out in all its tremendous force.
Miss Pickford's drudge is no mere matter of makeup, though the
physical difficulties of the role are obvious.   But she realizes the character with all her mentality, and sustains it without the slightest lapse.

Marshall Neilan directed the production, and made it exquisitely beautiful when opportunity offered, as well as sordid and relentlessly gripping when the theme was in minor key.   The supporting cast is in perfect tune.   Conway Tearle plays the journalist and
Camille Ankewich the besotted wife.

Stella Maris should prove a turning point in the history of
America's favorite star.   The public will never again be satisfied
with plays in which Miss Pickford is not given an opportunity to act.
                        --Randolph Bartlett in Photoplay,
                          Vol. 13, No. 5 (April 1918),
                          pages 69-70.

☐ STRAIGHT SHOOTING (Butterfly/Universal, 1917)

As the title very truthfully implies this picture is a western
melodrama.   Further than that it is filled with fine, effective western
action, containing thrilling climaxes that never allow the interest to
falter.   Superior locations were selected for its enactment.   The
long shots of the cattle herds and the numerous bands of horsemen
were picked with an eye to their appropriateness and in addition have
been superbly photographed.   The horsemen, incidentally, perform
with an unusual disregard for their respective lives.   In fact the
stunt stuff in the last fight between the cattlemen and the bandits is
loaded with sensational feats of daring that even go as far as to surpass most of the kindred action we have seen before.

George Hively, the author, has drawn upon reliably familiar
situations for his story, yet the new setting he has laid them in
sheds something of a new light over the whole.   The reform of the
bad man by the yearning look in the heroine's eyes paves the way
for the final rout of the villainous cattlemen who would drive the
settlers out of cabin and home.   The ride taken by Joan to warn the
settlers of the uprising of the cattlemen has all the thrill of Paul

Revere's famous gallop, while the succeeding fight in which the ma-
rauders ride round and round the lone cabin, until the kind-hearted
highwaymen arrive and save the day, is engineered on the style of
the Indian attack in the comparatively ancient pictures.

Harry Carey, with his very own mannerisms makes a likable
figure of "Cheyenne" Harry and Molly Malone is the typically sweet
heroine. Jack Ford produced and has laid great stress on terrifi-
cally fast action, particularly when he is dealing with horses and
riders. If he had left out a few of these riding scenes more connected results would have been attained but on the whole Straight
Shooting leaves little to be desired from the viewpoint of the fan who
devours the Westerns.

> --Peter Milne in Motion Picture
> News, Vol. 16, No. 10 (Septem-
> ber 8, 1917), page 1668.

☐ SUDS (Pickford/United Artists, 1920)

Miss Pickford's Amanda Afflick, the pathetic drudge of Suds,
is the better performance of the two. Her histrionic instincts are
truer than Doug's, and she has a better sense of character. But I
found the picture not particularly good entertainment. The pathos,
for one thing, is laid on a bit thick, forcing the suggestion of its
unreality. It is all artistically screened and beautifully pictured;
the dream of the little laundry girl, who sees in the clouds of suds
that rise from her tub visions of the grand young gentleman who is
one day to raise her from her lowly estate, is amusingly set in the
narrative and kept nicely in key with the slightly extravagant tone of
the story, and the broader comedy incidents of Amanda's turning
her room over to Lavender, the poor old delivery horse she saved
from the glue factory, delight the children. But Suds is an effort
to compromise between the real and the unreal, and to me such
compromises are never entirely successful. Little Mary proves
herself a fine little actress, however, and perhaps that is triumph
enough for one feature. Neither curls nor smirks nor Pollyanic aids
to sympathy are dragged in to help her, nor is she granted the sol-
ace of an altogether happy ending. Jack Dillon did the directing and
the supporting cast is competent. The story was taken from the
one-act play, 'Op o' My Thumb, which Maude Adams played a dozen
or fifteen years ago.

> --Burns Mantle in Photoplay, Vol.
> 28, No. 4 (September 1920),
> page 67.

☐ A TALE OF TWO CITIES (Fox, 1917)

No mimic representation of life, whether it be a laying-on of pigments or a carving of shadows, deserves to be called an art-work unless it arouses thoughts beyond itself. Does it slip the leash upon that dusky hound of mystery, Imagination? In the degree in which it appeals to Imagination, it is Art. In the measure in which it suggests a larger field of life than that its frame encompasses, it is a triumph for its creator.

For these reasons A Tale of Two Cities, a Fox production directed by Frank Lloyd, starring William Farnum, is the silver-sheet achievement of the month concerning whose visual fictions I write.

As big plays most often do, it came surprisingly as a shot from a dark doorway. Lloyd was assuredly of no special eminence; William Farnum has achieved celebrity and a fortune not as an actor of characters but as a purveyor of William Farnum; Fox is an industrious wholesaler of teary melodramas and vampires.

Lloyd permits Charles Dickens to retain a bit of credit, and keeps his title. Which was more than Henry Miller did, in his play upon the same subject, for Miller called his adaptation The Only Way.

Without renarrating in weaker and more desultory language a famous story, let us say, for clarity, that it concerns the gigantic comedy and tragedy of the French Revolution; the love of Charles Darnay, eventually heir of the hated Marquis St. Evrémonde, and the heroic self-sacrifice of his physical double, Sydney Carton, an Englishman.

Many as are the scenes of embattled Paris, our spiritual vision strays beyond the page. This is not merely a more-or-less convincing prop replica of the Bastile, shown by Mr. Lloyd; here are wider avenues than the shaded medieval streets; these gaunt and fantastic people, yapping at the heels of the Bourbon soldiery, are more than a crowd of energetically-driven supers. Almost as in the pages of Carlyle, we feel ourselves swept on the crest of the greatest awakening since Christianity.

Nor is this our genial friend William Farnum. The curly-headed, large-armed Bill disappears, and we are confronted by two distinct personalities; Darnay, the suave and silent aristocrat, direct and elegant as an arrow of silver in his discourse and his lovemaking; Carton, the rum-wrecked genius, abased to a gutter hell by his sloth and his appetite, fired with the passion of heaven by the eyes of Lucie Manette. Theoretically, Mr. Farnum is by no means the type for either Darnay or Carton. In fact, he is a tremendous realizer of both.

I wish the program gave us the name of that fair victim of "Citizen" wrath who, enroute in a tumbril with Carton to the guillotine, looks into his eyes with the sunrise of eternity in her own, and asks only that he hold her hand to the foot of the scaffold. In his treatment of this exquisite un-named character, as in the thrilling

death-exit of the Royalists, who march their ladies to the red cart
with high-arched hands and in the stately steps of a minuet, Lloyd
has approached the grandeur of true classic tragedy.   The stage,
this year, has nothing to offer which approaches the splendor of humanity in these scenes; and indeed, in his ability to hurl his ob-
servers head-foremost into an epoch, Lloyd reminds us of the gigantic power of Mr. Griffith, whose necromancy called back an utterly
forgotten civilization.

What an exquisite thing Jewel Carmen is, in her flowerlike
impersonation of Lucie!   She is her own first name.   Charles Clary,
as the elder St. Evremonde, sums up his Hohenzollern philosophy
as he watches the death-struggles of a girl destroyed by one of his
kind: "What life these common bodies have!"   Clary in his insolent
elegance and autocratic inhumanity could not be bettered.   Joseph
Swickard is very fine, too, as Dr. Manette; his is an impersonation
at moments of flashing contrasts, and again, of pastel tint.   A bit
of tremendous symbolism is supplied by Rosita Morisini as Mme.
Defarge, "the woman who knits death."   Great supporting values appear in the pictorial descriptions by Ralph Lewis, Herschell Mayall,
William Clifford, Marc Robbins and Willard Louis.

Having created a marvellous mob, Lloyd lapses strangely by
letting them, assembled, continually shake their hands or implements
above their heads in no human way.   Not even the members of a
mob do the same things; their end and larger movement may be the
same, but the physical expression of each man is individual.   In his
remarkable court-room scene, in which the drunken "Citizen" judge
woos order with a dinner bell, I think Lloyd has permitted bits of
grotesquerie which, while not in the least overdrawn, are viewed by
unthinking beholders as common attempts at cheap comedy.

                              --Julian Johnson in Photoplay, Vol.
                              12, No. 1 (June 1917), pages 91-
                              92.

☐   TARZAN OF THE APES (National Film Corporation, 1918)

Edgar Rice Burroughs, author of Tarzan of the Apes, has not
written another Robinson Crusoe or that other classic of adventure,
Cast Up by the Sea, but he has given to fiction a novel and interesting tale that loses none of its grip from the fact that it never did
and never could happen.   As shown on the screen, it is not always
a skillfully constructed piece of work.   Many of the scenes are laid
in England, and there is too much space devoted to them and they
smack too much of melodrama from the Surrey side of the Thames.
The merits of the picture, however, so far outweigh its defects that
it should duplicate the success of that other unique screen production,
Twenty Thousand Leagues Under the Sea.

Scott Sidney directed the picture.   Aside from the jungle

scenes his task was not at all difficult, but it is gratifying to be able to credit him with achieving such excellent results with the unusual and knotty problems presented in reproducing the portions of the story showing the personal side of Tarzan's life. They are handled with fine judgment, and the one regret will be that there are not more of them.

Gordon Griffith, a youthful actor of uncommon gifts, impersonates Tarzan as a boy. He is a fit subject for a sculptor, as he climbs through the trees in company with the apes, his naked body showing its grace of line in every move. Elmo Lincoln as Tarzan, the man, although not quite so unconventionally clad, moves about through the trees with the same ease and picturesque effect. The scene where he tracked a native in this manner while the black man travels on the ground below brought a round of applause from the spectators. The actor's understanding and playing of the part leave nothing to be desired. Enid Markey as Jane Porter has a number of difficult scenes with Tarzan and acquits herself with much honor. The other important members of the cast are True Boardman, Kathleen Kirkham, Thomas Jefferson, Bessie Toner, George French, Jack Wilson and Colin Kenny.

--Edward Weitzel in The Moving
Picture World, Vol. 35, No. 7
(February 16, 1918), page 1002.

*   *   *

Tarzan of the Apes, Edgar Rice Burroughs' fantastic story, has been put on the screen, despite obstacles which would, to the lay mind, appear insurmountable. But the thing has been so well done that it is convincing. An English boy is lost in the wilds of Africa and adopted by a tribe of apes. He grows to manhood with the simian strength and human intelligence. The picture was really filmed in South America, but the lions, leopards and other wild beasts are quite as fierce as they could possibly be in their native land. A remarkable child, Gordon Griffith, plays Tarzan the boy, with his ape-like proclivities. Elmo Lincoln is Tarzan the man, a giant creature who can, and does, wrestle single-handed with a huge lion and kill him. It is interesting if not advanced drama.

--Photoplay, Vol. 13, No. 6 (May
1918), page 104.

☐ TESS OF THE D'URBERVILLES (Famous Players, 1913)

At the Lyceum Theater on Tuesday afternoon there were gathered by invitation of Daniel Frohman and Harrison Grey Fiske many friends of Mrs. Minnie Maddern Fiske. The occasion was the initial showing of the five-part screen reproduction of Tess of the D'Urbervilles, in which Mrs. Fiske sustains the title role. The great actress repeats before the camera the success she achieved on the

stage. The unfolding of the absorbing story of Thomas Hardy was
followed by a silence that in itself was the best indication of the
spell thrown over the entire house by this film drama. There was
never a moment when the interest slackened. There was a steady
pull at the heartstrings, lightened on rare occasions by flashes of
humor, as for instance in the first part when the Durbeyfields are
convinced of their descent from the knightly family of the D'Urbervilles. Again, at the wedding of Tess and Angel Clare, there is
laughter through the tears as the three girl friends of the bride--
and unavowed rivals--refuse to speak to her.

        The interest in this picture will, of course, center about
Mrs. Fiske. Her admirers will not be disappointed. True it is
that the appealing voice will not be heard; but there will remain the
art of revealing through expression the tumult that surges in the
bosom. The face of Tess may be as a piece of stone, but the eyes
tell the whole story. You see, you feel, the tears. There are a
multiplicty of strong situations. One of the most pathetic is where
Tess, forbidden by her father to go for a clergyman that her un-
named child may not die unbaptized, awakes her sisters, and, in
the bare attic, herself performs a ceremony. One of the most dramatic is where the husband of Tess, informed by his wife on the
evening of the wedding day of her past in reply to a similar burst
of confidence on his part, flies into a rage and later falls asleep by
the fire. In a somnambulistic stroll he dreams that Tess is dead.
He goes to the bridal chamber and finds Tess on the couch at the
head of the bed. Picking her up in his arms he carries her downstairs, lays her by the fire, puts a candle at each side of her, and
then returns to his couch. The woman who is to be bride in name
only arises from the floor and places a mantle over the sleeping
figure. The fifth reel is the strongest of all. It is here where
Tess, deserted and her family in want, is again in the grasp of
Alec D'Urberville, the betrayer; she is sought out by her husband,
now of changed mind. It is too late. Tess goes to the room of
D'Urberville. She returns and tells Clare that she has killed him.
Clare takes his wife to the Temple of the Druids, where the two
are found in each other's arms the next morning by the officers of
the law.

        The support of Mrs. Fiske is uniformly excellent. Criticism
may be made as to the comparative youth of Raymond Bond, who
plays Angel Clare. Mr. Bond, however, has played in the company
of Mrs. Fiske and is said to have been her selection for the part.
David Torrence is strong as Alec D'Urberville. The father and
mother of Tess were played by John Steppling and Mary Barker.
They were the chief figures of the first reel, and their excellent
character work is deserving of high praise. Mr. Steppling is an
experienced camera player; his portrayal of the dissolute John Dur-
beyfield shows it. It was Mrs. Barker's first appearance in a picture. It is one of the tragedies of the screen that it also was her
last. She did not live to see projected the film in which is preserved
a record of the drama in which she had appeared in every speaking
performance. James Gordon, who will be recognized by picture followers, is excellent as the robust head of the dairy farm.

The backgrounds were chosen with rare good judgment.   In truth, it is in this factor of the picture, as well as in Mr. Murphy's artistic interiors, that will be noted one of its chief claims to distinction.   There is the great palace of the D'Urbervilles and its surrounding grounds.   The rose garden is a thing of beauty.   Many of the settings were applauded by the Lyceum audience, and all deserved it.   Some of the scenes of rural life, of meadow, stream and hill, will linger in the memory--even in the memory of those who see many pictures.   The photography matched the locations.   Not only was it exceptional in quality; but, by reason of the unusual skill displayed in the filming of sunsets and cloud effects, it will stand in a class by itself.

Taken altogether--considering the story, the acting, the direction, the backgrounds, the photography--Tess of the D'Urbervilles is a great picture.   Speaking calmly, the writer believes it one of the greatest ever made.   It will redound to the credit of American kinematography.   For this result we may thank Adolph Zukor, Daniel Frohman, Edwin S. Porter and J. Searle Dawley, whose splendid coöperation has made it possible.

--George Blaisdell in The Moving
Picture World, Vol. 17, No. 11
(September 13, 1913), page 1155.

☐   TESS OF THE STORM COUNTRY (Famous Players/Paramount,
1914)

In Hearts Adrift and A Good Little Devil, Mary Pickford had no opportunity to demonstrate her true value as a movie actress.   In Tess of the Storm Country, Grace Miller White's human heart story which the Famous Players Co. turned loose from its photoplay factory March 20, Little Mary comes into her own and her work in this five-part movie production so far o'ershadows her work in the other films there's no comparison.

As the little, expressive-eyed tatterdemalion of the Lake Cayuga shores, Miss Pickford sticks another feather in her movie crown which will help the Famous Players reap a benefit in more ways than one.   In photoplaying the Tess story the F.P. Co. has taken more care than it has done in some of its other Pickford pictures and gives the silent drama fans some realistic indoor and exterior scenes.

Tess has everything the bug's heart craves for and there is plenty of action from start to finish.   The characters are all real, or at least are taken from real life, and so well depicted by the camera players the film will leave a deep impression wherever shown.

Miss Pickford is the spirited, aggressive, mischief-loving Tess all the way.   Brought up amid an environment that brings out the sterner stuff and forces her to combat against realities that would

floor the average city girl, she surmounts all difficulties and finally
wins out.   It's a great part for Mary and she makes the best of it.

There are some big scenes--big moments--that give the picture the K.O. wallop so many movie producers strive for and it is
these climaxes that will carry the film along to unbounded success.

The theft of the Bible from the Mission, the fight with the
real murderers of the gamekeeper, getting milk by desperate methods for the baby, the struggle in the courtroom crowd, the hut fight
with the shore bully, the "break" with her sweetheart, and the big
situation in the church, where Tess, realizing the baby is dying,
makes a superhuman effort to have the kidlet baptized so that it can
enter the Kingdom of Heaven, are all well staged.   The photography
in the first part is somewhat indistinct, but the excellent filming
which follows makes up for all shortcomings in this respect.

                                    --Mark in Variety, Vol. 34, No.
                                    5 (April 3, 1914), page 21.

☐   THAIS (Goldwyn, 1917)

This is the début of Mary Garden, the famous prima donna,
into an opera of shadows.   Thais, you remember, is the story of a
great struggle between the desires of the flesh and the spirit.   It is
the story of the reclamation of a passionate, selfish dancing-girl's
soul by a Christian, who has to overcome not only her earthly desires, but his own for her.   Miss Garden is pictorially beautiful;
but it is the beauty of chiseled marble, of perfection of line and
form and accoutrements.   One admires her.   One thinks to oneself,
what gorgeous gowns, what a marvelous figure, what a handsome
face; but never do we sense an emotional appeal.   Miss Garden
seems quite conscious that this is Mary Garden having her picture
"took."   Towards the finale, however, when Thais has abandoned
her glittering robes and in the simple garb of the sisterhood has
sought peace and spiritual cleansing, Miss Garden strikes a sincere
and appealing note.

The street scenes of Alexandria have been visualized with
great care and realism.   In fact, the ensemble is one of richness
and artistry, but as to Mary Garden, because she is a great lady
in her own sphere of grand opera, every one will welcome a chance
to see her on the screen.   But Mary Garden is an acquisition to the
silversheet, and an addition to the art of pantomimic drama solely
in that another great name has been added to those who have heard
the call of the newest art and answered.   A review of Thais would
be incomplete without mentioning Crawford Kent, who makes the
small part of Lollius, Thais' forsaken lover, stand out in a manner
which proves Mr. Kent a master artist.   Hamilton Revelle as Paph-
nutius is also histrionically adequate.

                                    --Hazel Simpson Naylor in Motion
                                      Picture Magazine, Vol. 15, No.
                                      2 (March 1918), page 98.

*   *   *

Thais, which should have been a moving picture triumph, is
a moving picture misfortune. As produced by Goldwyn, it is one of
the severest blows the art has ever received, for this reason--it
will bring to the picture theatres, by reason of the presence in the
title role of Mary Garden, thousands who have scorned the movies.
Had the picture been well done, it would have made thousands of converts for the screen. Done as it was, it will still further alienate
the scoffers. Thais, one of the most purely spiritual stories in all
literature, in the hands of Goldwyn, comes out as an orgy of un-
lovely flesh. It is so tawdry, so crude, so vulgar, that it reminds
one of one of those sucker-catching advertisements, "Send ten cents
and get ten snappy pictures." Mary Garden brings to the screen
the tedious and dismal technique of operatic acting, which is not
acting at all, but slow motions made while waiting for the music to
catch up with the drama. Moreover--and this may seem brutal, but
if stars will trade upon reputations, the truth must be told--Miss
Garden is no longer the lovely creature of Louise. Careful study of
effects in draping might have done much for her, but that, seemingly, is not the Goldwyn way. With producers frantic for good stories,
one of the best in the world has been ruined to snatch a few dollars
by trading upon the international reputation of a star.

--Randolph Bartlett in Photoplay,
Vol. 13, No. 5 (April 1918),
page 70.

☐ 39 EAST (Paramount-Realart, 1920)

It has remained for the screen version of Rachel Crother's
successful play, 39 East, to present Constance Binney at her best.
The Realart star has been burdened with poor material aside from
Erstwhile Susan--material which has almost engulfed her. Her personality never had a chance. But now the personable and talented
actress comes forward in an adaptation of her own stage success
and scores as surely as in the spoken version. It is seldom that a
play can stand such a close translation without losing some of its
spark or vitality, but 39 East follows the original in every important incident and entertains without any padding being discernible.
The dialogue is the only element missing and since it is a play of
character studies and atmosphere one can truthfully say that the picture is every bit as entertaining as the original.

The boarding house which 39 East represents, the views of
Central Park--these are more significant in the silent version. The
peculiar types that compose the list of boarders are as real since
six or seven of the original company are enacting their parts again.
Indeed 39 East is a sample of faithful fidelity. The fact that practically the same company is interpreting the photoplay is an assurance that the characters are well depicted. The original offering

didn't strike us as particularly good screen material--as if it lacked
substance or vitality.

It is a feather in John Robertson's cap that he has been able
to give it so much life and to keep an audience constantly interested.
He has taken the spirit of the play and Miss Binney, knowing the
part so well, has given it animation. Her study of the wistful country girl who comes to the city to gain a livelihood and who has a
hard time keeping the wolf from the door is rich in sympathetic appeal. The gossips of 39 East endeavor to make her unhappy. But
she conquers in the end and finds romance with the youth who never
gave up believing in her. The picture builds to a satisfactory climax with Robertson showing good taste in not spoiling it with melodramatic hokum. 39 East may be obvious, but it is so perfectly
constructed, so well balanced with humor and pathos, and so finely
directed and acted, that every spectator will enjoy it. Certainly it
is Constance Binney's best bet.

--Laurence Reid in Motion Picture
News, Vol. 22, No. 14 (September 25, 1920), page 2497.

☐ TILLIE'S PUNCTURED ROMANCE (Keystone, 1914)

When Mack Sennett was in the East a couple of months ago
he confided to a friend that in the making of his six-reel comedy in
which Marie Dressler was starred he had given all that he had.
After viewing Tillie's Punctured Romance we are bound to say he
had a lot to give. At the time the Keystone producer was here he
was in doubt as to what the title of the comedy would be. When he
intimated to a party of film men that he was thinking of "She Was
More Sinned Against Than Necessary," there was hearty acclaim.
The advisability of incorporating "Tillie" in the title, that the star
of the piece by reason of previous associations might be more clearly identified, turned the scale.

Marie Dressler breaks into the story at the first jump. She
is in the scene every minute right to the finish. She fits into the
Keystone style of work as to the manner born. She kicks and is
kicked, she falls and gets up or is laboriously picked up; sober or
unsober she is inimitable. Trouble follows in her ample wake; if
at any moment there seems an insufficiency of disturbance she beats
a strategic retreat and takes a fresh stranglehold on everything and
everybody and starts something new. That she survives her strenuous experience is remarkable; it is a tribute to her vitality as well
as her agility. In fact, it is inexplicable that these boneless but
never spineless Keystone players live to play another day.

Charles Chaplin plays opposite Miss Dressler. In apposition
with the famous woman of the legitimate comedy stage, the screen
player suffers not a whit by comparison. The two constitute a rare

team of funmakers--the sort of combination that not only tempts but
impels an ordinary fallible reviewer to indulge in extravagant language. Chaplin outdoes Chaplin; that's all there is to it. His marvelous right-footed skid--and it seems to make no difference whether
he has under him rough highway or parlor floor--is just as funny
in the last reel as it is in the first. Chaplin's serious face is seldom crossed by a smile. With perfect confidence he leaves laughter
to others; and well he may.

Mabel Normand is the third principal in the large cast. She
has the role of the unsuccessful rival for Charlie's hand; that is,
she is unsuccessful for a short but exceedingly lively period ending
in the harried and bedraggled Tillie resigning her claim to the fickle
bridegroom. Miss Normand sustains in her own mirthful way the
quieter role--always speaking comparatively, of course--that falls to
her. Charles Bennett is the millionaire uncle who is not killed by
the fall down the snow-covered mountainside and whose return to the
scene of Tillie's rampage is the climax as it is also the dramatic
catastrophe of his sole heiress's flight in high society. We also
recognized Mr. Bennett in two minor characters.

The picture is finely staged. The interiors of the mansion
wherein Tillie and her husband entertain society are elaborate and
luxurious. The bit in the snow above the clouds makes an impressive contrast with the sunshine-flooded vegetation of the lower country. The photography throughout is of a high order.

There is no use talking about situations. In Tillie's Punctured Romance there are nothing but situations. There's a story,
of course, and it is sufficient. It shows how Tillie is wooed by
Charlie and is given the mitten in favor of Mabel. When Charlie
reads that through the death of the uncle Tillie is heir to three millions, he encompasses a hasty marriage before Tillie gets the news.
Of course, it afterward develops uncle is not dead, but very, very
much alive. Tillie, however, is pretty near dead by the time she
has removed from her expansive chest several matters that weigh
heavily upon it. Before the battle is over the Keystone "cops" have
the riot of their tempestuous, catlike lives, an automobile takes a
plunge into the Pacific--the only calm element in the show--and Tillie, after several tedious lifts and sudden immersions is finally
landed on the pier. Mabel falls in the arms of Tillie. Charlie is
"jugged."

Mack Sennett has done well.
                                    --George Blaisdell in The Moving
                                      Picture World, Vol. 22, No. 7
                                      (November 14, 1914), page 914.

☐ THE TOLL GATE (Paramount-Artcraft, 1920)

In the first reel of William S. Hart's The Toll Gate, Black

Deering, as brave a bandit as ever donned a mask, leads his gang
into the cave that was their meeting place and says to them, in effect:

"Boys, we're through. The hounds of the law are yipping at
our heels and we'd better beat it while the beating is good."

"Not on your life," replies a radical of the extreme left. "I
know a job that's got to be done. One more trick, boys, and we'll
split the $40,000 and quit."

Thus Black Deering is out-voted and another hold-up is
planned. Immediately you are interested in two possible twists to
that plot: first, the outcome of the hold-up undertaken against
Deering's advice; second, the effect it is going to have on his future.

From that point forward the picture proceeds logically, ex-
citingly and truly to its conclusion, which indicates that Mr. Hart
also realizes that good pictures cannot be thrown together hit or
miss. The Toll Gate is the most interesting Western I have seen
this month, because, granting its melodramatic premise, it is the
most plausible, the most intelligently directed and the best acted of
the melodramas I have seen. Being the first of Mr. Hart's own
pictures, it suggests that he has included in it all those features
that he has found most effective in his other photoplays. He is
again a bad, bad man, but with a "streak that's square," and when
in escaping from the authorities he comes upon the usual pretty
little Western woman living all alone in a cabin in the hills with
her four-year-old son, he is inspired to lead a better life. He
does not reform overnight, however, nor marry the girl and start
a general store. He merely sets things right with her, clears his
own conscience and rides away. It is the sort of story that convinces an audience that it has been well repaid for its visit to the
theater. Anna Q. Nilsson is an attractively passive heroine and
Joseph Singleton a convincing heavy. Many of the shots are fine,
particularly those picturing Deering's escape from the train.

--Burns Mantle in Photoplay, Vol.
18, No. 2 (July 1920), page 72.

☐ TOM SAWYER (Lasky/Paramount, 1917)

Immortal Tom Sawyer has been brought to the screen. Thanks
to the Lasky Company, who produced the picture, the visualization
of this world-famous American boy is a significant contribution to
the already long list of characters in our literature that have been
brought before the vision.

It will at once be appreciated that there is enough material
in Tom Sawyer to make an interesting picture of greater length than
the usual five reels, so it became necessary for the producers to

select only a part of the incidents, and in doing this they have used good judgment.   The beginning of the picture shows Tom with his Aunt Polly, and Cousins Sid and Mary as the "mischievous but not mean" member of the family group.   From then on we are treated to five reels full of good, healthy laughter, following him through the well-known episodes of the fence painting, the advent of the new girl in the village, the Biblical examination in the Sunday School, his declaration of love to Becky, the running away and finally the scene where he walks in on his own funeral services.   Of course Huck Finn and Joe Harper figure prominently all through the story.

Jack Pickford seems to have caught the exact spirit of the part of Tom Sawyer, and he has painted a portrait that is delight- ful.   Little artistic touches here and there added to a comprehen- sive understanding of the difficult role and an appearance that car- ries out the preconceived notion of how Tom should look fairly bring the boy to life again.   The supporting players are excellent and they add a deal of enjoyment to the picture.   A careful choice of types has been made and the costumes are picturesque.

Tom Sawyer was photographed in natural surroundings.   That is to say all the scenes were taken in Hannibal, Mo., where Mark Twain laid the story and some of the houses and their adjoining yards have remained the same and appear in the picture.   The atmosphere this gives can be appreciated.   The director has arranged the action at an even pace, and although the story is more or less episodic, continuity has been established and retained.   The detail work, in the interior scenes and where it has become necessary to place some properties in the exteriors, is an invaluable feature of the film.

Tom Sawyer is among the notable screen achievements of the year.   That it will draw capacity houses is certain.   The manner in which the picture should be advertised is obvious.

--F. T. in The New York Dramatic
Mirror, Vol. 77, No. 2034 (De-
cember 15, 1917), page 18.

*   *   *

Nearly two decades removed from my last previous reading of Mark Twain's classic of American boy life, Tom Sawyer, the Jack Pickford-Paramount reintroduction of this 100 per cent boy was a happiness not easily described.   The incident of the whitewashing of the fence, the love affair with the new girl in town, the fight with the "model boy," the clandestine friendship with Huck Finn the dis- reputable, the first smoke, the pirate adventure, the attendance at his own funeral--to mention the incidents alone is to revive memo- ries of pleasures that come once in a lifetime.   If Hood had been blessed with the privilege of seeing such a picture, he might not have written his plaint that he was farther from heaven than when he was a boy, because he had learned that the tops of the fir trees did not touch the sky.   The tops of my fir trees touched the sky

again as I watched this picture.   Boys and girls will enjoy it, but
only men and women will truly understand.

--Randolph Bartlett in Photoplay,
Vol. 13, No. 4 (March 1918),
page 72.

☐ TRAFFIC IN SOULS (Imp/Universal, 1913)

        It is with no light heart that a reviewer of motion pictures
with an ordinary sense of responsibility can approach this production.   Its theme is indicated in the title.   It is a big subject--one
that has been given grave consideration by many thoughtful men and
women.   These divide naturally into two groups--one favoring battling with the evil, or, as the more advanced would phrase it, the
evils of the evil, in the old-time secret way; the other would come
into the open and fight a condition as ancient as the beginnings of
history with modern weapons--and the chief of these publicity.   To
those who hold the latter of these opinions, Traffic in Souls will be
warmly welcomed.   The picture is bound to arouse bitter antagonism.
Surely its friends, and among these are the members of the National
Board of Censorship, are entitled to ask that the production be seen
before it is condemned.

        Walter MacNamara is the author of the script.   George
Tucker produces it.   These two as well as the more prominent
members of the augmented Imp Company which participated in filming the story gave much thought to matters of ethics and of policy.
Their work has been carefully reviewed by the censors.   Several
eliminations have been made.   The story as it stands contains practically nothing of the lure of underworld life.   It does show much
of the sordid and brutal side of it--of the scheming villainy of the
underling procurers and of the smug respectability of the man higher
up, and also of the wretched condition of the lash-cowed victims.
On the other hand, the forces of law and order, represented by
many fine types of policemen, are upheld throughout the six parts
of the picture.   The moral of the story is impressively clear; there
are contained in it warnings for the girl of the city as well as the
girl from the country--and for parents, also.

        On the dramatic side Traffic in Souls has unusual power.
There are many stirring situations--of heart interest and of suspense.   The action unfolds smoothly, coherently, and always inter-
estingly.   It is a story written for the screen--one of the few we
have had of its length.   Its advantage over many adaptations--those
made by any other than the most skillful--is apparent in the beginning.   You don't have to wait until the picture is half down before
you can place and properly identify your characters.   There is an
excellent cast and an unusually large one.   The interest will center
around the efforts of Mary Barton, splendidly played by Jane Gail,
to recover a younger sister who has been lured into the clutches of

a cadet. Mary's chief aid is Burke, her policeman-sweetheart, intelligently portrayed by Matt Moore.

The two girls, employed in a candy store, live with their father, an invalid inventor. The younger one attracts the attention of the System. A cadet is detailed to capture her. To establish an acquaintance over the counter is easy. Then comes the invitation to a dinner, then to a dance, then the employment of a "safe" taxi driver, and the drugged girl is behind locked doors in a brothel. The older sister is discharged when the kidnapping becomes public-- too much notoriety for the store. Mary is enabled through the intercession of one of her customers to obtain a position as secretary to a business man, so she thinks. When she puts to her ear the receiver of a dictagraph she recognizes the voice of the man who took away her sister. She follows the wires down the fire escape and sees the chief agents of the System at work. Mary goes to her father, who turns over to her and Burke his invention for intensifying sound waves and recording dictagraph conversations. The following day the apparatus, which has been installed in the offices, records on cylinders the conversation of the social outlaws and provides evidence that will convict. These bits of wax are turned over to the police captain, who sends out a detail of men, filling three automobiles. The house, which has been located before by the young patrolman, is quickly surrounded, the controllers are arrested after a fierce battle and the victims released. The head of the System, out on bail, arrives home to learn of the death of his wife and the insanity of his daughter.

Three scenes that markedly stand out are the fight of Burke when he follows, into the house, the two immigrant girls who have been misled--a melee in which bannisters are wrecked; the pistol battle on the stairs and on the roofs during the raid, and the assaults of the mob on the heads of the System as they are released under bail by the court. Many of the episodes in the house as the victims fight their captors are thrillingly realistic. The demonstrably easy fashion in which girls on incoming steamships, girls coming into the city by rail and those who live in large communities are brought into the clutches of powers that prey will serve to cause thought on the part of the most stolid. The treatment of the police side of the story is deserving of all praise. The views of the station are many. We get a look-in on the camaraderie of the bluecoats off duty and we see some of the dangers and temptations to which they are subjected when on duty.

William Welsh, as the man higher up, gives a fine performance. Others prominent in the cast are Howard Crampton, Ethel Grandin, William Turner, William Cavanaugh, Arthur Hunter, William Burbidge and Laura Huntley. All types are selected with rare discrimination. There may be diverse opinions as to the wisdom of exhibiting this picture. If such exhibition serve to quicken the official or public conscience in lethargic communities; if it help to preserve to society any one of the "fifty thousand girls who disappear every year"; if it tend to make more difficult the vocation of un-

speakable traders, then indeed will there have been substantial excuse for the making of this melodrama of today.

--George Blaisdell in The Moving
Picture World, Vol. 18, No. 8
(November 22, 1913), page 849.

*   *   *

[Traffic in Souls is a] six-reel feature drama with which the
manufacturer has taken the most detailed pains to present a true and
at the same time unsuggestive drama of the white slave traffic.
They have succeeded admirably in handling a subject of morbid interest and difficult situations with nothing that would pander to the
evil senses and everything that tends to bring out the finer feeling
of the spectator.   The story in brief is as follows: Mary and her
sister Lorna are employed at a fashionable candy store.   Lorna is
abducted through the wiles of a procurer, and is being starved into
submission.   The sweetheart of Mary is a bright young officer.
Mary secures a position in the office of a philanthropist, the latter
being the real head of the vice trust.   By means of a dictograph
improvement, Mary not only finds out where her sister is being
held, but also obtains evidence that later helps to convict the pseudo-
philanthropist.   In a thrilling rescue Lorna is saved from the hands
of the white slavers.   In an anti-climax that might well be shortened,
we see the tribulations of the man who posed as the benefactor, and
who in reality was the villain.   This in brief is the plot of the story,
which ends with the marriage of Mary and the police officer.   But
the value of this film is that it is a wholesome sermon in fiction
form, and as the director was only able to show one form of the
white slave peril with Lorna as a victim, he has the police officer
concerned in a number of other attempted abductions as well, and
teaches in a realistic and well directed series of scenes some of
the other perils of the white slavers.   The photography is excellent
and in some instances unique.   The setting of the scenes, and the
acting of a large and well-known cast, is admirable.   The interest
in this human drama is well sustained and is built with fine cumulative effect up to the point where the police break into the house of
vice.   With all the sensational action throughout the six reels, there
is nothing to stagger our credulity.   It is a film for children above
the age of fifteen to see.

--F. in The New York Dramatic
Mirror, Vol. 70, No. 1822 (November 19, 1913), page 33.

☐   TREASURE ISLAND (Paramount-Artcraft, 1920)

On the whole, Maurice Tourneur doesn't take Stevenson's
Treasure Island nearly as seriously as did Stevenson.   He gives it
to the silversheet with less of the adventure with which the printed
word endowed it and more of the whimsy.   Generally, it runs true

to the story with combination of incidents now and then and at times
a deviation which was evidently done for a better continuity in the
necessary length.   The settings are exquisite and the atmosphere
redolent of the yesterdays when the Jolly Roger flew from the mast-
head and the buccaneers' battle-cry was

> Fifteen men on a dead man's chest--
> Yo, ho ho and a bottle of rum.
> Drink and the devil have done for the
>   rest--
> Yo, ho ho and a bottle of rum.

The pirates?   They are quite frightful enough to instil fear
and awe into adult as well as childish breasts, and we vote it a happy
thought which brought this beloved book of American literature to the
screen.

Shirley Mason plays Jim Hawkins with a whimsical touch and
is always extremely good to look upon, altho she might have registered a little more terror when surrounded by the burly pirates.

Taken all in all, it is a good production and one which is
ideal for the family to enjoy together.

--Adele Whitely Fletcher in Motion
Picture Magazine, Vol. 20, No.
8 (August 1920), pages 110-111.

☐ TRILBY (World, 1917)

Trilby was a masterpiece of atmospheric achievement.   Why
the programme did not name the director, I don't know.   It had the
artistry, the infinite detail, that intangible feeling of situation that
only Jimmy Young seems able to throw into a screen story of alien
life.

Here was Paris!   Not only the quiet banks of the Seine, and
the majestic Church of Our Lady--actual views--but the Paris of the
Quartier made in the World Film studio, the street taken in New
York's MacDougal Alley, the Quartier ball, and the ateliers.

Wilton Lackaye's Svengali is such a stage classic that even to
screen audiences his impersonation seems a repetition.   He lived
the bearded life, and died the stagey old 'cross-table death that he
has died, on and off, these fifteen years.

I was disappointed in Clara Kimball Young's Trilby.   The
characterization seemed insincere.   She was pert rather than innocent and childish; there was little variation between Trilby O'Ferral
and La Svengali; and when she died it seemed not because the vitality
of her demoniac master had passed from her, but because she fell
down and bumped her pretty little head.

The dramatic ending to Trilby has never been satisfactory, in that it is inexplicable to those who have not read DuMaurier's novel. But this cannot be changed.

> --Julian Johnson in Photoplay, Vol. 9, No. 1 (December 1915), page 90.

☐ TRUE HEART SUSIE (Paramount-Artcraft, 1919)

The quaint tale of a quaint little country girl who waited, and waited, and waited ... and finally got him when he became a sod-widower. This piece is worth seeing solely because of Mr. Griffith's characteristic lacery of character and fine humanities.

> --Julian Johnson in Photoplay, Vol. 16, No. 4 (September 1919), page 117.

*   *   *

We haven't the heart to discuss Mr. Griffith's True Heart Susie, immediately after his Broken Blossoms. For they are a thousand miles apart. True Heart Susie is of the Hoosier caliber of A Romance of Happy Valley. It revolves around a young minister who fails to see the lovelight in simple Susie's eyes, marries a fickle little milliner, discovers her semi-infidelity after her sudden death, and who turns finally to Susie, who has waited thru it all. To us True Heart Susie hasn't one-tenth of the real country and small-town atmosphere of The Turn in the Road. Lillian Gish is quaint as Susie, but darned if we can like her weird country attire. We've lived in the country but never glimpsed anything as exaggerated as Susie's clothes in these mail-order days. Clarine Seymour again reveals surprising promise as the cutie milliner who loves jazz better than her fireside. And, considering the Willie Jenkins of Bobby Harron, we can't entirely blame her.

> --Frederick James Smith in Motion Picture Classic, Vol. 8, No. 6 (August 1919), page 60.

☐ THE TURN IN THE ROAD (Brentwood, 1919)

The Turn in the Road is not a human document, but it comes nearer being one than any photoplay we have glimpsed in a year of movie-going. King W. Vidor, hitherto known to fame as Florence Vidor's husband, wrote and directed the story for the new Brentwood Films. And, were we a screen magnate, we would have been sitting on Mr. Vidor's doorstep the morning after seeing The Turn in the Road--and a blank contract would have been in our hand.

For, in one single picture, Mr. Vidor steps into the front
rank of directors. The Turn in the Road touches upon a tremendous
theme. What is life? Paul Perry is dazed by fate when death takes
his little wife just as a child is born. Her father, a clergyman,
tries to comfort him by declaring it is God's will. His own father,
a man of wealth, has promised to do everything that money can do.
The boy turns from them both and disappears into the night. His
lonely wanderings in quest of the true God take him far, but finally
he returns and drags himself, half-dazed for want of food, into the
hayloft of a barn, when a little boy, his own child, crawls up the
ladder. Then, in a scene exquisitely touching, the embittered man
learns the truth of life from the tiny boy. "I've been hunting for
God," he says, and the child answers, "Why, I could have told you
that--God is love and light. He is everywhere." When the man
protests, the child goes on, "When you close the blind a room is
dark--Sorrow is where you never let love in." Then his dead wife's
sister, who has loved him always and cared for his child thru the
years, comes--and out of the wretchedness of the past appears the
foundation of a new happiness.

Mr. Vidor's doctrine is applied Christian Science, but The
Turn in the Road isn't a preachment. Twice it sweeps to superbly
moving climaxes. There is the love story of Paul and his girl wife
amid the gentle atmosphere of a small town. Here is a slice of
life itself. Again there is the return of Paul and his discovery of
the secret of life. Mr. Vidor has lapsed into melodrama in telling
his story, but his lapses are so far offset by the cumulative power
of his directness that they are forgivable. The Turn in the Road is
a mighty big thing.

The photodrama has able handling, from little Ben Alexander's
touching Bob and Helen Jerome Eddy's sincere June to the distraught
Paul of Lloyd Hughes and the brief but sweet little wife of Pauline
Curley.

--Frederick James Smith in Motion
Picture Classic, Vol. 8, No. 4
(June 1919), page 46.

☐ $23\frac{1}{2}$ HOURS LEAVE (Ince/Paramount-Artcraft, 1919)

The reviewer boldly pronounces this the best all-around comedy of the season and cannot just recollect that he ever saw a better
one. It is distinctively wholesome and 100 per cent pure, occupying
a pedestal all its own. There are no lagging moments and no vulgarities injected.

Douglas MacLean, Doris May and Thomas Guise give clever
performances and the entire cast represents perfect types. At its
premier release as a regular offering at the Rialto Theatre in New
York it provoked chuckles from its inception. These chuckles soon

developed into hearty laughter which became continuous and at the
conclusion the heavy applause which rewarded the picture was as
remarkable as it was unusual.

A silent offering must be considered very striking to be en-
cored in this fashion by a blase audience.   Direction, mounting,
story, continuity, photography and laboratory work were all above
par.   The action takes place in an army cantonment on this side.

Pulling possibilities and pleasing probabilities for respective
audiences are: Metropolitan, big puller and exceptionally pleasing;
Elite, strong puller and highly pleasing; Family, big puller and very
pleasing; Labor, good puller and entirely pleasing.
                        --Tom Hanlin in Motion Picture
                          News, Vol. 20, No. 20 (Novem-
                          ber 8, 1919), page 3502.

☐   UNCLE TOM'S CABIN (Famous Players-Lasky/Paramount, 1918)

The most popular play of the American stage, Uncle Tom's
Cabin can hardly expect to make a like record on the screen.   Conditions that gave the story its remarkable success when it first appeared no longer exist.   The version produced by the Famous
Players-Lasky Corporation, with Marguerite Clark as Little Eva
and Topsy, presents the story very attractively, however, and screen
patrons will find it worth their while to view the old classic in a
new form.   Directed by J. Searle Dawley, and all the celebrated
scenes reproduced with commendable realism, the Harriet Elizabeth
Beecher Stowe book, which contains such a powerful sermon against
slavery, is bound to prove entertaining to the public even at this late
day.

It is also interesting to note that Uncle Tom's Cabin is an
excellent example of a well made play, outside of the timeliness of
its theme when it was first brought out.   It was written to arouse
the entire nation, and the different elements of suspense, pathos,
humor, and strongly drawn characters are handled with great skill
in both the stage and the screen versions.

There is no necessity for retelling the familiar story.   The
histories of Little Eva, Topsy, Uncle Tom, Eliza, Simon Legree,
and the rest of the characters are known the world over.   Marguerite
Clark's double of the little white embodiment of goodness and the
small black shadow of mischief is among the most interesting of her
screen impersonations.   The range demanded is a wide one.   The
death of Little Eva might have been more impressive, but the admirers of this clever artist will be quick to recognize the sincerity
and skill that are to be found in her work.

Frank Losee as Uncle Tom, Henry Stamford as St. Clair,

Walter Lewis as Simon Legree, Mrs. Priestley Morrison as Ophelia, and Florence Carpenter as Eliza stand out prominently in the well chosen cast.

--Edward Weitzel in The Moving
Picture World, Vol. 37, No. 3
(July 20, 1918), page 453.

☐ THE UNPARDONABLE SIN (Harry Garson, 1919)

And now comes a regrettable duty, commenting upon Harry Garson's production of Major Rupert Hughes' The Unpardonable Sin. Major Hughes built his novel around the Hun invasion of Belgium and the story is one atrocity after another. In the main, it centers about the efforts of an American girl to locate her mother and sister in ill-fated Belgium, where they have been the victims of German ruthlessness in the most repulsive sense of the word. It is our personal opinion that The Unpardonable Sin is not a picture to be shown to audiences of both grown-ups and children. There is nothing to be gained at this time by reproducing wartime depravity and the possibility of cheap exploitation of a picture of this type savors nothing more nor less than of the commercialization by Americans of Hun atrocities. God forbid that Americans do this! Blanche Sweet returns to the screen after a long absence, playing both Dimny Parcot and her ill-fated sister, Alice. The characterizations, both keyed at a high and gruelling emotional height, apparently prevent shadings. At any rate there are no gradations to the performance and Miss Sweet does not touch us anywhere. More effective is Mary Alden's playing of the mother. Marshall Neilan directs The Unpardonable Sin without revealing any particular touch of imagination.

--Frederick James Smith in Motion
Picture Classic, Vol. 8, No. 5
(July 1919), page 81.

☐ AN UNSEEN ENEMY (American Biograph, 1912)*

There is hardly a consistent situation in this film, which tells the story of a degenerate woman who attempts to rob the place where she is employed. The conditions precedent are vague, causing the audience to sit through most of the picture before getting the thread of the tale. The mere question of why such a woman as the servant appears to be on the surface is retained in the house is rather too much of a question for the average spectator to solve. A young man and his two sisters, formerly under the protection of the grandfather,

_____

*An Unseen Enemy, directed by D. W. Griffith, was the first film to feature Lillian and Dorothy Gish.

are now left to face the world alone as a result of death. The young
man disposes of a portion of the estate left them and deposits the
money in a small safe in the house. The servant overhears him
tell his sisters about the money and straightway makes for the telephone to enlist the aid of a former male companion in her intention
to rob. Her companion responds and the robbery is attempted in
broad daylight, one of the inconsistencies of the piece. The story
derives its name from the action of the woman, who thrusts a gun
through a hole in the wall to quiet the two girls in the next room.
The girls manage to get to the telephone and inform their brother
of their plight, and an extravagant rescue is made. The only diversion the film affords is the childish love that exists between a youth
and the youngest girl. She has refused to kiss him good-by when
he is about to leave for school, but consents to the familiarity after
her fright. It is well acted.

> --G. in The New York Dramatic
>   Mirror, Vol. 68, No. 1761 (Sep-
>   tember 18, 1912), page 28.

☐ VICTORY (Paramount-Artcraft, 1919)

     Maurice Tourneur accomplishes a rare feat in the splendid
melodrama whose name is capitalized above. He puts Joseph Con-
rad--the absolute Joseph Conrad--on the screen, while very seriously
altering Joseph Conrad's story! That is to say, Tourneur has caught,
and conveys, the true spirit, the real philosophy, of the author. In
this respect the distinguished French-American has more unerring
capabilities, perhaps, than any other camera-master now at work.
Not since his great optic transcription of Sporting Life has he so
thoroughly caught the timbre, as a musician would say, of the thing
in which he has engaged. Every reader of Conrad's dark but superb
story remembers that it ended in a tragedy of hellish laughter: the
bullet intended for the fiend Ricardo hits that passionate saint Alma,
and with her dies the youthful philosopher Heyst, whom she has
drawn from an existence of self-immurement, only to an end of final
despair. In Tourneur's picture things go just the other way: Heyst
has killed Ricardo, and the anthropoid Pedro, in ultimate revenge,
dumps "Mr. Jones," face forward, into the fire, while out in the
tropic garden Heyst says the tender word, and Alma comes to his
arms as the organist pulls the stops for the exit march. Yet, though
the Conrad finale is so radically upset, the dark splendor of Conrad's thought is preserved in every scene, and in every episode you
get the slow, majestic, tense movement of his strange drama. It
is not a pleasant picture. It may best be described profanely, as a
heller. The internal glare upon the face of Mr. Jones, as he goes
over into the fire; the deviltry of Schomberg; the cold evil of the
aforesaid Mr. Jones; the leers of the serpentine Ricardo--none of
these are happy subjects for contemplation. Yet what superb characterizations! Wallace Beery as Schomberg, Lon Chaney as Ricardo,
Ben Deely as Jones, Bull Montana as Pedro: here is acting; acting

that you won't often find duplicated on stage or screen. Jack Holt
is very fine as the virile young philosopher, and Seena Owen is at
once sensuous and sensitive as Alma. Mr. Tourneur has made a
fine art of suspense in this photoplay.

--Julian Johnson in Photoplay, Vol.
17, No. 3 (February 1920), page
72.

☐ WAR BRIDES (Selznick, 1916)

        Judged solely by its greatest dramatic moments, War Brides,
the eight-reel screen version of Marion Craig Wentworth's one act
play, reaches a tragic height never before attained by a moving picture. Marred by an opening that is both incongruous and commonplace and hampered by slow development during the first four reels,
it then starts to gather force and, although the final situation is retarded unnecessarily and is open to further criticism, the climax
which marks the end of the drama is probably the most powerful
ever seen on the screen. After a plethora of endings where the
lovers entwine their arms about each other and roll up their eyes
to slow music, it is a positive relief to be given a finish that has
all the electric effectiveness of a flash of lightning. Such moments
are rare upon the spoken stage; they are rarer still upon the screen.

        War Brides is a tragedy. In strength of theme it may be
classed with the greatest dramas of all times. In certain portions
of the screen play the possibilities of the theme have been fully realized. Its story sounds the deepest depths of human suffering, and
the acting of Nazimova and the supporting company brings out to the
full the intensity of every poignant emotion that is felt by the devoted
women whose hearts are torn by the relentless hand of war. In ar-
ranging the story for the screen, Herbert Brenon has taken the play,
with its one act and simple cottage interior, and elaborated plot and
setting so that the action embraces a battle scene and the equally
absorbing moments which mark the preparation and the aftermath
connected with the harvest of death. Throughout the eight reels,
there are evidences of the care and skill of the director, every device that money and experience could employ has been used in making the picture, beautiful photographic effects are of frequent occur-
ance, but its most potent appeal is the bitter cry of suffering womanhood that rings through it and strikes on the heart of the spectator.
The screen, though it have no tongue--to paraphrase the line from
Hamlet--speaks with most miraculous organ!

        Many of the reading and thinking public of this country are
familiar with the theme of the picture. The spoken play was first
published in a leading magazine and, later, Nazimova used it as a
starring vehicle in vaudeville. Its scenes are laid in a hypothetical
country, and its characters have the idealism and mysticism of the
Russian peasant whose mind has been awakened. Realism and sym-

bolism go hand in hand through the play, and only a very strong story could triumph over so many repeats of scene. The Joan of Nazimova, in her fierce resentment of the war brides decree and her out-spoken determination that she and her sex in general shall rear no more children to become food for cannon, belongs to the band of social firebrands that have been exiled, imprisoned or executed in the cause of Nihilism. For a brief space, it resolves itself into an unmistakable piece of Woman's Suffrage propaganda.

Objection has been raised to the almost revolting realism of the episode where Joan pictures to herself her fear that the women of her family will become the victims of an assault at the hands of the invaders. Director Brenon has spared but few of the details, and is vindicated on truthful, if not on artistic grounds. The actions and facial contortions of the soldiers are those of fiends, not human beings, but, the scene does not actually take place--except in the over-wrought imagination of the fear-tortured Joan. Under such conditions it is not a distortion of fact at least. To return to the climax and the stricture that it is retarded and is open to further criticism; from the moment that Joan first sights the automobile of the king until she has gathered her hordes of followers, returned to the cottage for her revolver and stopped the car of the ruler upon the highway, the lapse of time is so long that the royal motor car would have been miles beyond the horizon before her plans were half completed. This prolonging of the situation almost results in an anticlimax, but when the king and Joan do meet, the impact strikes fire. From then on until the woman makes good her threat not to bear her child unless the king promises there shall be no more war, and her lifeless form, selfslain, is held aloft before the eyes of the horrified monarch by the arms of the frenzied women who have sworn to resort to the same desperate means, the movement sweeps the beholder along with overwhelming force. A striking contrast of emotions is invoked during a scene in a church crowded with wounded and dying soldiers, while a number of recruits hurry gayly up the main aisle with the laughing girls who are to become war brides.

To Nazimova and her associates belongs the credit of a fine artistic achievement in the acting of the play--a masterly control of the emotions and their expression by means of the silent drama. The Russian actress' one flaw is in giving too freely of her inward fire. A woman of her intellectual and histrionic breadth need but sit in judgment upon her own work to correct the faults incidental to a first attempt. She will study the impersonation that Gertrude Berkeley gives of the mother--an example of screen acting that for beauty, truth and quiet force has never been excelled--and the way for her to tread will be made clear. Nila Mac is an appealing bit of womanhood as Amelia, of fine moral texture and grateful to the eye. Charles Hutchinson, Charles Bryant, William Bailey and Richard S. Barthelmess as the four brothers of Amelia, who are killed in battle, justify their mother's pride in them. Alex. K. Shannon, Robert Whitworth, Ned Burton, Theodore Warfield and Charles

Chailies are the remaining members of the carefully balanced
cast.

--Edward Weitzel in The Moving
Picture World, Vol. 30, No. 9
(December 2, 1916), pages
1343-1344.

*   *   *

The theme of War Brides looms above its other merits as
its greatest. It deals with the war in Europe and dwells on the
suffering of war's women. The principles of war and drama when
analyzed prove to be the same. Both are founded on conflict. A
good drama has its conflict from start to finish and so has war.
So when the two are combined, intelligently combined as in War
Brides, the results must of necessity be unusually striking. But
War Brides is even greater. Its story is tremendous. It is founded
on the one-act play by Marion Craig Wentworth which created something of a sensation when played in vaudeville with Nazimova in the
chief role.

Nazimova makes her screen debut in the picture. She is an
actress of wonderful emotional ability and as the woman who rebels
against the command of her king and refuses to bear her child with
the thought of it growing to live for another war, she puts her whole
self in the part. The complete technique of the screen is not yet
the knowledge of Nazimova--that will come in time--but technique or
no technique she plays so wonderfully that we tremble at the thought
of naming another actress for the character. In screen makeup she
also has more to learn, but in all sincerity such minor details are
quite without the range of vision with respect to War Brides, for the
reason that the whole is so good.

Beyond the shadow of a doubt it is the best thing that Herbert
Brenon has ever done. His direction here is excellent. His straight
scenes are effectively arranged, the action is centered--easy to follow. He has utilized close-ups to advantage--employed subtitles and
excerpts from the plays effectively. The standard of production is
above criticism. Many of the exteriors are mindful of great paintings. The lighting is superb and the photography excellent.

The picture has so many intense dramatic episodes that one
hardly knows where to begin in their listing. The scene in which
the mother learns of the death of her three sons is remarkable for
its sustained, almost nerve-racking suspense. Its climax is terrific,
for the third son reported dead is the husband of Joan (Nazimova).
When Joan denounces the captain and the entire system of war in
the name of the women of the country, it is very likely that any audience will break into applause as the trade audience did at the picture's initial showing. The final scene is a wonderful piece of
stagecraft. In it Joan after bringing all the women of the town together stands and denounces the king of her country and then puts an

end to herself and her unborn child.   A terrific climax to an immense picture.

Miss Gertrude Berkeley as the mother of the four soldiers
did a wonderful part in a corresponding way.   Nila Mac was effective as the sister.   The rest of the cast counted forcefully and included Charles Bryant, Charles Hutchinson, William Bailey, Richard Barthelmess, Alex Shannon, Robert Whitworth, Ned Burton,
Theodora Warfield and Charles Chailies.

A line or so in reference to the distributor of the picture is
in order.   War Brides is not a program picture and doubtless Mr.
Selznick will offer it at advanced prices.   All we can say is that it
should be well worth any reasonable hire.   When all is said as to
its artistic points, there is the all-important fact of the box office
angle--the attraction offered by the title and the star, and frankly
we know of no better combination than Nazimova in War Brides,
produced by Herbert Brenon.

--Peter Milne in Motion Picture
News, Vol. 14, No. 21 (November 25, 1916), page 3331.

☐   WAR ON THE PLAINS (Bison/New York Motion Picture Company,
1912)*

This is second in the series of large spectacular war and Indian pictures that this company is putting out and is a remarkable
and notable achievement in revealing life on the plains as it was
during the early period of the West.   Perhaps the best praise that
one can give the film is to say that it gives the impression that it
would and did happen in just that way, for it is an essentially vivid
and real performance built on a large scale, showing views of the
entire scope of a valley with the settlers below and the Indian en-
campment hidden among the hills, and the large train of emigrants
winding their way over the valley and stopping to rest at a settlement, with other views both near and far of artistic and exciting
import.   The story deals with the end of a coward, who left his
partner on the desert without water and later by this very cowardice
in fleeing from the settlers when he might have been of the most
use, meeting death himself on the desert from the bite of a reveng-
ing serpent.   He had joined the settlers, but when the attack by the
Indians came, he refused to go for aid, and his place was taken by
the lover of the girl whose affections he had succeeded in winning,
but when she saw him in the midst of the fray, crawling to shelter,
she realized his true character.   The settlers who came to their

---

*Starring Ethel Grandin and Francis Ford, War on the Plains was
the first two-reeler to be produced in Los Angeles by Thomas H.
Ince.

aid called off the Indians by setting fire to their camp, which they
saw burning over the hill, and then the train continued on its way
with the lovers once more united. The production has been done in
two reels and is an exceptional and noteworthy achievement.

--Reviews of Independent Films in
The New York Dramatic Mirror,
Vol. 67, No. 1732 (February 28,
1912), page 37.

☐ THE WARRENS OF VIRGINIA (Lasky Feature Play Company/
Paramount, 1915)

The screen has seen the great American war drama "acted
o'er and o'er again," and it may be that audiences are somewhat
cloyed with civil war plays. The Warrens of Virginia has become
a classic on the speaking stage. Just what screen values are to be
found in the old play may be an open question. Of course in the
matter of spectacular effects the screen is a far better medium than
the stage. In the filmed version of the Lasky Company quite a good
deal has been made of the spectacular possibilities. One or two
scenes are especially worthy of note, such for example as the am-
bushing of the Confederate supply train and the destruction of the
powder wagons. There was, throughout, much evidence of a most
laudable desire to do things on a lavish scale. I noticed, too, that
attention to detail, without which a real feature is impossible.

As to the acting, the work of James Neill as General Warren, may be characterized as thoroughly capable and conscientious
and effective; House Peters as Ned Burton had a most trying part
which tested his art to the straining point; Dick La Reno made a
most acceptable "General Griffin." Blanche Sweet has a charming
personality, which has won her innumerable friends among patrons
of the screen, but in the part of Agatha Warren she is scarcely at
her best. In the great scenes which precede the discovery of the
forged dispatch there was a lack of fire and spirit. In the scenes
where sweet girlishness was needed Miss Sweet was at her best.
She fitted well into the refined but simple atmosphere of an old-
fashioned Southern home. All the outdoor scenes in the play were
extremely well chosen. Here and there I noticed a flash of the
skill which visualizes quickly and powerfully, but evidences of this
skill were less frequent than in other Lasky productions. The part
of Mrs. Warren was in the filmed adaptation of the play a minor
and not a very grateful one, but it might have improved under better
treatment. Touches of humor occurred occasionally and often they
were good, but once or twice they seemed labored.

Taken as a whole, the production will go well on most programs.

--W. Stephen Bush in The Moving
Picture World, Vol. 23, No. 9
(February 27, 1915), page 1268.

☐ WAY DOWN EAST (Griffith/United Artists, 1920)

There are two kinds of super-feature productions--the Griffith
kind and the others. But before you spiral to the conclusion that
all that Griffith does is superlative and all that the others do suffers
something by comparison let me assure you that that is not what I
mean. The things that Griffith does best he does better than any
other director in pictures; the things he does badly he cheapens
quite as noticeably. In Way Down East, which is certain to be the
most talked of and probably the most successful picture of the year,
the concluding scene of the drifting ice and the rescued Anna Moore
is probably the most stirringly realistic single scene that has been
screened, and on the other hand the bucolic comedy is as commonplace and colorless and trivial as any.

Personally, too, I quarrel with the Griffith lack of taste in
the development of such episodes as that in which Lillian Gish is
forced to writhe about a bed in the pain of childbirth and in the
forced dramatic emphasis of such scenes as the night-long vigil with
the corpse of the dead child--scenes that require the utmost delicacy
of treatment to relieve them of that stark realism which is frequently
revolting. And yet it is no more than fair to admit that there is effective tragedy even in these scenes.

There may be other directors who could have handled the age-
old story of Anna Moore's attainment of happiness through suffering
better than Griffith has handled it, but if there are I am unfamiliar
with their work. This Belasco of the screen has a definite gift for
detail on which he expends an infinite amount of pains. His backgrounds are never merely plastered in, or set up hurriedly and
carelessly shot. They are etched in and become not only photographically true, but atmospherically consistent and helpful to the building
of the story. For example, the bridal "suite" in the country hotel
to which the seducer took Anna Moore after the mock marriage, was
rather elaborate when compared with what one might reasonably expect from the exterior of the same hotel, but it was a real room,
perfect in detail and furnishings. And there was not an exterior
that did not exude the very scents and smells of New England.

Griffith, too, is particularly careful in his choice of actors.
After twenty years of Phoebe Davies on the stage Lillian Gish seems
a little immature and childish for the suffering Anna, but she is
thoroughly competent and her director, knowing so perfectly her histrionic limitations, is careful not to press her too far. She inspires
a quick sympathy and is able to carry the emotional scenes tellingly.
Richard Barthelmess is a good choice for the honest farmer boy and
Lowell Sherman adds one more to his lengthening lists of seductions.
Creighton Hale, in the one intelligently directed comedy scene of the
barn dance, was excellent, and little Mary Hay added a touch here
and there that seems to promise a screen future for her. Burr
McIntosh, Kate Bruce, Vivia Ogden and Edgar Nelson lent competent
support. Like all super-features, Way Down East would be a

stronger picture if it were not so extended--if it were eight reels
in place of twelve, say. But it is the one of the few super-features
that will be able to stand alone. Anthony Paul Kelly provided the
scenario, which some one has spattered with a mixture of good titles
and bad.

--Burns Mantle in Photoplay, Vol.
19, No. 1 (December 1920),
pages 57-58.

*   *   *

It was almost a foregone conclusion that Way Down East would
make an exceptional picture. Its long life and nationwide popularity
on the stage had already stamped it as an unusual play. As a rule
melodramas have a short lease of life and are easily forgotten.
When one of them succeeds in maintaining itself in the national rep-
ertory for a great number of years, it is safe to assume that the
human appeal of the characters or a touch of real poetry in the story
rises above the conventional effects at which melodrama usually aims.
A play of this kind is sure to attract the producer of pictures because melodrama is undoubtedly the favorite art form of the screen.
Mr. Griffith has a sure instinct for such things.

The story of Way Down East is too familiar to need complete
retelling. It is, in its way, a classic of American rural life and is
almost as widely known as The Old Homestead or Uncle Tom's Cabin.
There is a real and unaffected poignancy about the betrayal of a young
and ignorant girl by a sophisticated seducer which can easily be
brought home to vast audiences. Here the moving picture has the
advantage over the play. For photoplay art has resources which permit it to soften the crassness of melodrama and to disguise its shop-
worn qualities. The silent drama leaves our imagination more free,
and the girl's misery, which is none the less real for being one of
the oldest stories in the world, can still be brought to us with artistic freshness.

Mr. Griffith has gone to work with his usual lavishness. He
tells his story against a panorama of country life and manners full
of much delightful detail, and thus adds an element of spectacle to
what would otherwise have been indeed a "simple tale." Anna
Moore's visit to her rich relatives is translated into a gorgeous
fashion show and the simple farm of Squire Bartlett is turned into
somewhat of a show place. Mr. Griffith favors large gestures to
reach his screen public.

The climax of the picture is furnished by Anna's blind flight
into the snowstorm. Here Mr. Griffith has let himself loose, and
the result, to judge from the applause which greets this scene, justifies the method. But the scene becomes very long and the suspense
threatens to lose itself as the spectator begins to doubt the possibility
of David's ice-jumping feats. They are certainly enough to make
poor Eliza of Uncle Tom's Cabin fame turn over in her grave, and
any real country folk who know something about ice jams will probably

realize that they are being told a pretty tall story. But, as Mercutio said, "it will serve," and there is no doubt of its being a headline thriller. It is possibly the most spectacular thing, giving at moments a sense of real terror, that has ever been photographed for a dramatic picture.

Mr. Griffith could be depended upon for bringing out the full pathos of Anna's tragedy. His genius for this sort of thing has always been great. And, as usual, he has had the advantage of Miss Lillian Gish's unlimited cooperation. It is a truly astonishing thing about this young artist that one can always say that her latest work is her best. One wonders how high she can still climb on the ladder of superb screen acting. Or perhaps it is a question of how far Mr. Griffith and Miss Gish could go together, for it is often impossible to tell in their work where direction ends and interpretation begins. The rest of Mr. Griffith's cast is, as usual, well balanced, and shows some fine individual work.

Here and there, however, Mr. Griffith has lowered his artistic standard. Some of his comedy scenes, the country dances and the village store episodes, are carelessly done, as if taken in haste, and are not properly joined to the rest of the story. And the scene where Anna gives birth to her child throws the emphasis on the physical side to a degree which is decidedly in questionable taste. It is a pity that in this case the acting of Miss Gish is forced beyond the line of expression into sheer distortion. Nor can anything be said for the colored tintings which Mr. Griffith has introduced here and there into his landscapes. All the delicacy and mellowness which has so distinguished his landscape work in the past is lost by this fatal pink intrusion.

As for the scenes during the function in the home of Anna's city relatives, in which colored foreground portraits of Anna are introduced in contrast to the black and white backgrounds of the longer shots, one hardly knows what to think. To some the idea will appear as an artistic blunder. Others will forgive the incongruity on the theory that Mr. Griffith was endeavoring to create the color impression of a very gaudy and sumptuous social affair. At least one of these colored portraits--that which reveals Miss Gish in tones of blue and silver--is quite beautiful and satisfactory in itself. Perhaps here Mr. Griffith is on the track of an impressionism which has tremendously effective possibilities.

There is one thing, in addition, which may be pointed out. With all the various life and movement of Way Down East, there is sometimes a carelessness in the cutting and matching of scenes which certainly interferes with the illusion. There is no reason why a character should rise from a chair in a close-up view and in the succeeding long shot, which is supposed to be part of a continuous action, should appear rising from the chair again.

Yet there cannot be any doubt of the general effectiveness of the picture. Mr. Griffith cannot touch any story without putting his

stamp upon it.   His version of Way Down East will travel far and
long.   When it has travelled long enough he may perhaps again find
courage to try his hand at another Broken Blossoms.

--Exceptional Photoplays, No. 2
(December 1920), page 3.

☐ WHERE ARE MY CHILDREN (Universal, 1916)*

It is not often that a subject as delicate as the one of which
this picture treats is handled as boldly yet, at the same time as
inoffensively as is the case with this production.   It succeeds in
making its point, in being impressive, in driving home the lesson
that it seeks to teach without being offensive.   This is largely due
to the capable direction of the Smalleys and the superb acting of
Tyrone Power, aided by an excellent cast.

The picture is confusing to some extent, in that it deals with
two big subjects without there being a distinct line of demarcation
to show where one leaves off and the other commences.   It starts
off as an argument favoring the dissemination of knowledge regarding birth control, showing the deleterious effect on civilization of
permitting the birth of children into the world handicapped with physical and moral deformities.   This part of the picture was not convincingly presented, and whereas the educated person might compre-
hend the indirect suggestive trend of the argument, still for a picture that is to be shown to the masses, we believe that the method
of treatment should be made more direct, simple, and understanda-
ble.   In so far as the first part of the picture is concerned, there
is no differentiation made between birth control, race suicide, or
abortion.   We cannot believe this to be the purpose of the authors.

The second part of the production is a strong preachment
against race suicide.   It is convincing, strong, and impressive, with
a touch of realistic human nature that brings tears to the eyes of
the audience.   This feature of the picture has been mighty well handled, every meaning and argument coming across the screen in a
simple, direct and intelligible manner.   There is one place, however, which has a false touch.   When the district attorney finds the
reason why so many of the social set are without children he drives
the women from his house, remarking that he ought to prosecute
them for manslaughter.   He also accuses his wife of being a mur-
deress.   No lawyer would make remarks of this nature, especially
without detailed knowledge as to whether a crime in the eyes of the
law had been committed.   The law allows a period of three months

---

*Where Are My Children was directed by Phillips Smalley and Lois
Weber, known collectively as The Smalleys.   However, all available
evidence indicates that the credit for this and other films directed
by the Smalleys should go to Lois Weber.

before it recognizes a crime in this case, and there was nothing to show that such a time had elapsed.

We are somewhat surprised that one with the artistic ability of Lois Weber should have permitted such a crude and cumbersome arrangement as that used to suggest Eternity and the departure and return of the disembodied souls of little children. We believe that explanatory subtitles would have been much more effective. Otherwise, the picture has been most ably produced.

Much of the success of the production may be ascribed to the strong, convincing and artistic acting of Tyrone Power in the leading role of Richard Walton, the district attorney. Helen Riavme, as his selfish wife, pleased with her effective work, as did Rene Rogers, A. D. Blake, Juan De La Cruz, and Cora Drew. The photography was good throughout, with some beautiful and elaborate settings.

The story is intensely dramatic. It tells of a district attorney, whose greatest ambition in life is to have children. He is forced to prosecute a doctor for disseminating knowledge relative to birth control, and though a student of eugenics, he is forced to present the evidence and assist in the doctor's conviction. His wife, selfish and frivolous, has, unknown to her husband, patronized a doctor, bringing about the destruction of conceived children, and has sent several of her friends to him when they were "enceinte." The young, innocent daughter of her housekeeper is indiscreet with her brother, and when the girl gets in trouble sends her to the doctor practising in defiance of the law. This time he bungles and the girl dies. The district attorney brings about his indictment and conviction, and he is sentenced to fifteen years at hard labor. Before leaving for prison, however, the doctor forces the lawyer to examine his record book in which it shows the many times that the district attorney's wife has taken advantage of the doctor's services. He returns home, and in an intensely dramatic manner accuses his wife of being a murderer, and asks her "Where Are My Children." Repentent, she tries to bring about conception, but she has perverted herself too frequently and is forced to endure a sorrowful life robbed of the blessing of motherhood.

--E. in The New York Dramatic
Mirror, Vol. 75, No. 1948
(April 22, 1916), page 42.

☐ WHILE NEW YORK SLEEPS (Fox, 1920)

We are going to forget the first episode of this three-act drama of Manhattan. It should not have been done at all. The second act is satire, satire as clever and as keen as any ever screened. It has fun with you, with me, and even with the solemn man who plays the trombone in the orchestra. In it, we meet Estelle Taylor

as a sprightly vamp.   If sirens were not out of style (on the screen)
we'd term La Taylor the empress of them all.   We won't spoil the
surprise of this satire by pinning it to paper.   A thrill is handed
all inlanders in those scenes showing for the first time on any
screen a close-up of Ziegfeld's Midnight Frolic, with a gorgeous
glimpse of the stately Dolores.   This is Broadway--the very breath
of it.

The third of the three acts is by far the best.   It is the most
gruesome tragedy the screen has known.   It is not entirely original
in conception, with all due respect to the programmed authors of it.
Once French, this plot of the paralytic old father who watches his
only son murdered by an unfaithful wife and her lover is peppy pabu-
lum for the picture-goers accustomed only to sugar-coated sex drama.   Marc McDermott, after a long absence, returns to films as
the father, giving the best performance of his career and pretty
nearly the best characterization of its kind in celluloid.   Harry Sothern, nephew of E. H., is reminiscent of Raymond Hatton as the
son.   Earle Metcalfe comes back with a bang as the young gangster-
lover--a capital performance, this.   Estelle Taylor, the same sensuous young woman of act two, has her first big rôle here.   This
beautiful newcomer has a vast dramatic reserve; she fairly hurls
herself upon a part and tears it to pieces.   With very careful direction she should go far.   You will gasp, you will shudder all the way
through this three-ring circus.   For once the advertisements have
not exaggerated.   The suspense is well sustained--so well that you
could hear the proverbial pin drop if it ever did, not to mention
smothered shrieks from the women and soft-pedaled profanity from
the men.   William Fox will make money with this one, as he has
with so many others.   But this time he earns it.   He has not attempted here to sugar-coat his sex-theme or veil his violence or
mask his melodrama.   It is as frank and unashamed as the above
alliteration.   And we would advise you not to miss While New York
Sleeps, providing you're equipped with shock-absorbers and check
your nervous system with your hat.   It's a real thriller.
--Photoplay, Vol. 19, No. 1 (De-
cember 1920), pages 121-122.

*   *   *

Fox has presented a touch of novelty in its latest production,
While New York Sleeps, by offering three distinct chapters in the
sordid life of the metropolis and portraying realistic phases among
the upper, middle and lower classes of its inhabitants.   It differs
from a serial, however, in its adherence to truth and the fact that
it doesn't rely upon melodramatic thrills but presents three ideas
which are logically conceived and executed.   The wheat is separated
from the chaff here and one only sees the chaff.   In this respect
the city is held up to the light and depicted in all its sordidness
during the hours between midnight and dawn.

The ideas incorporated, titled as "Out of the Night, " "The
Gay White Way, " and "A Tragedy of the East Side, " are truly dram-

atizations of the back page of a newspaper. The authors know their
New York and Charles J. Brabin, who collaborated with Thomas F.
Fallon, has given it a production which is remarkably real. Every
detail is rich in its color and atmosphere and the ideas are perfectly
constructed so that every ounce of action and suspense is squeezed
out, thus keeping the interest and holding it to the conclusion. The
first chapter depicts a favorite one-act-play recipe with the background laid in the suburbs. A husband is forced to go to town one
night and during his absence his wife is confronted by a former
spouse whom she thought dead. Complications develop when a bur-
glar enters the house and shoots the other intruder. And the wife
permits him to go, promising to forget his crime if he will forget
what he has overheard. And the sanctity of the home is kept.

     A story well done and acted up to requirements. "The Gay
White Way" is a dramatization of the "badger game" and shows a
vampire and her parasite being caught red-handed by a detective
who had registered innocence. The surprise finish gives the chapter
a healthy punch and no little humor. The best of the stories is "A
Tragedy of the East Side," which for its grim realism, its authentic
detail, its fine interpretation by Marc MacDermott and his assistants,
comes near being a melodramatic masterpiece. The suspense is
overwhelming as the action progresses. It is quite original, and
stark, and vivid in its tragic development. The crime is solved by
the expressive eyes of MacDermott in the role of a paralytic. It's
a tale carrying the same sweep and vigor as Broken Blossoms.
And executed with the same spontaneity. Harry Sothern, Estelle
Taylor and Earl Metcalfe lend admirable support.

                              --Laurence Reid in Motion Picture
                              News, Vol. 22, No. 7 (August
                              7, 1920), page 1237.

☐ THE WHISPERING CHORUS (Famous Players-Lasky/Paramount,
     1918)

     To any one desiring a wholly miserable afternoon or evening,
we cheerfully recommend Cecil DeMille's production, The Whispering
Chorus, based on a story by Perley Poore Sheehan. The Whispering
Chorus is guaranteed to take the joy out of life. Herein John Trimble steals from his employer, deserts his wife, runs away when de-
tection threatens, and then fakes his own "murder." Trimble finds
the body of a drowned man, disfigures it so that it is unrecognizable,
dresses it in his own clothes, leaves various notes indicating a fear
of murder at the hands of a mysterious Edgar Smith, and disappears.
The body is found, and some years later Mrs. Trimble marries a
man who finally becomes Governor of the State.

     Trimble, now a derelict, is arrested as Edgar Smith, tried
and convicted of murdering himself. His plot has proven a boom-
erang, and he is actually sentenced to the chair for the crime he

faked. Trimble goes to his doom without telling his secret, thus
protecting his former wife's happiness. The whispering chorus of
the title is made up of the wee sma' voices which whisper in your
ear and mine when you think about doing something naughty.

Right now one of these wee sma' voices is whispering to us
to forget all about saying anything unkind of The Whispering Chorus.
But we are telling the sma' voice to beat it. The truth must be
told. The Whispering Chorus is well done, but it is the quintes-
sence of morbidness. There is only one antidote for its seven reels
of disfigured corpses, morgues, dope-wrecked derelicts, death-cell
glimpses and electric-chair moments. The antidote? About fourteen reels of Keystone bathing-girls. Raymond Hatton presents the
disintegration of Trimble in graphic fashion.

--Frederick James Smith in Motion
Picture Classic, Vol. 6, No. 4
(June 1918), pages 65-66.

*   *   *

Jeanie Macpherson prepared the scenario of The Whispering
Chorus, a seven-part screen version of the story by Perley Poore
Sheehan, produced by Cecil B. DeMille for the Famous Players-
Lasky Corporation. The picture will cause people to think. The
subject is a powerful one, and in the hands of a director less capable than DeMille might easily have become repellent. No detail
necessary to a clear understanding of several gruesome episodes
has been omitted, but the keen artistic sense of the man responsible for the production of the picture lifts even these portions of the
story above the merely sensational and dignifies them with a moral
force that makes sin and suffering and human frailty fit subjects
for a photoplay.

The shallow mind will not relish the story, more's the pity!
but the most superficial observer will be aware that he is looking
upon a truthful reflex of life and, long before the finish, will realize
that the souls of the men and women before him on the screen are
being tried as in a furnace. Should he find nothing of interest in
such a spectacle there are still garish cabarets where his sort of
entertainment is to be had.

This is a realistic age and most persons do not give much
thought to allegory, but it is used to fine effect in The Whispering
Chorus. The title refers to the good and the bad impulses of the
mind of man that keep constantly whispering to him when anything
of moment is to be decided. These counselors are visualized at
certain intervals in the picture, and their treatment is weirdly effective.

John Trimble, a young married man, robs his employer and
runs away. While hiding on an island he drags the body of a
drowned man from the water and changes clothes with him. Later,
he is mistaken for his own murderer. His wife marries again.

During a visit to his mother Trimble is taken by the police. He is tried and sentenced to be executed. Realizing that if he tells the truth he will wreck his wife's happiness and cloud the life of the man whom she now idolizes, Trimble finds strength to go to his death with sealed lips.

Baldly stated, the story is only so much melodrama. The author's knowledge of the human heart and the skill with which he has put together his chain of events turn his work into a moving tragedy that is touched to beauty by an act of unselfishness and noble sacrifice.

It is hardly necessary to set down the obvious fact that without the co-operation of a thoroughly competent cast the director of The Whispering Chorus could not have achieved the high standard reached by the picture. The names on the program disclose a long list of representative players. Chief honors go to Raymond Hatton for his acting of John Trimble. He is not very impressive until after Trimble's sudden departure from home. From then on his performance grows in power, and the deeper the emotion the stronger he portrays it. His are the greatest opportunities of the cast, and he never fails to take advantage of the fact. His acting in the drowned man scene and in the electrocution episode fully supplement the artistic insight of Director DeMille.

On the same level of excellence are the Jane Trimble of Kathlyn Williams, the George Cogeswell of Elliott Dexter, the Mrs. Trimble of Edythe Chapman, the H. P. Clumley of Tully Marshall, the Chief McFarland of Guy Oliver, the longshoreman of Noah Beery, and the Mocking Face of Gustav Seyffertitz. John Burton, Parkes Jones, W. H. Brown, James Neill, Walter Lynch and Edna Mae Cooper complete the cast. Alvin Wyckoff was the cameraman and has much fine photography to his credit.

                                        --Edward Weitzel in The Moving
                                        Picture World, Vol. 36, No. 1
                                        (April 6, 1918), page 128.

                          *   *   *

It is strange that, with one of the epic ideas of human history and experience as their theme, Cecil DeMille and Jeanie Macpherson, who are jointly responsible for The Whispering Chorus, could have blundered so completely in the last reel as to destroy the entire effect. A man, coward and weakling by nature, runs away from the results of a comparatively small misdeed, and in doing so his character disintegrates, and he becomes a pitiable thing. Yet when the final test comes, the spark of manhood awakes, and he rises to the ultimate possible sacrifice. But the entire value of this sublime idea of inherent "good in the worst of us" is lost because the sacrifice is made in order that a woman may keep her husband ignorant of certain facts. It is revolting, this contemplation of a noble deed performed that two persons may base their happiness upon a lie. Also the final scenes are unnecessarily terrible, with awful, subtle

suggestions that will drive sensitive spectators almost into hysterics.
Much of the tale has been splendidly told, with the shadowy repre-
sentations of silent voices handled in manner most artistic.   It is
supposed to be a non-star production, but Raymond Hatton is the
unmistakable star, in as brilliant a character study as the films
have ever produced.   Elliott Dexter, with more than his usual force,
bolsters up a conventional role.

--Randolph Bartlett in Photoplay,
Vol. 14, No. 1 (June 1918), page
51.

☐ WHOM THE GODS DESTROY (Vitagraph/V-L-S-E, 1916)

Ireland at the outbreak of the European war offered plenty of
opportunities for the imaginative scenarioist.   As far as we know
Cyrus Townsend Brady is the first to have utilized these.   And he
has utilized them to excellent advantage weaving a powerful drama
about an Irish revolutionist who thought to strike at his mother country in her greatest hour of need.   The tension created by the story
is invariably high.   Mr. Brady doesn't wait until the last reel to
spring a lone big scene.   His is a picture crowded with stirring
moments from the first reel to the last.

Whom the Gods Destroy is notable for other reasons than Mr.
Brady's unusual theme.   It marks the return of Alice Joyce to the
screen after a good many years of absence.   In a part that gives
her full play we doubt if Miss Joyce has ever been seen to better
advantage.   The other leads, Harry Morey and Marc MacDermott
do sterling work too.   The exhibitor may well take into consideration the popularity of these three players and boost them heavily.
Their work will do justice to even colored superlatives.

The story centers on Sir Denis Esmond (Mr. MacDermott)
who contemplates leading a band of Irishmen against England.   In
this he is aided by Mary O'Neil (Miss Joyce), the girl he loves.
St. George Leigh (Mr. Morey) another admirer of Mary's and a true
English patriot, is temporarily blinded on his ship and is sent to
Mary's home to recuperate.   Here he discovers Denis' plans and
succeeds finally in dissuading him from his purpose.   To do so he
is obliged to rip the bandage from his eyes--to see for a moment,
but to go blind again--for life.

But St. George has not worked quickly enough.   Denis is arrested, tried, found guilty of high treason and sentenced to be
hanged.   Here Mr. Brady has introduced the King of England and
given him the power to pardon the Irishman.   The King does, at the
instigation of St. George, and the latter then believed he must leave
Mary for ever, but she prefers him as a man nobler than the ram-
bunctious Irishman.

To our mind it is always bad policy to introduce any noted living figure in motion pictures, particularly if that figure be crowned head of a nation. Thomas Mills as the King is a good actor, but as soon as such a character is introduced, the player, try as he will, is unable to create the necessary illusion of reality and royalty. But this is a small point. Perhaps after all it is unfair to mention it. The King is not a lead here and the scenes in which he appears are few.

William P. S. Earle in association with J. Stuart Blackton produced the picture in a highly acceptable fashion. Logan Paul, Charles Kent, Mary Maurice and Bernard Siegel have other important roles.

> --Peter Milne in Motion Picture News, Vol. 14, No. 25 (December 23, 1916), pages 4040-4041.

☐ WITHIN THE LAW (Vitagraph, 1917)

Within the Law, with Alice Joyce in the part Jane Cowl created on the stage, lacks the great stream of human humor which swept the spoken play like a torrent--which made it great. Within the Law is simply a melodrama, one of many.

> --Julian Johnson in Photoplay, Vol. 12, No. 3 (August 1917), page 148.

☐ THE WOMAN GOD FORGOT (Paramount-Artcraft, 1917)

A compound of high art and truly marvelous artistry is The Woman God Forgot, probably the most notable cinema masterpiece of recent weeks. In this remarkable production you will find Geraldine Farrar interpreting a role which will give her a fixed position at the topmost rung of the ladder of histrionic success in either silent or spoken drama. Out of the legendary mists of an ancient civilization she is revealed as a feminine personality displaying all the rich, romantic charm of the semi-barbarous Tezca, a princess of the Aztecs, imbued with fiery life such as compels almost breathless interest from her advent onto the scene of the story to the highly powerful ending. Miss Farrar herself regards the new characterization as her best, and she has the following to say regarding it:

"You will like The Woman God Forgot, I believe. Her unusual appeal lies in the romantic mysteries of the Aztec race. We all know they represented the highest form of civilization among the natives of the American continent at that period. Careful research

into the many, and sometimes mythical chronicles of this ancient
people revealed in Tezca, the daughter of Montezuma, a personality
peculiarly adaptable to a unique characterization. Such a close
study of this character was required for a historically correct portrayal that I was put on my mettle to actually live the life of this
woman of a dead race, in her conflicting loves for Alvarado, the
Spanish captain, and her own people. "

In the judgment of the writer, The Woman God Forgot is one
photoplay every person should see, not only because it entertains
beyond measure, but because it reveals the zenith of the splendor
which the screen art can attain. Some of the features are absolutely
original. A great battle between Spaniards under Cortez and the
Aztecs takes place on a pyramid which is two hundred feet in height.
There are probably a thousand gorgeous costumes worn by the numerous characters, and there have been few plays to offer such a
unique sartorial exhibition.

Miss Farrar's dramatic work is superb. She is at all times
a veritable mistress of the maximum of Thespian art. Moreover,
she is given most praiseworthy support by Raymond Hatton as Montezuma, Wallace Reid as Alvarado, Hobart Bosworth as Cortez, the
conqueror; Theodore Kosloff as Guatemoc, the Aztec prince-lover;
Walter Long as Taloc, the high priest whose idea of a good time
was to supervise the cutting out of the hearts of his enemies after
they were helplessly bound on a stone slab for that purpose; Olga
Grey as Matina, favorite maid of the princess; James Neill, as a
Spanish priest, and Charles B. Rogers, as Cacamo, the giant slave.
                              --Bert D. Essex in The Photo-Play
                              Journal, Vol. 2, No. 7 (Novem-
                              ber 1917), pages 38-39.

                    *   *   *

The three outstanding features of The Woman God Forgot are,
first--Geraldine Farrar's superb performance in the title role; sec-
ond--the gorgeousness of the production, and third--the expert direction supplied by Cecil B. DeMille. Had Jeanie Macpherson provided
her scenario with a little stronger and more plausible love interest,
the story part of the film would have been made doubly interesting
and enjoyable. As it is, the bigness of the production, which includes pageantry, fierce battles on high city walls, and beautiful
scenes of old palaces and sacrificial altars, lifts it far above the
ordinary feature release. In fact, the most notable thing about the
film is the amount of spectacular interest crowded into the five reels.

The story is laid in the romantic days of early Mexican history and concerns the defeat of the idol worshipping Aztecs at the
hands of the Christian Spaniards. Tesca, the daughter of the Aztec
emperor, loves a captured Spaniard, Alvarado, and in order to save
him from being offered as a sacrifice to the War God, she lets in
the hordes of his people, who rescue him and then break their word
and storm the emperor's castle. The Aztecs meet with defeat in

the ensuing battle and Tesca is cursed by her dying father, who prophesies that she shall wander upon the face of the earth deserted by the gods of all peoples.   But Alvarado offers his love and the consolation of his religion and the picture ends with Tesca in his arms and with fair prospects of future happiness.

Geraldine Farrar's portrayal of Tesca was at all times graphic and convincing.   Very beautiful to look upon, she was ideally suited to the part of the alluring Aztec maiden.   Wallace Reid gave a sympathetic performance as Alvarado.   Others whose acting stood out in a cast of general excellence were Raymond Hatton and Theodor Kosloff.   The Helen Moller pupils added beauty and grace to the opening scenes of the film.

The name of Geraldine Farrar alone is sufficient guarantee for capacity houses.

> --H. D. R. in The New York Dramatic Mirror, Vol. 77, No. 2029 (November 10, 1917), page 18.

☐ WOMANHOOD, THE GLORY OF A NATION (Vitagraph, 1917)

The trouble with Womanhood, The Glory of a Nation, Vitagraph's preparedness film, is that it has not one new idea, and is bound together, not in a great emotional band, but as a loosely-tied collection of irrelated melodramatic incidents which are at best not very convincing.   When the tremendous plays and pictures of this war are finally staged, it is probable that the tensest scenes will be far from the double beat of the giant guns; bloody action is, in a way, its own anaesthetic; real tragedy and emotion's mighty convictions arise where the peace of nature ironically accentuates the wrack and storm of the human heart.   Womanhood is simply a wholesale melodrama in none of whose phases has there been much ingenuity; and in some things, too little care.   To it are given such sterling players as Alice Joyce, Harry Morey, Joseph Kilgour, Peggy Hyland, James Morrison, Naomi Childers, Mary Maurice and Templar Saxe.   I am not saying that Womanhood won't entertain; perhaps it will give you the Spring's thrilling evening, but don't look for another Intolerance.   In any event, here is a pictorial "Wake up America!"

> --Julian Johnson in Photoplay, Vol. 12, No. 1 (June 1917), page 97.

☐ THE WRATH OF THE GODS (New York Motion Picture Company, 1914)

Productions which combine a powerful fascinating story with

superb spectacular effects are still among the rare jewels in filmdom. Not the least sparkling of these gems is this feature of the
New York Motion Picture Company, directed by Thomas H. Ince.

I cannot help admiring the boldness of the direction, which
was not afraid to film the very elements themselves, not the elements at peace, but the elements in their fury. In The Wrath of
the Gods, the camera follows the path of destruction at close range,
and we see portrayed with equal and astonishing skill and facility
the majesty of the angry sea, the sublime wrath of fire and the
fearful quaking of the very earth itself.

In the elaboration of these impressive and at times overwhelming spectacular phases of the play there is a finish of detail
which must please the most critical. The coming of the typhoon is
described on the screen not at all in titles, but all in pictures--a
difficult feat, which required uncommon skill in direction, and which
speaks of years of hard work and observation and experience on the
part of the director. The typhoon approaches just as men who have
traveled in Eastern waters have told it in a thousand books, but no
book can grip us as these pictures do showing with such remarkable
fidelity the gradual gathering force of the storm and the final bursting of the sky. The same realism characterizes the screen depiction of the floods of fire and lava descending in never-ending tor-
rents from the angry craters of the Sakura-Jima. I never saw an
audience more plainly moved than the thousands that sat in the
Strand watching this kaleidoscope of elemental rage. The scene
where the earth yawned and engulfed men and women and houses in
one huge grave was overpowering.

I must award no less praise to all the out-door work and
scenery in this feature. The spell of the rocks and the surf is on
the screen. He who selected these seascapes had the eye and taste
of a seascape painter.

Having thus roughly tried to sketch the marvelous frame in
which the story is set, let me say a word about the story itself.
It has a strange appeal doubly effective by the fact that all but one
of the principal parts are taken by Japanese artists. The first
place belongs to the handsome, talented and conscientious woman
who played the part of Toya San. Toya San is the daughter of Lord
Yamaki, who is the sole survivor of an old Samurai family which,
according to an old Japanese legend, was accursed of the Gods. An
old prophet delivers this tradition to the young men of that country,
warning them to keep away from Yamaki and his daughter. He tells
his people that if Toya San ever marries the Gods will open the fiery
mouth of the volcano and destroy every living thing within many miles.
Consequently, Toya San is shunned by all and lives in solitude with
her father, inhabiting a wretched hut near the coast and living pre-
cariously upon the food afforded by the sea. Yamaki himself believes
in the truth of the cruel tradition and vainly seeks to obtain forgive-
ness from the Gods, who had been incensed by a sacrilege of his
father. When Toya San hears of the strange decree of the Gods she

refuses to accept it, saying that no just God would seek to punish
the innocent.   One day an American vessel is wrecked on the coast
near their hovel.   Only one of the crew, a sailor named Wilson, is
lucky enough to be saved.   He is washed ashore half dead, and is
found by Yamaki.   The latter brings him to his hut and with the
ministrations of Toya San, nurses him back to life and strength.
The sailor proposes marriage to the Japanese maiden.   She tells
him of the dire prophecy and when he assures her that his God is
more powerful than the idols of the heathen she listens with eager-
ness and asks her father's consent.   The consent is given, but only
after long hesitation and after the simple preachings of the sailor
have converted Yamaki to the faith of the cross.   The sailor then
marries Toya San.   The people are furious to hear of this marriage;
they destroy the hut of Yamaki and murder him beside the rude
Christian altar he had erected.   And now the visitations of the
wrath of the Gods come upon the country and her people.   Toya San
and her Christian husband alone escape from the universal destruction, and despite the evil prophecy the seed of the ancient Samurai
survives beyond Yamaki's daughter.

        The parts of the old prophet Takeo and of the Jinrishka driver
and of Yamaki were rendered with an earnestness and power which
are rarely witnessed in the average screen performer.   The photography is worthy of the great subject, being excellent throughout.
                                    --W. Stephen Bush in The Moving
                                        Picture World, Vol. 20, No. 12
                                        (June 20, 1914), page 1665.

☐ YANKEE DOODLE IN BERLIN (Sennett, 1919)

        Whether Sennettry becomes a little watery strung out to five
long reels, or whether there is too much fooling and too little plot,
I leave for soberer diagnosticians than I to decide.   I am usually in
such a carnival of yelps at one of Mack's manifestations that I forget all analysis.   And yet this picture, crammed full of the regular
hokum, disappointed me.   I won't put in the stock line that it needed
a story; I'll say instead that it needed a little common-sense attention to detail, and a little less coarseness in one particular.   This
is a war-time hokus-pokus on the Hohenzollerns, but without delving
more than skin-deep into monarchical affairs and Potsdam facts, the
makers certainly might have honored our intelligences more while
sacrificing not a bit of their travesty.   It is a high crime to compare comedians' efforts, I know, but I cannot but remember that
when Mr. Chaplin felt called upon to say something about the war
he chose that very ticklist subject, the American doughboy, and, for
the purposes of his masque, perfected a paraphrase of camouflage
that startled even the scientific.   There is no such artistry shown
here, there is exhibited no will to really take off in laughter really
true things; the whole thing is thin as tissue paper and superficial
as a yellow-journal headline.   The only two performances of note

are Bothwell Browne's very creditable and inoffensive female impersonation, and hard-working Ford Sterling's replica of a well but
not favorably known sojourner in Amerongen. Mr. Browne enacts
an American aviator detailed to secure important information in
Berlin. He flies to the enemy's country, and, remembering "his
college days"--of course that was the easiest of the old ones to
pull--dons a damsel's garb, and tricks successively Hans und Fritz,
their officers, the generals, the string-bean Kronprinz, and Gott's
partner, Wilhelm II. I regret that into his fantastic fracas the
playmaker felt obliged to pull a georgemunroeish burlesque of the
German empress; not that I am for the empress, but vulgar acro-
bacy by a gray-haired woman does not strike me in any event as
funny or necessary. There is so much else that he could have done.
In no place does the sketch rise to anything that compliments the intelligence of the beholder, as did--throw your eggs at the reviewer
now, please--Mr. Chaplin's Shoulder Arms. Of course this affair
was never intended for peace-times. It was a catchpenny stirabout
for war days. The Sennett Follies bring their frolicking legs across
the screen line anon, and Marie Prevost plays something that faintly
resembles a part now and then. With what nature has done we have
no complaint; nor with what Mr. Browne and Mr. Sterling have done,
but the rest will add nothing to comedy history nor win any converts
to the screen.

--Julian Johnson in Photoplay, Vol.
16, No. 4 (September 1919),
page 85.

☐ APPENDIX A

THE SHADOW STAGE: THE YEAR'S ACTING,
A REVIEW OF PERSONAL PERFORMANCES*

by Julian Johnson

THE "fiscal year" is not the only twelvemonth which makes a face
at the calendar and ends topsy-turvily in early summer.   The first
flash of hot weather sees the end of the theatrical year; and while
the movie camp boastfully proclaims itself perpetual as a Klondike
palace of chance, there are no more reasonable days in which to
survey the grand collection of impersonative reflections than the long
days, the lazy days, of July or August.   The daylight platform is
not completely dissevered from the sunless stage.   So, as the theatrical managers are now making their 1916-17 plans, rehearsing their
new pieces and hiring their actors, the photoplay padrones are casting about for wider fields, mechanical innovations, bigger productions,
new people.

Considered en masse, the interpretative performances of the
camera year aggregate more acting than the English-speaking theatre
ever saw in a decade.   As an artistic distillation, this vast volume
shrinks prodigiously, but there remains an essence of much good
acting, some very fine acting, and a few really great characterizations.

The most significant single event has been the complete col-
lapse of the notion that a fairly good footlight performer must necessarily be great before the camera.   A few actors made genuine
screen successes.   The majority made themselves ridiculous, and
almost broke their awe-stricken movie managers.

AMONG the really distinguished performances of the year what shall
we first consider--Wilfred Lucas's marvellous characterization in
Acquitted, or Mabel Normand's bulwarking of all the Keystone comedy with her own slender shoulders?   Ethel Clayton's inimitable human portrait, in Dollars and the Woman, or Charlie Chaplin's un-
faltering rise to world-wide fame?   We might with propriety make
any of this quartet the opener; while some of the year's acting

*Reprinted from Photoplay, Vol. 10, No. 4 (September 1916), pages
119-128.

achievements have been concentrated in single parts, other triumphs have been the quieter but no less certain victories of steady, consistent playing.

Very few people outside the profession realize what Mabel Normand has meant to the Keystone organization; not that her comic excellencies are not apparent in any given part, but who, among the merely entertained, asks why and wherefore? The theory that the playgoer asks only to laugh, or to emote, is, rightly or wrongly, the cornerstone of the show business. It is neither exaggeration nor personal tribute to say that Mabel Normand knows more about screen comedy, and has made better screen comedy, than any woman actively photographed. This statement is merely a cool appraisal. Who pulled My Valet through the breakers of failure? Mabel Normand. Who put the legerdemain of appeal into Stolen Magic, and the charm of the romantically ridiculous into Fatty and Mabel Adrift? Mabel Normand. And who--if you'll pardon a backward jump of more than a year--gave lovely relief to Chaplin and Dressler in Tillie's Punctured Romance? Normand, surnamed Mabel. Her few Fort Lee pictures have made us wish for more frequent appearances.

You have not seen on any silversheet a single piece of acting surpassing Wilfred Lucas's impersonation of the persecuted bookkeeper in Acquitted. If I may quote the eminent Photoplay Magazine: "Lucas's marvellous fidelity to type has never been surpassed in photodrama. Here is a man you and I know. He belongs to every American town. Let calamity hit him, and he performs according to programme. Otherwise, he brings up his decent, inconspicuous family in a decent, inconspicuous way. He never does anything worthy of note. He gets his name in the local papers when he is born, when he is married, when his firm gives him a dinner or an uncomfortable watch on the twentieth anniversary of his faithful service--and when he dies." A simple annal!

I can think of only one companion-piece to Lucas's bookkeeper: Kathlyn Williams's Mrs. Cortlandt, in Colin Campbell's production of The Ne'er-Do-Well. Here was an impersonation of the subtlest and finest kind; an impression painted in almost invisible strokes; a pantomimic character devoid of gesticulation; an optic creation in which the creator vouchsafed psychic effects instead of the sign-language of motion.

Ethel Clayton I have mentioned. There was nothing Claytonianly new in the purveying of author Terhune's heroine; Ethel Clayton did much the same work in her own domestic drama series last season, but latterly this play and The Great Divide--to a far less degree--alone served to indicate what fine arts are slumbering within her well-coiffed head.

George Beban's viol of talent seems to have a single string, yet what beautiful variations, what harmonics, what chromatics of laughter and tears he can summon from it! The simple, child-like Breton peasant of The Pawn of Fate was the simple, childish Italian

grocer of Pasquale, yet so exquisitely drawn was each character
that each seemed absolutely individual.   Here was shadow-acting with
the abundant character of a well-worded book personage.

The only criticism we can level at Mr. Chaplin's comediettas
is a lack of finish and a lack of that serious touch which Mr. Chaplin can so superbly bestow.   What, after all, is the Chaplin seriousness?   Merely his natural sincerity applied to a serious situation.
The proof of comedy is a situation not funny.   Your insincere, get-
the-money "artist" vanishes in thin air when asked to put over anything except the vacant guffaw.   Mr. Chaplin can, if he will, summon the tear as deftly as he can lure the smile.   He is a fun-maker
not ashamed of his happy business.   Our hat is off to him; may he
go farther, slower, a little more thoughtfully.   He is original.   And
he is what no other screen player of any country has ever been: he
is universal.   He can summon a laugh from an Arab or a Chinaman,
an Igorrote or an Eskimo, as easily as he does from the American
peace-eater and the European soldier.

Speaking of comedy: the dumb stage has never had so quick,
big and wholesome a triumph as that of Douglas Fairbanks.   And
that without especially good vehicles.   Fairbanks' success has been
in his assumption of brisk American boys who were blind to obstacles, deaf to the quavering voice of fear, ready with the left hook,
strong for chicken garnished with marriage license, and constantly,
completely ablink in dazzling smiles.   When Fairbanks came to the
screen he was the most popular young American actor of virile type
--playless.   In his first year on the screen he has always played
himself.   Won't someone please write a regular two-dimension classic for D. F. ?

An even more boyish type of boy found its ideal, this year,
in lovable "Charlie" Ray.   No actor has had a greater personal success than Ray's in The Coward.   No play of his since has approached
that thrilling adventure, though The Deserter has an appeal which
even its morbidity cannot dim.

Mary Pickford has accomplished an eerie feat: she has remained the photoplay queen, the regal personage of black-and-white--
without any plays!   Her few vehicles this season have been of no
moment; her subsequent vacation, distractingly long.   Yet, such is
the Pickford individuality, so compelling is her gentle art, that she
is still the arch-actress of pictures.   The new amalgamation in
which she has just found herself vigorously afloat should do real
things for her in the year to come.

Lillian Walker's performance in Green Stockings is of a piece
with Wilfred Lucas's sudden flash in Acquitted.   Both were players
of experience, reputation, long and steady endeavor.   Both, quite
unexpectedly, offered an interpretation which was a gem of humanity
as well as flawless technique.   Miss Walker's repose, her elegance,
her surety of touch should make Green Stockings a permanent record.

So with the misbegotten Don Quixote, Fine Arts' most unworthy attempt among the masterpieces.   From this welter of key-
stonery by an undertakers' convention, Fay Tincher's Dulcinea
shines like a starbeam from another century.   The thing should
live for this jewel of impersonation alone.   Fay Tincher visualized
Cervantes.   She became the little serving maid of the dying Middle
Ages; in her eyes was humble wonder, and when the senile knight
caressed her cotton stocking with his lips it was as though repentant Kundry had seen The Grail glow crimson.

Theodore Roberts earns a place as one of the really impressive performers of the year by no one perfect part, but by many.
We are not decrying the Lasky excellence, nor the DeMille thorough-
ness, nor the valiance of the Hollywood ensemble, when we say that
the camp on Selma avenue is inexpressibly fortunate in the posessor
of the most reliable, most intelligent all-around character-maker in
motion pictures.   Robert's parts have not been of equal vitality, but
in every one of them--father or fiend, Russian or Iowan, Thespian
or diplomat--he has injected indescribable power, clarity of expression and a learned understanding quite foreign to character parts in
the films.

Tyrone Power, traveling from Selig to Universal, hits third
speed under the direction of Lois Weber.   As an embodiment of
austere and authority, mature force and iron gentility Power stands
alone.   It is a significant note that he has not yet played any part
which approaches his possibilities in characterization and power.
All he needs to make a nationwide explosion is a two-fisted author.

Harry Morey, a name it has been the pleasure of this cack-
ler's corner to feelingly inscribe more than once, appeared to enter
a new phase in the recent play, The Law Decides.   To this piece
he brought all of his old, indescribable virility, buckled into a visualization of the primitive man in the corsets and lingerie of civilization.

Geraldine Farrar's three Lasky plays were inground more
than a year ago; yet as her face and figure are now autographing
much more celluloid, a résumé of the gift she gave the screen is
not inapropos.   As a blazing expression of physical beauty, of the
dramatic value of movement, and as a demonstrator of real pantomime, Geraldine Farrar is alone and unequaled.   New to the screen,
she made a lasting and immediate hit, a hit apart from her operatic
celebrity, because she brought to the canvas tints it had never reflected.

IT is hard to draw the line of correct demarcation between work
which is excellent and work which is really surpassing.

However you rank them, you will admit that this year's end
finds the reputation and popularity of these people distinctly and de-
servedly advanced.

For instance: the Drews, Sidney and Mrs. Sidney. A year
ago floundering in rather uncertain mediums, the Drew advent at
Metro marked the arrival of comedy scripts which were really au-
thored. Now, this husband and wife are presenting problems of
everyday domesticity which often wax uproarious in the untangling.
We are sort of funny, after all, in our relations with the butcher,
the baker, the cook and the swell family next door. Drew is putting a microscope on an apartment-house.

For instance: Roscoe Arbuckle. Half a dozen years ago
Arbuckle was learning the Shakespearean essentials by being bumped
all over cheap stock opera stages. Some time later he began filling
up the celluloid. A little after that he floated under Mack Sennett's
wand. He was not ashamed to be a pupil. He has been an apt pupil. He is now the best of Keystone's sub-directors and one of the
cleverest of Keystone's funsters. The Keystone Fort Lee episodes
are all his.

We might take all of good Keystonia and dispose of it at
once. Chester Conklin's "Mr. Walrus" is more than a misfit suit,
a sly wink and a motorman's eyebrow on the upper lip. It is a
real and uproarious character. Fred Mace and Charles Murray are
on the credit side of the ledger. So is Minta Durfee, the shapely
Mrs. Arbuckle.

At the World studios Alice Brady has done much fine and
consistent work. There is a frightened little note of pathos, a bird-
like insistence to please, which is half the charm of this girl's acting. Gerda Holmes, coming out of a year's lethargy, shows splendid possibilities in The Chain Invisible. Frances Nelson, in such
plays as What Happened at 22, has proven an ingenue of serious
dramatic ability as well as statuette size and 1800-volt sex. Frank
Sheridan shows in The Struggle, and in a few other pieces, what he
can accomplish in portraits of middle-aged men.

Is Tom Mix no more than a rough rider? I believe he is
an actor. Wait for his Light of Western Stars. His past year's
work in drama and comedy-drama has been fitting him for real
rôles. Bessie Eyton has held her place, and has distinctly advanced, though she has plainly shown the need of another Spoilers.
Perhaps she will find the vehicle in The Crisis.

Theda Bara has gained--what? A world-wide box-office following. Dramatically, she has not approached the mark she set
under Herbert Brenon's direction in The Clemenceau Case, and The
Kreutzer Sonata. Virginia Pearson, whom we may describe as a
college-educated "vamp," evidences a worthy desire to put character into her evil portrayals. In Blazing Love she grew old before
one's eyes--grew old more truly and terribly than any actress whom
we have ever seen essay public ageing. Dorothy Bernard, one of
the loveliest of young leading women, has not only doubled, but has
at least trebled her popularity as well as her artistic effectiveness
since she has entered the Fox ranks.

At Laskyville the interpretative institution seems to have moved ahead en masse. A year ago, who had heard of the generally adored "Wallie" Reid? This brief word of appreciation may also serve as a croak of warning--Reid's great acting with Farrar has not been duplicated in recent photoplays. Why? Sessue Hayakawa has carved an ivory niche of appreciation in which he sits securely. Hayakawa is wiser than Reid in that he works for a new "rep" in every piece. So does his wife, that Oriental doll in Lucile frocks: Tsuru Aoki. Victor Moore, despite a vehicle or two of deadly dullness, wields laughter pretty much as he will. Raymond Hatton, the chronic mean guy, has dispensed an adorable double distillation of villainy from California of the Bear Flag day to Petrograd, the revamped Petersburg. And as a modest and faultless orchestral instrument in this fine ensemble, let us not forget James Neill. Blanche Sweet is emerging from her sulks. Cleo Ridgely has responded to the directoral megaphone with beauty plus dash. Thomas Meighan is making distinct advances, and Tom Foreman has, on the whole, done admirable acting.

From Inceville William S. Hart has blazoned across the motion picture sky a newer, finer type of Westerner than the screen ever knew. Louise Glaum, the champion dance-hall "vamp," has wrought artistic destruction in many a fictional camp. Bessie Barriscale, giving a lot of splendid characterization to many fairly good pieces, appears to wait only the sterling vehicle for a repetition of her Cup of Life sensation. J. Barney Sherry has been as staunch in Ince's service as Roberts in Lasky's.

At Fine Arts pieces like The Penitentes have demonstrated the spiritual fineness of Seena Owen's dramatic sensibilities. Lillian Gish has been completely outclassed, lately, by her roguish little sister Dorothy; Susan Rocks the Boat, Little Meena's Romance and Betty of Greystone are a fine trio of Dorothyisms. Norma Talmadge, too, has put the best of her shapely feet forward in her longest stride of accomplishment. (Which is Norma Talmadge's best foot?)

At Essanay, despite a desperately bad serial, Edna Mayo has more firmly intrenched herself in popular favor than ever. Much credit is due, too, to those sterling actors E. H. Calvert and Ernest Maupain.

Really--the list of progressors and progressees is quite illimitable. We have Helen Holmes and J. P. MacGowan, forsaking mechanical thrills for real drama in the Spearman stories; John Barrymore, in such uproarious concoctions as The Red Widow; "Dot" Kelly, a splendid actress full blown from the ingenue bud, in The Law Decides; Bushman and Bayne, a progress sometimes uncertain artistically, but undoubtedly large in the favor-general. There is that darling ingenue, Marguerite Courtot, now sheltered in the Famous fold.

As a type of the younger actors who are not stars and will

not be, but whose painstaking delineations are the underlying substance of the profession, I might mention Nigel DeBrullier, a young
Californian with a grave liking for character--and a knack for it,
too. DeBrullier's wide range of work is best shown in his Felipe,
in Ramona, and the Italo-American banker, in Pasquale.

DO you realize how many stage celebrities have come screenward
during the past year? I don't believe you do! I didn't, until I began to foot up a list which is only representative.

I should say that the most brilliantly successful of all is
Fannie Ward. Here is a woman whose first bloom of youth has
long since passed, according to the calendar--a bloom which she is
just entering if we are to believe every evidence of the camera and
every iota of personal appearance! Never has a stage person thrown
such enthusiasm, such abandon, such personality into her work as
Miss Ward brought to pieces like The Cheat, and Tennessee's Pard-
ner.

Marie Doro is working valiantly, but has yet to equal the
spontaneity and charm of her Morals of Marcus, an old Famous
Players photoplay. Pedro de Cordoba flashed forth lithe and sinister alongside Farrar; then again into his theatrical scabbard. Charlotte Walker has made several good plays.

At Inceville William H. Thompson has tellingly put over character after character. William Desmond, a Morosco speaker, flings
the C. Gardner Sullivan uniforms about the silversheet with magnificent abandon. H. B. Warner, as a serious performer, has done
the best work of his life in front of the same cameras which canned
Civilization.

Truly, the list of the season's successes is long, your patience and these pages short! Frank Keenan, in his tense plays of
war or modern life; Forrest Stanley, a likable Morosco lover;
Frank Campeau, Virginia-eternal; Tully Marshall, a contriver of
deviltry in odd make-ups; H. Cooper-Cliffe, suavest of roués; Arthur Ashley, awful until he became a villain; Lewis S. Stone, Essanay's superbly virile capture; Frederick Warde, unforgettable as
Silas Marner; Willard Mack, Lou-Tellegen, Charles Ruggles, Orrin
Johnson, Herschell Mayall--all have spoken loudly through the si-
lences!

Among pretty, potent women behold Jane Grey, Grace Valentine, Olga Petrova, Gail Kane, Mabel Taliaferro.

Harry Watson brought his one make-up and three uproarious
expressions from burlesque and The Follies.

Ham and Bud, permanent screen possessions that they seem
to be, were recruited from the land behind the asbestos curtain.

NOT all the famous folks hit the bull's-eye when they shot at it with a camera. With most of them, it seems to have been a case of too much fame--anything would be easily won in so childish and puerile a sport as photoplay-making!

There was Willie Collier. Ince pulled him through once with the funniest set of captions ever shot through the magic-lantern. His own son Buster beat him to a frazzle in that juvenile hurricane, The Bugle-Call. Otherwise--muffled drums, please.

There was Raymond Hitchcock, for whose success Mabel Normand was a vicarious sacrifice.

There were Weber and Fields, funny in one picture, but as doleful in the rest as a couple of grave-diggers during a season of unexampled health.

There was Eddie Foy, who had a contract, and got his big money notwitstanding. Mr. Fitzgerald--for such is his quiescent monaker--is alleged to have murmured, as he stood against a Key-stone fence, baffled, blinded, all but strangled during a preliminary pie-hurling: "Throw 'em, you— — —! Throw 'em, for it's going to cost you $1,000 a pie!" And it did, or thereabouts.

And last of all: that delightful gentleman, grand curtain-speaker, and footlight veteran--also that celluloid lemon and shadow ruin--DeWolf Hopper. Let us forbear.

A baffling tragedy is Billie Burke's. Peggy, with Tom Ince's personal direction and every opulence of equipment, did not get over. Gloria's Romance, equally sumptuous, now seems doomed to the dis-card of unworthy things.

And here are notables who did not get far in the land of story-telling shades: John Mason, Valli-Valli, Donald Brian, Anna Held, Constance Collier, Sir Herbert Tree, Edna Goodrich, William Gillette.

IN the bright list of real stars the year has created I think Bessie Love stands first. Here is a talent more direct, simple and sweetly sincere than any discovered since Mary Pickford. Mary Pickford and Bessie Love slightly resemble each other, physically; spiritually there is a much stronger resemblance; mentally--I don't know Bessie Love, so here I cease.

Edna Purviance is more than the loveliest blonde in picture comedy; she is that wonderful creature, a pretty girl with brains.

Gladys Brockwell brought glowing youth and a tremendous dramatic talent out of Fine Arts early in the season. She has not done so much lately, but with the right play and the right director she is an artistic wager than which there is no better.

Louise Fazenda possesses the ornamental physique without which no Keystoness seems fitted for that studio's spirituelle atmosphere--plus that supreme comedy gift, an ability to draw the smile which is brother to a tear.

Adda Gleason's rendition of Ramona is a more than ordinarily fine effort.

Speaking of girls--why shouldn't we forget them and say something nice about that apotheosized jumping-jack, Al St. John, youngest and in some ways livest apostle of St. Sennett?

HERE are some of those who have maintained their places without special advance: a statement which is of no final significance, for even before these lines are printed any one of these popular men and women may have had a masterwork cranked in.

It seems almost impossible for Holbrook Blinn to find a good play. Here's an actor who's fairly colossal--bound to the rut of the commonplace by a lack of scripts. Of his most recent effort, The Weakness of Man, a Chicago critic wrote, "Why waste so much celluloid when there's such a demand for washable collars?" Contemptuous and perhaps flippant, but it was the answer.

Harold Lockwood seems tied to plays more or less uninspiring, as does William Russell. Anna Little is where she was three years ago--a Western rider. Art Acord started a series of promising comedies, but the spotlight turned elsewhere. Will Mary Miles Minter, she of the motionless age, simply keep flashing the fine promise which doesn't come to fulfilment? Nance O'Neill, by ferocious swimming in a sea of choppy scripts, just manages to keep above water.

William Farnum, at $75,000 a year, remains on the sea-level, though his popularity is doubtless ever widening. Tom Santschi, Stuart Holmes, William Shay, House Peters and Bruce McRae; five dissimilar men who are standing still.

Lovable Tom Moore, Jack Standing, J. Warren Kerrigan, Eddie Lyons, Lee Moran, Owen Moore, Dustin Farnum--about as they were, a year ago.

The ladies: Pearl White, for instance, is too grown-up to keep on in physical melos like The Iron Claw. One such she can pull up; another will pull her down. Edith Storey is standing still. Marguerite Clark, Hazel Dawn and Pauline Frederick, potential persons and royal princesses in following, need real vehicles. Frederick has had none since The Spider; Clark and Dawn none in immemorial months.

Eulalie Jensen, Ruth Roland, Nell Craig: afloat in the actor ladies' Sargasso Sea.

THE most cruel thing to wish upon a player is a great success.
The star who has once touched a mile-a-minute gait must keep the
pace or be spoken of as a has-been.   Let's call the roll of people
who've subsided a bit in the past six or eight months.   Is it, even
in a majority of cases, the fault of their acting?   Not at all.   Great
plays make great actors very often, and their big parts haven't been
repeated.   The Fine Arts people, now quiescent, may blaze forth
more splendidly than ever in Griffith's new picture.   It's all in the
George Bernard Shaw aphorism: <u>you never can tell</u>.

Mae Marsh has never had a part to compare with Little Sister, in <u>The Birth of a Nation</u>.   Edward Earle can lay his present
inconspicuousness to Edison.   So with Mabel Trunnelle.   Lillian
Gish is pigeonholed with Mae Marsh.   Where is Bobbie Harron?
Mack Swain seems to be left out of the shifting styles of Keystone
cutupery.   Anita Stewart, Vitagraph's maiden-queen, hasn't had a
real play in many months.   If Earl Williams has done anything notable lately we've missed it.   Marc McDermott, a really great character actor, seems to have been forgotten by the dramatists as far
as real plays go.

More conspicuous than any of these is Henry Walthall, a year
ago acclaimed the screen's very finest intellectual-poetic male product.   Walthall is still Walthall, but where are his plays?   Echo answers, Essanay wails.   Somehow, his ventures have been flashpan
misfires.

The list of those whom the parts won't hit might be continued
for pages--Charles Richman, Joseph Kilgour, Thomas Holding, Richard Travers and Herbert Rawlinson.

There are other fellows, other complaints.   Carlyle Black-
well, essentially one of the cleverest of leading men, is altogether
too prone to carelessness.   Crane Wilbur is just solemnly absurd.
Robert Warwick carries on as no human being ever carried on over
land or sea.   So does Francis Ford.   Robert Mantell upon the
screen is a sort of scene-eating monstrosity.   King Baggott belongs
to the old school of gesticulative grandeur.   Courtenay Foote gets
nowhere.   Billie Reeves ought to get somewhere--just where, we
won't say.

Ethel Barrymore, a really great actress, has been only tiresome and absurd upon the screen.   Florence La Badie has made no
progress whatever in a year.   Cleo Madison, though continually acting, means nothing to interpretative art.   Neither does Grace Cun-
ard, nor Violet Mersereau, nor Ormi Hawley, nor Rosetta Brice.
Enid Markey, with her golden chance in <u>Civilization</u>, was a bitter
disappointment.

HOW long since you've seen--at least in new roles which impressed
you--Charlotte Burton, Miriam Nesbitt, Mae Hotely, Grace Darmond,
James Cruze, Spottiswoode Aitken, Marguerite Marsh, Mary Alden,

Morris Foster, Maurice Costello, Julia Swayne Gordon, Margarita
Fischer, G. M. Anderson, Hobart Bosworth or Mary Fuller?

HERE are some babies, either in age or film experience, who'll
bear watching. They're possibilities.   Ann Pennington, Doris Kenyon, Marjorie Daw, Camille Astor, Margery Wilson, Dorothy Green.
Extend this list and exercise your fancy by adding your own selections.

THE SCREEN YEAR IN REVIEW*

by Frederick James Smith

An infinitely interesting year it has been, one vibrant with fine promises for the future. True, the twelve months possessed their disappointments, but, upon the whole, the production average has been well sustained.

The weakness of the American cinema still remains manifestly the same; i.e., a lack of literary discernment and story discrimination. Most of the stuff produced in this country is absolutely banal.

The photoplay is developing its technique slowly and painfully. Here and there may be detected indications of the film drama of tomorrow; vital, human, close to life and far from the average melodramatic screen entertainment of today.

As for direction, the American average is high--in point of treatment and studio workmanship. But, while the average is uniformly high, the men who can vivify a story into silversheet fire can easily be numbered upon the fingers of one's hands.

Before we digress further, let us name our selection of the ten best photoplays of the film year ending July 1, 1920:

1. The Miracle Man.
2. The Gay Old Dog.
3. Pollyanna.
4. Why Change Your Wife?
5. On with the Dance.
6. Male and Female.
7. Dr. Jekyll and Mr. Hyde.
8. $23\frac{1}{2}$ Hours' Leave.
9. Humoresque.
10. Mrs. Drew's After Thirty stories.

A second list would consist of:

---

*Reprinted from Motion Picture Classic, Vol. 10, No. 6 (August 1920), pages 44-45, 78 and 88.

1. <u>Romance</u>.
2. <u>Blind Husbands</u>.
3. <u>The Right of Way</u>.
4. <u>The Devil's Passkey</u>.
5. <u>The Idol Dancer</u>.
6. Harold Lloyd's comedies.
7. <u>Jubilo</u>.
8. <u>Behind the Door</u>.
9. <u>Scratch My Back</u>.
10. <u>The Six Best Cellars</u>.

Our biggest disappointment of the year lies in the fact that David Wark Griffith has contributed nothing material to the screen during the twelve months. For the first time in three years he fails to head our list of best photoplays. Just now, when the photoplay needs a courageous leader more than ever before, he has failed to follow his epic of Limehouse, <u>Broken Blossoms</u>, with anything worthy of himself. <u>The Idol Dancer</u>, a trite chase melodrama of the tropics, came nearest in points of poetry and beauty, but it fell a thousand miles short. Griffith had his biggest theme in <u>The Great Question</u>, dealing with the psychic problem of the existence of future life, but he lost his subject in a maze of stale melodrama. <u>Scarlet Days</u> belonged to the old Biograph period of Southwest romantic melodrama.

Actually the most important development of the year has been the splitting of the screen world into two factions: independents and-- but what shall we term the others? Without question, Wall Street interests are bringing the bigger producing organizations together in what may develop into a gigantic combine, controlling the film theaters of America, or possibly the world. There are indications everywhere of this movement. While this has been under way, the photoplay world has seen a steady breaking away of the bigger forces and the formation of independent organizations. This has manifested itself in the United Artists, the Associated Producers, etc. It is very clear that business interests cannot easily tie the hands of artistic development on the silversheet.

But to return to our selection. But six were original stories written for the screen and eleven were photoplays in which there were no stars.

Here let us register another disappointment. King Vidor, who, since he produced <u>The Turn in the Road</u>, last year, seems to us the most promising single force in films, did not repeat himself. Yet we have not lost faith in this young crusader for the close-to-the-soil drama.

Cecil DeMille continued along his luxurious primrose path of sex and divorce. There is no questioning the popularity of this director, whose eye is that of the theater and not of the sympathetic observer of life. Lavish and picturesque is his style, but the human note of tomorrow is not there. Then, too, DeMille is running rife in boudoir negligée. His dramas are as intimate as a department store window.

The one directorial surprise of the year was Erich von Stroheim, heretofore a player of Teutonic scoundrels in war thrillers. Von Stroheim put over a flashing--if soulless--thing in Blind Husbands and then duplicated it with another study in passionate intrigue, The Devil's Passkey. Von Stroheim brings a new, Continental and uncannily cynical viewpoint to our screen, hence his sudden success. His is the eye of the Viennese boulevardier who adventures in romance, the Parisian connoisseur in love. He possesses surprising directorial dexterity, technically second only to Griffith. The soul of life itself is alone lacking, for his characters still fall short of the breath of reality.

Here we turn naturally to Mrs. Sidney Drew, who worked with Hobart Henley upon The Gay Old Dog, that well-nigh perfect visualization of Edna Ferber's story. Mrs. Drew also produced a number of the After Thirty stories of Julian Street. These are all marked with a rare human note, a fine insight into life and a splendid ability to reflect it upon the screen. Mr. Henley's work upon The Gay Old Dog alone would justify careful observation of his future progress. Here let us draw attention to the fact that The Gay Old Dog is not rated as a financial success and that destructive conclusions regarding motion picture audiences have been drawn from it. To which we answer that The Gay Old Dog was released thru a channel familiar with the handling of melodramatic serial thrillers and the like. It failed for this reason and none other. We stand firm in our belief that audiences want the best--if they can get it.

It is rather late to comment upon George Loane Tucker, whose The Miracle Man holds first place in the screen year. If Tucker does nothing else, he has contributed much to the photoplay's progress. We judge him as possessing a fine sense of the drama, a welcome disregard of non-essentials and a remarkable ability to make players act. Many months have passed and we still await his next production.

George Fitzmaurice, master of screen light and shade, is coming along with splendid strides. He is at the very top of our directorial leaders. Frank Borzage leaped into attention with his Humoresque, which, if long-drawn-out and tiresome at times, had a promising human touch.

The season's histrionic level has been singularly high. First of all, we place Betty Compson's superb playing of the greedy and sensuous Rose of The Miracle Man, the underworld girl whose spirit finally awakens. Here was a vibrant and human portrayal worthy of the highest praise. Mary Pickford's dear and touching Pollyanna wrung our hearts. Shall we ever forget the moment when she steps from her wheel-chair and walks?

There were other admirable performances. John Cumberland's lonely and sacrificing Jimmy Dodd in The Gay Old Dog was splendid in its subtlety. Charles Ray invested a half-dozen inconsequential plays with life thru his matchless sincerity. Bert Lytell was excellent as the arch-cynic, Charles Steel, in The Right of

Way. John Barrymore contributed a flashing and haunting performance in the ghoulish Dr. Jekyll and Mr. Hyde.

    Then, too, we might mention several of Thomas Meighan's
characterizations. Striking, also, were Vera Gordon's lovable Jewish mother in Humoresque; poor little Clarine Seymour's piquant
half-caste girl, rife with the love of life, in The Idol Dancer; Mae
Murray's butterfly Russian in On with the Dance; Mae Busch's playing of the grisette in The Devil's Passkey; Myrtle Stedman's sincere
Cherry Mellotte in The Silver Horde; Noah Beery's well-thought-out
characterization of The Sea Wolf; Lon Chaney's remarkable character work in The Miracle Man and Victory; Gibson Gowland's primitive French-Canadian in The Right of Way and Lewis Stone's dual
playing in The River's End. Also we would add Hedda Hopper's
playing in The Man Who Lost Himself.

    Probably the biggest individual advance of the year--at least
in the item of popularity--was registered by Harold Lloyd, whose
farces have hit a high average. Lloyd is rapidly overtaking Chaplin.
Wallie Reid has been growing steadily in favor, now that he is devoting himself entirely to swift-moving comedy. Charles Ray has
lifted himself to the acting leadership of the drama, this in the face
of fearful vehicles. Richard Barthelmess is fast developing along
the lines of romanticism--and he is now a star. Thomas Meighan
made steady progress all year.

    Of the feminine contingent, Clarine Seymour seemed most
promising, just when death entered the field. Wanda Hawley, Gloria
Swanson, Bebe Daniels and one or two other promising younger folk
of the previous year already have their names in stellar electric
lights. Constance Binney, to our way of thinking, bids fair to achieve
limitless popularity if she guides her celluloid career carefully.

    Here a few words about the cinema leaders are in order.
Mary Pickford did her finest work since Stella Maris with Pollyanna.
Douglas Fairbanks is still young America's idol. Charles Chaplin
did nothing in particular all year. Here is comic genius going to
waste. Please, Mr. Chaplin, do something about Charlie! William
S. Hart is still the reforming bad man. His nearest above-the-
average vehicle was Wagon Tracks, at least atmospheric of frontier
days.

    Norma Talmadge has had one namby-pamby character after
another all year. Right now she should be at the zenith of her career. We repeat our words of last year with added emphasis. Miss
Talmadge needs real dramatic material or--How long can she maintain her present popularity if she persists in milk-and-water vehicles?
Nazimova has done nothing distinctive all year. Here is an instance
of temperament running wild. We have well-nigh given up hope of
ever seeing another Revelation.

    Now for specific comments upon the various releasing organi-
zations:

Famous Players-Lasky still easily maintain far and away the best average in general workmanship. The once so popular Marguerite Clark seems to be voluntarily dropping from sight, having deliberately chosen retirement. Elsie Ferguson, sometimes lacking stories and other times failing to have sympathetic direction, has gone backward rather than ahead. Her best vehicle was The Witness for the Defence, well done by George Fitzmaurice. Charlie Ray was steadily handed inane scripts, but he triumphed thru his own unique ability. Wallie Reid is at last getting the right sort of stuff. Dorothy Gish's bright and boisterous comedy methods did a lot to overcome fearful material. Dorothy Dalton continues her way thru hectic emotionalism, minus her old clinging appeal. Ethel Clayton is still the victim of the scenario department. Robert Warwick, no longer a F. P.-L. star, apparently failed to "get over." Violet Heming as yet has not established herself at all definitely. Bryant Washburn suddenly began to get good stories just before he left the fold. Another Six Best Cellars would have lifted him to the forefront of comedians. Mrs. Irene Castle still appears now and then.

Enid Bennett has somewhat improved, but at no time has she electrified in anything. The Maurice Tourneur productions have been interesting series of photographically beautiful tableaux--and nothing more. Treasure Island was his best, Victory his worst. The last completely missed the spirit of Conrad. Douglas MacLean got away in a flying start with $23\frac{1}{2}$ Hours Leave and hasn't equalled it since.

Metro--Every effort seems to have been made to put over Bert Lytell, who at first seemed rather light for the big material entrusted to him. But he justified their faith with The Right of Way and did very well with Alias Jimmy Valentine. Metro believes it has a real find in Alice Lake. So far we pronounce her competent--and nothing more. Metro started the year by seeming on the verge of doing interesting things, but, with the entrance of new capital, the trend is now frankly towards melodrama. We certainly wish they would give better opportunities to May Allison. Viola Dana continues about the same. We have already commented anent Nazimova.

Selznick--A youthful battery of stars appearing in passable stories directed by less passable directors. Our chief interest in the forthcoming year centers in William Faversham's work under the direction of Hobart Henley and in what Louise Huff may do. The stolidly piquant Olive Thomas is apparently the most popular of the Selznick constellation, altho the powers-that-be there seem to expect big things of Elaine Hammerstein. We doubt it. Eugene O'Brien--my! my! Owen Moore--we like him better than we did last year.

First National--Of Norma we have spoken. Constance Talmadge continues along the line of thin-ice comedies, to which she lends a sparkle and verve. She's doing nicely, thank you. Anita

Stewart seems to slip more and more with each production. Micky
Neilan's productions fluctuated, from the well-sustained Arctic Circle
melodrama, The River's End, to the awful farce, Please Don't Marry. We have commented elsewhere upon other First National stars
and productions.

Goldwyn--Radical changes are going on here. Of all the
"eminent author" stuff emanating from these studios, we like the
Rex Beach productions best. Gerry Farrar and Pauline Frederick
have ceased to be Goldwyners. Tom Moore, Madge Kennedy and
Mabel Normand continue uneventfully. Jack Pickford is spending
money lavishly but without particular effect. Goldwyn is wasting
Will Rogers in conventional melodramas. Give him a chance, as
in Jubilo, and watch him burn up the road. Going back to the trio
we just mentioned, Tom Moore is slightly bettering his average of
1919. Miss Normand is retrograding. The early Edgar short juvenile comedies of Booth Tarkington's promise something delightful.

Vitagraph--Won't somebody do something about stories and
directors there? Vitagraph apparently refuses to believe that the
photoplay has advanced since 1915. Alice Joyce and Corinne Griffith continue to be wasted in features and Tony Moreno, the most
picturesque of all male film stars, is buried in serials. They allowed the promising Gladys Leslie to depart after manhandling her
career. Earle Williams and Harry Morey are still present. Vitagraph certainly needs a far-seeing and vigorous directorial hand to
lead it out of its cobwebby retreat.

Pathé--Serials seem to be the pièce de résistance here as
before. We pass on hastily, for our endurance balks at serials.
The best things on the Pathé program have been the Harold Lloyd
farces and Mrs. Drew's comedies, vastly dissimilar, but each admirable in its individual field. We have spoken anent The Gay Old
Dog. Blanche Sweet is waning.

Fox--We hear that changes are under way here and that the
trend will be away from melodrama. Pearl White's first Fox features have not yet been released. Shake-ups have been regular
events until apparently only a star or two remain.

Robertson-Cole--This organization seems to be handicapped
by various things, including a difficulty in getting into the leading
theaters. Sessue Hayakawa is easily its ablest star.

Cosmopolitan--All interest is centered in Marion Davies.
Which makes us realize just how difficult--or shall we say impossible?--it is to manufacture a star. Alma Rubens has had little opportunity thus far.

Universal--Erich Von Stroheim's productions are the biggest
factors by all odds. The one other big "U" production, The Virgin
of Stamboul, will make lots of money, but it is inconsequential from
a literary or directorial standpoint. We fail to see Priscilla Dean.
Of the numerous other "U" stars we cannot talk authoritatively.

United--The stellar fever seems to be breaking up the Griffith family. Lillian Gish is going a-starring. Bobbie Harron and
Dick Barthelmess are becoming stars. Who will be the Griffith
players of the coming year? Other United stars and productions
are mentioned elsewhere.

Hodkinson--As presented in Sex and other vehicles, Louise
Glaum is not the seductive siren of Triangle days. Doris Kenyon
is pretty and pleasant to look upon. J. Warren Kerrigan is quite
the same, altho practically minus popular interest.

Realart--We are betting on Constance Binney. Mary Miles
Minter is doing her best, but she will never approach Mary Pickford. That's definite. Alice Brady is a plugger. Allan Dwan's
productions have been workmanlike, but not meteoric anywhere.

Many screen stars seem to have been absent most of the
year. Theda Bara has been devoting herself to stage work. So
has Alice Brady. Dorothy Phillips has done nothing since leaving
Universal. Mae Marsh is back before the Cooper-Hewitts, but her
first vehicle is yet to be released. The same refers to Bessie Love.

We pause to consider film farce. We have been noting our
enthusiasm regarding Harold Lloyd. "Fatty" Arbuckle has been improving. The Sennett comedies continue along their own way. Charles
Murray stirs our risibilities as possibly no one else does. And
there's no two ways of looking at Ben Turpin's natural comedy. The
Christie comedies are ambitious but purposeless. And William Fox's
Sunshine comedies--ye gods! Words fail us!